TRANSFORMING UNDERGRADUATE EDUCATION

TRANSFORMING UNDERGRADUATE EDUCATION

Theory that Compels and Practices that Succeed

Edited by Donald W. Harward

Case Studies Edited by Ashley P. Finley

ROWMAN & LITTLEFIELD PUBLISHERS, INC.

Lanham • Boulder • New York • Toronto • Plymouth, UK

Published by Rowman & Littlefield Publishers, Inc.
A wholly owned subsidiary of The Rowman & Littlefield Publishing Group, Inc.
4501 Forbes Boulevard, Suite 200, Lanham, Maryland 20706
http://www.rowmanlittlefield.com

Estover Road, Plymouth PL6 7PY, United Kingdom

British Library Cataloguing in Publication Information Available

Library of Congress Cataloging-in-Publication Data

Transforming undergraduate education : theory that compels and practices that
succeed / edited by Donald W. Harward.
     p. cm.
   Includes bibliographical references and index.
   ISBN 978-1-4422-0674-8 (cloth : alk. paper) — ISBN 978-1-4422-0676-2 (ebook)
   1. Education, Higher—Aims and objectives—United States. 2. Education, Higher—
United States—Philosophy. 3. Education, Higher—United States—Administration.
4. Universities and colleges—United States. I. Harward, Donald W.
LA227.4.T73 2012
378.73—dc23   2011020661

∞ ™ The paper used in this publication meets the minimum requirements of American
National Standard for Information Sciences—Permanence of Paper for Printed Library
Materials, ANSI/NISO Z39.48-1992.

Printed in the United States of America

Contents

Foreword

Julie J. Kidd

We all have lofty goals for higher education, whether we are directly connected to the education field or are parents of students or students ourselves. Very often, however, the undergraduate liberal arts experience of today falls short of meeting its objectives, or its objectives fall short of the needs of the students.

Beset by the confusion of an increasingly complex world, pressured to think about education primarily in competitive terms, and often feeling more valued for their instrumentality than for their individuality, many of our students graduate from college ill-prepared both academically and emotionally for the world they will face. Significant changes are needed on our campuses if we are to serve our students well, not only in the strictly academic sense but also in recognizing our students as complex individuals with many challenges in all realms of their lives.

What the needed changes are and how to go about making them are the difficult questions facing higher education, questions that the Bringing Theory to Practice Project, out of which this book has grown, has nobly and boldly addressed throughout the past decade. The goal of this book addresses no less a challenge than helping students perceive their relationship to the world in deeper, richer ways that allow them to use their talents, their imaginations, and their empathy more meaningfully.

In its clarion call to transform campus cultures in a manner that deepens and broadens learning while addressing the student as a whole person, this book is both theoretical and practical in its approach, both current and forward-looking, with relevance long into the future. This compilation of essays is both a manual and a source of inspiration, drawn from the concerns and experiments of many of our most dedicated educators, both here and abroad.

After close to thirty years as president of the Christian A. Johnson Endeavor Foundation, founded by my father in 1952, it is gratifying indeed to be asked to write a preface to this important work. Many years ago, when the foundation's trustees and I were thinking through the areas of human endeavor to which we would devote our energies and resources, we all agreed that the development of human potential through education would be the most important contribution we could make. Hence, we have focused on undergraduate liberal arts programs ever since, both in the United States and overseas.

It is our view that higher education must assist students in realizing their potential as human beings over the full course of their lives. It is not acceptable to allow students to graduate without the inspiration and depth of vision they will need to carry them through life's challenges, not just as survivors but as active participants, participants who possess empathy, high ethical standards, and a sense of self that allows the best in each to come through and shine.

The insistent pressure of change that began in the last quarter of the twentieth century has made this goal significantly harder to achieve. The promise of education has suffered from the difficulty of understanding and properly reacting to the effects of societal changes for which we were unprepared and which are coming too fast to process at a desirable rate. At Endeavor, we have witnessed firsthand the effects of this swiftly changing landscape on the enterprise of higher education and the resulting challenges to its mission. *Transforming Undergraduate Education* emanates from the recognition of these challenges.

When I think back to my childhood, one of my most vivid memories is of my father, sitting by the fireplace, with my young cousin David perched upon his knee, talking to David about the thrill of mathematics, with David's attention captivated by every word. Beyond that, my father's actions embodied in numerous ways his deep commitment to education, from sending me to the encyclopedia at least once during almost every dinner, by banishing sloppy thinking from all mealtime conversation, by reading extensively throughout his life, and by helping many of my friends find their way to the college of their choice. He was as committed to education as he was to breathing, and he was committed to the highest values in human behavior with equal passion.

The contributors to this book share my father's commitment to high principle. How refreshing it is to encounter in the adult world the passion and energy that lie behind the work described here! Many people have contributed in numerous ways, giving generously of their time and energies to test and illuminate the ideas contained herein. That is indeed an inspiration to the Endeavor Foundation to continue its work in higher education.

All contributors deserve our thanks and commendation, but I cannot end these comments without singling out the leadership of Donald Harward. He engaged the all-important work of framing the challenges, bringing together the educators, and supporting the development of their many ideas and perspectives. His effort represents a deep commitment to seeing that our campuses promise all students that if they apply themselves to the task of learning with energy and enthusiasm, they can indeed make strides toward becoming the very best they can be.

Foreword

Sally Engelhard Pingree

This book is the culmination of years of dedicated efforts on the part of many great colleagues, all of whom believe, as I do, in the promise and importance of liberal education.

A decade ago, Don Harward, former president of Bates College; Tad Roach, headmaster of St. Andrew's School in Delaware; and I met to discuss our concerns and aspirations for students attending American colleges and universities. We collectively believed that studies, discussions, and research could not only identify how students were struggling on our campuses but also identify specific ways to create communities of engagement and learning worthy of our mission statements. We set to work and along the way met a brilliant, gracious, and creative group of colleagues who made Bringing Theory to Practice come alive.

The strategy adopted by the Bringing Theory to Practice Project was to encourage the use of institutional and academic strengths of engagement to determine if their use would have positive and confirmable effects or influences on the learning, behaviors, and dispositions of students. Resources from the Charles Engelhard Foundation, the Christian A. Johnson Endeavor Foundation, and many others have provided over the last decade multiple opportunities for research, campus projects, conferences, and workshops as well as monitored demonstration sites examining, within and across cohorts and time, the linkages among forms of intensive academic learning, the well-being of students, and their civic development.

In more recent years, the attention and resources of the project have been concentrated in helping institutions make the changes, often transformative changes, that they determine necessary to fulfill their mission of learning and discovery and their commitment to the wholeness of the lives of their students.

This book in part reflects the successes of those years of work by hundreds of institutions and the leadership of many. Some are authors contributing chapters to this book; others have been significant supporters, advisors, evaluators, sponsors, advocates, and colleagues. As one of the project's founders and primary supporters, I want to thank them all. What occurs in the contents that follow would not be possible without them.

Our hope is that this book will inspire and guide those who set priorities for the engagement and education of students on college campuses everywhere.

Acknowledgments

It is with much gratitude that I acknowledge the authors and coauthors of the chapters and case studies that collectively make up this major study. Their insights, analyses, and perspectives provide the very best of what the book offers.

Ashley Finley has, as my editing colleague, performed the essential task of selecting and organizing the case studies as well as authored a significant chapter. I want also to acknowledge Mr. Dylan Joyce, assistant to the Bringing Theory to Practice Project (BTtoP), whose positive attention to the multitude of editing and organizational details was indispensible. Mr. David Tritelli, editor at Association of American Colleges & Universities, and Mr. Michael Ferguson, editor at American Association of University Professors, provided consultation and many helpful edit suggestions.

Jennifer O'Brien, project manager for BTtoP, has, with this book, as she has with all the project's work over the last five years, been our source of most competent management and leadership.

From the inception of the scope and plan of the book, I have been encouraged by Ms. Sally Engelhard Pingree, president of the S. Engelhard Center, and by Ms. Julie Johnson Kidd, president of the Christian A. Johnson Endeavor Foundation. Their support and unflagging commitment, as friends and educators and as philanthropic leaders, to the value and championing of creating this book have been essential.

To all I extend appreciation and respect for their assistance and significant contributions. The book is not a "last word," but hopefully it does provide a pathway and the encouragement for needed conversations for "next words"—and the reasons and evidence needed to both construct and act on them.

Introduction

This book emphasizes a blend of rationale, argument, and evidence with the realities of campus initiatives and practices. It offers to those who are considering whether, why, and what changes need to be made in higher education generally, and their own campus specifically, the evidence and arguments for moving from stasis. For those ready to participate in making transformative changes, the chapters and case studies that follow suggest how steps can be taken and progress made. For those who are currently involved in, perhaps leading, changes to their own campus cultures, the book offers support and encouragement. And for those who are pausing—looking positively but cautiously at what needs to change and at the prospects and challenges that may be encountered—the book offers a guide. Our intention is to address a wide and receptive audience who look forward to making the efforts and sustaining them—rather than look only backward to the prevailing constraints, policies, and practices that are likely not to characterize higher education's future but may well be elements of what are amply described in the chapters that follow as causal conditions for the crises in higher education.

We do not think that additional alarms are needed to alert readers to the challenges and omissions in higher education. We do think that what is needed, and what this book intends to supply, is a set of arguments, theories, and evidence sufficient to encourage significant—transformative—changes, as well as examples of campus initiatives that document such changes (from directional nudges to major shifts of emphases and resources), combining theoretical consideration and analysis of fundamental issues related to learning and liberal education with studies of particular practices and modes of evaluation.

This book is designed to advance broad-based campus and off-campus discussions of how institutional structures; curricular and pedagogical emphases; and prevalent priorities, expectations, and reward systems contribute to the intensity and intentionality of specific cultures for learning. We believe that it is through such wide and inclusive discussions, combining consideration of both theory and practice, that transformative institutional changes lead to the creation of more viable campus cultures for learning. In sum, this is a book that provides both arguments and evidence for changing what is decried as multiple "crises" in higher education—and then suggests ways of sustaining what we know works and is valuable. It looks forward to ways of supporting campuses and their efforts.

Part I outlines the broad issues and identifies the areas where most agree that change is needed, while also recognizing the accomplishments and long-standing successes that many institutions have already achieved. In addition, part I describes the conceptual sources of the issues and considers various approaches for strengthening the campus culture for learning, as well as anticipates what may result.

Parts II and III explore the more specific issues involved in actually making profound changes and examines some of the implications. Each of the twenty-four scholars, administrators, policy designers, faculty members, researchers, and practitioners who have contributed to these chapters has kept in mind that readers will approach this book with their own histories and with varying levels of awareness of ongoing discussions within higher education. The common intent is to offer enduring insights or emphases while building upon but not duplicating the rich body of information and work that is already available. Our hope is that the book will have a long shelf life, that it will serve a considerable length of time as a stimulant of ideas and as a resource for practices and initiatives. Moreover, we hope and expect that the insights and emphases offered here will be broadly applicable to all institutional types and cultures.

Part IV of the book is devoted to the discussion of specific practices and to the presentation of relevant evidence from a set of ten case studies. The transferability and utility of the case studies are emphasized, making clear how others can adapt and adopt particular or systemic changes to meet the conditions and expectations of their own campus history and culture.

PART I

THE THEORETICAL ARGUMENTS AND THEMES

Donald W. Harward

The ideas presented in this book reflect multiple major themes, four of which receive separate consideration in part I. These themes have arisen from conversations and insights offered by the contributors (and others) and from the work of the Bringing Theory to Practice Project (BTtoP) over the last decade. Taken together, they connect most of the strands (with their practical consequences) that are explored more thoroughly in the chapters, case studies, and policy discussions that follow.

Theme One: The Campus Context or Culture Can Be Transformed

A campus context or culture can be made more conducive to encouraging and supporting learning. Because we can alter the campus culture, and because we have garnered evidence sufficient to show that campus cultures significantly influence learning (as determined by assessing behaviors, attitudes, and outcomes of wide ranges of definable populations of students over periods of time), an assessment of how those cultures affect learning can be accomplished across campus sites and silos, done in integrated and interesting ways, and meaningfully described and compared within and without the institution. Accordingly, the patterns of assessment an institution uses become exemplary of what the campus understands the nature of learning to be, of how and where learning occurs, and of how learning connects to changes in pedagogy, structure, and even reward systems.

Campus cultures, and the expectations they influence, have documentable significance for whether and how students achieve the integrated outcomes at the core of liberal education. The overarching conclusion is

3

that no matter the point from which an institution begins (with its multiple qualities and its unique history), an even more intentional campus context or culture for learning can be realized, learning that is critical and substantive, transferrable to new situations, and sustained—learning that is at the heart of liberal education.

Developing the means to alter the campus culture for learning should be neither a mystery nor an idealistic hope. In many contexts it may mean altering dominant policies, practices, and priorities. The patterns, practices, evidence, leadership, expectations, encouragement, and rewards— the what, the why, and the how of changes to a campus culture—are described in the chapters, case studies, and research profiles that follow.

The call for change to the campus culture includes the admonition to place liberal education at the center, as a core dimension of undergraduate education. This call is not new, but the necessary changes—to structure, access and cost, curricula, pedagogy, expectations, reward systems, and much more—have never before had more numerous or forceful advocates.

A recent critic argued that the fundamental problem is "consumers are being forced to shop for higher education on the basis of a college's reputation rather than the quality of the education . . . [C]olleges spend huge sums of money on new facilities, state-of-the art fitness centers, big-name researchers, and winning sports teams. Such visible investments help buoy a school's reputation, but they don't help students learn."[1] Many holding this or a similar view argue that the solution lies in making individual testing results more transparent so as to make higher education more accountable by comparing the achievements of students as they progress through a particular institution. Such results, they argue, should be the basis for institutional rankings.

This charge and the solution posed are, I believe, misguided. It is not unfair to charge that institutional priorities are driven disproportionately by image and marketing; indeed, it is apparent that "keeping up with peer institutions" is one, if not the most intense, of the drivers of priorities and resultant costs. Nor do I think it is mistaken to propose that institutions should attend more closely to student learning or use reliable means of assessing institutional qualities. The effort to concentrate attention to measuring outcomes of individual learners, however, fails to recognize that such an approach may rest on two category mistakes. The first mistake is to conflate teaching and learning. Teaching and learning are not points on a singular continuum. Instead, they represent different categories—separate, even if often considered co-continua. I am reminded of the quip by Gilbert Ryle that "She left in a car and a flood of tears does not mean she left by two modes of transportation."[2] There is no direct causal relationship between teaching and learning—as those who teach know so very well.

There is no evidence that an "increase" in teaching is proportional to increases in student learning. Rather, it is the character and the context of the teaching that bear on learning. The second category mistake is to conflate an increase in, and transparency of, the data arising from the assessment of particular students' experiences (no matter how large a pool) with the assessment of the overall quality of learning at the institution.

The search for meaningful, measurable, and comparable individual learning results overlooks the reliable assessment tools that are already available to gauge the campus culture for learning—to assess what is meaningful and connected to the likelihood of greater, deeper, and more useful student learning. Using both qualitative and quantitative measures and means, several research and campus-based projects have compared collections of learners in intensive contexts and cultures with random collections, with control groups, and over time. The findings suggest that it is the learning context or culture—the means, the opportunities the institution uses, and the priorities it sets in order to establish and foster a stronger campus culture for learning—that makes a difference.

This is not simply looking at more subtle "inputs." Changes in the campus context can make a real difference for students—for their learning as collectively determined, their attitudes, and their behaviors. At many institutions, faculty members consistently address the right questions: What does an intensive writing experience mean? What outcome do we want for our students when we ask them to be more adroit at quantitative reasoning? What form does the argument in a given text take and why? What role should faculty play in determining how students are progressing, beyond offering grades in our courses? How are we to normalize students' responses and expectations? How are new expectations to be structured and made explicit?

All these questions, and others like them, are asking for ways to address the campus culture. They should and can be considered independently of how we try to measure student learning for any particular student in any particular time of the individual's experience. However, to capture information and answers to relevant queries regarding the campus culture is likely to require changes to the ways information is gathered and the types of information gathered. Assessing a campus culture for learning is also likely to require an increase in communication within the institution and a corresponding decrease in the sense of ownership of information within particular silos.

The comparative data now used to rank institutions have everything to do with marketing, reputation, endowment levels, deferred maintenance, and "inputs" such as student aptitude scores, school rank, and retention. These factors have little or nothing to do with actual learning or with the conditions under which deep and profound learning occurs. Perhaps we should expect nothing more, given that we have all too often allowed higher education to be framed as a commodity or a service and have referred to students as "customers." In this way, we have reinforced the popular understanding of higher education as a private gain to be achieved through the accumulation of seat time and course credits. Insofar as marketing truly has become the dominant mode of institutional presentation, does it make any real difference to student learning and development which college or university the student attends? Perhaps if we moved the compass needle to the campus culture for learning, we would be addressing that question and decreasing attention to the misleading nature of current directions.

We might remind ourselves that there is little that is "customer friendly" about learning. On some economic models, teaching and administrating may appear as services, but learning is never simply a "service." Perhaps it would be more helpful for the current ranking systems to identify themselves as what they really are—comparisons of marketing, resources, and reputations—and then to run comparisons from volunteered, documented data regarding the campus culture for learning. Those data would be relevant, and they would be supported by the confirmation of increases in learning at the ranked institutions. As a first cut of such information, institutions could characterize their campus cultures for learning by responding to such inquiries as the following:

- What percentage of each class year of students participates in a guided research experience?
- What percentage of each first-year class has successfully completed multiple courses requiring significant writing, critical thinking, and methodological emphases (e.g., mathematical, empirical, interdisciplinary)?
- What percentage of students, regardless of major or year of study, participates repeatedly in identified engaged learning experiences? Are these experiences optional or expected?
- How do student reports of what they expect to find challenging (or expect to find in meaningful conversations with multiple faculty members) compare with what they actually experience?
- Are there civic learning expectations? In what form do they occur?
- What is spent per student on contexts that support teaching and learning beyond the classroom—for example, for community-based learning or applied research?
- What percentage of the full-time faculty serves as advisors, beyond their interaction with advanced students in the major?
- What changes—when using flourishing and resiliency scales or when tracking behavioral patterns, attitudes, and dispositions from

survey data—are revealed when collections of students are compared throughout their undergraduate careers?
- How has the campus intentionally documented the connection of student well-being measures with learning?
- What is the evidence, qualitative and quantitative, that the civic mission stated in the institution's catalog is being achieved?

By focusing on the significance of altering the campus context or culture for "higher" learning, we can develop new ways to measure learning outcomes. A campus that is transforming its culture for learning is one where faculty are involved from the start in identifying outcomes and considering what should constitute sufficient evidence of their achievement. On such a campus, the context or culture for learning is thoroughly and carefully evaluated, and the work of all is punctuated with ongoing discussions of what has been effective—and what has not been.

Separating the feasible though complex task of assessing a campus culture for learning from the issue of how to assess the gains or progress of a particular learner—which is usually thought to involve measuring the retention of a readily quantifiable body of information or a particularly measurable skill—recognizes what faculty have long known, namely, that the very liberating experience of individual learning has much to do with individual student motivation, expectations, capacities, and readiness. These factors are often quite independent of teaching, yet they can be shaped by the campus culture—the intensity of that culture being the faculty's primary responsibility. Students are then expected and encouraged to engage in that culture—and in doing so, liberate themselves. Persistent failures to recognize the relation between the culture for learning and student expectations, efforts, and accomplishments help explain faculty hesitancy regarding the evaluation of teaching and the multiple appeals for its assessment. Teaching is not superfluous, of course, but it does not stand in direct causal or linear relation to learning.

Our institutions are established on the confirmable premise that teaching and teachers are among the most influential factors in the context or culture for learning that the campus provides. Effective teaching comprises complex and subtle acts. The sort of effective and deep learning experiences that are at the core of liberal education—experiences that go well beyond memorization, skill development, and the capacity to retain complex information—are, in fact, expressions of individual liberation and choice that originate in supportive and encouraging contexts.

If the campus context or culture can be transformed, it can be made more conducive to deep learning. To be sure, some institutions already succeed in creating and sustaining such campus cultures and have made the campus culture a defining element or an institutional priority. The campus culture can be transformed in connection with greater expectations of engagement—by students and faculty—in shared research, in dialogue, in courses that require frequent and assessed major writing experiences, in deep and thorough textual examination or empirical inquiry, in quantitative analysis, and in the scientific method. The campus culture can be transformed through such diverse efforts as an understanding of the utility and aesthetics of both logical and empirical analyses and models, through service learning, and through structured communities of learners. It can be transformed by expanding the context for learning beyond the classroom and by putting teachers and learners in positions of reciprocity of responsibility.

Contexts and expectations affect learning—learning that is simultaneously critical and substantive, analytic and synthetic, transferrable to new situations, and sustained for a lifetime. But this is learning freely achieved. To make a campus culture more conducive to learning is not to confuse learning with indoctrination or training, nor is it to confuse learning as the objective of higher education with the social and economic needs for job preparation. Learning and the campus culture, and the intentional cultivation of expectations that affect learning, are not incompatible with training or job preparation; indeed, they can be inclusive of them. But they are not identical to them. In many ways it is this broader perspective, and the changes and expectations that flow from it, that should be championed publicly and within our institutions.

Theme Two: The Epistemological, Psychosocial, and Civic Dimensions of Liberal Education Are Interrelated and Essential—Both in Practice and as Core Purposes

Discussions of liberal education often suffer from variations in the history of the uses of the term itself. Originally, liberal education was defined in terms of the curriculum or content—in classical terms, the *trivium* (grammar, logic, and rhetoric) and the *quadrivium* (arithmetic, geometry, astronomy, and music). Later there emerged a humanistic definition that emphasized self-realization and the basic reality of learning as a political or communal act. This definition goes as far back as Aristotle's characterization of human agents (he limited his definition to "free" citizens) as *zoon politican* (political or community beings). Liberal education was understood as "liberating"; the emphasis was not exclusively on what was studied but included specific and sustained outcomes—forms of learning that liberated the individual from prejudice or opinion and that remained a dimension of how one lived one's life. Following the Enlightenment, "liberal education" connoted not only self-liberation (i.e., self-awareness) but also being "critically minded," challenging judgments by authority, appealing to reason or evidence, and suspending judgment when neither sufficient evidence nor logic indicated a conclusion. This interpretation of the liberal learner as an engaged, but privileged, skeptic led some to conclude that liberal education was appropriate only for a few. The abiding misconception that liberal education is conjoined with the political and social ideology of liberalism can also be traced to this elitist and contrarian understanding of the enterprise—perhaps a partial explanation for why the phrase "liberally educated" has recently come to be used as a way of casting disdain or aspersions on those to whom it is said to refer—to the politically liberal and the critics of conventional institutions. And all too often, for those so described, the accusation was considered confirmation of the anti-intellectualism of the nonliberally educated. There was no point in mounting an informed and constructive response—so the language (and thereby part of the promise) of liberal education was surrendered. Both the language and the promise of liberal education need to be recaptured.

Liberal education has been relegated to the margins of higher education. At many institutions—though certainly not all—it has been translated into a modest set of course requirements often referred to as "general education." Although students in all disciplines may be required to take these courses, most do so without understanding why they are germane to their primary interests. Even when pursued as an area of concentration, liberal education has moved to the category of the "boutique" and has been made available only to the comparative few with the leisure to pursue it.

Today, the language of liberal education is still found in virtually every institutional mission statement, though often as unexamined rhetoric. Less frequently found is any characterization of what the institution means by the term or how, specifically, such an education is accomplished—except in terms of seat time or course credits. The objectives or purposes of liberal education need explication: Why is liberal education important? Why is it a vital dimension of higher education? Why is it an education for everyone? In what sense does it embody what makes university or college education "higher"—that is, not simply postsecondary but of a categorically different sort? What follows is an effort to provide such an explication, an effort that has been informed by the work of the Association of American Colleges and Universities and other higher education associations, as well as the thoughtful writings of teachers, scholars, and college presidents.

Liberal education comprises three interrelated and essential dimensions: the epistemic, the psychosocial, and the civic. It bears asking whether there really is wide institutional support for student achievement along each of the three dimensions. Do parents and students see these dimensions as impractical and prefer to hold the institution accountable for providing the training and skills needed for employment? Can the proclaimed centrality and interdependency of these dimensions be realized—that is, can they be moved functionally beyond their status as the topic of occasional faculty conversations to become clear institutional priorities and to inform expectations across the campus? To sort through these issues, it is necessary first to "unpack" this dimensional triad and to examine each dimension separately, what it means and what it suggests. Like all complexities, when the several "strands" of the complexity are examined, the "hooks" they suggest make drawing connections even more apparent.

Teaching and learning are distinct aspects of a complexity, a gestalt of intellectual, emotional, behavioral, and civic development. Over the last several decades, evidence from many disciplines (including behavioral psychology and empirical studies of enhanced magnetic resolution imaging of brain behavior) justifies suspension of the formerly prevalent Cartesian model of wholly separate zones of identity—for example, cognitive versus emotional and behavioral—and the implication of that "divide" that wholly separate service centers were needed in colleges and universities to address them. This book speaks to the interdependency of the connections between liberal education and the full, integrated self. It is in this respect that the call for transformative changes to campus cultures and structures also holds the promise of the "transformation" of the learner—of the campus culture for learning positively affecting the whole student.

Taken together, the epistemological, psychosocial, and civic dimensions of liberal education reflect the sum of the purposes of "higher" learning, project the categories of effects and affects for learners, and characterize the objectives at the core of the institutional mission—if the institution is indeed offering a liberal education.

Before addressing how they are connected, it will be useful to characterize each dimension briefly. These are oversimplified characterizations (and there is much literature bearing on each) but may be sufficient for our purposes to reveal the "hooks" that make connections possible.

The first, or epistemological, dimension itself can be understood as a complexity made up of three distinguishable components or categories, each of which is essential:

- *"Knowing that."* This form of knowing includes propositional knowledge, information, and facts—the elements of the "what" that is to be studied—and, most often, is thought to dominate the content of a curriculum.

- *"Knowing how to."* This form of knowing entails the acquisition of skills, practices, and methodologies of discovery and research that provide the means to join learning and patterned inquiry; it is obviously essential to scholarship, discovery, and the ongoing addition to what we know.
- *"Judgment."* Distinct from both "knowing that" and "knowing how to," judgment characterizes the relation of knowledge to action.

The second dimension, the psychosocial (referring to the student's well-being or the eudemonic dimension of liberal education), focuses on the integration of learning and its connection to the full development of the learner. The learning at the heart of liberal education positively affects the flourishing, the sense of identity, the persistence and resiliency, and the self-realization of the learner—behaviors, dispositions, and actions that point away from the presumptions of dualism and argue for the consideration of the learner as an integrated whole.

The third dimension, the civic dimension of liberal education, focuses on the integration of learning, the self, and awareness of what is "other." Knowing "takes" an object—be it the world, or a state of affairs, or a fact or process. To know anything, including oneself, is to recognize what is other—what is not self—and to know anything deeply is to become clearly aware of that relationship and what may be a responsibility to sustaining it. Knowing and learning become ethical acts—by their very nature connected to the awareness of other and to the civic and community—acts guided by "virtue" and expressed in the universality of the moral principle to treat what is other as an end in itself and not solely as a means. This notion of the guiding of the relation of education to the civic has, of course, its own long history. It goes partway, however, in noticing that without "the guidance of virtue" the connection of education to the civic could (as the world has sadly seen) lead to tyranny. A major point of inquiry in several of the chapters that follow is how we are to understand that relationship between self and other today. Is recognizing and valuing what is other a necessary condition for civic responsibility and development within an open, democratic, and highly diverse society? Does higher education foster this link between knowing and its object, and in so doing, does it point to a core connection between learning and the civic?

Beyond drawing out some subtleties of these dimensions of liberal learning, we find that certain practices foster greater understanding and support for each of these three interrelated dimensions. We could begin by exploring how each dimension of learning championed by liberal education can be better expressed in a campus culture.

- How do particular pedagogies create or maximize conditions for learning?
- What evidence do we have that "engaged learning" pedagogies (e.g., dialogic experiences, research involvement, service learning, intensive writing, and critical thinking or reflection) actually make a substantial, positive difference?
- How are we to construct and evaluate experiences and opportunities that extend beyond the classroom?
- What confirms that not all the aspects of learning inherent in liberal education are linked to the teaching acts of faculty?
- How is the learning inherent in liberal education better understood metaphorically as being "horizontal" rather than "vertical"?
- Just how does the integration of multiple forms of experience require understanding the learner as a whole, as a gestalt?

Recent attention within colleges and universities has tended to focus not on core purposes or dimensions (and their relatedness) of liberal education but, instead, on structural or institutional management issues and, more broadly, on the "enterprise of higher education": How do we assure that the institution persists? How do we open it to more? How do we continue to finance it? How do we prepare those who will maintain it in the future? These questions raise important issues, but so, too, do the following less frequently asked questions:

- What basic objectives, or core purposes, of our mission derive from our avowed commitment to liberal education? What is promised to the learners who participate in liberal education and to those who support it?
- Is there a preferred view of liberal education? Do we continually reinvent it to meet the needs of our age, whatever we determine those needs to be?
- Is it enough to say that the objective of liberal education is for students to acquire the particular skills needed to participate in a technologically driven society or in a global economy?
- Is it enough to say that the objective of liberal education is for students to acquire breadth, for them to have more freedom to choose from a multitude of existing courses in order to gain acquaintance with methods of analysis and inquiry that can encourage discovery across disciplinary boundaries?
- Is it enough to promise access to information, to special services, or to special facilities— important as many of us think these are to the strength of our appeal and relevance?

The argument, the evidence, and the practices discussed in many of the following chapters suggest that liberal education is a necessary condition for the realization of the full and whole self. Reasserting this argument might mean that we are likely to revisit, and in many cases to transform, the structural and institutional dimensions of liberal education that we have built. We might begin by reconsidering the need to participate in the "arms race" of providing more services and facilities "because the market demands it"—and then question whether the market is the appropriate compass for determining the direction and purposes of higher education. We might begin by asking, "Who, or what, should define academic quality, and how should that definition direct the campus culture and the expectations of those who participate in it?" "How are our teaching and our students' learning inextricably connected to their intellectual, emotional, behavioral, and civic development?" These inquiries would not be peripheral or beyond our mission; rather, they would flow from our understanding of the core objectives of liberal education.

Regrettably, multiple surveys have revealed that the outcomes of an integrated and intensive undergraduate liberal education are not widely understood or highly valued by the general public today. While the college degree is universally recognized as the key to economic and social mobility, the quality of the educational experience that lies behind that credential is more or less ignored. And because of its complicity in the neglect of the full core purposes of liberal education, the academy itself bears some responsibility for popular misconceptions or ignorance of what liberal education promises.

Many in the academy have lost track of the full complexity of undergraduate education by giving concentrated attention to teaching in discrete fields and giving less consideration to student learning or to the concept of learning itself. And even though many faculty do focus with good will and great intentionality on the "knowing that" dimension of their disciplines and, subsequently, its centrality in the curriculum, most give less attention to the complexity of other epistemological dimensions of liberal education.

Recently, the nearly exclusive focus on just one aspect of learning—the gaining and transfer of knowledge—has begun to be redressed through the development of pedagogies that emphasize other epistemological elements such as "knowing how" and "judgment." As a result of advocacy on behalf of pedagogies that involve undergraduates in research, for example, more institutions and individual faculty members are now developing research methods (patterns for "knowing how") and discovery processes both within and across disciplines. Service learning and community-based research experiences are growing rapidly, and they have proven to be viable means of expanding teaching and learning beyond the classroom and of introducing opportunities for judgment and for the application of knowledge to practice.

Notwithstanding these promising changes and exemplary improvements that engage students in learning, the lack of attention to the core purposes of higher education other than the epistemological remains largely unaddressed. Many faculty members continue to value the theoretical over the applied or practiced, and it remains a stretch for them to intentionally foster self-discovery and well-being or to make evident the relationships between knowledge and the responsibility to act for the common good. Within and without the university, the prevailing view has long been that attention to student well-being and to the relation of education to the civic is the province of other cultural institutions, such as religion or the family, or that it is the work of counselors and other trained professionals. Often, we have failed to adequately acknowledge what we have intuitively understood as educators, namely, that liberal education is unique in that it contributes to the achievement of these multiple core outcomes and reveals their interdependency. The connections between liberal education and these outcomes are not accidental; rather, they reflect the essential or core dimensions of learning and their observable effects on student attitudes, dispositions, behaviors, choices, and actions.

However, there is a persistent pattern that ignores or denies these connections. Departments represent fields and are separated from each other. Student affairs is separated from academic affairs; research from teaching; the curricular from the extracurricular; the university from the community. The evidence shows that these separations ignore the reality of the organic, the gestalts of learners and of learning. And so, why do they prevail? Why does the suggestion that we change provoke precaution, if not outright resistance? Is our reluctance to consider change a matter of examining the current structures of separation and determining that they are more efficient and economical than the alternatives? Or does the reluctance merely reflect the inertia found in all complex organizations, where the preservation of the default structure is seen as identical to the preservation of the organization itself? Regrettably for our students and their families, opportunities to explore these questions are rare, and the complexity of the core purposes of liberal education is seldom considered. More often, students and families reflect back to us what many in higher education have been emphasizing over the last several decades, namely, the extrinsic uses of education, the networks of alumni, and the acquisition of a credential needed to take the next step on a social or economic ladder.

Many who lament this state of affairs conclude that higher education has become "commodified," that it has become just one more product or service offered to consumers at a market-sensitive price and valued solely for its subsequent economic utility. Moreover, treating higher education as a commodity has fit well with those who choose to characterize liberal education as political and social liberalism and faculty as ideologues, with the implication that liberal education has been further marginalized as a "politicized" product that is certainly not for everyone and is not at the core of higher education.

Liberal education is not ideological indoctrination. There is, however, an "ideal" of liberal education. At its best, liberal education enables students to develop critical thinking skills and disciplinary competence and to distinguish categories of information, acknowledge ambiguity, and eschew easy certainty. It encourages students to be both reasonable and passionate—to link learning with action—and, in that respect, to champion the cultivation of the civic and the responsibilities of citizenship and leadership. Liberal education does respect contrarian ideas and challenge the status quo. And if expectations are held high and students are truly valued, the consequences of liberal education are deeply relevant to students' lives. Faculty members have always known this. In many respects, this book serves as a reminder of the changes that are needed in order to assert liberal education's relevancy and to realize its potential to affect the well-being of students.

This powerful ideal of liberal education can be realized if it is articulated and emphasized, if it is consistently expressed in curricula and pedagogies, if it is truly reflective of institutional priorities and practiced mission, if meaningful evaluations are studied and made apparent, and if the full integration of the core dimensions and purposes of liberal education (the intellectual, psychosocial, and civic) is permitted to shape the expectations of those within and beyond the institution—including parents, friends of the university or college, and those invested, internally and externally, in its future. Changing expectations changes attitudes and perceptions, and those changes lead, in turn, to changes in choices and behavior.

Theme Three: Certain Behavioral Patterns, Exhibited by Students and Expressive of Disengagement, Can Be Modified Through an Increase in Their Academic Engagement

The genesis of the Bringing Theory to Practice Project (BTtoP) arose from the exploration of a hunch a decade ago. That hunch emerged from an abundance of what might be termed "negative evidence" that the behavioral patterns so obvious on our campuses (as expressions of disengagement) could be modified by intentionally increasing the opportunities for and expectations of academic engagement. By *engagement* we meant not busy work or additional stress over paper assignments and examinations but greater involvement of the student in the patterns and dimensions of learning—specifically, greater involvement in judgment, in seeing the relation of knowing to the practical issues they encounter in the community beyond the campus.

Multiple surveys between the early 1990s and 2010, historical studies, editorial observations, and the popular press have focused on student behaviors that are self-abusive—or, at best, self-indulgent. The commonly advanced explanatory thesis is that these behaviors are expressions of various forms of disengagement and of cultural and social inducements for postponing development and responsibility.

All current students have been stigmatized by what is reported as rampant, and this breadth of the implicit indictment is particularly unfortunate. The actual state of affairs on our campuses is both more complex and more positive, a fact that has been revealed by BTtoP surveys and conferences that have attracted scores of students from institutions of all types and locales. Yes, the patterns of disengagement are real. But so, too, are patterns of full and meaningful engagement—intellectual, social, and civic. And as one would expect given the diversity of backgrounds and motivations at play, both patterns are, to a significant extent, blended on our campuses. However, this blending does not relieve our obligation to examine the various opportunities, activities, programs, and expectations—implicit or explicit—that have the potential to reorient the campus culture toward greater engagement and learning for all our students.

Numerous studies and commentaries have shaped both scholarly and popular impressions of student culture since the 1990s. Helen Horowitz's 1987 study, *Campus Life: Undergraduate Cultures from the End of the Eighteenth Century to the Present*, describes the various and evolving worlds that undergraduates make and, to an extent, why some emerge as dominant.[3] Faculty influence on those worlds has always been significant, she argues—even recently, as faculty members have withdrawn from their once prevalent role in the full lives of students. And while emotional and economic dependence on parents appears to be greater for today's students than for previous generations (excepting "returning student" populations), it remains unclear what impact greater attention to diversity has had on the worlds students form.

In the mid 1990s, Willimon and Naylor used their direct acquaintance with the culture of Duke University as a starting point for consideration of what they referred to as "the symptoms": alcohol abuse, sexual aggression, the attitude that "we work hard so we're entitled to play hard," and the preponderant view that the undergraduate years are simply the time for gaining the techniques and contacts required to be "a moneymaker."[4] Regarding the sources of these symptoms, Willimon and Naylor saw a prevailing sense of meaninglessness (certainly purposelessness) among students and a failure of the college or university to provide the "glue" that gives greater meaning to the undergraduate experience. The solution they offered was to emphasize teachers who teach, to revisit the curriculum and make it more relevant to students' lives, and to develop "learning communities" within institutions.

Tom Wolfe's novel *I Am Charlotte Simmons* and Barrett Seaman's presentation of campus life in *Binge: What Your College Students Won't Tell You* may have overstated for literary and dramatic coherence the intimate structure and disturbing qualities of what they characterized as the prevalent campus culture.[5] However, we know that at least parts of our campuses are, in fact, marked by the negative features depicted by both authors—the abuse, the self-indulgence, the peer pressure that reinforces those behaviors and attitudes, and a seeming disinterest on behalf of the "adult" population of faculty and administrators as they distance themselves from the full lives of students. Today, all of us in higher education recognize the patterns as present, if not prevalent, in any honest description of our campus cultures. It was that honesty, and not the hyped extremism of a jeremiad, that pointed to a possible way to cultivate broad recognition of campus reality—its complexity and its extent—and then to change those elements of the culture that led away from learning and its connections to student well-being and civic development.

Although they are evident on all campuses (some to a greater degree than others), certain patterns of behavior and related forms of disengagement remain the "elephant in the room": disengagement through substance abuse; self-reported episodes of depression sufficient to inhibit or prohibit academic work; evidence of withdrawal from civic engagement; and the prevalence on some campuses of a tacit bargain struck by students and faculty—"If I don't ask much of you, you won't ask much of me." Often, we don't speak of these patterns for fear of creating a singular "marketing" problem. But they are present in the minds of every college or university president who receives a call in the middle of the night informing her or him of a student crisis.

The BTtoP "hunch" was that one especially promising way to approach student disengagement might be to explore the use, practice, and expectation of greater engagement in learning and then to document how that engagement positively affects the whole student. We, in effect, thought we might confirm Dewey's arguments with the evidence of actual practices.

Listening to student and other voices on many campuses, and drawing from national studies (some commissioned by BTtoP), we documented patterns of student disengagement, behavioral disengagement (particularly exhibited in substance abuse), emotional disengagement, and civic disengagement. While these patterns were apparent to many faculty members and to most professional student affairs and counseling staffs, they were infrequently being addressed as systemic issues. As they responded to liability and security concerns, many institutions struggled with ameliorating symptoms but not the contributing causes.

Initially, the BTtoP Project called on campuses to address the underlying causes of these patterns—and, in doing so, to test our hunch that the patterns shared important connections and that strengthening student academic engagement would have implications, effects and affects, for student behavior, well-being, and civic development. This was not a hunch regarding therapy for the subset of students who exhibit patterns of serious illness or alienation; rather, the hunch suggested that more deeply engaged learning and community involvement (at multiple levels) had contributing effects and affects for most, if not all, students—that their well-being, their flourishing, resilience, adaptability to difference, identity, and civic development, would be affected.

As the project began to commission research and national studies, we refined the hunch to a hypothesis. To study the specific forms of engaged learning and the capacity of affects and effects defined as possible outcomes, we identified national demonstration sites and, concerned about the potential for bias in small samples, eventually supported national intensive sites where entire student populations were involved. In addition, scores of campuses received small programmatic or research grants to explore in their own context the possible relationships between active academic engagement and student well-being and civic engagement. All of this has led to a preponderance of evidence confirming the hunch that behavior, attitudes, and the well-being criteria of flourishing, resiliency, persistence, and identity are directly connected to the campus culture for learning.

We asked why it is surprising to discover that liberal education is necessary for the development of the habits, resiliency, dispositions, and patterns of choice that are relevant to healthy and productive lives. Could transformational changes at our colleges and universities put the co-objectives of student learning, student health or well-being, and student civic development at the center of what we do and what we value?

Doing so is likely to require recognition of both the whole student and the reality of multiple and interconnected elements of student experience and development. Liberal education is encouraged within a context—a learning community—that reinforces the gestalt of the multiple aspects of the student's experience. Practically, this means, for example, identifying—with equal attention to curricular and pedagogical matters—where and when students gather beyond the classroom. What is encouraged by such spaces and times? Who is available for interaction? What opportunities do students have to apply elements of what they learn to examples beyond the classroom? What models for the application of knowledge do they encounter? And how are they held responsible for applying what they learn in ways that encourage further engagement?

If the call for knowledge, the call for civic engagement, and the call for individual realization (well-being) come together to form the full purpose of liberal education, then attention to two out of three is insufficient.

If liberal education is the messy work of creating a culture or context for learning, that work is done so that learners can choose to liberate themselves. And when engaged, students can choose to encounter what they are trying to understand. Through such encounters, students' own views and privileges can be exposed and examined. Thinking about the basic or core purposes of education helps us understand our work as the crafting of contexts within which learners can achieve realization and prepare to act—and to change behavior, attitudes, and dispositions.

It is our fundamental promise to our students that we will provide the context in which they can liberate themselves. The best way to deliver on this promise is to expect and, indeed, insist that students be engaged academically, to provide ample opportunities for them to engage, and to value their engagement.

Theme Four: What Is Meant by Transformative Change in the Academy, and What Does Achieving It Entail?

This last major theme begins with a conclusion. Transformative (institutional) change will mean at least the following:

- "Shifting the paradigm" from teaching to learning and then fully attending to whether learning occurs
- Prioritizing pedagogies of engagement, connecting knowledge and discovery to judgment and practice
- Rejecting the operative myth of Cartesian dualism and structuring what we offer to students with the realization that they are whole persons with intellectual, emotive, and civic dimensions
- Reenvisioning and reordering reward structures for faculty and staff that align with our core purposes

- Addressing the socialization patterns that currently dominate the preparation of our faculties and academic leadership, as we define for ourselves and for our institutions the meaning of being a "teacher/scholar"
- Deepening the contexts for learning and for strengthening what faculty can do best by practices and support systems
- Recognizing that not all learning occurs in the classroom and that not all teaching occurs by faculty
- Most importantly, restructuring priorities, resources, and practices, including the financial, so that changes are brought from the periphery to the center of the institution, and to what it delivers, and to what its publics then expect

Current discussions are replete with the grammar of change. But if those discussions are to serve as a credible source of support or as a reliable guide to any actions, then it must be clear what is meant by "change"—and especially "transformative change." Is a paradigm shift of the academy's attention required—from teaching to learning, for example? What is sufficient to produce change, and what is necessary? Who leads change, and who resists it?

To consider change is to consider one of the framing notions we have of reality, our actions, and their purpose. Heraclitus claimed that change was the only true character of reality; his critics denied change ever occurred. Because of fundamental shifts in the educational enterprise, it is uniquely appropriate now to make changes to the structure, pedagogy, curricula, rewards, and other parts of a campus culture for learning. How profound is the call for change in higher education? I believe the recent proponents of neopragmatism have it right: "The substantive struggles [in higher education] have to do with changing notions concerning the nature and sources of knowledge; with changing notions concerning what it means to know and understand; with changing conceptions of the processes by which teaching and learning are mediated; and with changing conceptions [provided by current neuroscience research] of the affective and cognitive mechanisms and meanings of human mental activity."[6]

Whatever one may consider the theoretical bases for such changes, the evidence clearly supports the transformative effects of changes that engage, educate, and affect the full lives of students—individually and as a collection of civic agents. This evidence is derived largely from the practices—and the thorough assessment of them—that have been developed through the work of the BTtoP Project; the Association of American Colleges and Universities' Liberal Education and America's Promise initiative; the American Association of State Colleges and Universities' American Democracy

Project; Imagining America; Campus Compact; the Bonner Foundation; Project Pericles; and the independent work of scholars, other institutes, and foundations, as well as initiatives on hundreds of campuses.

How does transformative change happen, and why? How can its effectiveness be evaluated? What does it take to restructure an institution, to reprioritize budgets, to rethink curricula? What does it take to reinvest in the faculty design of pedagogies and the use of out-of-class resources, or to reconsider faculty preparation, dominant patterns of socialization in the profession, and reward systems? And most importantly, what does it take to alter the expectations of students, their families, and the public at large—including expectations regarding the relation of liberal education to job preparation?

All these questions point to issues and strategies of promise that are at the heart of ongoing work in higher education—and that inform the themes and theses of this book. The variety and complexity of these expressions of change reflect the proper answer to the question "What is transformative change?"

Whether as a conceptual construct, or simply as a graphic characterization of the complexity of change, an arc can be used to display a series of positions that individuals within the campus (or the institution in general) may occupy. The metaphor of "taking steps" suggests moving individuals or groups to new positions on the arc, reflecting the dynamic quality of change in higher education. The metaphor is particularly relevant to transformational change, through which established paradigms—complete with their own inertia—are confronted; conditions of disequilibrium are noticed; and the paradigm is reconsidered, altered, or replaced, and around which new practices, policies, and priorities are established. The curve of the arc can represent direction and steepness as well as recognize that new paradigms will themselves eventually be positioned on an arc of change, challenged, and then reconsidered.

In figure I.1, the initial position on the arc is that of confronting the current paradigm. Actually doing this is most complex and certainly context dependent. In some contexts, calling attention to current barriers, failures, and inadequacies is heard as a jeremiad and, consequently, ignored. In others, the very evidence of student disengagement (or "out of control" cost increases, or "new uses" of technology) is recognized as a clear sign of a paradigm that has failed, or at least one that needs urgently to be addressed. For many campuses, however, conversations regarding what it would mean to alter the campus culture—to make students' educational experience truly transformational; to significantly affect student learning, well-being, and civic development—are an effective means of at least examining the prevalent paradigm and asking what would follow if an alternative were put in place.

Arc of Change

An "arc" of change identifies stages in creating a campus culture for learning—a campus culture supportive of transformative student experience. The efficacy and wisdom of reordering priorities—costs and rewards—rather than only using additional resources to move the campus on any "arc" of change is both the challenge and the unique opportunity provided by the financial constraints all institutions face.

Sustainability/ Priorities: At this stage institutions are addressing how they will sustain changes and how they will have the campus culture reflect, in practices, policies, priorities, rewards, and finances, the transformation they've achieved.

Assessment/ Evaluation of effectiveness and costs: Institutions are in the midst of thorough evaluation and assessment of initiatives.

Implementation/ Investment in means, processes and models: At this stage, institutions are implementing major new initiatives.

Understanding/ Considering strategies and clarity of objectives: Suggests institutional exploration of the rigorous clarification of objectives and the strategic steps they should take to affect change and/or address current paradigms.

Awareness/ Confrontation with current paradigm: The initial position on the arc is complex and context dependent. At this stage campuses may call attention to current barriers, failures, inadequacies, marginalization of purpose, or evidence of student disengagement. Institutions may initiate or extend campus "conversations" regarding what it would mean to alter the campus culture in a way that makes the educational experience truly transformational in its implications for student learning, well-being, and civic development.

Figure I.1. Arc of Change.

Steps on any arc of change are rarely linear; before progressive change occurs, some steps may mark returns to earlier positions on the arc. Some campuses are well beyond recognizing current barriers and inadequacies of the predominant paradigm; they have begun the rigorous clarification of objectives and have taken the strategic steps that should follow next. Still other institutions are even further along—implementing major new initiatives or engaging in thorough evaluation and assessment. And some campuses are already addressing how to sustain the changes—how the transformation they've achieved will be reflected in the campus culture through practices, policies, priorities, rewards, and finances.

In many respects, the appropriate forms of encouragement and support along the arc of change must be determined on a case-by-case basis. History and institutional culture always shape the steps. Nevertheless, the several available campus models demonstrate that theory can indeed be brought to practice and that new paradigms do emerge—often in spite of, or perhaps even enabled by, the severe limitations on funding that force a reordering of priorities rather than an adding on. Our experience with the hundreds of campuses—large and small, public and private—that have been involved in the BTtoP Project has shown that the most likely route toward transformative change and a shift of paradigms is through careful examination of evidence, legitimation of "counter cases," and conversations rooted in both the faculty and the student body. It's helpful to bear in mind that paradigms tend to shift gradually, over long periods of time. (Heliocentric theories were espoused by Leonardo da Vinci long before Copernicus and before Galileo, for instance, and the Roman Church didn't adopt the paradigm shift until several centuries later.)

In explaining transformative change, the paradigm shift metaphor can usefully be complemented by a very different metaphor arising from economics—that of intentionally designed "guides" or "nudges," as presented in the work of Cass Sunstein and Richard Thaler.[7] Robust change can be encouraged, facilitated, and explained by directional nudges or intentionally designed guides that, although seemingly inconsequential in themselves, act like a "hand on the back" guiding the change process. The exciting consequence of this metaphor is that it presents the necessary changes as intentional, well conceived, well designed, well evaluated, and well coordinated rather than as dramatic, wholesale, and potentially disruptive and unsustainable.

Many of us have long defended a "libertarian" approach to higher education. That is, we do not seek to liberate our students; we seek, instead, to provide a campus context or culture that is supportive of student choices that enable our students to liberate themselves. Controlling all choices, or influencing them in ways that prohibit freedom of action, is incompatible with education. However, the conditions of free choice and action, while necessary for education, do not make the campus context wholly neutral. Subtle, culturally specific guides or influencers of choice and action operate within every campus context. These are not directly causal, but they do affect individual behaviors nonetheless. Accordingly, a campus culture, like other community contexts, can be both paternalistic and libertarian. Choices remain free, even as educators guide or steer students in directions that are likely to improve their lives—intellectually, emotionally, and civically.

We can begin to exert this positive influence—to "nudge" or "guide" our students—by recognizing the existence and pattern of the influences or guides that currently prevail on our campuses. The issue is not whether there *are* guides or influences but rather what they are and what they encourage. Can we be intentional in substituting some influences for others—without prohibiting student choice? Can we replace some prevailing influences, not with explicit admonitions from authority but with subtle, context-dependent influences that affect the behaviors and freely made choices of students and faculty? At many campuses, the prevailing influences are disproportionately directed toward narrow self-interest and forms of disengaged behavior. The economics literature asks us to consider, for example, a cafeteria line where, because they are placed in a highly visible and readily accessible position, french fries are frequently chosen—even when they are understood to be unhealthy.

The BTtoP Project has encouraged the presence and development of counterbalancing influences. It has encouraged choices and behaviors that are directed toward transformative change; that reflect the gains maximized by collective self-interest; that lead to the development of the whole student; and that suggest the common good can, in the long term, positively affect self-interest. To reprise the cafeteria-line example already given, the BTtoP Project has moved the carrot sticks to the prominent place previously occupied by the french fries, thereby encouraging—but not forcing—diners to select the healthier option.

There is a wide range of potentially effective influences. For example, an institution might allow students to receive their financial aid when studying abroad, while limiting foreign venues to inherently challenging contexts. This would create the opportunity for all students to experience a condition that challenges them to adapt and to question their own long-held views. Or an institution might create faculty reward structures that encourage service learning, community-based research, and other less conventional pedagogies that insist on greater student engagement. Neither of these examples would restrict choice, yet both would affect behaviors and actions. Those best able to craft such positive influences are those who know the campus culture most intimately—the faculty and the student affairs and counseling staff.

Finally, communities—campus communities as well as the broader civic community—can be considered metaphorical social organisms that undergo developmental changes and adaptations that preserve and sustain them. One role of higher education, then, could be to identify prevailing influences and substitute guides that lead to behaviors that are not necessarily in an individual member's immediate self-interest but that are in the interest of the common good. And a significant aspect of civic engagement could be to identify the specific social construction of the community and those factors—from direct causes to nudges—affecting the behaviors that sustain it. The goal would be to understand their influence and to find ways of enhancing them while still preserving the unique culture of the community and the liberty necessary for meaningful choice. One result would likely be that the academic institution and the community (at any level) would develop a reciprocal partnership so that the social construction of the community and the encouragement of meaningful civic engagement and development could be fostered for both those making up the campus and those in the larger community.

If basic attitudes and behaviors are to change, and if our campuses are to realize their full promise, I believe fundamental shifts are needed. These shifts should engage us all and support all our efforts as laborers in the messy process of initiating and sustaining steps—large or small steps and nudges. Over the past decade, through its support for institutions, the BTtoP Project has demonstrated that faculties, staff, and students welcome the conversations that begin the process and that estimates of entrenched opposition to change are most often overstated. There is no villainous element. There is likely no single enlightened view. As educators, we know that what we promise really can be delivered.

As we think about the nature and extent of change, we would do well to consider the Faustian bargain we must avoid, namely, to diminish the relationship between faculty and students. This relationship is inherently precious—not precious in the sense of fancy or rare, but rather in the sense of profoundly important and fragile. The Faustian bargain would have us make changes that stress only presenting information, in ever more efficient ways, rather than assessing the operable campus culture for learning and insisting on engaging students in the messy processes—for the former is cheaper and easier than the latter. Under the terms of this Faustian bargain, changes would reinforce the view that making teaching more "efficient" would have the consequence of making more time available for those things that are regarded as more important—and are rewarded accordingly. The bargain would also reinforce the view that no constituency is responsible for the whole student. Such a Faustian bargain must be rejected, and on many campuses it already has been.

Recent campus initiatives have demonstrated that shifts in institutional resources and priorities make transformative change possible. Such shifts lead to the adoption of practices and expectations and to the alignment of resources and rewards. They also emphasize engaged or high-impact learning experiences for all students, the integration of education within and beyond the classroom, the elevation of expectations for student potential, and the realization of students' full development—cognitive, emotional, and civic. Where such shifts occur, the campus provides the opportunities, the resources, and the culture that make a liberal education not just possible but likely for every student. To these ends, many institutions have implemented some version of the following very practical steps:

- Holding relevant internal conversations regarding the institution's commitment to a call for campus change (or intensification) for learning
- Establishing a rooted leadership or planning team and charging it with initiating plans that fit the institutional culture (including the perspective of those off campus) and ensuring that those plans gain widespread understanding and ownership
- Finding relevant means of placing messages about the need for and the promise of transformational change at the very center of the institution's attention
- Taking intentional action steps, appraising their effectiveness, and building on what works

The realignment of campus priorities can yield needed resources; it is not necessary to await external or "soft" funding to begin. As a broad-based cost study of multiple campuses, developed by Ashley Finley for the BTtoP Project, makes evident, opportunities for significant change can be gained simply by understanding where separate and uncoordinated expenses are currently being used to respond to crises rather than to address basic changes in altering the context for learning.[8] Because parents and alumni have a clear stake in the institution's addressing the whole student, their dedicated support could become a viable source for funding initial efforts. Endowment campaigns can characterize how the institution meets challenges by constructively building on its strengths and culture, thereby leading to transformative changes that assert institutional excellence. When the objective is truly central to the mission of the institution, those beyond the campus can readily see the potential of change.

Given the increasing demands on scarce resources and the competitive environment in which colleges and universities function, it can certainly be challenging to prioritize resources in order to make engaged learning and its documented outcomes the core objectives of the institution, its faculty and staff, and its programs and opportunities. It is unlikely that individual campuses can meet this challenge and make the needed shift in priorities without collective support and encouragement. But those institutions that are leading the way in finding affordable means for shifting priorities do provide successful models that can be adapted to fit the cultures and financial realities of other campuses.

Recent discussions of transformative change address the potential role of computer-based social networking. Online networks such as Facebook and Twitter introduce a "horizontal" dimension of change (like ripples in a pond) insofar as their influence derives from the rapid dispersal of information and perspectives and from the potential to yield a high level of participatory action. It is far too early in the development and use of social networking to speculate reliably about its full role in effecting change. Social networking may be very effective in increasing participatory action, but of what sort? The participation may involve little understanding, commitment, risk, or even self-reflection, and thus the potential impact on future choices or actions may not be significant. Or the lessons may be dramatic and the explosion of changes in areas of political suppression profound and relevant. It remains unclear whether, in contexts where freedom of expression is not prohibited, a widely dispersed request to sign a petition, or to vote, or to "tweet" a civic leader leads to substantive change or whether those participating gain a full sense of engagement in change.

In the arena of generating changes in higher education, forms of participation and action, such as active strategic involvement, may by necessity be organized quite differently than is social networking. Participation may be more "vertical," requiring of a few a relatively high level of accountability and action steps that are intentionally demanding. For example, the needed change may require sustained participation in a drafting group for developing policy change, or accepting an internship or mentoring assignment that is based on contributing a significant skill without conventional compensation.

It would seem that the most desirable way to intensify the conditions needed to effect change, and perhaps even to accelerate change, would be to combine social networking on one level—somewhat disorganized but widely dispersed—with a more strategic and critically organized apparatus and leadership. In other words, the best way to intensify and advance transformative change on campus may be to work vigorously on both aspects simultaneously. Create means for the rapid involvement of many through Twitter or Facebook and, thereby, make possible levels of participatory action that fit such networking (e.g., attending town meetings, signing petitions, volunteering time, voting, and surveying colleagues). At the same time, create the more vertical patterns of leadership needed for significant and durable change—including those patterns of participation that may put reputation and rewards at risk, such as the risk of having to explain and defend one's views. The access to a more hierarchical, but nonetheless necessary, structure makes it possible to champion a contrarian voice, organize colloquia and seminars, and empower task forces that are representative of all campus constituencies (trustees, students, faculty, alumni, invested deans and presidents). Without a vertical dimension, the potentially more inclusive involvement that results from social networking may remain shallow—context forming but not determinant. But without a horizontal dimension, without the rapid involvement of many, the vertical strategic structure for change could easily be marginalized—described as simply the "current vogue" for a marginalized few, or "too radical" for many, and thereby dismissed.[9]

A Few Specifics, Some Evidence, and Some Promising Initiatives

Finally, because it provides a professional vocabulary for summarizing many strands of the previously presented arguments, what follows is a taxonomy of transformational learning excerpted from Lynn Swaner's commissioned report to the BTtoP Project in 2008. Such learning is:

> Developmental—During the college years, students experience fundamental shifts in their perceptions of self, others, and community. Changes in these three areas have profound implications for the ways students make meaning of their learning and experiences, as well as their functioning in relationship to other individuals and to society. These transformations are along the lines of what psychologists call "developmental" change, in which challenges in the environment cause individuals to move toward new—and generally more complex—ways of being in the world (Perry 1999; Baxter Magolda 2004; others).
>
> Holistic—Research confirms that most college students gain substantial academic knowledge and skills through college participation, as well as identify and move toward a career path during their time at college (Pascarella & Terenzini, 1991, 2005). However, change during the college years is not limited to the academic and vocational realms, while these areas remain the focus of much of the academic enterprise. Rather, by crisscrossing the cognitive, affective, psychosocial, and behavioral

domains, learning that is transformational encompasses multiple aspects of the self (Chickering & Reisser, 1993). This kind of learning is not limited to an acquisition of specific content or mastery of a set of skills, but is "deep" in engaging the learner's capacities for understanding, feeling, relating, and action.

Integrative—Transformational learning involves the integration of experience, reflection, and action in a learning cycle that is iterative rather than having a definite endpoint (Kolb, 1984; Hutchings & Wutzdorff, 1988). In a Deweyan sense, transformational learning is distinguished from other types of learning by being active and involving ongoing experimentation, rather than a passive absorption of information. In addition to fostering integration of these learning processes, transformational learning also integrates learning from multiple settings.

Contextual—Rather than occurring in the "vacuum" of the individual, transformational learning requires engagement with social contexts. Through transformational learning, students come to understand the interdependence of self and society, engage in the construction of shared meaning in collaboration with others (Wenger, 1998), and negotiate for shared action that benefits the common good (Jacoby, 2004). In this way, transformational learning ultimately develops civic capacities for democratic participation and engagement in community life.

Transactional—All learning involves interaction between the individual learner and the specific learning environment. This interaction occurs through continual, mutually-shaping "transactions" between the individual learner and the environment, as suggested by Bandura's (1986) concept of reciprocal determinism. Transformational learning is more likely to occur when the potential of these transactions is maximized through the intentional design of learning environments. The confluence of multiple trends, campus achievements, research studies, and the successes of experimental projects is sufficiently powerful to create a context for maximizing efforts to initiate (or to extend current successes on many campuses now in progress) campus transformative change.[10]

Given that transformative learning as here described is both desirable and achievable, it is lamentable that national surveys indicate that few students report having transformational experiences during their undergraduate years. Worse still, most students did not expect to have them. Simply put, the relevance of transformational learning experiences is not widely recognized.

Swaner's analysis, which articulates the perspective of the scholarly learning theory community, is amply supported by evidence of the effectiveness of high-impact educational practices: first-year seminars, service learning courses, writing-intensive seminars, student involvement in faculty research, integrated community-based research experiences, senior research and theses, integrated capstone seminars, and other engaged learning experiences that lead to transformational change. The evidence is persuasive. Students who have one or more of these experiences are retained to graduation at higher rates, have higher grade point indices than had been projected from their entry qualifications, and report far higher levels of satisfaction with their education than those who do not have such experiences. And from some BTtoP demonstration sites, the evidence indicates that these positive effects are even more significant for students with only modest entrance qualifications.

All the evidence now available—from BTtoP demonstration sites, campuses involved in AAC&U's Liberal Education and America's Promise initiative, and elsewhere—suggest that, when engaged (high-impact) learning experiences are significant and repeated parts of a student's education, the positive effects and affects are intensified. This is especially true when at least some of those experiences have been infused with content that is directly relevant to the lives of students and to the challenges of disengagement they face. At Georgetown University, as part of their Engelhard Curriculum Infusion Project, a math course uses group investigation to predict alcohol absorption rates; a first-year philosophy seminar explores self-realization as a function of the categories and limitations of knowledge; and a service learning course in sociology examines and compares the intensity of depression within homeless populations to that found within campus populations. Evaluations of infused courses suggest it is especially relevant that these experiences include not only faculty but also counseling staff and off-campus experts or practitioners as part of an instructional "team."

The available evidence also indicates that, among the outcomes of undergraduate education, the well-being of students is truly transformative. As use of flourishing scales attest, the "full flourishing of students" recognizes that the emotional and mental health of students is a dynamic element in their learning and development.[11] Dr. Daniel Silverman, vice president and chief medical officer at Sinai Hospital of Baltimore (and LifeBridge) and former executive director of University Health Services at Princeton, adds that mental health and mental illness are not poles on one scale. A student can be, and indeed many students are, mentally healthy but far from flourishing!

When counseling staff and faculty work together to develop programs that identify, destigmatize, and directly affect student well-being through integrated academic approaches, including the pedagogies of engaged learning, student flourishing and well-being are positively affected. Professor Kathy Low of Bates College has documented this in her studies of college populations over several years, and flourishing scales have become a ubiquitous tool of institutional research data.[12]

An arbitrary segmentation prevails on most campuses; some aspects of student development are relegated exclusively to the faculty, and other aspects are relegated exclusively to a separate category of service providers. When this segmentation is replaced by an interdisciplinary and integrated approach that recognizes the whole of student learning and development, student well-being becomes an outcome that can be documented—it becomes more than a claim in a mission statement.

Moreover, many institutions have recently made advances in securing the connection between their academic programs and the civic engagement and development of their students. For this reason, as well as to foreshadow major dimensions of several chapters that follow (see particularly chapters 5 and 12), some brief additional examples of this direction of engagement and intentional change may be helpful.

Volunteerism and service work by faculty and students are now both valued and frequently expected, even when there are difficulties in defining the essential academic dimensions of the experience. Even so, it remains unclear precisely how these initiatives and practices are linked to greater civic development and engagement, what those terms mean and suggest to each constituency (both within and outside the institution), how we document the connection of learning to any obligation to be responsible to and for others, and how these initiatives and practices actually strengthen an open, democratic society. The current attention to the civic mission of higher education often includes exploration of the relation of our institutions to their communities—local and beyond. Some see the relationship, or want to see it, as an economic "engine"; others seek to break down long-standing barriers between town and gown. Most are simply trying more carefully to examine the nature and the possibilities of conceptual and practical linkages that can join the academic and the civic—including the practices of civic action that have long been the interest of community organizers as well as social theorists.

For example, attention to the civic dimension of liberal education has often led to an exploration of the relationship between volunteerism, service, and service learning, on the one hand, and robust civic practices that stem from considering education as a common good, rather than simply a personal gain, on the other.

In addition, we learn more about this relationship of the civic to liberal education from initiatives undertaken in other parts of the world—particularly recognizing the cultural relativism inherent in our notions of service, service learning, and the common good. The history and culture, for example, of Poland create a distinctive context for understanding how pedagogies of engagement link to the civic, a context within which the very notion of a common good that is served by education takes on a different meaning. In that context we ought to be considering whether contrarian independence is more connected to the civic than is service. The point is that we are likely to learn from initiatives that do not reflect the typical U.S. models of liberal education. In addition to asking what we can export to these initiatives, it would be worthwhile considering what we may need to import from them.

Although clearly contextualized within the overarching themes discussed in part I, the chapters in parts II and III of this book add considerably to the threads of argument presented here. There are formative chapters on the meaning of liberal education, on the conditions for change, on engaged learning, on the relation of learning to practice, on the often ignored objectives of student well-being and civic development, on the learner as a whole or a gestalt, and on the role of faculty in leading changes. These chapters present as well as constitute the arguments and evidence for change—for theory that compels and for practices that transform.

Part III also provides extended discussion of the multiple implications of transformative change—implications for financing higher education, implications of change for secondary education, of the changes needed in the preparation and socialization of the professoriate, and of public policy implications. These are controversial but illuminating discussions.

Part IV is made up of ten case studies. The cases have been chosen for the "takeaways" they offer—some clear, successful strategies; some clear, systemic obstacles that limited success. Many of the cases deal with the complexities of assessment and offer model processes for using assessment results to make new discoveries or to identify opportunities within campus cultures for learning.

Like the short strands that overlap to form a common piece of hemp rope, intentional direction and shared objectives do not require a single unifying thread. This book is about such short strands and the connections they make in theory and in practice.

Notes

1. Kevin Carey, "The Old College Lie," *Democracy* 15 (Winter 2010): 8–20. Reviewed in *Wilson Quarterly* (Spring 2010): 73–74.

2. Gilbert Ryle, *The Concept of Mind* (New York: Harper and Row, 1949), 22; Ryle's argument notes the mistake made by Cartesian dualists of treating mind and body as both substances—one empirically accessible, the other not—a historic "category mistake."

3. Helen Lefkowitz Horowitz, *Campus Life: Undergraduate Cultures from the End of the Eighteenth Century to the Present* (Chicago: University of Chicago Press, 1987).

4. William H. Willimon and Thomas H. Naylor, *The Abandoned Generation: Rethinking Higher Education* (Grand Rapids, MI: Eerdmans, 1995).

5. Tom Wolfe, *I Am Charlotte Simmons* (New York: Farrar, Straus and Giroux, 2004); Barrett Seaman, *Binge: What Your College Students Won't Tell You* (Hoboken, NJ: Wiley, 2005).

6. Bruce A. Kimball, "Toward Pragmatic Liberal Education," in *The Condition of American Liberal Education* (New York: The College Board, 1995), 3–122.

7. Richard H. Thaler and Cass R. Sunstein, *Nudge: Improving Decisions about Health, Wealth, and Happiness* (New Haven, CT: Yale University Press, 2008).

8. Ashley P. Finley and Lynn E. Swaner, *Bringing Theory to Practice (BT-toP) Cost-Study: College and University Expenditures in Addressing Patterns of Student Disengagement* (2008), www.aacu.org/bringing_theory/documents/COSTSTUDYFINALREPORT_R.pdf.

9. A most insightful article by Malcolm Gladwell, "Small Change: The Truth about the Twitter Revolution" in *The New Yorker* (October 4, 2010), discusses strategic models for social and political change.

10. Lynn Swaner, *Campus Change for Learning: Leading a Category Shift in Liberal Education* (November 10–11, 2008), www.aacu.org/bringing_theory/documents/2008StrategyforChange.pdf.

11. Ed Diener and Robert Biswas-Diener, "Flourishing Scale" (2009), http://s.psych.uiuc.edu/~ediener/FS.html.

12. Kathy G. Low, "Flourishing and Student Engagement," *Bringing Theory to Practice Newsletter* (May 2010).

PART II

THE ISSUES, RATIONALE, CONSTRAINTS, AND PRACTICES

1

A Copernican Moment

On the Revolutions in Higher Education

David M. Scobey

> Having become aware of these defects, I often considered whether there could perhaps be found a more reasonable arrangement of circles.
>
> —Nicolaus Copernicus, *Commentariolus*

Change does not take place in a vacuum; and neither do calls for change. The chapters in this volume offer a vision of educational renewal that is grounded in a shared sense of discontent with the current state of the American academy. The crux of that vision, in my view, is a commitment to educating undergraduates as complex, integral, social beings: educating them through practices that braid their studies *outwardly* with the world of civic responsibility and purposeful, productive work and *inwardly* with ethical reflection, emotional development, and self-authoring. The chapters draw appreciatively on some of the deepest traditions in American liberal education and some of the best practices on American campuses. Yet they compose, as the title of the book underscores, a call for transformation, not rededication.

My aim here is to set that call in historical relief, to illuminate the context in and against which it has emerged. As a partisan for change and a historian whose trade is to study it, I want to offer a map of the present moment—in the academy and in the academy's relationship with the larger society—to which the ideas and proposals in this book pose a response. How is the educational landscape evolving? To what extent do troubling trends in undergraduate education reflect larger conditions—institutional, economic, demographic, technological—that enable and constrain the possibilities of innovation in the academy? In the face of such conditions, what type of educational reform is desirable (or possible, or inevitable) at this moment? Even under the best of circumstances, when the story is long past, historical perspective is difficult. A history of the present is much more fraught. But that is what I aim to sketch.

The most fundamental aspect of the current situation, however, is as clear as it is complicated. This book's brief for change comes at a time when the academy is in the throes of change. Partisans in current education battles may strenuously debate how to design curricula, assess learning outcomes, or make college affordable; but there is widespread agreement that higher education faces a sea change in its intellectual, institutional, technological, and economic organization. The knowledge, skills, and values for which students should be educated; the ways in which teachers are trained, certified, hired, and arrayed into faculties; the intellectual landscape of disciplines and degrees; the geographies and networks by which educational institutions are organized and sustained; the funding of teaching, learning, and research—all this promises to be profoundly different in twenty years. Some forces of change have resulted from our own inertia in the academy (for instance, the push from policy makers and funders for accountability and degree standardization). Others represent the consequences of our very success (for instance, the globalization of student bodies and curricula). Still other forces reflect broad political, market, and technological developments not primarily of our making (for instance, the growing centrality of digital media to teaching and research). Yet, taken together, these factors define a moment in which—to quote Thomas Kuhn's account of political and scientific revolutions—"existing institutions have ceased adequately to meet the problems posed by an environment that they have in part created."[1] In such a moment, the question is not *whether* the academy will be changed, but *how*. Defending or merely tweaking our current arrangements is not an option.

This mix of inevitability and uncertainty is unnerving—and not only for loyalists to the academic status quo. Even for critics of mainstream practice, it is tempting to assume the stability of an older, established paradigm against which, like a whetstone, our ideas for reform have been honed. That "official" model took as normative an undergraduate regime of full-time postsecondary students and full-time tenure-stream faculty; a four-year, two-stage course of study in which general education segues into advanced majors defined by disciplinary specializations; a curriculum segmented into fungible units of labor, effort, and time called *courses*, *credit hours*, and *semesters*; a campus world segregated into academics and extracurricular student life. During most of the twentieth century, from the triumph of the system of majors and electives through the postwar expansion of public and land-grant education, this *was* the paradigmatic architecture of baccalaureate education in the United States.[2] For those of us who have struggled with its negative effects—the narrow bandwidth of professors' attention to students, the instrumental goals of students, the research and status incentives of disciplinary professionalism, the siloed structure of our institutions—it made sense to critique undergraduate education as *stuck*. The goal of reform was then to act as an Archimedean lever, dislodging the academy from its satisfied, secure inertia.

Yet this is *not* the moment in which higher education finds itself. In almost every particular, the conditions that were taken for granted by the older paradigm no longer hold; and the educational assumptions that it instituted no longer seem self-evident. Only about one-third of undergraduates are recent high school graduates, attending a single four-year institution; twice as many faculty work on term contracts than in tenure-stream positions.[3] The for-profit sector is burgeoning, as is online learning across *all* sectors (to my mind, a more consequential change).[4] At the same time, the educational practices that seem to make the most difference to student engagement—so-called high-impact practices such as interdisciplinary learning communities, experiential and community-based learning, study abroad, and capstone research—are precisely those that tend to *disrupt* the established ecology of atomized courses, disciplinary courses of study, and the separation of curricular from cocurricular experience.[5] The problem is not that the "official" paradigm of undergraduate education is constricting yet effective; it is that the paradigm is constricting and exhausted. Higher education is not in stasis but in crisis; and what is needed is not an alarm clock to awaken the academy from its dogmatic slumber but rather a star chart by which to navigate an uncertain future. We are in Kuhn's "revolutionary" moment when a new paradigm—a new institutional and epistemological regime for organizing educational practices and educational communities—feels necessary and imminent yet inchoate and up for grabs. It is a Copernican moment.

In the annals of American higher education, of course, talk of crisis is cheap. It is also persistent. For two centuries, a whole host of Cassandras and Jeremiahs have variously decried the academy's corruption, shallowness, commercialism, mandarin exclusiveness or social irrelevance, loss of moral compass or intellectual rigor or civic responsibility or nerve. Yet there is something different, I want to argue, about the current moment; the discourse of discontent is more widespread and wide ranging. "It is time to be frank," warns the 2006 report of Secretary of Education Margaret Spellings' Commission on the Future of Higher Education:

Among the vast and varied institutions that make up U.S. higher education, we have found much to applaud but also much that requires urgent reform. . . . We may still have more than our share of the world's best universities. But a lot of other countries have followed our lead, and they are now educating more of their citizens. . . . History is littered with examples of industries that, at their peril, failed to respond to—or even to notice—changes in the world around them. . . . Without serious self-examination and reform, institutions of higher education risk falling into the same trap.[6]

The Spellings Commission report takes aim especially at the problems of assessing learning outcomes and enforcing institutional accountability; by contrast, Mark Taylor's *Crisis on Campus* decries what he sees as the looming intellectual (as well as fiscal) bankruptcy of the educational status quo. Taylor's provocative proposals for deconstructing the disciplinary collegium in favor of problem-based curricula and electronically networked learning communities could not be further from the commission's concern with standards and standardization. Yet his framing of the current situation is strikingly resonant with the commission's rhetoric:

American higher education has long been the envy of the world. . . . But in the past four decades, this situation has gradually deteriorated. The quality of higher education is declining; colleges and universities are not adequately preparing students for life in a rapidly changing and increasingly competitive world.[7]

These texts offer almost incommensurable accounts of what is wrong with higher education, what is coming, and what needs to be done. Yet—just because of that—what is most striking is their shared sense of the moment in which U.S. higher education finds itself: a threshold moment of decline or disorienting adaptation.

This discourse of discontent is diverse, in part, because "the education crisis" that it registers is actually a manifold of different problems. It may help to tease them apart. Most obviously, higher education is in fiscal crisis. Over the past quarter century, we have seen a shrinkage of public funding at just the same time that academic institutions have expanded their scale and the complexity of their missions—and at precisely the same time, again, as they have faced rising costs in health care, energy, campus infrastructure, and faculty salaries. There has been, to use the cliché, a perfect storm of fiscal pressure; and it has yielded the sharp rises in tuition that seem so irrational and are so burdensome to taxpayers, tuition payers, and other stakeholders.

Beyond the direct costs to students and institutions, the fiscal crisis has imposed secondary effects that undermine educational quality and equity.

It has amplified the need for colleges and universities to rely on part-time and contingent faculty labor. It has encouraged undergraduate "credit shopping" and transfers, incentivizing students to make instrumental choices in crafting their course of study at the expense of community, continuity, and shared reflection. The fiscal crisis has also reamplified class divides thought to have subsided during the decades of educational expansion after World War II. It has reinforced the tendency of selective colleges and universities to jockey for status according to the dynamics of luxury-goods markets rather than Smithian cost discipline. These pricey, price-inelastic institutions assert their desirability by driving *up* costs through a "rankings arms race" for the best amenities and services, star professors, and merit-based scholarship aid. Even more important, the tuition bubble has tended to shut poor and working-class students out of college altogether or to displace the burden of paying for it onto student loans. Anya Kamenetz has persuasively argued that the expansion of student borrowing over the past two decades is a core element of the academy's growth model—and an unsustainable one.[8] One need not concur with her alternative vision of "do-it-yourself universities" with informal, electronically mediated learning networks to second her trenchant analysis of the centrality of debt to our current situation—and the threat it poses to democratic access, student well-being, and educational community. For too many students, the most important cocurricular "others," the activities that preoccupy them when they are not at study, are not sports or Greek life but loans and work. Any reform agenda must engage and change that reality.

Put another way, the costs of the crisis are more than just monetary. Budget cuts, tuition hikes, and debt burdens make manifest (and to some extent obscure) a crisis of *legitimacy*: a growing sense that, as the "official" undergraduate paradigm has frayed, the academy has betrayed its commitments to, and turned away from, the larger society. This legitimation crisis has a complex etiology, rooted in both the historic achievements and recent problems of higher education.[9] After World War II, universities and university systems grew vaster and more opaque; disciplinary professionalism enforced a hiring and tenure regime that prompted scholarship to become hyperspecialized and esoteric. At the same time—and partly in reaction against this specialization—technical and political shifts in the production of knowledge destabilized the organization of disciplines, catalyzing interdisciplinary fields such as neuroscience and gender studies. And after the 1960s, these institutional and intellectual developments took place in the context of a deepening political gulf between a progressive professoriate and an increasingly conservative public.

There is always a social compact that regulates the relationship between the academy and the larger society, a compact that legitimizes the enormous claims we make on resources and autonomy. By the 1990s, that compact had grown frayed. Culture wars, tuition hikes, declining government support, and a kind of high-minded defensiveness on the part of campus leaders and scholars magnified the divide between higher education and its publics, bringing long-simmering resentment at the arrogance and unaccountability of the academy to a boil.

This crisis of legitimacy represents, I think, one of the most crucial factors in our current situation. It has fueled the atmosphere of mistrust that pervades public debates over higher education and the current rash calls for external assessment and accountability. Within the academy, it has generated a broad literature of complaint and reform, not simply from conservative dissenters such as Allan Bloom and radical critics such as Marc Bousquet but also from mainstream scholars and leaders. [10] Books such as Derek Bok's *Our Underachieving Colleges*, Charles Muscatine's *Fixing College Education*, and the recent *Academically Adrift*—not to mention this volume—base their specific (and quite disparate) critiques in the assumption that undergraduate education as a whole has failed to deliver on its promise and its promises.[11] "[C]ollege costs too much . . . [and it is] impossible for many students of low income to attend at all," laments Muscatine in *Fixing College Education*:

> But there is terrible irony in the fact that these are not . . . even the most serious defects in the system. . . . [T]he truth is that the teaching and learning that go on in our colleges are actually not very good at all. The main problem of our colleges is poor education.[12]

Precisely what needs fixing, however, is highly contested. For some critics—we might call them traditionalist reformers—the purely curricular and cognitive goals of the "official" undergraduate paradigm have remained tried and true: the teaching of critical thinking, communications skills, and subject mastery that leads to professional or career preparation. The problem is that higher education has abandoned these goals in fostering a faculty culture of research and disciplinary status seeking and a student culture of low expectations. The majority report of the Spellings Commission, with its call for uniform, objective standards enforced by strict assessment and accountability, represents one voice in this camp. So does *Academically Adrift*, whose authors argue that more time in class, more demanding academic work, more stringent assessment, and more consequences for failure are needed to change an anemic culture of "limited learning" on campus. For another set of critics, by contrast— pedagogical radicals such as Mark Taylor and Charles Muscatine—the crisis of legitimacy requires more than a renewal of rigor or an enforcement of standards. What is needed is "a new curriculum for the twenty-first century" (to use Muscatine's subtitle), a kind of Liberal Education 2.0, more intellectually holistic, personally integrative, and integrated with the larger world of work and citizenship.

It is among these reformers—for whom liberal education represents an unfinished and transformative educational project—that I would situate the contributors to this volume. They do not focus on the fiscal or policy ramifications of the current moment of crisis and change. Rather, they are concerned with its distressing effects on the minds and hearts of undergraduates, the practices of teachers, the shape of curricula, and the local organization of campuses. The book maps an educational landscape marked by students' disengagement and instrumentalism toward their studies; by alarmingly high levels of student depression; by a disciplinary balkanization that has thinned out faculty-student relationships; by a reward system that privileges research and disciplinary status over teaching and campus leadership; by the segregation of the life of study from "student life," understood as a domain of customer service rather than educational growth; by the disconnection of both the (specialized) curriculum and the (consumerized) extracurriculum from community and civic bonds. Taken together, the chapters in *Transforming Higher Education* offer a portrait of the dysfunctional consequences of the older undergraduate paradigm and its decomposition under the pressure of change.

And yet this is all too bleak a picture of the current situation. For if the past quarter century has eroded the taken-for-granted assumptions, economic stability, and sheer self-confidence of the academy, it has also been an era of remarkable (and often unremarked) innovation. The rise of academic civic engagement and community-based learning offers a vivid example. What began in the 1980s as an earnest but often unreflective commitment to community service and service learning—more broad than deep—has grown into a mature academic movement, characterized by a broad network of campus-based centers and programs and national consortia. Faculty, staff, students, and community partners have developed models of sustained, collaborative projects and courses that are at once academically rigorous and socially transformative. Indeed there is a broad commitment to public engagement *not only* in individual courses but also across the curriculum and the institution as a whole—as well as a commitment to engagement that links community work to systemic issues of policy, power, and justice.

The "civic turn" is only one of a broad array of educational innovations that have emerged (with striking simultaneity) over the past twenty-five years. I have already mentioned the scholarly development of new interdisciplinarities: some grounded in social justice and identitarian movements (women's studies, ethnic studies), some in scientific cross-pollination (bioengineering, neuroscience), some in theoretical and interpretive boundary crossing (cultural studies). Other innovations were more strictly student centered: writing across the curriculum; first-year courses that melded interdisciplinary themes, seminar (and sometimes writing) pedagogy, and academic advising; multicourse or residential learning communities; undergraduate research programs (and the concomitant expansion of capstone research); internships and other forms of experiential pedagogy; and study abroad programs. Nearly all these initiatives followed developmental patterns similar to the growth of civic engagement: pioneering experiments, proliferation via scholarly and institutional networks, national convenings or associations, and the coalescing of a community of practice that debated best practices and deepened program building.

The result has been a record of change that dramatically enlarged the possibilities of undergraduate teaching and learning. My oldest son's experience at an urban university can serve as an example. A narrative of the most significant chapters of his undergraduate career would include a first-year seminar on urban homelessness, which presented collective research on the local shelter system to municipal officials; a study abroad semester in South Africa; an urban studies major in which he interned for a city councilman and was required to compose a senior seminar paper—on the theme of "justice"—using graphic-novel software; and a capstone thesis that drew on focus group research and media theory to analyze the representation of urban crisis in *The Wire*. He had fallow times, to be sure; but at its best, this was an undergraduate experience marked by the kind of active, collaborative, exploratory, and integrative opportunities that the voices of reform aim to nurture. Hardly a single one of those opportunities was available when I attended college thirty-five years ago.

The history of the current moment, in short, is one of creativity, not simply change and crisis. Indeed it is a story of creativity responding to, and sometimes making use of, the conditions of change and crisis sketched in the first part of this chapter. First-year seminars and learning communities, for instance, were designed precisely to overcome the balkanization and disengagement that have plagued undergraduate learning and campus culture. Civic engagement courses were designed to repair the breach between the academic classroom and the larger society, activating learning in public problem solving and culture making. Study abroad programs have served as a pedagogical laboratory for how best to impart intercultural and global competencies in an interdependent world. To be sure, these innovations have too often been siloed and ad hoc. Yet they constitute a creative response to both the discontents of mainstream campus life and the dislocations of a brave new academy of globalization, digital networks, and culture wars.

Two aspects of this more hopeful side of the current moment are notable. First of all, the innovations I have sketched correspond almost exactly with the repertoire of high-impact educational practices that, according to George Kuh's influential research, have proven most consequential for undergraduates.[13] They are not simply creative but also *effective* in engaging and transforming students. Second, they have done so largely on the margins or in the interstices of mainstream rules and structures. I do not mean that ordinary faculty, staff, and administrators have opposed innovation. Quite the opposite. The new practices have been a labor of love for thousands of academics. But sustained innovation has generally succeeded by working around, and sometimes against, the protocols of departments and curriculum committees, the grid of distribution and concentration requirements, the temporal ecology of credit hours and semesters, and (perhaps most of all) the incentives of the faculty reward system. High-impact practices tend to live simultaneously within, across, and against the traditional disciplines; within, across, and against the traditional academy calendar; within, across, and against the boundary that separates the campus from local, global, and digital publics. To a disheartening extent, the most exciting and effective initiatives of the past twenty-five years have had to swim upstream, so to speak, against the inertial habits and repetition compulsions of ordinary academic practice. Georgetown literary scholar Randy Bass, a leading theorist of campus pedagogical innovation, hilariously titled a conference workshop Low-Impact Practices (Formerly Known as the Curriculum).

How does it feel to be at a threshold in time, on the cusp of transformations that may turn out to be revolutionary? When Nicolaus Copernicus began developing his radical new model of the cosmos, early in the sixteenth century, the inadequacies of the Ptolemaic system had grown increasingly clear. Ptolemy and other ancient astronomers had from the first constructed an elaborate theory of planetary "epicycles," "eccentrics," and "equants" to explain the discrepancies between the geocentric model and their observations of the night sky. During the Renaissance, an explosion of new astronomical research further documented and amplified these anomalies, dimming the aura of authority that had surrounded the Ptolemaic system; scholars and scientists (most famously, Leonardo da Vinci) were beginning to speculate about a heliocentric theory without being able to discern or elaborate its lineaments. It was in this moment—the exhaustion of the older system in the face of anomalous new phenomena, the intuition of a new system toward which the anomalies gestured—that

Copernicus undertook his work. "Having become aware of these defects [in Ptolemy's system]," he writes in the preface to the *Commentariolus*, his early précis of the heliocentric theory, "I often considered whether there could perhaps be found a more reasonable arrangement of circles."[14]

U.S. higher education is on the threshold, I believe, of such a Copernican moment. As I have argued here, an older "official" paradigm of undergraduate education has exhausted itself, partly under the pressure of external revolutions (economic, political, technological, intellectual) that undermined its structures and norms, partly under the weight of mounting evidence (whether from depression rates, student surveys, or external assessments) that underscored its educational inefficacy. Reformers and critics have anatomized these failures from a variety of viewpoints and warned—or crowed—of dramatic changes to come. Meanwhile, in just the same years that the older paradigm was fraying, an array of new educational practices has emerged. Disparate and unassimilated, at odds with traditional practice, and yet remarkably robust, these innovations are something like the anomalous points of light that the Renaissance astronomers observed in the night sky. They illuminate the inadequacies of the older undergraduate system, and they point the way toward "a more reasonable arrangement of circles," as Copernicus put it.

What will that future paradigm look like? I am not so foolish as to offer anything like a full answer. Even if I could, it would surely be wrong, for educational models, perhaps more than astronomical ones, need to be tested and revised iteratively. Yet it seems to me that we can discern something of the future possibilities by extrapolating from the double story of disruptive change and counternormative creativity I have offered here. How do we build out from the achievements of the current moment? How do we respond to its crises?

On the one hand, I would argue, we want an educational future that draws on, and draws out, the implications of the new high-impact practices. Such a model would provide students with an arc of learning experiences—active, collaborative, boundary-crossing, and integrative—that interweave intellectual, professional, civic, and personal growth. Faculties and courses of study would be organized around interdisciplinary issues or domains of cultural practice—perhaps remapping them periodically—rather than a fixed, departmental topography of specialized fields. The professoriate would be trained and rewarded for teaching and advising more fully than today's faculty. Many more would be expert in project-based, collaborative, and interdisciplinary forms of pedagogy. Academic institutions would encourage heterodox forms of knowledge creation, culture making, and creative work—including public, practitioner, and digital scholarship—that are generally devalued by disciplinary professionalism.

Students would be expected to develop a broader array of proficiencies than simply the writing requirements of the old paradigm: digital literacy, civic practice (including public speaking), the application of their studies to professional practice, and teamwork. Their course of study would engage them in learning communities that extend beyond the boundary of the classroom or lab: work-based networks, community partnerships, global or intercultural encounters, and online classes. Knowing how to learn from, learn with, work with, and argue with a wide array of significant others would be a key learning outcome of the liberally educated person. And just as the classroom would no longer be privileged as the spatial "atom" of learning, so too the new model would emancipate itself from an academic calendar in which the semester course and its metronomic rhythm of weekly meetings were the atomic building blocks of educational time. Semesters, courses, and contact hours may be efficient ways to administer faculty labor and student credit acquisition; but they militate against the integration of learning experiences into shared, reflective pathways. The new calendar would be flexible and distributed, weaving together synchronous and asynchronous curricula, long-form and intensive learning experiences.

In short, we might extrapolate from the "creative anomalies" of the current moment to sketch a sort of Liberal Education 2.0. On the other hand, however, we need to extrapolate from the crises and dislocations of the current moment as well: to include in our account of the future a tough-minded acceptance of the realities that are transforming the educational landscape. Our new paradigm must meet the needs of a student majority that will attend more than one institution and balance studies with wage earning and borrowing. That may mean slimming down the amenities of liberal education to lower its costs; it will certainly mean embedding liberal learning with opportunities for paid work and professional apprenticeships. Similarly we will need to create promotional pathways, professional support, and intellectual collegia for faculty who will not, by and large, work on tenure tracks. And we will need to create curricula, pedagogical styles, and forms of sociability for institutions in which online learning and networked student communities compose as important a context as campus-based and on-site experiences. Too often, reform-minded liberal educators have simply abstained from figuring out how to include nontraditional students—adult or part-time learners, working-class transfers, online students—within the ambit of our vision. In the future, we will need to commit ourselves to creating models of teaching and learning that can flourish when the taken-for-granted conditions of liberal education—compact campus places, expansive student time—are absent.

I have ventured here a historical account of our current situation in higher education, paying special attention to the weave of change, crisis, and innovation that has characterized the past quarter century. When the next quarter century is over, and a new generation of historians and critics look back, to what situation will *they* have to respond? The landscape of academic life will surely be dramatically altered; *someone's* new paradigm will have taken hold. Will it be an economistic and instrumental regime, efficiently driving masses of students to degree completion and populating them across that era's global division of labor? Will it have instituted an "American Bologna Process" in which standardized disciplinary degree programs have been "tuned" in siloed isolation from one another? Or will we have created a model of undergraduate education in which (like the Polish monk's epic act of decentering and recentering) both the new conditions and the creative anomalies of our present moment will have moved from the margins to the heart of academic practice? Will we have created a "Copernican revolution" worthy of the name?

Notes

1. Thomas S. Kuhn, *The Structure of Scientific Revolutions* (Chicago: University of Chicago Press, 1996), 92.

2. Frederick Rudolph, *The American College and University: A History* (Athens: University of Georgia Press, 1962), 287–482; John R. Thelin, *A History of American Higher Education* (Baltimore: Johns Hopkins University Press, 2004), 205–316.

3. Association of American Colleges and Universities, *Greater Expectations: A New Vision for Learning as a Nation Goes to College* (Washington, DC: Association of American Colleges and Universities, 2002), 1–10; American Federation of Teachers, *The State of the Higher Education Workforce 1997–2007* (Washington, DC: American Federation of Teachers, 2009), 10.

4. Elaine I. Allen and Jeff Seaman, *Online Nation: Five Years of Growth in Online Learning* (The Sloan Consortium, 2007).

5. George D. Kuh, *High-Impact Educational Practices: What They Are, Who Has Access to Them, and Why They Matter* (Washington, DC: Association of American Colleges and Universities, 2007).

6. U.S. Department of Education, *A Test of Leadership: Charting the Future of U.S. Higher Education* (Washington, DC: U.S. Department of Education, 2006), ix, x, xii.

7. Mark C. Taylor, *Crisis on Campus: A Bold Plan for Reforming Our Colleges and Universities* (New York: Knopf, 2010), 3.

8. Anya Kamenetz, *DIY U: Edupunks, Edupreneurs, and the Coming Transformation of Higher Education* (White River Junction, VT: Chelsea Green Publishing Company, 2010).

9. I give fuller treatments of this view that a legitimation crisis characterized the history of U.S. higher education since the 1980s in "Legitimation Crisis: The

Spellings Commission and the Civic Engagement Movement" (unpublished manuscript, 2006) and "The Arts of Citizenship in a Diverse Democracy: The Public Work of the Arts and Humanities" (unpublished manuscript, 2007).

10. Allan Bloom, *The Closing of the American Mind* (New York: Simon and Schuster, 1987); Marc Bousquet, *How the University Works: Higher Education and the Low-Wage Nation* (New York: New York University Press, 2008).

11. Derek Bok, *Our Underachieving Colleges: A Candid Look at How Much Students Learn and Why They Should Be Learning More* (Princeton, NJ: Princeton University Press, 2006); Charles Muscatine, *Fixing College Education: A New Curriculum for the Twenty-First Century* (Charlottesville: University of Virginia Press, 2009); Richard Arum and Josipa Roksa, *Academically Adrift: Limited Learning on College Campuses* (Chicago: University of Chicago Press, 2011).

12. Muscatine, *Fixing College Education*, 1–2.

13. Kuh offers the following catalog of "high-impact educational practices," based on analysis of student response data from the National Survey of Student Engagement (NSSE): first-year seminars; common intellectual experiences; learning communities; writing-intensive courses; collaborative assignments; undergraduate research; diversity/global learning; community-based learning; internships; and capstone courses and projects.

14. For a good nontechnical introduction to the context and key elements of Copernicus's work, see Jack Repcheck, *Copernicus' Secret: How the Scientific Revolution Began* (New York: Simon and Schuster, 2007). Additionally, an English translation of Copernicus's *Commentariolus* is available at http://dbanach.com/copernicus-commentarilous.htm.

2

The Ideals of the Liberal Artisan: Notes toward an Evolving Group Biography

Catharine R. Stimpson

Anyone watching YouTube during the first part of 2009 could have clicked on video clips of demonstrations in France. Their purpose was to denounce the president of the republic, Nicolas Sarkozy, and the reform in French universities that he and his education minister had initiated in January of that year.[1] *Ah*, a cynic might shrug, *what's new?* What's new is what the demonstrators were doing: giving a group reading of a canonical text in French literature, a novel, *La Princèsse de Clèves*, that a woman, the Countess de La Fayette, had published anonymously in 1678.

The protestors were liberal artisans. This is a term I have invented for people who practice and advocate for the liberal arts. An artisan is a craftsman who makes and shapes things, here the liberal arts. These French liberal artisans were engaging in a struggle about what matters in their national culture. In 2006, Sarkozy had made some ill-tempered comments, *boutades*, about the novel. His boyhood reading experience, he had said, had proved that it was indeed unreadable. Only "an imbecile or a sadist could have chosen to set it" as an examination text.

However French these protesting liberal artisans might have seemed, they also exhibited some of the more transnational contemporary features of the liberal arts. First and perhaps foremost, I saw the demonstrations on YouTube. Our technologies of communication transmitted them far beyond France and French speakers. A far-flung community of liberal artisans, some French, some not, could share the thoughts and feelings of the protestors. Next, the icons that were being defended were a novel about a woman and a writer who was a woman. They were no longer excluded from nor marginalized in culture. On the contrary, they were revered—except by a philistine, vulgar, sexist male president. He revealed a sickening gap between official culture, which the liberal artisans were

51

protecting, and official power, which he embodied. Such a chasm was yet more evidence that the liberal arts, especially the humanities, were beleaguered and that the default position of liberal artisans was defensive.[2]

My purpose is to offer some notes toward a group biography of liberal artisans in colleges and universities and their ideals, to sketch a "then" for the "now" of YouTube, especially a "then" for America.[3] Liberal artisans have a twofold relation to the past. First, they provide our primary composers of history who are responsible for its thick descriptions and complex analyses. Next, liberal artisans can learn from their own past, both its defiling cautionary failures and its more uplifting, sustaining values. What Peter J. Gomes wrote of the American residential liberal arts college might also be true of the liberal arts in general. "The way of the future for such institutions may well come from a reappropriation of aspects of their past."[4]

In the West, the group history of liberal artisans is an evolving, changing one. What history is not? The much translated, interpreted, and misinterpreted Greek philosophers whom we read today are not the same as the flesh-and-blood men who walked beneath the trees and porticos that sheltered them from a Mediterranean sun. Any group biography of liberal artisans will show change in their ideals—as well as support for change and, in contrast, lacerating doubts, anxieties, and miseries about it. However, in response to the inevitabilities of change, liberal artisans can struggle, argue, and experiment with new life forms. They can defend historical novels but do so on YouTube.

A historical, common perception is that liberal artisans are universally genteel, high minded, and airy with abstractions, that these strolls in the shade always were and always are tranquil. This is a misperception. Their group history has terrible bouts of violence. The fittest have not always survived. In part, this is so because a common method of doing the liberal arts has been aggressively dialogic and disputatious. In part, this is so because of battles over intellectual propriety, property, and turf. In far greater part, this is so because the liberal arts and liberal artisans are a part of their times, with their vicious factions, quarrels, and wars. Think of that iconic figure of the Western liberal arts—Cicero, the Roman politician, lawyer, orator, and writer. Born in 106 BCE, he was murdered during the Roman civil wars in 43 BCE, throat cut, head severed.

The YouTube of the French demonstrations—with its mixture of the new technologies of communication, the subsequent instant global circulation of ideas and images, the respect for diverse voices and talents, and the conviction that the liberal arts are dangerously peripheral to society—represents the situation of many liberal artisans in their current period of change. It is a grating irony that liberal artisans—in the arts, humanities, social sciences, sciences, and interdisciplinary endeavors—are generating important and influential ideas. Nevertheless, endorsements of them from some of the politically powerful, student interest in them, and faculty positions for them are demonstrably shaky—especially in the humanities and social sciences. Moreover, in the United States and elsewhere, many assessments of the worth and impact of liberal artisans mechanically impose grids of evaluation that measure quantity but not quality. This is one feature of the contemporary U.S. treatment of higher education. Since 1945, the United States has created the most remarkable system of higher education in the world, but having built it, the nation is careless or skeptical about supporting it, especially its public institutions. How sickening it is to watch one's country choke the goose that has laid so many golden eggs.[5]

Yet, past and present are bound together. The deep identity of the liberal arts and the purpose of liberal artisans have been persistent. The liberal arts are a profound human creation, as magnificent in their way as a Shakespearean play or an Indian epic and just as ambitious. Liberal artisans have constructed one influential, systematic way of exploring, mapping, and knowing our interwoven worlds. They include the human world that we form and the natural world that we shape or deform. Thinking is valued for its own sake, learning for its own sake, but also for the sake of understanding—be it of the ways of the gods, god, or us.

Significantly, the liberal arts are more than "the humanities" or, more largely, "the arts and humanities," or even more largely, "the arts, humanities, and social sciences." They conjoin what we now call the arts, humanities, social sciences, and sciences. Even if liberal artisans now understandably cleave to their individual disciplines, the inspiring ideal of the liberal arts is to accumulate the materials of a holistic picture or vision of reality. Think of the Greek philosopher Aristotle (384–322 BCE). A polymath, he wrote about drama and literature, politics, ethics, metaphysics, logic, and the sciences. His mind, I suggest, was a microcosm of the macrocosm of the liberal arts. As Adele Wolfson has written, "It is stating the obvious to say that the sciences and the humanities are just two approaches to seeking knowledge. . . . [They] share a goal of understanding the world and our place in it, out of curiosity and wonder and in search of answers to large questions. . . . Scientists and humanists should be working together to encourage broad liberal education."[6] If, she adds, students are in professional schools and the professions, the values of the liberal arts should migrate there. Few liberal artisans today have the multitasking genius of an Aristotle, but the lack of such a rare capacity need not atrophy nor amputate curiosity and wonder.

As such, the liberal arts are an epistemic structure. Such structures do not exist in cold isolation, orbiting the earth as if they were a data-capturing and -categorizing computer. Liberal artisans are also said to enable a good and valuable life, although the meanings of *good* and *valuable* are variable and have waxed and waned over time. Some might claim that teaching well in the classroom is sufficient unto itself.[7] In contrast, Professor Gomes writes of the need for "moral education" and the "formation of conscience."[8] Because they carry the double hope of serving epistemology and ethics, liberal artisans have a third task as well: to become embedded in the structures and processes of teaching and learning, of forming the young. A Latin root of the word *discipline* means a group of masters and students. Liberal artisans shape schools, classrooms, and curricula as they inquire into the true, the beautiful, and the good.

Epistemology, ethics, education: At their most copious and vital, the liberal arts overflow the classrooms and flood into homes, the mind of a lonely child in an isolated area, the media, or the backpacks of soldiers in the field. At their most begrudging, liberal artisans turn the classroom into an evaporated moat and salty well in the landscape of knowledge. Then life must flood over and renew them. Liberal artisans are often at their most perplexed and quarrelsome as to whether they should say yes or no to their current practices. Is a piece of work new but promising, or is it new and fraudulent? Is a piece of work traditional but strong, or is it traditional and tired? Are the ranks of liberal artisans open to the new but talented, or are they closed to the new, talented or not? Read the complaints of the great twelfth-century philosopher Peter Abelard about his jealous master in the schools of Paris. As a result, any group biography of liberal artisans can evoke both admiration for their talents and dismay at their wrongheadedness, snobbery, mean-spiritedness, arrogance, and impotence in the face of cruelty.

When liberal artisans are at their most dismaying, it is instructive to remember the story of the emperor's new clothes. Once there was an emperor who notoriously cared only about himself and his wardrobe and finery. Then two weavers come to town and bamboozle and steal from him while they pretend to weave the most magnificent set of new clothes for him. The unique selling proposition about these garments is that they will be invisible only to people who are too stupid or incompetent to hold their offices. When people come to visit the looms of the new tailors, they see nothing, but as they rub their eyes, they mutter to themselves, "If I say I see nothing, I will be judged to be stupid and incompetent, and I will lose my job." Then the emperor, claiming that he is wearing his new clothes, parades naked through the town. And a little child cries, "But he has nothing on." The child's voice breaks the spell. A lesson of this story for a group biography of liberal artisans is that a child or an outsider must often proclaim their intellectual and academic nakedness. However, the story is only partially instructive, for the liberal arts are never wholly without warp and woof, without texture, without providing some clothing for the body of thought and action.

The threads and patterns of the Western ideal of liberal artisans grew out of Mediterranean and Near Eastern cultures. Though I say a childish "No" to aspects of this heritage, and though I read the classics in translation, I love them. I return to the Platonic dialogues, the myths, the tragedies, the histories, and the literature and letters, again and again. They always surprise, teach, and renew me, a capacity that shapes my definition of "a classic." Famously, the antecedents of *liberal arts* are in the Latin *artes liberales* and *disciplinae liberales.* Significantly, as Bruce Kimball suggests, they embody not one but two ideal ways of thinking, both rooted in the Greek *logos*, "the term that the Greeks applied to the human faculty that was thought to be the source of learning and civilization." One emphasizes reason, the faculty and act of thinking; the other emphasizes speech, how we talk and communicate.[9] In Greek philosophy, this marks the difference between Plato and Aristotle, on the one hand, and the rhetors and orators on the other. If the tension between two modes of thought leads to quarrels among liberal artisans, it also prevents the brain-aging hegemony of a single method.[10] The classics also gave us the ideal of the liberal arts as an alliance of wisdom and virtue that the young can usefully learn before assuming their rightful place in the social order. Exemplified by a Cicero, the liberally educated were best prepared to become statesmen, leaders, great and well-trained voices in the public square.

However, the very term *artes liberales* embodies what many modern liberal artisans consider a "con job" of the classical ideal. *Liber* means free. The liberal artisan was free from menial labor, servitude, and slavery in order to pursue these arts. As such feminist scholars as Elizabeth Kamarck Minnich and Jane Roland Martin have argued, the liberal arts reflected and sustained relations that were at once dualistic and hierarchical—for example, between mind and body, inquiry and utility, citizen and less than citizen, man and woman. Much of the labor of modern liberal artisans has been to rip these dualistic hierarchies from the liberal arts and to prepare all students to be democratic, freedom-loving citizens.

The next task for liberal artisans, after the rise of Christianity toward the end of the fifth century, was to blend classical culture and Christian learning. Liberal artisans codified the liberal arts into seven (*septem artes liberales)*, consisting of the three ways of the *trivium* (grammar, rhetoric, logic or dialectic) and the four ways of the *quadrivium* (arithmetic, astronomy, geometry, and music).[11] The seven bring together what we would call the humanities and the sciences. Supplementing and overlapping them was philosophy, which Isidore of Seville (c. 560–636) defined as "the understanding of matters both human and divine joined to the study of the good life."[12] Philosophy was threefold: natural (or physics); moral (or ethics); and, for Isidore, "rational" (or logic).

Ironically, if the liberal artisan was primarily gendered male, the personifications of the liberal arts and philosophy were gendered female. Like the Muses in classical thought who emblemize the arts and history, or like the goddess Athena who nourishes learning, the seven liberal arts were allegorized as women. The perhaps mythical philosopher St. Catherine could also be patron of the medieval faculty of liberal arts. Arguably, the traditional metaphorical linkage of women with learning made their real-life demands for the status of publicly active liberal artisan more plausible, but getting those demands met was the arduous work of centuries. In doing so, women and their male allies invented three strategies: the creation of a history of learned women that gave women liberal artisans a genealogy; the creation of women's spaces, the convent and later the school and college, in which women liberal artisans could thrive; and finally, the imaginative yet empirical, tough-minded yet supple advocacy for women as liberal artisans in education, including colleges and universities.

The liberal artisans in medieval and early modern Europe next participated in the growth of communities of learning outside of well-born homes, courts, and monasteries. In the eleventh century, the cultivation of cathedral and parish schools helped lead to guilds of masters and students, *universitas*, the beginning of that institution of higher education that was to become a global force. The work of the liberal artisan and the curriculum were invigorated (one might more accurately say redeemed) by the arrival of Islamic thought, including its study of ancient Greek culture and Jewish thought. For liberal artisans, Aristotle became the ideal philosopher. Their universities were intellectual centers, providers of authorized credentials, and sites of training for advanced careers. Indeed, the seven liberal arts were an introductory curriculum, offering a bachelor's and master's degree to students who might be quite young. They could then obtain a license to teach, the *licentia docendi*. The liberal arts were a bridge to the higher faculties of law, theology, and medicine, themselves an avenue of mobility for service to the church or governments. From time to time, the junior liberal artisans seem to anticipate the attitude of some contemporary students to their general education requirements: Get me through this so I can go on to my major and professional courses. In 1255, the "Rules for the Liberal Arts Course" at the University of Paris were forced to decree:

> Let all know that we, all and each, masters of arts by our common assent, no one contradicting, because of the new and incalculable peril which threatens in our faculty—some masters hurrying to finish their lectures sooner than the length and difficulty of the texts permits, for

which reason both masters in lecturing and scholars in hearing make less progress—worrying over the ruin of our faculty and wishing to provide for our status, have decreed and ordained for the common utility and the reparation of our university to the honor of God and the church universal that all and single masters of our faculty in the future shall be required to finish the texts which they shall have begun on the feast of St. Remy [October 1] at the times below noted, not before.[13]

Given how secular or nonsectarian modern liberal artisans are, we may forget how tightly bound the universities were to the Roman Catholic Church for the religious justification of their activities and their unifying theological and moral frameworks, definitions of orthodoxy and heresy, daily routines, status and privileges, and misogyny and anti-Semitism. The deeply influential late-sixteenth-century Jesuit plans for liberal arts institutions, which include the arts, are brilliantly organized. They both design institutions and bring together the liberal arts ideals of the past, those of classic liberal arts, medieval scholasticism, and Renaissance humanism. The purpose of education is clear: to teach the disciplines that "arouse knowledge and love of our Maker and Redeemer."[14] During and after the sixteenth- and seventeenth-century warfare and turbulence of the Reformation and the Counter-Reformation, in which the Jesuits were powerful actors, the liberal artisans placed themselves within a spectrum of confessions, be they Catholic or one of the varieties of Protestantism. Nevertheless, the spectrum was within a Christian cosmology and society.

Religion accompanied the two immensely important evolutions of the work of liberal artisans in the early modern period—Renaissance humanism and the new science. Crucially, they were the consequence of liberal artisans inside the university but outside of it as well. They invented such cultural forms as the fifteenth-century Platonic Academy of Florence (for humanists) and the seventeenth-century Royal Society of England (for scientists). I hope that we contemporaries have the devotion to learning, the skills, and the courage of these predecessors, and that we contemporaries who are professional liberal artisans within the academy have the ability to reach and collaborate with colleagues outside of the academy. For they are everywhere—in book clubs, reading groups, and, so extensively, on the Internet. Wikipedia is a twenty-first-century academy.

To oversimplify, Renaissance humanism, its origins placed in the fourteenth century, reshaped and reidealized the trivium and philosophy. Its rebirth of literary culture and the rediscovery of texts reformed education. [15] Plato and Cicero took a place with Aristotle as authoritative models of thought. Supplementing Christian education, the *studia humanitas* sought to shape rulers and princes as well as scholars and professionals through Greek and Latin texts. In that famous representation of English

Renaissance humanism, Hamlet is both scholar and warrior, a gallant prince who is a university man at home with a book and a sword. To Ophelia, he is a "noble mind," courtier, scholar, soldier, the "rose of the fair state/The glass of fashion and the mould of form" (III, 1, 159–161). The second evolution, the growth of modern science and empiricism, reshaped and reidealized the quadrivium after the late fifteenth century. In different ways, both profoundly altered the philosophies.[16]

For American liberal artisans, the founding of Harvard College in 1636 is of signal importance. Symbolically, of the now idealized humanists, Erasmus, born in 1466, died in 1536, an exact century earlier. Bacon, of the now idealized scientists, was born in 1561 and died in 1626. Galileo, born in 1564, died in 1642. Harvard was the beneficiary of both humanism and the new science. By 1636, there were two universities in the Americas, both in the Spanish colonies (in Mexico City and Lima), as well as a Jesuit institution in Quebec. All were Roman Catholic in orientation. However, Harvard was the first collegiate foundation in the English colonies and defiantly Protestant in orientation, the creation of Puritan immigrants, many of whom had studied at English universities, primarily Cambridge. The charter of 1650 gives the purposes of Harvard as "the advancement of all good literature artes and Sciences." This would provide "knowledge and godliness," and so doing, train new leaders for a new land. They would include but not be limited to ministers who could "expound the Sacred Scriptures from the original Hebrew and Greek, and be cognizant of what the Church Fathers, the Scholastic Philosophers, and the Reformers had written, in Greek and Latin."[17] This ambition demanded a curriculum that would bring together languages, the seven liberal arts, the three philosophies, and a cadre of liberal artisans who could propound it.

Crucially, Harvard aligned the liberal arts with the education of undergraduate men, more accurately gentlemen, in a morally righteous residential setting. Faculty and students, living and studying together, would form a community. Although Harvard's early days were often financially precarious, its model of how liberal artisans were to teach proved sturdy. Given the resources available to Harvard's founders, the creation of another Cambridge University with a cluster of colleges would have been a pipe dream. All the other colonial colleges that were founded before the Revolutionary War, the basis of the Ivy League, followed its model. They varied by their exact Protestant religious affiliation, which helped bring a degree of religious tolerance to Colonial American higher education, but they were united in their conflation of a liberal arts curriculum, training in moral and intellectual leadership, and a self-conscious community. The curriculum was tightly structured. An account of the Princeton curriculum in 1764 shows morning and evening prayer; a freshman year of Latin and

Greek; a sophomore year of languages, plus sciences, geography, rhetoric, logic, and mathematics; a junior year of mathematics, natural and moral philosophy, metaphysics, chronology, and Hebrew for some, especially if they were to have a career in the church. But this requirement was "so unhappily unpopular." Interestingly, the account gives clues to some support of critical thinking, the necessity of which is now an article of faith among contemporary liberal artisans. "In the instruction of youth, care is taken to cherish a spirit of liberty, and free inquiry, and not only to permit, but even to encourage their right of private judgment, without presuming to dictate with an air of infallibility, or demanding an implicit assent to the decisions of the preceptor."[18]

Before and after the Revolutionary War, the ideals of liberal artisans had to evolve to both guide and respond to shifts in history's massive tectonic plates. One, cultural and political, was the Enlightenment. Today, we may also forget that the Enlightenment, for which liberal artisans inside and outside of universities fought, was no cakewalk. In 1798, when Kant published *The Contest of the Faculties (Der Streit Der Fakultäten)*, it was a jarring document. For, he submitted, the great faculty should be not theology but philosophy, where reason can work freely. In the United States, conventional liberal artisans still abided by Protestant Christianity. A common capstone course in the colleges was Evidences of Christianity. Here the teacher, usually the president, would show undergraduates how the learning of their previous four years could be reconciled with and made coherent by Christian teaching. Yet, Enlightenment thought gave liberal artisans the increasingly desirable ideals of reason and intellectual freedom.

The second great shift, which Enlightenment thinking famously influenced, was the American Revolution and the birth of the United States. What role were liberal artisans to take on to be of value in the new republic? In addition, how were they to respond to the ever-increasing presence of science and the need to bridge a gap (or gulf or abyss) between theory and its application?[19] Gentlemen should and could be interested in Copernicus as well as Cicero. The calls for reform in the colleges are fascinating reading, written under the urgent compulsion to build a new, independent nation and an educational system from primary schools through colleges that would serve it. These liberal artisans also had a rigorous liberal arts education that prepared skilled, confident rhetoricians.

One sign of the public debates about education and the liberal arts is the 1795 essay contest that the American Philosophical Society sponsored. Its subject was the best system of "liberal education and literary instruction, adapted to the genius of the government of the United States; comprehending also a plan for instituting and conducting public schools in this country, on principles of the most extensive utility."[20] One winner was Samuel H. Smith (1772–1845), a graduate of the University of Pennsylvania at the age of 15. In the liberal arts tradition, "A System of Liberal Education" calls the great hope of a "correct education" the making of men who will be "virtuous and wise" in a republic. Their "general education" will consist mostly of prescribed books that will give them "what it is necessary [that] every man should know." To have utility, this common curriculum will include mathematics, geography, and science. The essay ends with a prophetic vision of the United States, its citizens liberally educated, that will be safe and benign, radiant with "dignity, humility, and intelligence." It will be "too enlightened and virtuous" to go to war—unless forced to do so. Smith's last sentence is a rhapsodic tribute to the alliance of a liberal education that has accepted science and the creation of the blessed and peaceable kingdom. "Let us, then, with rapture anticipate the era where the triumph of peace and the prevalence of virtue shall be rendered secure by the diffusion of useful knowledge."

One must ask with what rapture an American slave would greet this flourish. To be sure, some of the educational visionaries of the new republic were abolitionists. Among them was the notable Dr. Benjamin Rush—a doctor and scientist who founded Dickinson College. In 1786 he had declared that we must educate a class of leaders appropriate to our form of government and "lay . . . the foundations for nurseries of wise and good men."[21] However, efforts to limit the pool of trained liberal artisans who could play an active role in public life to Christian white men became morally and socially unsustainable. The nineteenth century saw two great strategies for enlarging the pool, both entailing hard work and patience. The first was slowly to admit the Other into the institutions for the higher training of liberal artisans. This began before the Civil War at such colleges as Oberlin, Knox, Genesee, Antioch, Lawrence, and Alfred (though it was chartered as a university). Public institutions also became coeducational—although vicious racial segregation persisted. For example, Purdue, established in 1874, admitted its first women in 1875. No one should confuse coeducation with an absolutely equal education. At Purdue, no more than 10 percent of the students were women until 1920. Nevertheless, the ideal of who a liberal artisan might be was reforming itself.

The second strategy was to establish alternative educational systems. The first Catholic institution was Georgetown, founded in 1789. Next were colleges for women. I am the beneficiary of my liberal arts college for women, the blue-stocking Bryn Mawr. The school's second president, the formidable M. Carey Thomas (1857–1935) terrified generations of undergraduates with her maxim "Our failures only marry," which we transmogrified into "Only our failures marry." Immediately after the Civil War, a third system, this for African Americans, was created.

One of the most famous arguments in the history of American higher education was over the purpose of what we now call the historically black colleges and universities and the place of liberal artisans in the struggle to end racism, discrimination, and segregation. One antagonist was Booker T. Washington (1856–1915), born a slave, educated at Hampton Normal and Agricultural Institute, and, in 1881, the first leader of the Tuskegee Institute where he became nationally prominent. The other was W.E.B. Du Bois (1868–1963), born a free black, educated at Fisk University, a black institution, and Harvard University, who was to achieve great eminence as well. How were blacks to be free men? What, then, was the education that would serve this end? Washington stressed moral, vocational, and practical training. Du Bois argued that a liberal education should be given, especially to the "Talented Tenth" of the race—linking the acquisition of liberal education to leadership of racial salvation. *The Souls of Black Folk* (1903), Du Bois' magnificent combination of autobiography, anthropology, and politics, is an extended quarrel with Washington. Eloquently, Du Bois claims the liberal arts tradition as his as well. "I sit with Shakespeare and he winces not. Across the color line I move arm in arm with Balzac and Dumas. . . . From out the caves of evening that swing between the strong-limbed earth and the tracery of the stars, I summon Aristotle and Aurelius."[22]

If a constricted, limited ideal of *who* the liberal artisan might be became unsustainable, so did the ideal of *what* the liberal artisan should do in the classroom and *where* that classroom should be located. To be sure, the classical curriculum has never wholly disappeared. However, it has been radically displaced. Significantly, in the eighteenth century, the learning of Latin began to decay—despite classical language requirements for admission to the colonial colleges. In the mid-eighteenth century, the requirement at Yale to speak only Latin once there disappeared. Students nervily expressed discontent with the amount of their classical studies. Later, as the system of public education grew, the inability of many high schools to offer Greek and/or Latin made the requirements of classical languages for entrance to college unrealistic for those colleges who wanted to enroll public high school graduates. Today, when liberal artisans must fight for learning of the modern languages, let alone the classical ones, it may be hard to imagine how great the stature of Latin was. For it was nothing less than the traditional common language of liberal artisans and the mark of the elite educated man.

The most formidable defense of the classical curriculum was *The Yale Report* of 1828, much of it written by President Jeremiah Day. Clear, vigorous, it is conscious of designing new institutions for a new nation.[23] Yes, it admits, new subjects—the sciences, political economy—can enter the ideal curriculum, but the overarching purpose of a college must guide change. A residential community, the college is to "LAY THE FOUNDATION OF A SUPERIOR EDUCATION" that will be "broad, and deep, and solid" (p. 6). This will inculcate the "*discipline*" and "*furniture*" of the mind that will enable further study of the practical arts and professions. For, together, the disciplines show a student "*how*" to learn. Only a fixed curriculum will guarantee that the liberal artisans-in-training will encounter "those subjects . . . which ought to be understood by everyone who aims at a thorough education" (p. 18). Those subjects include the classics. They are not the abused "dead languages" but the foundation of all European literature. To read them is to "relish . . . what is elevated, chaste, and simple" (p. 35). Indeed, the report recommends, Yale should raise its admissions standards so that matriculates will know more Greek and Latin and need less remedial education.

Articulating and reinforcing an ideal, *The Yale Report* was influential. Enrolling about 300 students, Yale was one of the largest colleges in the country. Many of its graduates became educators who carried the report's message with them. Despite such power, *The Yale Report* was an American report, sent forth to a changing nation that increasingly believed that providing access to education was a democracy's responsibility. In turn, educated citizens built democracy. Moreover, the United States was turning to the university as a supplement to the college. In 1862, Congress passed the Morrill Act, which helped states establish the land-grant institutions that would teach the practical arts and sciences. Throughout the nineteenth century, liberal artisans were also importing and adapting the exhilarating model of the then-new German research university. Over 10,000 Americans traveled and studied in Europe. They returned to support its mission of generating new knowledge and of organizing a much freer, nonsectarian, and futuristic curriculum.

Existing institutions set up reforming themselves. Harvard established its graduate school in 1872. New institutions, with visionary leaders, were created: Cornell University, partially land grant, in 1868; Johns Hopkins, a graduate institution, in 1876. The university was to be a structure that oversaw undergraduate, graduate, and professional education. Liberal artisans were to do their research and teaching in departments that housed disciplines. Disciplines then clustered into the modern constellations of the sciences, social sciences, and the humanities.[24] During this process, modernity may have stripped the faculty, especially in the value-free sciences and social sciences, of a historic responsibility of the liberal artisan: to embody and teach morality.[25]

The roots of the American liberal arts college were hardly yanked up; the buildings were hardly smashed; the faculty were hardly replaced;

compulsory chapel was hardly abolished everywhere. The ideals of the college and of the university might collide, but they might also collude. The career of Henry S. Tappan, D.D. (1805–1881) is instructive. He served as the president of the University of Michigan, from 1852 to 1863. The university, founded in 1837, was still new. Tappan believed in universities. His book, *University Education*, is an act of advocacy.[26] His models are the Protestant universities of Germany and Scotland, which believe in freedom and freedom of thought. Attentive to liberal undergraduate education, he established a Department of Literature, Science, and the Arts (now a powerful school), although its focus was the modern languages, science, and mathematics rather than Greek and Latin.

Yet, liberal artisans within the college had a formidable rival: liberal artisans within the modern research university and its ideals. The clash of ideals still resonates—carried on the struggle between "teaching" and "research." Of the extraordinary men who built the American research university in the nineteenth and early twentieth centuries, perhaps none is more extraordinary than Charles William Eliot (1834–1926). If the leaders of higher education had a Mt. Rushmore, Eliot's would be the first face to be carved there. A chemist, he was another young president, who had done his European tour. He started at Harvard in 1869 and left forty years later. Of his many reforms, he brought electives to the undergraduate curriculum. He was not the first to want to abolish requirements in favor of student choice. Henry Wayland, the president of Brown from 1827 to 1855, had defended the addition of new subjects and electives in *His Thoughts on the Present Collegiate System in the United States*. Eliot made it happen. Like the old defenses of the liberal arts, Eliot's justification for his actions was both epistemological and ethical. Epistemologically, he argued that because research impels growth and change in knowledge, the university must offer many more subjects that the faculty wish to teach. Ethically, he supported the liberty and freedom of students. Let them choose their subjects. In so doing, they will get the training and character formation that individuals need in order to create habits and customs for themselves.

The elective system grew. Eliot's justifications for it are still plausible. Yet, liberal artisans also led a revolt against it. Freedom was not an ideal but the primrose path to haphazardness, professionalization, overspecialization, and faculty and student self-indulgence. Where was the ideal of the unity of knowledge, let alone coherence and structure? Let alone a common undergraduate experience? Was there no core in this curriculum? Liberal artisans and their leaders embarked on a series of experiments that were both retrenchments and innovations. In this process the vocabulary of "the liberal arts" mutated to include "liberal learning" or "liberal education."

Eliot's successor as the president of Harvard, the far more socially and politically conservative A. Lawrence Lowell (1856–1943), immediately instituted one major reform. Beginning with the class of 1914, courses were to be grouped into "concentrations" (majors and minors). Undergraduates would first have breadth, then depth. The quest for breadth commonly took the form of the still-popular distribution requirements. In the same decade, Columbia was responsible for the initiation of two other highly influential ideals of education by and for liberal artisans. The first, in 1917, was a general honors course that focused on classic texts. The Great Books movement in liberal education is perhaps now most closely associated with Robert M. Hutchins (1899–1977), another of those young presidents who forged a tradition of strong administrative leaders. President of the University of Chicago from 1929 to 1951, Hutchins advocated a "Great Conversation" with the classics, which form "permanent studies" and revealed a human nature that we all share. These "Conversations" could occur inside and outside of the university. Among liberal artisans, the "Great Conversation" had competed with ideas about the "progressive college," associated with the philosopher John Dewey (1859–1952). Liberal learning was to be an unfolding journey, concerned with students, interested in problems.[27]

The second Columbia-initiated reform was general education. Like so many accomplishments by liberal artisans, it was related to war. The government needed a training course for the Student Army Training Corps in World War I. The result was Contemporary Civilization, which slowly evolved into three broad common courses for undergraduates: Contemporary Civilization, humanities, and sciences. Daniel Bell, the sociologist, has given three great reasons why Columbia was so important in general education. First, the college, always a center of the university, was rebelling against the professionalization of the university as a whole. Next, the college was responding to the abandonment of the classics as a requirement for admission and graduation, a process that was completed in 1916. Finally, the student body at this urban university was changing, admitting many more children of immigrants. Student homogeneity was no longer a given.[28] In response to this threat of immigrants from Southern and Eastern Europe, especially those whose children were academically promising, some of the United States' most prestigious universities instituted quotas for the admission of Jewish students. These lasted for decades. The pool of liberal artisans in training was, it was hoped, to consist primarily of the Protestant sons of immigrants from Northern and Western Europe.[29]

World War II profoundly changed the United States. Perhaps a "core curriculum" or "general education" was to continue to provide training in the democratic values that the United States had successfully defended, academic coherence (to one degree or another), and moral explorations for the undergraduates whom many feared, and still fear, were neglected or badly taught in the large universities.[30] Yet, after World War II, the limitations on the workplace of liberal artisans seemed as unsustainable as they did during the nineteenth century. The number and kind of institutions grew, including the community colleges in which about 50 percent of U.S. students are now enrolled. As unsustainable were the constrictions on the identity of the ideal liberal artisan. That pool had to grow, a demographic change that the federal government enabled. After the passage of the Servicemen's Readjustment Act in 1944, popularly known as the G.I. Bill of Rights, millions of veterans entered colleges and universities. In 1946, President Harry Truman created the President's Commission on Higher Education. It was responsible for a six-volume report that "did not hesitate to identify the economic, social, racial, and religious barriers that stood in the way of the nation's commitment to equal opportunity."[31]

For liberal artisans, the 1960s were the decade in which such barriers, including those against women, were dismantled. The 1960s were the setting for the protests against the war in Vietnam and for the increasingly intense and successful civil rights movements. Education was an urgent, even passionate, cause for them. Liberal artisans—faculty and students— were to include far more women and members of racial and ethnic minorities. Especially but not exclusively in the humanities and social sciences, the curriculum was to explore, even embrace, their experiences in disciplinary and interdisciplinary women's studies, black studies, or ethnic studies. For many, it was necessary but not sufficient to know more. Moral and ethical choices were to be made as well. Moral and ethical ideals were to be followed. Simultaneously, the academy was studying profound cultural changes in such emerging programs as Cultural Studies, Performance Studies, and Cinema Studies, and later, GLBT Studies. The very use of the word *studies*, which had begun after World War II with *area studies*, was a marker of the blurring of disciplinary boundaries and the rising of interdisciplinary ambitions.

In brief, the quest for *diversity* and *inclusion* as an ideal of liberal arts education had begun. It was deeply, bitterly entangled in the "culture wars" in the United States and elsewhere. I believe that the culture wars, which took place in the media and a wide variety of publications, were fought over the linked issues of historical meanings of the United States and its role in the world as a superpower; race and racial discrimination; gender and gender discrimination; and sexual norms. At the end of the Vietnamese war, the struggles shifted to what its history and that of the United States as a whole should be. The consequences for liberal artisans and their ideals were unsettled, even viciously so. What should be read?

What should be taught? What were we to consider our "cultural capital"? Liberal artisans were once again partisans.

A sophisticated, edgy replay of the 1930s between the ideals of the Great Books and progressivism began when Allan Bloom, a classicist and political philosopher, then at the University of Chicago, published a wondrous jeremiad, *The Closing of the American Mind: How Higher Education Has Failed Democracy and Impoverished the Souls of Today's Students*, in 1987. It excoriated contemporary liberal artisans for representing an anti-idea, lacking in depth, respect for classical learning, seriousness, and moral and intellectual standards as they were. In the midst of the mixed acclaim and skepticism it received, an equally publicized struggle took place at Stanford University over the revision of a core course on Western culture, to be known as Culture, Ideas, Values. Mary Louise Pratt, a humanities professor who supported the revisions, asked if ideally we wanted to be a multicultural, multiethnic, multilingual nation, or if we wished to "create a narrowly specific cultural capital that will be the normative *referent* for everyone, but will remain the property of a small and powerful caste that is linguistically and ethically unified." [32] Then, in 1996, the historian Lawrence W. Levine brought out a riposte, *The Opening of the American Mind: Canons, Culture, and History*. It pointedly argued for the values of our pluralism. [33]

In the 1980s, the quest to implement the ideal of diversity and inclusiveness expanded to include global as well as national differences and the meanings of the economic, social, and cultural forces of globalization. In part, liberal artisans call for a historical exploration of patterns of globalization. In part, they promulgate the ideal of hearing a diversity of voices. Gayatri Spivak, a scholar of comparative literature who was born in India but who works in the United States, prizes the knowledge and perspectives of those most marginal to globalization—for example, an illiterate peasant woman in Southeast Asia. Living in the world at large, we must fully comprehend the Otherness of Others, and, as Kwame Anthony Appiah suggests, construct an ethics in a world of strangers.

Then, in a book that is a superb example of useful knowledge, Martha Nussbaum synthesizes the ideals of the classical curriculum and of the new learning about diversity and globalization. Studying fifteen U.S. colleges and universities, Nussbaum could outline a norm of democratic citizenship in a multicultural and multinational world and examine the liberal arts curricula that serve it. Her examples connect Western classical culture and its traditions to non-Western cultures and to such new fields as women's studies. In doing so, Nussbaum shows us, the liberal arts embody the deep values of leading an examined life, which entails the admission of one's own ignorance; the liberation of the mind from custom and habit; the possession of a "narrative imagination"; and the capacity to become that cosmopolitan "citizen of the world."[34]

The task then for many liberal artisans, if they do not wish to defend the legitimate powers of a classical curriculum, is to integrate national and global diversity into a core or general education curriculum.[35] The faculties of undergraduate colleges of arts and sciences—whether part of a university or independent—debate strenuously about how to do this. The current Morse Academic Plan, the resolution reached at my home institution, New York University, is a good example of this work. It prescribes areas of study rather than a sequence of courses, an acknowledgment of student interest and, perhaps, of the difficulties of scheduling for nearly 10,000 student enrollments. Students can gain exemptions from or substitutes for the required areas of (1) Expository Writing; (2) Foundations of Contemporary Culture (Texts and Ideas, Cultures and Contexts, Societies and the Social Sciences, Expressive Culture [arts]); (3) a foreign language; and (4) Foundations of Scientific Inquiry, which are courses in natural and quantitative sciences.[36] Each of the lecture courses has recitations or a lab.

Drawing on both nineteenth-century and early-twenty-first-century commentary on liberal arts ideals, MAP provides a "core academic experience for undergraduates" or "an integrated general education curriculum in the liberal arts"; gives undergraduates a "common experience"; and offers an "academic foundation for . . . future studies." The outcomes of MAP ought to be a heightened "cultural awareness"; better "critical reading skills"; the promotion of "creative and logical thinking"; broader "perspectives; . . . new pathways for intellectual inquiry; . . . and the skills, background and social awareness to thrive in dynamic circumstances." As citizens of a diverse, mobile, volatile world, they will be "equip[ped] . . . for lives as thinking individuals and members of society." The graduates of the liberal arts in MAP will have both intellectual training and preparation for a global world.

However good MAP is, it is probably not tautly coherent enough for another set of contemporary liberal artisans who seek the ideal of *integration* of the liberal arts. This is not a discovery of the hidden unity of knowledge or of God's deepest plans; rather, it is a deliberate effort to do two things: first, to put the act of learning itself into play with other activities, and next, and perhaps more narrowly, to put the academic disciplines into play. Both efforts value establishing *connections* and networks. William H. Newell, summarizing major developments in integrative learning, calls on Julie Thompson Klein for a spacious definition, "an umbrella term for structures, strategies, and activities that bridge numerous divides, such as high school and college, general education and the major, introductory and advanced levels, experiences inside and outside the classroom, theory and practice, and disciplines and fields." [37] Integrative learning also prizes intentionality, the process on the part of all learners, coming into consciousness and awareness of how one teaches and learns.

The implications of integrative learning for liberal artisans within the academy are vast, even scary—if one is as rooted in current practices as I am. How, for example, should we reform the major, which was so innovative a century ago during President Lowell's time at Harvard? In a tightly argued essay, Carol Geary Schneider makes a comparatively modest but important proposal. She submits that students do need a major. In order to think well, they need its exposure and depth. She is right to say this so plainly. A danger of integrative and interdisciplinary activities is superficiality. One must bring something of value—ideas, information, "content," and "expertise," if you will—to the table. As a result, a certain asymmetry may mark the exchanges around the table. X may know a lot about the construction of gender in medicine; Y about the construction of gender in law. X cannot chatter on about the law without listening to and learning from Y. Y cannot chatter on about medicine without listening to and learning from X. Only then can they begin to understand together what the construction of gender in the professions might be. The fallacy of misplaced originality, of naively believing that what one is saying is new and true, is only too common.

A major, Schneider continues, is an act of "enculturation." Students may be learning the protocols, codes, rhetoric, and rules of evidence of that particular field. However, the "focused discourse" of an interpretative community does result in an increase in cognitive skills. The more knowledge and disciplinary consciousness a student has, the more material he or she has for analysis and argument. That said, a major, although necessary, is not sufficient for a student who is preparing for a modern world that "requires practice in translating languages, negotiating differences, rethinking one's understandings in light of alternative conceptual frames and points of view." A major should become "integrative and translational or intercultural." This will happen if a student can move back and forth between double majors, majors and minors, and the acquisition of knowledge inside and outside of the classroom.[38]

Given the convictions of interconnections, it is not surprising that a persuasive, elegant picture of the ideal liberal artisan is called "only connect," a reference to *Howards End* (1910), E.M. Forster's novel about modern loss, fragmentation, alienation.[39] William Cronon gives these characteristics of the liberal artisan, practitioner of the liberal arts. Interestingly, they combine both aspects of the "logos" that Kimball described: first, the capacity to use speech and to enter into communicative acts, and next, the capacity for thought, logic, analysis.

There is an ancient proverb, anonymous, that has mistakenly been attributed to the great Greek playwright Euripides. If the gods wish to destroy you, they will first drive you crazy, mad (my paraphrase). Madness is frenzy, destruction, the id in charge. Let's add a corollary. If the gods wish to destroy you, they will also make you stupid. The liberal arts, because they demand thought, for its own sake and for the sake of other principles that have changed over time, are tough garments of the mind. They must be worn in the wild weathers of madness and the torpors of stupidity. The liberal artisans create these garments, and re-create them, and re-create them. If we let the liberal arts atrophy, or fall into disrepair, we are inviting madness and stupidity. We are also abandoning the proof of our human capacities for thought and creativity. This will not be the choice of the gods, but of human beings, including a smug president of France.

Notes

1. Among the reforms were an apparent privileging of applied over basic research; taking away of national appointments to university faculties; assessing staff on a four-year cycle; and giving universities more autonomy under strong executive leaders. Robin Briggs, "President Sarkozy, *La Princèsse de Clèves,* and the Crisis in the French Higher Education System," *Oxford Magazine,* Second Week, Trinity Term, 2009, 4–6.

2. The literature about the marginal position of the liberal arts in U.S. society, with a special emphasis on the humanities, is too large to note here.

3. I regret that I will not be mapping the liberal artisans in secondary schools, their ideals, and their relations with liberal artisans in higher education, but I recommend for a general history of American schools Patricia Albjerg Graham, *Schooling America: How the Public Schools Meet the Nation's Changing Needs* (New York: Oxford University Press, 2005), 273. Diane Ravitch, *Death and Life of the Great American School System: How Testing and Choices Are Undermining Education* (New York: Basic Books, 2010), especially chapter 11, offers a persuasive defense of a liberal arts curriculum in the schools.

4. Multiple helpful contributions to the discussion of liberal education appear in a dedicated issue of *Daedalus,* 128, No. 1 (Winter 1999).

5. Interwoven with the difficulties of the liberal arts, except at their most utilitarian, is the well-documented decline in the number of liberal arts residential colleges. However, that number is growing outside of the United States.

6. Adele Wolfson, "The Straw Man of Science as Enemy of the Humanities," *Teagle Liblog,* August 16, 2010, http://teaglefoundation.org/liblog/entry.aspx ?id=258. Teagle is a foundation that supports education. Significantly, in the twentieth and twenty-first centuries in the United States, foundations and organizations have supplemented the voices of powerful individual liberal artisans, of major university presidents, as advocates and explainers of the liberal arts.

7. Stanley Fish, an important voice, frequently writes on this point more fully and intelligently.

8. Peter J. Gomes, "Values and the Elite Residential College," *Daedalus* 128, no. 1 (Winter 1999): 118.

9. Bruce A. Kimball, *The Liberal Arts Tradition: A Documentary History* (Lanham, MD: University Press of America, 2010), 9. This 511-page text provides an excellent overview.

10. A common metaphor that described logic and rhetoric shows their commonality as well as their differences. Logic is "the closed fist," a tight argument; rhetoric is the "open hand," a more discursive one. However, the human hand, body, and brain operate both.

11. *Trivium* means where three ways meet, *quadrivium* four ways.

12. Kimball, *The Liberal Arts Tradition*, 79.

13. Kimball, *The Liberal Arts Tradition*, 135.

14. *Ratio Studiorum: The Official Plan for Jesuit Education*, trans. Claude Pavur (St. Louis: Institute of Jesuit Sources, 2005), sec. H1 (7), www.slu.edu/colleges/AS/languages/classical/latin/tchmat/pedagogy/rs/rs1.html.
A recent paper by Mark O'Conner, director of the honors program at Boston College, speaks eloquently to the use of the Jesuit tradition in the classroom. Students are encouraged to share an intellectual conversation and debate across the disciplines. They are to ask how they learned what they learned and to work sequentially, to see how their explorations build on each other. This is true of many contemporary liberal arts classrooms, but O'Conner also adopts the Jesuit tradition of *discernment*, "a fuller awareness of the consequences of our actions—on ourselves, on others, on the world around us." Being aware is unending, "the liberal/liberating process is lifelong." Mark O'Conner, "What Country, Friend, Is This?" (unpublished paper), 2. I thank Professor O'Conner for permitting me to read his paper.

15. Scholars from Byzantium, coming to the West before and after the fall of Constantinople in 1453, renewed the study of Greek.

16. Johannes Gutenberg (1398–1468), by inventing the Western printing press, also irrevocably changed the work of liberal artisans by giving them a wonderful new tool, the equivalent of our computers and electronic technologies of communication.

17. Samuel Eliot Morison, *Three Centuries of Harvard 1636–1936* (Cambridge, MA: Belknap Press of Harvard University Press, 1965), 1. Morison is a model of bringing the history of an institution alive.

18. The literature about the American curriculum and the colonial colleges is extensive, but these quotes are from Kimball, *The Liberal Arts Tradition*, 236–37.

19. One of the powerful pre–Revolutionary War influences was the scientist Joseph Priestley (1733–1804), an Englishman who immigrated to the colonies, and his 1765 *An Essay on a Course of Liberal Education for Civil and Active Life*.

20. My quotes about and from this contest are in Kimball, *The Liberal Arts Tradition*, 238–50. The American Philosophical Society extends the tradition of gatherings of liberal artisans outside of the university who contribute to national and international academic life. Founded in 1843, with Benjamin Franklin as a primary

advocate, it was the first learned society in the colonies, promoting "useful knowledge" in the sciences and humanities.

21. Benjamin Rush, *Thoughts upon the Mode of Education Proper in a Republic* (Philadelphia, 1786), www.schoolchoices.org/roo/rush.htm.

22. W.E.B. Du Bois, *The Souls of Black Folk: Authoritative Text, Contexts, Criticism*, ed. Henry Louis Gates Jr. and Terri Hume Oliver (New York: Norton, 1999), 74.

23. Committee of the Corporation and the Academical Faculty, *Reports on the Course of Instruction in Yale College* (New Haven, CT: Hezekian Howe, 1828).

24. A common and usually derogatory term for individual disciplines and their disciplinary clusters is *silos*.

25. Julie A. Reuben, *The Making of the Modern University: Intellectual Transformation and the Marginalization of Morality* (Chicago: University of Chicago Press, 1996), 363. Reuben also traces a wave of reform that instituted student services, "student life," and evocations of "community" to take on the job of forming character and moral values. In 1891, Harvard appointed the first dean of students. Reuben's book is necessary reading in the history of the modern research university.

26. Henry P. Tappan, *University Education* (New York: George P. Putnam, 1851).

27. One of the farthest reaching of the experiments was simply called the Experimental College, which Alexander Meiklejohn (1872–1964) established in 1927 at the University of Wisconsin. For men only, it was an interdisciplinary, residential adventure with no fixed grades and six-week curricular models. It lasted until 1932, but the university in 1948 set up a version of the college, Integrated Liberal Studies.

28. Daniel Bell, *The Reforming of General Education: The Columbia College Experience in Its National Setting* (New York: Columbia University Press, 1966), quoted in Kimball, *The Liberal Arts Tradition*, 381.

29. Jerome Karabel, *The Chosen: The Hidden History of Admission and Exclusion at Harvard, Yale, and Princeton* (New York: Houghton Mifflin, 2005), 711. This is a magisterial account of Jewish quotas in admissions.

30. Post–World War II reports on general education (and its permutations) were both national and local (i.e., produced by individual colleges or universities). Among the national reports, in addition to Bell's *Reforming of General Education*, were Faculty of Arts and Science at Harvard, *General Education in a Free Society* (Cambridge, MA: Harvard University Press, 1945) (never adopted); Association of American Colleges, *Integrity in the College Curriculum: A Report to the Academic Community* (Washington, DC: Association of American Colleges, 1985); Ernest L. Boyer, *College: The Undergraduate Experience in America* (New York: Harper and Row, 1988); and Association of American Colleges: Task Group on General Education, *A New Vitality in General Education: Planning, Teaching, and Supporting Effective Liberal Learning* (Washington, DC: Association of American Colleges, 1988).

31. William G. Bowen, Martin A. Kurzweil, and Eugene M. Tobin, *Equity and Excellence in American Higher Education* (Charlottesville: University of Virginia Press, 2005), 34. The book also documents the constraints that segregated states put on returning black servicemen who sought to utilize the benefits of the GI Bill.

32. Catharine R. Stimpson, "The Culture Wars Continue," *Daedalus* 131, no. 3 (Summer 2002): 36–40.

33. Mary Louise Pratt, "Humanities for the Future: Reflections on the Western Culture Debate at Stanford," in *The Politics of Liberal Education*, ed. Darryl J. Gless and Barbara Herrnstein Smith (Durham, NC: Duke University Press, 1992), 15; Lawrence W. Levine, *The Opening of the American Mind: Canons, Culture, and History* (Boston: Beacon Press, 1996), 10ff.

34. Kwame Anthony Appiah, *Cosmopolitanism: Ethics in a World of Strangers* (New York: Norton, 2006), 196; Gayatri Chakravorty Spivak, *Death of a Discipline* (New York: Columbia University Press, 2003), 128; Martha C. Nussbaum, *Cultivating Humanity: A Classical Defense of Reform in Liberal Education* (Cambridge, MA: Harvard University Press, 1998), 328.

35. One study showed that by 1992, more than a third of all colleges and universities had a multicultural general education requirement. Arthur Levine and Jeanette Cureton, "The Quiet Revolution," in *American Higher Education Transformed 1940–2005*, ed. Wilson Smith and Thomas Bender (Baltimore: Johns Hopkins University Press, 2008), 194.

36. Samuel F.B. Morse was a great scientist and NYU faculty member in the nineteenth century. Morse Academic Plan has the benefit of becoming the acronym MAP.

37. William H. Newell, "Educating for a Complex World: Integrative Learning and Interdisciplinary Studies," *Liberal Education* 96, no. 4 (Fall 2010): 6. For a highly technical study of interdisciplinarity, see Robert Frodeman, Julie Thompson Klein, Carl Mitcham, and J. Britt Holbrook, eds., *The Oxford Handbook of Interdisciplinarity* (New York: Oxford University Press, 2010), 580. An important, sophisticated exploration by leading academic liberal artisans of interdisciplinarity and disciplinarity, at once theoretical and empirical, is James Chandler and Arnold I. Davidson, eds., "The Fate of Disciplines," special issue, *Critical Inquiry* 35, no. 4 (Summer 2009).

38. Carol Geary Schneider, "Enculturation or Critical Engagement?" in *Foundations of American Higher Education*, ed. James L. Bess and David S. Webster (New York: Simon and Schuster Custom Publishing, 1999), 245–56. Schneider's essay was first published in 1993.

39. E.M. Forster, *Howards End* (New York: Putnam, 1910).

3

The Theories, Contexts, and Multiple Pedagogies of Engaged Learning

What Succeeds and Why?

Lynn E. Swaner

Ask higher education faculty and administrators to define engaged learning—as I have at many colleges and universities I've visited as part of my work with the Bringing Theory to Practice Project—and the response is often, "We don't know exactly how to define it—but we know it when we see it." For those of us involved in the higher education enterprise, our descriptions of engaged and disengaged students prove that we do indeed know what "it" looks like: Engaged students ask intelligent and probing questions; they integrate what they learn from class discussions and reading into well-crafted course assignments; they effectively collaborate with their peers both in class and in campus leadership positions they hold; and they have a clear sense of the value of their college experience in crafting a meaningful career and life. By way of contrast, we typically describe our disengaged students as slumped over in their chairs on the verge of sleep, either because they spent the previous night partying or because they've been locked in their rooms chatting on Facebook into the wee hours (certainly their lethargy is not attributable to our enthralling efforts to educate them!). Even more troublesome are those students whose names are on our class, advising, or residence hall rosters, but we have no idea where—or perhaps most importantly, who—they are. We assume they are "lost" in the myriad of temptations offered by college life or are floundering, directionless, in an existential limbo between adolescence and adulthood.

The fact that most of us in academe—across departments, divisions, and institutions—can describe in similar terms what engaged learning looks like is significant, because we have a shared sense of what "higher" learning, and by way of implication "higher" education, should be about. We agree it's more than accumulation of academic concepts or skill development for a career, although these have an appropriate place in a college education; engaged learning, however, is somehow transcendent, evidenced by deep involvement in one's learning process and in actively and purposefully shaping one's life direction. And it is the polar opposite of missing class as a result of alcohol or drug use—something to which nearly a third of college students attest.[1] So we have engagement as a shared goal, and even if we can't crisply define it, we do know it when we see it.

But therein lies a problem, upon which we might find a second area of agreement—*we don't see it as often as we would like*. Excepting the few students each semester who tend to be on the verge of burnout (also known as overengagement) in both their learning and campus involvement, we are generally dissatisfied with the engagement level of our students. Some of this disengagement is attributable to factors beyond our control: in addition to being less prepared for college work than their predecessors, today's students are "coming to college overwhelmed and more damaged than those of previous years" as evidenced by the sharp rise in psychological services over the past two decades.[2] But to attribute all of students' disengagement to these factors is problematic in two ways: First, it leaves us as educators feeling largely powerless; and second, it contradicts those experiences we have of genuinely influencing students in their learning (e.g., when we provide mentorship to at-risk students, and as a result students become perceptibly more engaged and more successful in their learning). So while we perceive disengagement from learning as a reasonably widespread problem, we wish more students were (healthily) engaged in their learning and college life. And we hope, sometimes against hope, that we might have a role to play in encouraging this engagement.

In light of these areas of consensus—a shared sense of what it means to be engaged in one's learning, and a desire to help our students become more engaged in that learning—the goals of this chapter are twofold. First will be to frame our collective observations and intuitive understanding of engaged learning in terms of learning theory, from the fields of both higher and adult education research—thus hoping to attempt to answer the question "What is engaged learning?" through the lens of theory and research. The second goal is to try to move beyond our assumptions about the causes of student disengagement to examine known "best practices" for encouraging engaged learning. In doing so, we move in the spirit of "as far as depends on you"[3]—or taking up our end of the educational bargain. Perhaps the degree to which we are intentional about creating contexts for engaged learning will determine how much we actually see it, which is the central thesis of the Bringing Theory to Practice Project.

Dimensions of Engaged Learning

If there is uncertainty about what is meant by engaged learning among college educators, there is likewise a lack of a crystallized definition among theorists and researchers. Yet, a great deal of literature in the fields of higher and adult education describes various *dimensions* that enrich, deepen, and intensify students' learning. While they are not discrete and often transact with each other, there are four such major dimensions: the *developmental* dimension (fostering intellectual complexity); the *holistic* dimension (encompassing multiple domains in learning—e.g., cognitive, personal, and social); the *integrative* dimension (integrating types, sources, and temporality of learning); and the *contextual* dimension (promoting interdependence and engagement in community). Each of these dimensions, when activated in a learning setting, has the potential to make a student's learning experience transformational in nature—which, put simply, means that students are never the same (in a good way!) as a result of their learning. Put less simply, educational settings that activate these dimensions not only facilitate gains in knowledge, real-world application of learning, and intellectual complexity but also harness these gains to help learners progress toward what Keyes describes as "flourishing" (emotional, psychological, and social well-being).[4] When these dimensions converge in educational practice, they facilitate the transformational experiences we might consider engaged learning.

The Developmental Dimension

During the college years, students experience fundamental shifts in their perceptions of self and others. Changes in these areas have profound implications for the ways students make meaning of their learning and experiences as well as their functioning in relationship to other individuals and to society. These transformations are along the lines of what psychologists call *developmental* change, in which challenges in the environment cause individuals to move toward new—and generally more complex—ways of being in the world.

Pioneering the theory and research on college student development, Perry found that as students become more capable of recognizing and incorporating diverse perspectives into their worldviews, they in turn develop increasingly complex ways of thinking, knowing, and making meaning.[5] Through the positions of Perry's model, or "scheme," students move from a dualistic worldview that endorses simplified either/or thinking to a recognition of multiple and potentially valid perspectives, and then to a contextually relative approach to judging the adequacy of these differing perspectives. This developmental path is foundational in the work of Belenky et al., who describe women's development in terms of increasingly complex ways of knowing and understanding self.[6] In this view, students shift from relying on external authorities for self-knowledge to recognizing themselves as authorities and finally to reconstructing knowledge generated both external to and within the self. Similar development is also described by King and Kitchener, who examine how students learn to comprehend and address the complexity inherent in ill-structured problems, and is echoed in work by Baxter-Magolda, who focuses on how students develop a more complex sense of knowledge and self.[7] Still other theorists have used a similar developmental arc to examine areas such as moral development, faith development, racial identity development, and response to multiculturalism and difference.[8]

Key to the developmental dimension is the balancing of what Sanford called "challenge" and "support" in the educational environment.[9] Such a balance encourages developmental movement toward complexity in cognition, whereas imbalance can result in what Perry identified as developmental "pause" or even "retreat." In light of this need, Knefelkamp conceptualized a model of developmental instruction variables based on Perry's work in order to, as Knefelkamp states, "understand the underlying characteristics of the student-as-learner so that we could design instructional environments that were characterized by a balance of intellectual challenges and supports."[10] According to Knefelkamp, cognitive development can be fostered by titrating four environmental variables to learners' developmental needs: the level of diversity experienced; the amount of structure provided; the amount and type of experiential learning; and the level of personalism (or the degree of respectfulness, of collaboration, and of connection made between content and students' lives). Thus, student learning, development, and meaning making can be directly facilitated by the conditions of a given learning context, particularly by the balancing of developmental challenge and support.

The Holistic Dimension

While the academic and vocational realms remain the focus of much of higher education, and research confirms that most college students experience substantial gains in these areas, change during the college years is not limited to these realms.[11] Learning that is engaged intentionally crisscrosses the cognitive, affective, psychosocial, and behavioral domains, thereby encompassing multiple aspects of the self. This kind of learning is not limited to an acquisition of specific content or mastery of a set of skills; rather, it is *holistic* in that it engages the learner's capacities for understanding, feeling, relating, and action.

One of the most widely read theorists of college student experience and development, Chickering provides a thorough cataloging of psychosocial change in college through seven vectors, or "major constellations of development during adolescence and early adulthood": developing intellectual, physical, and interpersonal competence; managing emotions; moving through autonomy toward interdependence; developing mature interpersonal relationships; establishing identity; developing purpose; and developing integrity.[12] While it may be hard to imagine a psychosocial domain that does not find its place among these vectors, Chickering's theory offers more than an organizing principle; rather, it offers a kind of holistic map of potential areas for personal growth and development in college.

It is true that students cover a good deal of this map's terrain simply as a result of attending college; personal growth and development are spurred on for residential students, for example, by being removed from familiar home surroundings and having to live communally in a residence hall with diverse strangers (as we've all witnessed, this can be quite the psychosocial challenge for an eighteen-year-old!). Yet many educators, particularly those in student affairs divisions, have found that intentionally planning and programming with these vectors in mind can make not only for highly effective programs but also significant student learning. It also offers a means of consciously balancing developmental challenges and supports so that students do not become overwhelmed (in the aforementioned example, a learning community structure with mentoring and reflective discussion opportunities might provide the support the residential student needs to succeed in the transition to college life). Likewise, faculty can structure the classroom environment for holistic learning by incorporating activities that encompass the cognitive, affective, psychosocial, and behavioral domains—for example, through research projects that also incorporate reflective journaling, group collaboration, and off-campus application of learning, respectively. While this requires intentionality and effort on the part of faculty, students consistently report in the research that holistic learning experiences—those that enable them to both learn and apply that learning toward their personal development—are the most impactful.

The Integrative Dimension

While the holistic dimension refers to the incorporation of multiple domains of self in learning, the integrative dimension deals directly with the *learning process* itself. Engaged learning involves the integration of multiple types of learning acquired in and through varied sources of learning. It also entails the integration of immediate learning with past learning, all of which serves as the foundation for future lifelong learning. The integrative dimension thus helps students build a latticework of meaning making across learning types, sources, and temporality.

In a Deweyan sense, engaged learning is active and involves ongoing experimentation rather than just passive absorption of information. When learning is active, the nature of students' educational experiences—as well as what they do with those experiences—becomes critical. Based on the work of Dewey as well as Piaget and Lewin, Kolb's model of experiential learning offers a way of understanding how various learning processes can be integrated to help students learn from experience. The model depicts four such processes—experience, reflection, integration, and application of knowledge—as arranged in an iterative cycle: "[Students] must be able to involve themselves fully, openly, and without bias in new experiences . . . to reflect on and observe their experiences from many perspectives . . . to create concepts that integrate their observations into logically sound theories . . . [and] to use these theories to make decisions and solve problems."[13] Certainly, diverse learning sources—such as the classroom, online learning platforms, laboratories, practicum experiences, and so forth—provide rich opportunities for the operation of this cycle as opposed to a singular site of learning (e.g., the traditional lecture hall). Students must have chances to engage in what Hutchings and Wutzdorff call the "dialectic" between "knowing" a subject of study and actually "doing" the subject (e.g., through lab experiments, a biology student comes to understand photosynthesis not only as an abstract concept but also as a concrete process).[14] This dialectic also involves the integration of knowledge gained from others (e.g., faculty who share their expertise) as well as knowledge gained through self-directed study or collaborative learning with peers.

Thus through the dialectic of knowing and experience, mediated by reflection, students come to integrate their learning on an ongoing basis into more complex and complete understandings. One significant challenge to this process in the college setting is the bounding of most learning experiences by the beginning and end of a semester (with the notable exception of cross-semester experiences, such as first-year learning communities or capstone courses). We do not need research (only our own experiences as learners) to tell us that our students' learning is not that discrete or linear. This is particularly important as several theorists, such as Schön and Mezirow, highlight the critical role of reflection in learning—and reflection is a process that requires both intentionality *and* time.[15] With intentionally structured experiences that are sufficient in duration, new learning can serve as the basis for future experimentation; critical reflection on that experimentation can occur; and students can craft new, resultant ways of being and doing in the world. The integrative dimension thus leads to a rich, developing knowledge base in which to live—and continue to learn—in the world.

The Contextual Dimension

In discussing the developmental, holistic, and integrative learning of individual students, we mustn't forget that an individual's learning does not happen in a vacuum. Rather, learning requires engagement with social contexts (whether the classroom, laboratory, residence hall, or community) in collaboration with faculty mentors, peer groups, supervisors, and many others. When these social contexts are harnessed and shaped for learning, students can come to understand the interdependence of self and society, engage in the construction of shared meaning, and negotiate for action that benefits the common good.

Learning is a "fundamentally social phenomenon reflecting our own deeply social nature as human beings" that occurs within the context of multiple communities in which students are situated, according to Wenger.[16] Communities such as colleges and universities, as well as those that lie beyond the campus gates, are places where students "develop, negotiate, and share" the ways they understand the world. Participation in these communities shapes not only students' meaning making but also their behaviors and their sense of identity.[17] This participation involves a dynamic "negotiation" process between the environment and the individual, and to this end Wenger asserts that educators need "inventive ways of engaging students in meaningful practices," which entails "involving them in actions, discussions, and reflections that make a difference to the communities that they value."[18]

By coming to see themselves in relation to larger contexts, and by thoughtfully and critically aligning their actions and identities within those contexts, students gain skills needed for community membership. They learn interdependence between self and others. This is critical in the immediate college environment as well as the broader communities in which students will find themselves throughout their lives. Intentionally engaging students in these communities prior to graduation (through structured experiences such as service learning) can help students develop a commitment to civic engagement, which Jacoby describes as "a heightened sense of responsibility to one's communities . . . and [to] benefiting the common good."[19] In this way, the contextual dimension of learning fosters capacities for democratic participation and lifelong engagement in community.

Engaged Learning Pedagogy

For engaged learning to involve these four dimensions—the developmental, holistic, integrative, and contextual—it likewise requires pedagogies that foster intellectual complexity, encompass multiple domains of self, integrate diverse learning processes and sources, and foster interdependence in and commitment to community. Yet, engaged learning pedagogy is fundamentally different from much of the teaching and learning that occurs in academe, as Edgerton explains:

> The dominant mode of teaching and learning in higher education [is] "teaching as telling; learning as recall." . . . This mode of instruction fails to help students acquire two kinds of learning that are now crucial to their individual success and critically needed by our society at large. The first is real understanding. The second is "habits of the heart" that motivate students to be caring citizens. Both of these qualities are acquired through pedagogies that elicit intense engagement.[20]

Such engaged pedagogies, while not yet normative in higher education, have gained some traction over the past two decades—which is to say they are receiving increased attention both in practice and research. Kuh identifies a number of such high-impact practices that tend to foster student engagement in learning, such as service learning, first-year seminars, learning communities, undergraduate research, and capstone courses and projects (still other examples of engaged learning pedagogies are community-based research, collaborative learning, problem-based learning, intergroup dialogue, and internships).[21] These pedagogies can be considered engaged because they tend to foster complexity in students' thinking, feeling, relating, and acting (developmental and holistic dimensions) as well as create connections between students' learning experiences and with social contexts and communities (integrative and contextual dimensions).

For the purposes of this chapter, three of these pedagogies—service learning, learning communities, and undergraduate research—are discussed, along with a summary of their known outcomes (as described by Brownell and Swaner in their analysis of research on these pedagogies).[22] Although the body of research on these and similar pedagogies is relatively new and is methodologically limited, it provides suggestive evidence that the pedagogies contribute positively to the four dimensions of engaged learning.[23] Finally, moderating variables—defined by Swaner and Brownell as "those factors unique to each practice which impact outcomes"—are outlined for each pedagogy, as certain formulations, structures, or emphases in each appear to make for more successful student learning experiences.[24]

Service Learning

Benson and Harkavy describe service learning—a pedagogy that integrates community-based service experience with classroom learning and reflection—as one of "a handful of creative, active pedagogies . . . that enhance a student's capacity to think critically, problem solve, and function as a citizen in a democratic society."[25] Similarly, Jacoby explains: "Service-learning is a form of experiential education in which students engage in activities that address human and community needs together with structured opportunities intentionally designed to promote student learning and development."[26] This type of integrative service learning has been implemented in a wide range of academic disciplines and professional fields and is generally offered for academic credit, though the length of these experiences may vary.

As implied by its name, service learning involves a reciprocal relationship between the activities of service and learning. In regard to service, students are generally involved in nonpaid work in a community setting, whether on a local, national, or global level. Examples of service learning sites include early literacy programs, Head Start centers, homeless shelters, immigrant centers, community health clinics, or legal aid agencies; regardless of the setting, the more relevant the service to the student's course work, the more meaningful the learning experience.[27] Zlotkowski explains that in contrast to "traditional cocurricular volunteerism," service learning is integrated within the academic enterprise with the aim to "promote faculty involvement and to establish a reliable curricular base."[28] Practically speaking, this means faculty articulate the rationale, purpose, and learning goals of service activities as well as ensure that the specific tasks of service are relevant to these goals. In terms of course activities, much of the service learning literature points to structured opportunities for reflection (such as journal writing and group discussion) as the hallmarks of the pedagogy. Reflection enables students to make intentional connections between their classroom learning and their service experiences.

In a review of higher education research, Brownell and Swaner found that participation in service learning benefited students academically (in terms of higher grades, higher persistence rates, and higher levels of academic engagement) as well as across the four dimensions of engaged learning. In terms of the developmental dimension, research indicates student gains in critical thinking, writing skills, and moral reasoning as accompanying service learning participation. From a holistic dimension, students engaged in service learning experience greater interaction with faculty and report increases in social responsibility. Service learning also leads to greater application of course learning, indicative of gains in the integrative dimension. And finally, in terms of the contextual dimension, service learning participation is correlated with greater levels of civic behavior, understanding of social justice, sense of self-efficacy, tolerance, and commitment to a service-oriented career. The positive gains of service learning participation appeared to be mediated by characteristics of both the service experience (quantity of hours and direct service contact; quality of supervision) and the learning experience (opportunities for reflection; the degree to which faculty connected course material with the service experience).

Learning Communities

Learning communities generally involve a group of students who share common classes and/or cocurricular experiences, but they vary greatly from campus to campus in terms of the number of linked classes, the incorporation of a residential component, and the use of a thematic focus (e.g., environmental conservation, social justice). Additionally, the duration of participation in learning communities can vary by campus; some experiences may be a semester long, while others can extend over a single or multiple academic years. For example, Tinto and Goodsell describe first-year interest groups that operate on a learning community model and facilitate connections with peers and faculty for new students (thus first-year seminars, depending on their structure, may be considered a subtype of learning communities).[29] Pascarella and Terenzini explain that regardless of their particular formulation, "the purpose of structured learning communities is to facilitate active over passive learning, collaboration and cooperation as opposed to competition, and community instead of isolation."[30] Learning communities achieve this through shared or collaborative learning (enrollment of the same group of students in common courses) and connected learning (organization of learning around a theme or large topic). Thus, learning communities not only utilize engaged pedagogies but also institutionalize them in the collegiate structure.

In their analysis of higher education research, Brownell and Swaner identified a range of positive effects of learning community participation. These included gains in academic indicators (higher grades, higher persistence rates, higher levels of academic engagement) as well as across each of the dimensions of engaged learning, including developmental (self-report of critical thinking gains, gains in intellectual development, gains in writing and reading skills); holistic (greater interaction with faculty and peers, perception of campus as more supportive, ease of college transition); integrative (higher levels of assimilating information and making connections among classes); and contextual (greater appreciation for and engagement with diversity and different viewpoints, higher rate of civic engagement). These gains appear to be moderated by several variables, including the intensity of the learning community experience (e.g., the number of linked courses and whether a residential component is included) as well as the degree of positive student and faculty interaction.

Undergraduate Research

Kinkead explains that undergraduate research "is defined broadly to include scientific inquiry, creative activity, and scholarship."[31] Depending on the discipline, undergraduate research can range from laboratory investigation, to development of an artistic portfolio, to the creation and evaluation of a community outreach program. Undergraduate research opportunities are generally structured in nature and are often sponsored or administrated by a student's major department. Some institutions have undergraduate research centers or may house related programs within broader teaching and learning centers. Regardless of where these research opportunities are situated, a faculty mentor plays a crucial role in guiding students' research—from the selection of a topic, to conducting the research, to disseminating the results (often through a conference presentation or publication). Nationally speaking, the majority of formalized undergraduate research opportunities have been extended to students in the sciences, to students of color, to academically disadvantaged students, and to honors students.

As a pedagogy, undergraduate research is fundamentally different from traditional forms of learning in the academy. This is underscored by the Boyer Commission's report, *Reinventing Undergraduate Education: A Blueprint for America's Research Universities*, which describes the learning in undergraduate research as "based on discovery guided by mentoring rather than on the transmission of information," thereby representing a "profound change in the way undergraduate teaching is structured."[32] In such a model, undergraduates are responsible for cocreating knowledge through the process of inquiry, as opposed to receiving, memorizing, and re-presenting knowledge from faculty experts.

One subtype of undergraduate research is community-based research, which, as Strand et al. describe, is a unique "partnership of students, faculty, and community members who collaboratively engage in research with the purpose of solving a pressing community problem or effecting social change."[33] Where community-based research differs from undergraduate research is that it considers students as equal partners with faculty and community members on the research team. Students are empowered in their learning to think critically about community concerns; to engage in collaborative problem solving; and to design, implement, and evaluate real-world solutions. The final "products" of community-based research differ from traditional undergraduate research as well, in that they are collaborative and are of direct benefit to the community (e.g., a team of faculty, students, and community members develops a health and wellness program and together conduct an evaluation of its efficacy).

Compared to service learning and learning communities, the research on learning outcomes of undergraduate research—including community-based research—is minimal. Brownell and Swaner did find evidence of academic gains related to undergraduate research participation, such as higher rate of persistence, higher rate of graduate school enrollment, and improvement in research skills. Some developmental gains were also identified in the research, such as increases in problem solving and critical thinking. In terms of the contextual dimension, students who participated in undergraduate research experienced increased interaction with faculty and peers and a greater sense of connectedness to the academic enterprise (not surprisingly, the two moderating variables identified in the literature were the role of the faculty mentor and the quality of the mentoring relationship). One might speculate that participating in undergraduate research would help students integrate their learning from their course work and the research experience, and that activities such as community-based research would yield gains similar to service learning (e.g., increases in civic engagement); these remain, however, areas in need of research.

Creating Cultures of Engagement

Although further research on the outcomes of engaged learning pedagogies is needed, we can confidently say they show promise in promoting gains across the four dimensions of engaged learning. This is not to forget that students also demonstrate gains in the traditional academic outcomes, such as grade point average and persistence to the degree. Yet despite this potential, few students across all of American higher education have the opportunity to participate in engaged learning settings, as they are offered on a limited and elective basis on most campuses. Furthermore, those students who are able to participate may do so only once during college, which itself is problematic as Eyler and Giles explain: "The learning goals in higher education are complex, and students are affected by many of life's experiences; no single intervention, particularly over the course of a semester, can be expected to have a dramatic impact on student outcomes."[34]

If the added value of these pedagogies to higher education writ large is limited by their isolated use and duration, the question becomes how to increase student engagement in systematic ways. Certainly as individual or small groups of educators have opportunity to implement engaged learning pedagogies, the benefit accrues to each successive student who participates (thus, we shouldn't "despise the day of small beginnings"). From a field-level perspective, we also might view individual engaged learning efforts throughout higher education as weights that, with continual stacking, will eventually bring academe to the "tipping point"—where engaged pedagogies move from the periphery to the center in the ways faculty "teach" and students "learn" in higher education.[35]

There is, however, another approach we might consider. If we understand learning to be the result of interaction between the individual learner and the specific learning environment, we can view this process in terms of mutually shaping "transactions" as suggested by Bandura's concept of reciprocal determinism.[36] The learning environment and students within are continually, and reciprocally, engaged with each other. It follows that employing the dimensions of engaged learning in these transactions is more likely to occur and be maximized through the intentional design of learning environments. By contrast, an environment that is unintentional or "piecemeal" in its approach to student learning would likely fail to harness its transactional potential for engaged learning or leave the process largely up to chance.

Most colleges and universities have engagement as a priority in their institutional mission statements, but it requires intentionality, diplomacy, and (for lack of a better term) grit to translate engagement into the dominant models of teaching and learning at colleges and universities. By shifting engaged pedagogy—and as important, its philosophical base—from the periphery to the center of educational practice, institutions move toward establishing what I have termed *cultures of engagement* that can harness the full promise of engaged learning.[37] Kuh and Whitt define cultures in higher education as "patterns of norms, values, practices, beliefs, and assumptions that shape the behavior of individuals and groups in a college or university and provide a frame of reference within which to interpret the meaning of events and actions on and off the campus."[38] Applying this definition, a culture of engagement would involve establishing engaged learning as (1) a normative experience for students; (2) a shared value among members of the campus community; (3) a common practice across all sites of learning; and (4) an affirmed belief and assumption in the curriculum and cocurriculum.

Such a reordering would have profound implications for the frame of reference with which all members of the campus community view education and its purposes. And specific engaged pedagogies—such as service learning, learning communities, and undergraduate research—would shift from exceptions in teaching and learning to the building blocks for these cultures of engagement. There appear to be some colleges and universities that have already experienced success along these lines; for example, Kuh et al. name twenty institutions that are highly effective in terms of promoting student engagement,[39] and Colby et al. identify twelve institutions as "building moral and civic education into the heart of their undergraduates' learning."[40] These colleges and universities are working to make engaged pedagogy, in Edgerton's words, "part of their overall institutional identity."[41]

If we understand the core purposes of higher education as transcending unidimensional academic knowledge and transferable skills to encompass students' full development as individuals, then at each level of academe we must actively attend to students' intellectual and personal development, to their overall well-being, to their crafting an integrative foundation for lifelong learning and action, and to their capacity for living committed and purposeful lives in community. To this end, we need to encourage the expansion of engaged learning pedagogies and corresponding research on their efficacy, but we also must work toward building cultures of engagement across higher education, thereby harnessing the full potential of engaged learning.

Notes

1. Core Institute, *2006–2008 National Data: Core Alcohol and Drug Survey Long Form, Executive Summary* (Carbondale: Southern Illinois University, 2010).

2. Arthur Levine and Jeanette S. Cureton, *When Hope and Fear Collide: A Portrait of Today's College Student* (San Francisco: Jossey-Bass, 1998), 95; Richard Kadison and Theresa Foy DiGeronimo, *College of the Overwhelmed: The Campus Mental Health Crisis and What to Do About It* (San Francisco: Jossey-Bass, 2004).

3. Rom. 12:18 (New International Version).

4. Corey L.M. Keyes, "Promoting and Protecting Mental Health as Flourishing: A Complementary Strategy for Improving National Mental Health," *American Psychologist* 62, no. 2 (2007): 95–108.

5. William G. Perry Jr., *Forms of Ethical and Intellectual Development in the College Years: A Scheme* (New York: Holt, Rinehart and Winston, 1970).

6. Mary F. Belenky, Blythe Clinchy, Nancy Goldberger, and Jill M. Tarule, *Women's Ways of Knowing: The Development of Self, Voice, and Mind*, 10th anniversary edition (New York: Basic Books, 1997).

7. Patricia M. King and Karen Strohm Kitchener, *Developing Reflective Judgment: Understanding and Promoting Intellectual Growth and Critical Thinking in Adolescents and Adults* (San Francisco: Jossey-Bass, 1994); Marcia B. Baxter-Magolda, *Knowing and Reasoning in College: Gender-Related Patterns in Students' Intellectual Development* (San Francisco: Jossey-Bass, 1992); Marcia B. Baxter-Magolda, "Self-Authorship as the Common Goal," in *Learning Partnerships: Theory and Models of Practice to Educate for Self-Authorship*, ed. Marcia B. Baxter-Magolda and P.M. King (Sterling, VA: Stylus, 2004), 1–35.

8. Lawrence Kohlberg, *The Psychology of Moral Development: The Nature and Validity of Moral Stages*, vol. 2 of *Essays on Moral Development* (San Francisco: Harper and Row, 1984); Carol Gilligan, "In a Different Voice: Women's Conceptions of Self and Morality," *Harvard Educational Review* 47, no. 4 (1977): 481–517; James Fowler, *Stages of Faith: The Psychology of Human Development and the Quest for Meaning* (San Francisco: Harper and Row, 1981); William E. Cross, *Shades of Black: Diversity in African-American Identity* (Philadelphia: Temple University Press, 1991); Janet E. Helms, "Toward a Model of White Racial Identity Development," in *Black and White Racial Identity: Theory, Research, and Practice*, ed. Janet E. Helms (Westport, CT: Greenwood Press, 1990), 49–66; Milton J. Bennett, "Intercultural Communication: A Current Perspective," in *Basic Concepts of Intercultural Communication: Selected Readings*, ed. Milton J. Bennett (Yarmouth, MN: Intercultural Press, 1998), 1–34.

9. Nevitt Sanford, *Self and Society* (New York: Atherton Press, 1966).

10. Lee L. Knefelkamp, introduction to *Forms of Ethical and Intellectual Development in the College Years: A Scheme*, by William G. Perry (San Francisco: Jossey-Bass, 1999), xi–xxx.

11. Ernest T. Pascarella and Patrick T. Terenzini, *How College Affects Students: A Third Decade of Research*, vol. 2 (San Francisco: Jossey-Bass, 2005).

12. Arthur W. Chickering and Linda Reisser, *Education and Identity*, 2nd ed. (San Francisco: Jossey-Bass, 1993), 44.

13. David A. Kolb, *Experiential Learning: Experience as the Source of Learning and Development* (Englewood Cliffs, NJ: Prentice Hall, 1984), 30.

14. Pat Hutchings and Allen Wutzdorff, "Experiential Learning across the Curriculum: Assumptions and Principles," *New Directions for Teaching and Learning*, no. 35 (1988): 5–19.

15. Donald A. Schön, *Educating the Reflective Practitioner: Toward a New Design for Teaching and Learning in the Professions* (San Francisco: Jossey-Bass, 1987); Jack Mezirow, *Transformative Dimensions of Adult Learning* (San Francisco: Jossey-Bass, 1991).

16. Etienne Wenger, *Communities of Practice: Learning, Meaning and Identity* (Cambridge: Cambridge University Press, 1998), 3.

17. Wenger, *Communities of Practice*, 48.

18. Wenger, *Communities of Practice*, 10.

19. Barbara Jacoby, "Advancing Education for Civic Engagement and Leadership in a Large Research University: Excerpts from the Report of the Team on Civic Engagement and Leadership at the University of Maryland, College Park" (paper presented at the Pedagogies of Engagement conference of the Association of American Colleges and Universities, Washington, DC, 2004), 10.

20. Russell Edgerton, *Higher Education White Paper* (unpublished paper, Pew Charitable Trusts, 1997), 67.

21. George D. Kuh, *High-Impact Practices: What They Are, Who Has Access to Them, and Why They Matter* (Washington, DC: Association of American Colleges and Universities, 2008); Lynn E. Swaner, *Linking Engaged Learning, Student Mental Health and Well-Being, and Civic Development: A Review of the Literature* (Washington, DC: Bringing Theory to Practice Project of the Association of American Colleges and Universities, 2005).

22. Jayne E. Brownell and Lynn E. Swaner, *Five High-Impact Practices: Research on Learning Outcomes, Completion, and Quality* (Washington, DC: Association of American Colleges and Universities, 2010). Note that this review of the literature also includes an analysis of known learning outcomes for underserved students; where available, research on engaged learning experiences generally indicates academic and personal gains for these students.

23. It should be noted that while the research generally shows positive gains for students who participate in these engaged learning pedagogies, Swaner and Brownell identified "substantial limitations" to this research: Most studies were descriptive in nature, involved only a single institution, did not control for selection bias or utilize adequate comparison groups, were short-term studies versus longitudinal, and involved self-report versus direct measures of outcomes. Thus the evidence described for each pedagogy is "moderate" and in need of further confirmation through systematic research that addresses these issues.

24. Lynn E. Swaner and Jayne E. Brownell, *Outcomes of High-Impact Practices for Underserved Students: A Review of the Literature* (Washington, DC: Association of American Colleges and Universities, 2008), 128.

25. Lee Benson and Ira Harkavy, "Academically-Based Community Service and University-Assisted Community Schools as Complementary Approaches for Advancing, Learning, Teaching, Research and Service: The University of Pennsylvania as a Case Study in Progress," in *Learning to Serve: Promoting Civil Society through Service Learning*, ed. M. Kenny, L.A.K. Simon, K. Kiley-Brabeck, and R.M. Lerner (Norwell, MA: Kluwer Academic Publishers, 2002), 362.

26. Barbara Jacoby, "Service Learning in Today's Higher Education," in *Service-Learning in Higher Education: Concepts and Practices*, ed. Barbara Jacoby and Associates (San Francisco: Jossey-Bass, 1996), 5.

27. Janet Eyler and Dwight E. Giles, *Where's the Learning in Service-Learning?* (San Francisco: Jossey-Bass, 1999).

28. Edward Zlotkowski, "Pedagogy and Engagement," in *Colleges and Universities as Citizens*, ed. R.G. Bringle, R. Games, and E.A. Malloy (Needham Heights, MA: Allyn and Bacon, 1999), 97–98.

29. Vincent Tinto and Anne Goodsell, *A Longitudinal Study of Freshman Interest Groups at the University of Washington* (Washington, DC: Office of Educational Research and Improvement, 1993).

30. Pascarella and Terenzini, *How College Affects Students*, 109.

31. Joyce Kinkead, "Learning through Inquiry: An Overview of Undergraduate Research," in *Valuing and Supporting Undergraduate Research*, ed. J. Kinkead (San Francisco: Jossey-Bass, 2005), 6.

32. Boyer Commission on Educating Undergraduates in the Research University, *Reinventing Undergraduate Education: A Blueprint for America's Research Universities* (Stanford, CA: Carnegie Foundation for the Advancement of Teaching, 1998), 15–16.

33. Kerry J. Strand, Sam Marullo, Nicholas Cutforth, Randy Stoecker, and Patrick Donohue, *Community-Based Research and Higher Education: Principles and Practices* (San Francisco: Jossey-Bass, 2003), 3.

34. Eyler and Giles, *Where's the Learning in Service Learning?* xvii.

35. Malcolm Gladwell, *The Tipping Point: How Little Things Can Make a Big Difference* (Boston: Little, Brown, 2000).

36. Albert Bandura, *Social Foundations of Thought and Action: A Social Cognitive Theory* (Englewood Cliffs, NJ: Prentice Hall, 1986).

37. Lynn E. Swaner, "Linking Engaged Learning, Student Well-Being and Mental Health, and Civic Development: A Review of the Literature," *Liberal Education* 93, no. 1 (2007): 16–25.

38. George D. Kuh and Elizabeth J. Whitt, *The Invisible Tapestry: Culture in American Colleges and Universities*, ASHE-ERIC Higher Education Report 17, no. 1 (Washington, DC: George Washington University, Graduate School of Education and Human Development, 1988), iv.

39. George D. Kuh, Jillian Kinzie, John H. Schuh, Elizabeth J. Whitt, and Associates, *Student Success in College: Creating Conditions That Matter* (San Francisco: Jossey-Bass, 2005).

40. Anne Colby, Thomas Ehrlich, Elizabeth Beaumont, J. Stephens, and Lee S. Shulman, *Educating Citizens: Preparing America's Undergraduates for Lives of Moral and Civic Responsibility* (San Francisco: Jossey-Bass, 2003), 49.

41. Edgerton, *Higher Education White Paper*, 30.

4

Reuniting the Often Neglected Aims of Liberal Education

Student Well-Being and Psychosocial Development

Dessa Bergen-Cico and Joyce A. Bylander

Our careers in higher education have been spent almost equally divided between the academic realm and student life administration. As observers and investigators of human and organizational behavior, we have tried to move our institutions toward articulated goals—including that of developing global citizens. All that we have seen and read leads us to the conclusion that unless we intentionally begin to reintegrate our own work on behalf of students, we cannot maximize the impact of our learning environments for students. Like you, we want to foster the kind of environments that provide young people with the freedom to test their limits and potential, while at the same time safeguarding individuals and the community from careless, unlawful, or dangerous behavior. And like you, we've worried a great deal about the consequences of not integrating the realms of academic and student life within the predominant structure of higher education. So, as we work, we are about posing such questions as "How can we reintegrate the lives of students and accomplish the true goals of higher education?" And "How do we reassert the often neglected aims of student well-being, psychosocial development, and civic development, confirming how they are integral to the missions of our institutions?"

More than ever, the health and economy of a nation and the achievements of its citizens depend on the quality of higher education and its association with increased aptitude, higher productivity, and enhanced human capacity to improve quality of life. But it has become an increasing challenge, even among top schools, to put into place the resources, the pedagogical commitments, the faculty energy, and the expectations needed from students that would assure the quality of an undergraduate experience.[1] Coupled with the external pressures to produce employable alumni are the internal student pressures to assess their education solely on grades and the management of their social interactions.

The core objectives of liberal education are not only job preparedness but also a certain character of learning, inherently connected to the students' psychosocial well-being and to their civic development. We, like most educators as well as parents, consider a student's holistic development as equally important to, if not in the long term more important than, the acquisition of a credential for a first job. Higher education has always held out for more and should continue to do so.

We examine the connections among students' well-being, their intellectual and social development, and the broader liberating purposes of liberal education. Those purposes are not just mastery of a specific content of study but are focused on learning that truly "liberates" the student as a knower and discoverer, as a citizen, and as a fulfilled and whole person.

A Profile of Undergraduate Students in U.S. Higher Education

The proportion of high school completers who enroll in two- or four-year colleges in the fall immediately after completing high school is at an all-time high of nearly 70 percent.[2] In many ways, American college students' are a representative mirror of our nation, and yet the experience of college can often magnify differences between those who attend college and those who do not. Beyond the perception that college is the pathway to economic and social success, we are always impressed when students tell us they come to college because they realize they "aren't finished yet" and because colleges and universities hold the promise of answers or some insights into the questions that capture them—"What will I become?" "Who will I become?" as well as "Will this college prepare me to do something?" In this respect, we should remember that what many students sense is at stake in their educational experience—and what they desperately expect to gain—has much to do with matters well beyond job preparation, even as they function in the midst of the prevailing clamor for such preparation.

Today's undergraduate students are increasingly diverse and predominantly female; however, differences in enrollment rates based on parental education, racial/ethnic group, and family income have persisted over time. Higher education enrollment rates for black, Hispanic, and Native American high school graduates are lower than those of their white peers. Low-income families trail the rates of those from high-income families by 20 percentage points, and high school completers whose parents have not earned at least a bachelor's degree are less likely to go on to college.

These demographic and socioeconomic differences between students who do and do not enroll in college underscore the prospect that students able to enroll in higher education are among the nation's more auspicious in terms of well-being and psychosocial development. The young people who make it to our campuses represent some of our country's best talent (this is true whether they show up at the most elite institution or a community college). These young people are the survivors who managed to stay focused long enough to get themselves into our institutions. Yet a growing number of college students struggle with depression, anxiety, and substance abuse problems that disrupt their academic progress. Among all students who attend a four-year institution full time in pursuit of a bachelor's degree, less than 60 percent actually complete a bachelor's degree, or its equivalent, at that institution within six years.[3] The reasons for the lack of persistence to graduation have as much to do with the students' psychosocial support and development as with their intellectual and cognitive aptitude. We are all too aware of the fact that college students' substance abuse and mental health problems have a negative impact on academic performance, retention, and graduation rates.[4]

Over time, because of the civic activism and engagement of a wide array of outsiders—women, minorities, people with disabilities, and gay and lesbian individuals—the number of people able to be included as members of an educated citizenry has greatly expanded. As higher education has become more representative of the population, more people have access to educational resources that provide greater opportunities and the capacity to actively and productively participate in civil society.

It is just this broadening of participation in higher education that has been conjoined with the professional schism—the growing split between the spheres of academic and student affairs. Because of the complexities of today's students, their success and retention are often dependent on a careful balance and blend of their experiences inside and outside the classroom. However, more often than not there is limited collaboration and intentionality between the two spheres, which are literally referred to as academic affairs and "the division of" student affairs. Faculty members are asked to teach, concentrating on the epistemic aims of higher education. Student affairs professionals are asked to contribute to the well-being and civic aims of student development through cultivation of community engagement and guiding student participation in the cocurricular and the extracurricular life of the institution. The implicit assumption is that these areas of attention are separate and separable. The result has been a perceived, and real, chasm or split of spheres of responsibility, and with that split has come the general neglect of the interdependency and integration of learning and student development—and the bolstering of the erroneous judgment that their integration should just "happen" without the institution's intentionality.

From our own experience, there were times when we worked in environments that encouraged collaboration and applied scholarship between student affairs and academic affairs. However, when we moved from one side of the academic house to the other (i.e., from student affairs to academic affairs), we turned around only to find that the bridge that had connected the two units had been taken away. When the academy split its responsibilities to students in the late 1960s and 1970s, when student protests and demands helped put an end to *in loco parentis*, a new category of faculty and higher education professionals emerged. Some might say that this came as a result of the growing demands for research in a country that had entered a race for intellectual supremacy with the Soviet Union. Some might argue that this bifurcation came as a result of the growing challenges and demands of students and their increasing unwillingness to do things "just because someone said so." Whatever the reasons, we did split the lives of students at our institutions. But since there really aren't two student bodies, one academic and one social or developmental, did we consider how our compartmentalization of students' lives might have unintended consequences?

The core educational mission of our institutions has been accompanied by an equally important, though not always implemented, championing of the civic through leadership and citizenship that support the common good. Shouldn't that common good first be applied to the lives of the students on our campuses? Yet we divided students' lives and asked faculty to teach and student life professionals to "entertain"—making the application of the common good for students impossible. Student affairs professionals were admonished to keep them busy, happy, and safe. As former deans of students, we cannot tell you how much sleep we lost worrying about the problematic behavior of students. Despite our best intentions and our investment in programming and judicious action, we've all spent too much of our resources managing the consequences of alcohol and other drug misuse and abuse. Few of us stopped problem or illegal consumption and abuse of substances, and each year too many of us had to manage the aftermath of some alcohol-related tragedy.

Scope of the Problem

We first began to notice the sirens in the mid-1990s. Did you hear them too? They warned us of the dire changes to come in the youth population. From *Newsweek* to *Nightline*, the *New York Times* to the *LA Times*, alarms were going off. At every turn we heard about the selfishness, pathology, and apathy of youth. The label of self-centered slacker was assigned equally to children of the inner cities and the suburbs, to the dropout as well as to the college student. Dozens of books elucidated the topic: *Generation at the Crossroads* by Paul Rogat Loeb, *Generation X Goes to College* by Peter Sacks, *The Abandoned Generation* by Willimon and Naylor, *Generation Me* by Jean Twenge, and *Binge* by Barrett Seaman, to name a few.[5] These books, written in the mid- to late 1990s and early 2000s, outlined the problems of the emerging generation. They told the story of the deteriorating state of higher education and our failure to engage students in deep learning. Some lamented the growing disconnect between institutional goals and student expectations. Many placed much of the blame on student failures and fragilities. The stories were accompanied by a great deal of hand-wringing. College students weren't the same. They were pampered, apathetic, and lazy. Some of these authors seemed to be asking how such enlightened parents had been saddled with such ungrateful, unfocused, and fragile children.

As educators deeply connected to the lives of young people, we worry about what the statistics are saying. Even more we worry about the young people in need of guidance and care who show up in our offices and on the radar of faculty and student life professionals. Are these students really more fragile than those who came before them? Does the fact that so many of them come to us with better diagnosed problems, long-term treatment histories, and delicate spirits say something about them or about us? What would it take to truly assist these talented young people on their journeys to wholeness and health? As members of the faculty, administration, or student life division, we worry that, because of our separating zones, we might be part of the problem rather than the solution.

Depression, anxiety, substance abuse, and suicide are significant problems affecting college students. Among U.S. college-age youth (twenty to twenty-four years), suicide is the third leading cause of death, with approximately 1,100 suicides occurring on campuses each year.[6] Not surprisingly, campus counseling centers have reported increased demand and increasingly complex mental health needs of students seeking counseling services.[7] Despite concerted efforts over the past fifteen years to reduce alcohol use among college students, the rate of heavy or binge drinking has remained around 44 percent among students at four-year colleges who reported drinking.[8] Over the past decade, the percentage of college students who report experiencing anxiety on a level that affects academic and social functioning has nearly doubled. According to the 2008 National College Health Assessment (NCHA) study, 13.2 percent of students reported experiencing anxiety in the preceding twelve months, up from just 7 percent of college students for the same survey in 2000.[9] Moreover, female college students reported experiencing anxiety at rates nearly double their male counterparts, 15.8 and 8.5 percent, respectively.[10] A substantial proportion (15.3 percent) of college students report their academic performance has been negatively affected by anxiety, depression, seasonal affective disorder, or a combination thereof. However, just 9 percent report having been diagnosed with anxiety disorders, and only a small percentage of students who report recently experiencing anxiety also access counseling services, suggesting that most students struggle to cope with anxiety on their own.[11] Together these factors demonstrate an increasing need for clinical support services for indicated populations while also pointing to the need for supportive resources for nonindicated populations of students who are not likely to access clinical services.[12] As in the general public, college students' anxiety manifests broadly, from generalized anxiety disorder to debilitating anxiety and panic attacks. These problems have significant implications for students' well-being, academic performance, and behavior. Whereas, college campuses are complex communities with relatively dense populations, the behavior of each member of the campus community greatly affects the tenor and well-being of the campus culture as a whole.

The point is that the pursuit of greater emphasis on engaged learning within our campus cultures is not to be considered a therapy for a subset of students who are not healthy but a condition of higher learning and developing for all students.

There is an important leadership role for faculty in facilitating effective learning environments and human connection in the classroom. Faculty can engage students in the study of related campus health issues as curricular subject matter. The subject matter and learning experiences need not be analyses of the students' lives to be effective. High-leveraging educational practices in the classroom can cultivate mindfulness as a trait through exploration of divergent perspectives, introducing ambiguity, analysis of social issues, and critical thinking.[13]

There is a noted need for reciprocity of responsibility and greater expectations of engagement between faculty and students. On the one hand, faculty may not be particularly present-centered in their teaching as they are increasingly under pressure to publish and bring in external funding to demonstrate their value to their institution. Likewise, students focused on their GPA, or on their preparation for graduate study, or on their life after college are rarely engaged in the learning process itself. "Our best work must begin with the students . . . *not the student body*, but to the very undivided student. You don't teach a class. You teach a student."[14]

Mindfulness, Positivity, and Well-being

Researchers have noted that high levels of psychological distress among college students are significantly related to poor academic performance. Specifically, students experiencing greater psychological distress characteristically have higher test anxiety, lower academic self-efficacy, and poor management of time and study resources.[15] Faculty and student affairs professionals have also observed that college students display decreasing capacity for distress tolerance of any type. In relation to this, there is a mounting tendency for college students to engage in mood-altering behaviors and activities as a means of distraction from stress, boredom, anxiety, and other unpleasant feelings. College students divert their mental attention through activities ranging from a preoccupation with text messaging, surfing the Web, and mindless eating to abuse of prescription medications, alcohol, and illicit drugs. These are not only indications of distracted thinking but also reflective of a culture that has a low threshold for distress of any type. One may argue that an important part of the learning process in higher education engages students with a level of cognitive discomfort and distress necessary to cultivate new and expansive ways of thinking. The move beyond black and white views and clear-cut right and wrong judgments requires students to swim in the gray areas and sit with the uncertainty that will eventually lead them to new ways of seeing and knowing. This mindfulness helps cultivate the cognitive and emotional skills necessary to remain engaged in the moment-to-moment awareness needed for this type of transformative learning.

The operational definition of mindfulness is a present-centered state of consciousness that involves attending nonjudgmentally to one's moment-to-moment experiences, on purpose and in a particular way, which stands in opposition to the future-oriented cognition of anxiety.[16] Acting with awareness is defined as engaging fully one's current attention with undivided interest, or focusing with awareness on one thing at a time. Mindfulness practices are essentially attention-enhancing techniques that cultivate present-moment attunement and enhanced self-awareness. Among the most widely practiced and studied is the Mindfulness-Based Stress Reduction (MBSR) Program, which has been found effective in treating anxiety, depression, substance abuse, and eating disorders and in self-management of stress.[17] It is important to note that the mindfulness and meditative practices referred to in literature researching their efficacy in higher education are the secular practices that do not require adherence to particular cultural and religious beliefs.

Effective higher education assists in the holistic development of students through intentional cultivation of their social, psychological, physical, and intellectual growth. The cultivation of mindfulness among college students is one progressive example of advances in higher education to cultivate student well-being and effect change at the individual and community level. Research conducted at Syracuse has found that college students who participate in an academic course that includes weekly mindfulness-based meditation, modeled after the MBSR Program, as part of their classroom activities show significant improvements in self-reported psychological health and well-being through the reduction of trait anxiety and a concurrent increase in mindfulness and self-compassion. In contrast, students enrolled in a course taught by the same professor that did not include discussion of mindfulness or meditation practice reported constant levels of anxiety at the beginning and end of the semester, with moderately rising levels of anxiety and distress midsemester.[18]

In this study, student mindfulness was calculated using the Kentucky Inventory of Mindfulness Skills (KIMS), which measures four facets of mindfulness: observing, describing, acting with awareness, and nonjudgmental acceptance.[19] Both groups had similar scores for mindfulness at baseline, 123.13 ± 12.9 for the control group ($n = 65$) and 122.09 ± 5.3 for the course that cultivated mindfulness ($n = 35$). By midsemester, significant differences were present in the mindfulness scores; the students in the course integrating mindfulness practices had significantly increased their KIMS score to 130.08, whereas the control class remained virtually unchanged at 122.15 ± 13.9. The final surveys were taken two weeks after the end of the semester and showed continued growth in mindfulness among the students who had been enrolled in the course that cultivated these techniques (132.03 ± 18.4), whereas the KIMS scores of the students in the control class remained in line with their baseline score at 123.05 ± 13.3.

Figure 4.1 provides a visual display of the comparative changes in mindfulness as measured by the KIMS score over the course of the semester for these two groups. Here we see that the cohort of students without any study or practice of cultivating mindfulness had a generally constant low level of mindfulness throughout the semester, whereas the students who studied the concept and engaged in practice to cultivate mindfulness increased their mindfulness throughout the course.

In addition to measuring mindfulness, the study also measured the students' anxiety over the course of the semester using Spielberger's State-Trait Anxiety Inventory-Trait form (STAI-T), a self-report assessment tool that measures trait anxiety with a range of scores from 20 to 80; higher scores indicate greater anxiety. The mean national scores are 38.30 ± 9.2 for male college students and 40.40 ± 10.2 for female college students.[20] The mean baseline anxiety scores in the study were 40.03 ± 8.5 for students in the control course and 41.36 ± 8.9 for students enrolled in the course that included mindfulness meditation practice. The latter group had a slightly

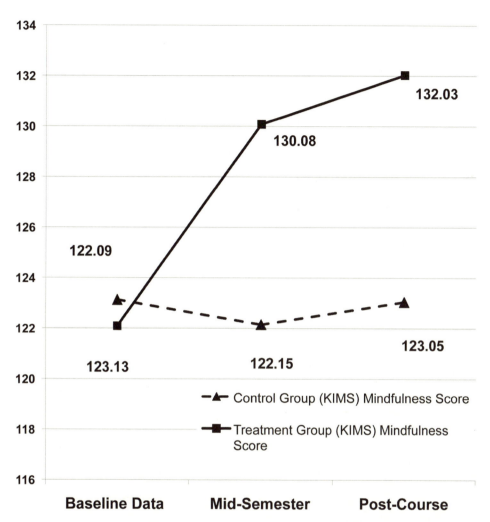

Figure 4.1. Source: Bergen-Cico, Cheon, and Abe, "Examining the Mediating Role of Mindfulness on Trait Anxiety and Self-Compassion." Mindfulness (under review).

higher mean than the national average; however, the differences between the two groups were not significant at baseline.

Figure 4.2 shows that by midsemester, the students in the control class reported a level of anxiety (41.39 ± 8.8) above the STAI-T anxiety mean. The students in the course that incorporated mindfulness meditation reported significant reductions in their trait anxiety, with a mean of 38.12 ± 7.3. The follow-up survey conducted after completion of the course demonstrated retained benefits in trait anxiety reduction for the students who had cultivated mindfulness techniques, as their scores had dropped to 37.97 ± 8.45 and remained below the national average for college students.[21]

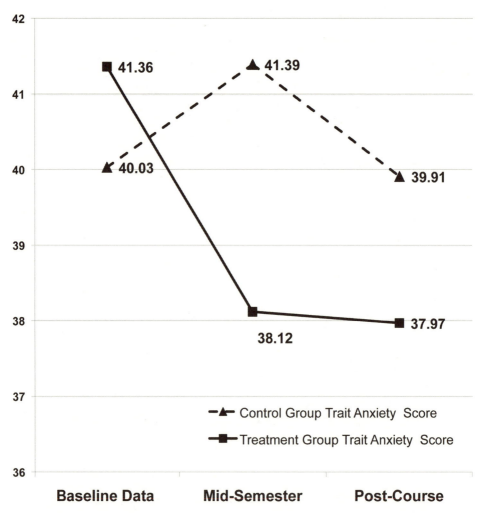

Figure 4.2. Source: Bergen-Cico, Cheon, and Abe, "Examining the Mediating Role of Mindfulness on Trait Anxiety and Self-Compassion." Mindfulness (under review).

The students' trait anxiety outside of class was also assessed. Trait anxiety is a relatively stable characteristic that measures anxiety proneness, as reflected in the frequency of a person's anxiety states and the individual's tendency to respond with anxiety to perceived threats in the environment.[22] Trait anxiety is also one of the most widely investigated outcomes in mindfulness meditation studies. Thus, trait anxiety reduction is considered a representative measure of improvement in psychological distress symptoms that occur through the cultivation of mindfulness. Among the reasons anxiety was the central measure of this study, and is a core measure in mindfulness meditation research, is the interdependent connection of anxiety's impact on the mind and body. Anxiety is understood holistically as a psychological problem with cognitive origins (racing thoughts, distracted cognition) that can result in physiological reactions (e.g., increased heart rate, muscle tension, headaches, profuse sweating) caused by complex biological reactions.[23]

The study's findings provide evidence of positive changes in mindfulness and a reduction in trait anxiety among the nonclinical population of college students who engage in mindfulness practices as part of their academic course. This demonstrates an integrated means of improving student well-being and shows that disposition and state mindfulness predict self-regulated behavior and positive emotional states. The outcomes of meditation practice applied to higher education complement and enhance academic skills and thus support educational goals. For example, mindfulness meditation involves conscious regulation of attention and development of an attitude of open curiosity. As for personal development, this practice supports affective and interpersonal aptitude, psychological well-being, and cultivation of the "whole person." The personal benefits and interpersonal skills fostered through mindfulness meditation include an attitude of openness and nonjudgmental acceptance and present-centered attention.

Of note is how this integrated study incorporated faculty interest in linking learning patterns to the content in the course, gave students an opportunity for participatory research, and exposed students to methodology and matters understood to have real implications. Studying cohorts of one's own students in this way, with appropriate research methodologies and protections in place, is itself a means of bridging the divide between academic and student affairs. The research presented here on mindfulness is evidence of inquiry that successfully crosses boundaries for faculty, professional staff, and students. This challenges the prevailing assumptions and practices of separate silos of responsibility for student development and academic inquiry.

With the increasing rates of anxiety and depression among college students negatively impacting their academic persistence and encumbering the limited campus-based clinical resources, providing mindfulness and meditation programs to students across campus may be an effective means of addressing the challenges of this generation. Mindfulness and meditation programs are increasingly prevalent on college campuses. Student response has by and large been very positive. Participants in the flourishing campus programs learn through experience about a variety of mindfulness practices such as gentle yoga; sitting and walking meditation; and focusing on breathing to reduce stress and anxiety, increase attention, and enhance well-being. The offerings range from open drop-in sessions to structured eight-week programs. The noncourse programs are offered through recreation and wellness centers, counseling centers, health services, and campus religious affiliates. Students self-select to enroll and are sometimes referred by campus counselors or health care professionals.

Mindfulness and the interventions studied come out of the emerging field of positive psychology, whose founding pioneer was Martin Seligman, a former president of the American Psychological Association. He currently directs the Positive Psychology Center at the University of Pennsylvania. Since the 1970s, he has been working to redirect the field's focus from mental "illness" to a more balanced focus on assets and debits, strengths and weaknesses, and the stressors and resources in the environment that lead to resilience and flourishing.[24] According to Dr. Barbara Fredrickson, a positive psychologist, resiliency is marked by emotional agility and the ability to recover from setbacks. It is a quality that she contends is our birthright. While some personalities are more resilient than others, Fredrickson believes resiliency can be enhanced. The mental habits that come with being positive and resilient foster mindfulness—"open-minded awareness marked by its focus on the present moment coupled with a nonjudgmental attitude." Fredrickson's research and experience helped her come to another important insight: Resilience is not just something an individual does or does not have—it "runs through the social fabric of communities."[25] Resilience contributes to flourishing because it can be enhanced and expanded through interactions with other people in your community. In examining the beneficial attributes of resiliency and mindfulness, we see parallels with the aims of a liberal education: open-mindedness, awareness, a nonjudgmental attitude, and open curiosity unfettered by prejudice of outcome.

Students arrive on our campuses with what one set of researchers called "a coping reservoir."[26] This reservoir, built over a lifetime, can provide students with the tools that support good mental health and well-being. Students' own personality traits and dispositions make them more or less resilient. They respond to external stressors in the environment (stress, internal conflicts, demands on time and energy) in ways that either add to or deplete this reservoir. Our environments also add positive inputs to the reservoir. This happens through psychosocial support, social and healthy activities, mentorship, and intellectual stimulation.[27]

This model is pertinent because it supports our experiences of working with undergraduate students. Regardless of intellectual capacity or success levels, students often seem to be "running on empty" and focused elsewhere. Most often it is through personal conversation that we are able to ascertain the sources of stress, dysfunction, or confusion. The model requires positive inputs including psychosocial support and mentorship from family, peers, and most importantly faculty and other administrators. Those in authority must be willing to provide some degree of personal disclosure to model for students the mentor's own methods for approaching work and coping with stress and competing demands.[28] We have each found it important to disclose some aspects of our own personal journeys with students. This carefully selected sharing, connecting our own humanity with theirs, can often provide the kind of support that helps move students forward. This cultivation of the reservoir is essential for student well-being.

It is through coming to know students as whole human beings with lives outside our classrooms and institutions that we learn enough about them to support their intellectual and psychosocial development. Helping to establish and replenish our students' reservoirs while in our company can set students up for more positive inputs as they mature and interact with others. In order to strengthen resilience, we must be partners and collaborators in this endeavor. Our students will be more resilient, more positively engaged in their learning, and more willing to do the work and take the risks involved in deep learning both in and out of the classroom, and they will flourish if we are willing to give of ourselves. "Flourishing is not a solo endeavor. It's scientifically correct to say that nobody reaches his or her full potential in isolation. Every person who flourishes has warm and trusting relationships with other people."[29] As many of our colleagues confirm, the very liberating experience of individual learning is affected by a campus culture—the intensity of which is determined by faculty and teaching—yet learners are also affected by quite independent factors.

Our capacity to keep our students engaged "hinges on the establishment of a healthy, *caring* environment which enables individuals to find a niche in the social and intellectual communities of the institution."[30] So who is responsible for creating these healthy, caring environments? Whose job is it to ensure that students find social and intellectual community? We can't simply expect them to grow up, get serious, and be adults if we aren't willing to show them the way. Students need caring adults and supportive peers in order to successfully navigate their journey to adulthood.[31] Helping students move through their intellectual and emotional journeys—from being externally defined during periods of doubt and disequilibrium toward a more wholly integrated self who understands that knowledge is constructed—provides the platform on which students will begin their lives and complete their journeys toward self-authorship, well-being, and positive mental health. This process is what "removing silos" or "building bridges" can effectively mean.[32]

Many forces in our culture work against us. Characteristics of this particular generation of young people lead to some of the isolation, risk taking, loneliness, and depression so prevalent among them. They have been shuttled around from activity to activity by ever more busy and rushed parents or caretakers. Or they have been left to their own devices far too much, and the lessons they've learned haven't always been good ones. Moreover, their ideas about "reality" and human interaction are too often formed by reality TV and its over-the-top, exploitive, unhealthy portrayals of human behavior and interpersonal dynamics—displaying contrived and convoluted models of what constitutes critical judgment and how to appropriately manage emotions.

Faculty and student life professionals have the opportunity and choice to create reality by becoming "keepers of meaning," an adult developmental task outlined by George Valliant.[33] As a keeper of meaning, we can use our knowledge and perspective on the workings of the world to guide young people, "linking the past to the future."[34] In fact, one of the most powerful aspects of our work with college students is our capacity to touch the future we may not know. That is what makes this work sacred for us. The kind of collaborative, trustworthy work being imagined is labor intensive. It will require more from us at a time when we already feel overworked. We are asking faculty to engage in work that their reward structure doesn't honor. But we would argue, as many others have, that it is just this kind of trustworthy, labor-intensive work we must do from our perspectives, positions, and professionally protected "pulpits."

In *Student Academic Services*, Gary Kramer asserts, "Traditional age students come to college at a developmental time in their lives when they must answer these questions: 'Who am I? What will I do with the remainder of my life? Who will I share my life with? How do I make meaning of what I hear in class, read, and observe? How do I reconcile conflicting information, methods of inquiry and value systems?'"[35] Our goals for the questions that will be asked and answered mirror theirs. Kramer states, "We must create a seamless educational experience for students. The word seamless suggests that what was once believed to be separate, distinct parts [or *in* and *out* of the classroom; academic and nonacademic; curricular and cocurricular] must now be of one piece bound together so as to appear whole or continuous."[36] What would it take to create these whole experiences for students? How did their lives and our work get so disconnected in the first place?

We are, and should be, concerned about students' engagement with the learning process. But the disengagement that should worry us the most is a student's disengagement from the self. At the same time that we have been engaged in the activities of protection and rescue, we have also been building positive outlets and exploring promising practices that have the potential to connect students in our care to their purpose and passion. Leadership initiatives, service learning, diversity initiatives, learning communities, spirituality and religious life efforts, volunteer and community service, and residential colleges have all been efforts to engage students more fully with the reasons we say we exist and ultimately why they *pay* to come to college. But because of the isolated ways we behave in the academy, even on the same campus, those of us, faculty and staff, who work with students around engagement, learning, and well-being issues often do not talk to one another.

Civic engagement, coupled with reflective and applied learning, prepares students for citizenship by engaging them in problem solving for self and society. When this type of applied scholarship is intentionally constructed to foster civic (not simply service) aims, it is reciprocal in nature and cultivates sustained engagement with local and global constituent communities. Civic engagement and applied scholarship can cultivate a shift in thinking, which increases intrinsic thinking and intrinsic capacity for value of self rather than personal roles and value of others regardless of their roles or labels.

Experiential learning fosters present-centered attention, which contributes positively to student well-being. Intentional cultivation of expectations that affect learning is not incompatible with the social and economic need for job preparation. Moreover, a campus environment that is conducive to fostering insight over simple information transfer supports faculty and students in their pursuit of the transformative learning that leads to individual liberation, broadening of perspectives, and creative critical analysis.

The best educators foster personal and intellectual development, and effectual mentoring requires carefully balanced guidance and pointed questioning while enabling students to take the lead and assume responsibility. Faculty have a clearly assumed responsibility to educate students; however, we would argue that everyone on campus has an important role to play, for higher learning is inextricably linked to the social, emotional, and personal development of the learner—all of which are critical elements of a meaningful education. It is just this understanding of the developmental work (both intellectual and emotional) that must contribute to an integrated whole that will help us "reunite" students. The research is clear that "colleges and universities that exemplify linked academic and student affairs divisions place student learning at the center of their joint enterprise and create institutional *coherence* about student success."[37] Faculty and student affairs professionals must partner in support of the development of the whole student.

Notes

1. Ron Ritchart and David Perkins, "Life in the Mindful Classroom: Nurturing the Disposition of Mindfulness," *Journal of Social Issues* 56, no. 1 (2000): 27; Howard Gardner, *The Unschooled Mind: How Children Think and How Schools Should Teach* (New York: Basic Books, 1991).

2. U.S. Department of Education, National Center for Education Statistics, *The Condition of Education 2010* (Washington, DC: National Center for Education Statistics, 2010), www.nces.ed.gov/fastfacts/display.asp?id=51.

3. U.S. Department of Education, *The Condition of Education 2010*, www.nces.ed.gov/fastfacts/display.asp?id=40.

4. Martha Anne Kitzrow, "The Mental Health Needs of Today's College Students: Challenges and Recommendations," *National Association of Student Personnel Administrators Journal* 41, no. 1 (2003): 165–79; Suicide Prevention Resource Center, *Promoting Mental Health and Preventing Suicide in College and University Settings* (Newton, MA: Education Development Center, 2004).

5. Paul Rogat Loeb, *Generation at the Crossroads: Apathy and Action on the American Campus* (New Brunswick, NJ: Rutgers University Press, 1994); Peter Sacks, *Generation X Goes to College: An Eye-Opening Account of Teaching in Postmodern America* (Chicago: Open Court, 1996); William H. Willimon and Thomas H. Naylor, *The Abandoned Generation: Rethinking Higher Education* (Grand Rapids, MI: Eerdmans, 1995); Jean M. Twenge, *Generation Me: Why Today's Young Americans Are More Confident, Assertive, Entitled—and More Miserable Than Ever Before* (New York: Free Press, 2006); Barrett Seaman, *Binge: What Your College Student Won't Tell You* (Hoboken, NJ: Wiley, 2005).

6. National Mental Health Association and the Jed Foundation, *Safeguarding Your Students against Suicide: Expanding the Safety Network* (Alexandria, VA: National Mental Health Association and the Jed Foundation, 2002).

7. Kitzrow, "The Mental Health Needs of Today's College Students."

8. Henry Wechsler, Juan Eun Lee, Meichen Kuo, and Hang Lee, "College Binge Drinking in the 1990s: A Continuing Problem," *Journal of American College Health* 48, no. 5 (2000): 199–210; National Institute on Alcohol Abuse and Alcoholism, "Changing the Culture of Campus Drinking," *Alcohol Alert* no. 58 (October 2002); American College Health Association, "American College Health Association–National College Health Assessment Spring 2008 Reference Group Data Report (Abridged)," *Journal of the American College Health Association* 57, no. 5 (2009): 477–88, www.acha-ncha.org/docs/ACHA-NCHA_Reference_Group_Report_Sprin2008.pdf.

9. American College Health Association, "National College Health Assessment Spring 2008"; American College Health Association, "American College Health Association–National College Health Assessment: Reference Group Data Report Spring 2000" (Baltimore: American College Health Association, 2000), www.acha-ncha.org/docs/ACHA-NCHA_Reference_Group_Report_Spring2000.pdf.

10. American College Health Association, "National College Health Assessment Spring 2008."

11. American College Health Association, "National College Health Assessment Spring 2008."

12. American College Health Association, "National College Health Assessment Spring 2008."

13. Ritchart and Perkins, "Life in the Mindful Classroom."

14. Ken Bain, *What the Best College Teachers Do* (Cambridge, MA: Harvard University Press, 2004), 97.

15. Barbara E. Brackney and Stuart A. Karabenick, "Psychopathology and Academic Performance: The Role of Motivation and Learning Strategies," *Journal of Counseling Psychology* 42, no. 4 (1995): 456–65; Kitzrow, "The Mental Health Needs of Today's College Students," 165–79.

16. Jon Kabat-Zinn, Ann O. Massion, Jean Kristeller, Linda Gay Peterson, Kenneth E. Fletcher, Lori Pbert, William Lenderking, and Saki Santorelli, "Effectiveness of a Meditation-Based Stress Reduction Program in the Treatment of Anxiety Disorders," *American Journal of Psychiatry* 149, no. 7 (1992): 936–43.

17. Kabat-Zinn et al., "Effectiveness of a Meditation-Based Stress Reduction Program"; Randye J. Semple, Elizabeth F.G. Reid, and Lisa Miller, "Treating Anxiety with Mindfulness: An Open Trial of Mindfulness Training for Anxious Children," *Journal of Cognitive Psychotherapy* 19, no. 4 (2005): 379–92.

18. These numbers and figures are based on datasets as of November 2010 from research conducted for Dessa Bergen-Cico, Sanghyeon Cheon, and JoAnn A. Abe, "Examining the Mediating Role of Mindfulness on Trait Anxiety and Self-Compassion," *Mindfulness* (forthcoming).

19. Ruth A. Baer, Gregory T. Smith, Jaclyn Hopkins, Jennifer Krietemeyer, and Leslie Toney, "Using Self-Report Assessment Methods to Explore Facets of Mindfulness," *Assessment* 87, no. 1 (2006): 27–45.

20. Charles Donald Spielberger, Richard L. Gorsuch, and Robert E. Lushene, *STAI Manual for the State-Trait Anxiety Inventory* (Self-Evaluation Questionnaire), (Palo Alto, CA: Consulting Psychologists, 1970).

21. See note 18.

22. Spielberger, Gorsuch, and Lushene, *STAI Manual for the State-Trait Anxiety Inventory*.

23. Kabat-Zinn et al., "Effectiveness of a Meditation-Based Stress Reduction Program"; Semple, Reid, and Miller, "Treating Anxiety with Mindfulness"; Ruth A. Baer, "Mindfulness Training as a Clinical Intervention: A Conceptual and Empirical Review," *Clinical Psychology: Science and Practice* 10, no. 2 (2003): 125–42; John J. Miller, Ken Fletcher, and Jon Kabat-Zinn, "Three-Year Follow-Up and Clinical Implications of a Mindfulness-Based Stress Reduction Intervention in the Treatment of Anxiety Disorders," *General Hospital Psychiatry* 17, no. 3 (May 1995): 192–200.

24. Charles R. Snyder and Shane J. Lopez, *Positive Psychology: The Scientific and Practical Explorations of Human Strengths* (Thousand Oaks, CA: Sage, 2007), 9.

25. Barbara Fredrickson, *Positivity: Groundbreaking Research Reveals How to Embrace the Hidden Strength of Positive Emotions, Overcome Negativity, and Thrive* (New York: Crown, 2009), 117.

26. Laura B. Dunn, Alana Iglewicz, and Christine Moutier, "A Conceptual Model of Medical Student Well-Being: Promoting Resilience and Preventing Burnout," *Academic Psychiatry* 32, no. 1 (2008): 44–53.

27. Dunn, Iglewicz, and Moutier, "A Conceptual Model of Medical Student Well-Being.

28. Dunn, Iglewicz, and Moutier, "A Conceptual Model of Medical Student Well-Being.

29. Fredrickson, *Positivity*, 191.

30. Vincent Tinto, *Leaving College: Rethinking the Causes and Cures of Student Attrition* (Chicago: University of Chicago Press, 1987), 181.

31. Tinto, *Leaving College*.

32. Marcia B. Baxter Magolda, *Making Their Own Way: Narratives for Transforming Higher Education to Promote Self-Development* (Sterling, VA: Stylus, 2001).

33. George Valliant, *Aging Well: Surprising Guideposts to a Happier Life* (Boston: Little, Brown, 2002).

34. Snyder and Lopez, *Positive Psychology*, 116.

35. Gary L. Kramer, *Student Academic Services: An Integrated Approach* (San Francisco: Jossey-Bass, 2003), 7.

36. Kramer, *Student Academic Services*.

37. Kathleen Manning, Jillian Kinzie, and John H. Schuh, *One Size Does Not Fit All: Traditional and Innovative Models of Student Affairs Practice* (New York: Routledge, 2006), 122.

5

Renewing the Civic Purpose of Liberal Education

Barry N. Checkoway, Richard Guarasci,
and Peter L. Levine

Civic engagement is any process or situation in which people participate in public work to address issues and create change at the civic level. The process can include initiatives in which people organize for social action, plan local programs, or develop community-based services. They might become active members of a neighborhood association, contact public officials about an issue, speak at a public hearing, or join others in a protest demonstration outside the building where the hearing is held.

Civic engagement also can include initiatives at the national, global, or other civic levels. *Civic* is a term with limitless units of practice, whether as a place in which people reside, a group of people with similar social or cultural characteristics, or a common cause that people share. As long as people are addressing issues and creating change through public work at the civic level, civic engagement is taking place.

Higher education is ideally positioned to prepare people for civic engagement. Many colleges and universities were established with statements of civic purpose in their founding documents; most of them have courses or programs with civic content; and some of them have strategies, institutional infrastructure, professional staff members, and curricular and cocurricular activities for civic learning.[1] We believe that if more colleges and universities were aware of the benefits of civic engagement for students and faculty members as part of their core mission and liberal education, they might strengthen their commitment to this purpose.[2]

Liberal education, according to the Association of American Colleges and Universities, is "a philosophy of education that empowers individuals with broad knowledge and transferable skills, and a stronger sense of values, ethics, and civic engagement . . . characterized by challenging encounters with important issues, and more a way of studying than a specific course or field of study."[3] It can include a general education curriculum featuring social sciences, humanities, and other academic disciplines and can be found in small and large public and private colleges and universities nationwide.

Today's colleges and universities differ widely in their orientation to civic engagement, but many of them are narrow in their conception. Thus members of these institutions may consider civic engagement solely as a type of volunteerism, community service, or service learning rather than recognizing the many forms it might take, both on campus and in the community. Thus when students collect cans of food and take them to a homeless shelter—or stay and serve meals in the shelter, or reflect upon their trip to the shelter and seeing homeless people eating the food—and then discuss their observations through a facilitated discussion on campus in a service learning course, students, faculty, and administration alike often view these activities as the only approach to civic engagement. They may be aware of other possibilities on campus (such as in anthropology or history courses, or in integration of academic disciplines and professional fields) or in the community (such as organizing an action group for affordable housing, or becoming advocates for a new national housing policy, or presenting their ideas at the public meetings of a nongovernmental organization in the global housing arena), but they still tend to focus on volunteerism, community service, and service learning as what constitutes engagement.

However, we believe that civic engagement can include curricula and courses in several disciplines and fields, and it can promote public work to address issues and create change. Volunteerism, community service, and service learning might contribute to these objectives as part of a comprehensive strategy, but too often they look like "doing good" rather than "public work." Doing good is good, but it is not necessarily good enough in itself to create change.[4]

We believe there are special opportunities on campus for strengthening engagement and learning, and when taken together, engagement and learning can form a comprehensive approach for enabling higher education to express its civic purpose in ways that contribute to student learning and faculty scholarship, an approach that has been demonstrated at the University of Michigan and other institutions.[5] Because of its centrality to the educational process, liberal education is especially situated for this purpose.

The Case for Civic Learning

The alignment of civic engagement and liberal education is intimate, and the combination provides a powerful approach to learning. When combined with a deep commitment to community collaboration, they produce a heightened civic awareness, an appreciation for the arts of democracy, a zeal for intellectual discovery, and a reaffirmation of democratic purpose. Joining civic engagement and liberal education opens lines of inquiry that promise new pedagogies, ones that place the student and learner as an agent and author of learning and knowledge. This union allows the teacher to link ideas and experience through a process of reflective practice and allows colleges and universities to renew their commitment to their core missions of combining the freedom to learn with service to human well-being and social advancement.[6]

Liberal education, and the liberal arts and sciences in particular, provides students with knowledge of the width and breadth of the human experience. Founded on the essential practices of open inquiry, critical thinking, and evidence-based arguments, liberal education allows learners to engage the constellation of our human intellectual heritage. It focuses students on diverse historical epochs and the variety of distinct cultures as well as the mysteries and dynamics of the natural world. Liberal education "liberates" students from the parochialism of their own autobiographies by offering the enchantment of discovery and the romance of acting in and on the world around them.

By engaging the broad intellectual and scientific vistas, liberal education opens students to the world. In this regard it is liberating, but although the students are open to the world, they are not necessarily engaged with that world. Ideas that lack experience or integration with action can limit the value of learning—although learning for its own sake has often been seen as an ideal for liberal education.

Experiential learning as a pedagogy was long held suspect by passionate advocates of liberal education on the grounds that it reduced learning to vocationalism, provincialism, or both. Some advocates also caution against community service and service learning, as if to suggest that alternative approaches such as these do not measure up to ones that are traditional in the academy. Experience for its own sake could easily lead to false impressions born from the limitations of personal observation, they argue.[7]

However, higher education has evolved dramatically in the last fifty years. Traditional liberal arts do not enroll most of our students. It is more typical to find institutions characterized by numerous preprofessional programs that depend heavily on experiential learning and other alternatives. These approaches are perceived by some as outside of the domain of liberal education. Ardent supporters of the traditional canon see these programs as utilitarian, applied, and vocational. In this sense, they are seen as not transformative or "liberating" in the traditional sense.[8]

In *The Reflective Practitioner*, Schön eloquently deconstructs these criticisms by outlining in detail how applied fields have many of the same needs for critical thinking, cultural contexts, and problem solving as the liberal arts. Applied learning, and its necessary cognate experiential learning, draws on many of the same attributes of liberal education.[9] The fact remains that, within the academy, professional and liberal education are understood by many as remote, if not distinct, modes of learning. While this dichotomy can be argued endlessly, it frames the context for the attempt to reconcile liberal education and civic engagement. The inability of too many higher education leaders to integrate field-based learning into a meaningful philosophical framework is a definite barrier to transforming undergraduate education.

A new type of liberal education is required. At Wagner College, for example, it is called Practical Liberal Arts, an approach in which professional programs and the liberal arts disciplines are integrated into a vibrant dialogue. Where the liberal arts provide the aforementioned breadth and depth of the human experience, professional education promotes conceptualization, design, implementation, assessment, reflection, and revision. When joined, both modes of learning are ways to know and engage the world more formidably. This provides the opening for building the foundation for the conjunction of civic engagement and liberal education. Civic engagement may deepen understanding of the discipline by providing a real-world cultural, political, economic, and physical context for the essential intellectual and moral issues embedded in the course texts and ideas. Civic education may provide the benefits gained from direct student involvement when community projects, linked to the intellectual project, are conceptualized, implemented, assessed, and revised. Civic engagement opens up the possibility of enhanced reflection on the interplay of the course ideas and the experiential engagement. The involvement with community members and institutions may allow for greater understanding of the impact of the issues studied from the perspective of others and how their interpretation creates alternative meaning and response—not a small attribute of liberal learning.

Such learning outcomes result from an enriched undergraduate experience designed to reconcile liberal and professional education, whose ideas and experience are compared and contrasted through a process of reflective practice that calls upon critical thinking, openness to the social and physical context, engaged listening, the gathering and reliance on evidence, the formulation of arguments, the rejection of unfounded opinions, the use of intellectual interpretation, and personal discretion in decision making. When done responsibly and with a comprehensive use of pedagogical tools, civic engagement holds great promise for transforming liberal education.

In addition, other learning outcomes become possible. Civic learning is distinct from civic engagement, but when taken together, they promote personal growth. When students participate in community-based learning, emphasizing substantive reflection, they engage in a new level of civic learning. Students contextualize their field-based experiences with community organizations, distinct cultures, and people who are different from themselves and who help them think about the phenomena in ways, or with perspectives, the academy is not always able to provide. Civic learning allows students to ask critical questions about their field experience when accessing the larger intellectual heritage provided by the arts and sciences. Students begin to ask, "How have social institutions shaped the particular dynamics and personal destinies of the very people and organizations with which I am engaged?" "How was this particular equation of social, personal, and environmental possibilities arranged?"

Civic learning allows for the larger impact of combining liberal education and civic engagement, namely, the building of a democratic culture. When done with a deep respect for intellectual growth and open inquiry and in partnership with the local community, civic learning evokes for students a deeper connection with communities and individuals usually unique in their personal experiences. They encounter individuals who differ from them in age, race, ethnicity, culture, class, religion, sexuality, or any number of social categories. These "border crossings" establish the basis for interpersonal connections that introduce or strengthen a mutual sense of understanding, empathy, and reciprocity. In short, civic learning mobilizes civic connections and strengthens democratic culture. Taken alone, this is a significant contribution to the larger civic mission of the university. When connected to the historic promise of American higher education to enhance civic development of a democratic society, the impact of civic engagement joined to liberal learning fortifies one of the cornerstones of democratic progress.

Democracy is a dynamic political and social system requiring active, effective, and articulate citizens. As one of the essential goals of higher education, educating learners for democracy extends beyond the provision of a deep and substantive intellectual program. It also calls for civic learning where students acquire the arts of democracy; where they learn that effective civic action requires developing openness to others, active listening skills, collaborative work, social mediation, political negotiation, active engagement, deliberate action, impact assessment, and revision and refinement.[10]

Many of these arts of democracy are closely linked to the traditional values and practices of liberal education, specifically the development of critical thinking, evidenced argument, effective communication, and a deep respect for the diversity of thought as well as the rigor of intellectual inquiry. The absence of these democratic arts will lead to a democratic culture that is less informed; likely incapable of respecting cultural and social difference; and unable to forge active debate and dialogue into meaningful, effective, and sustainable public policy. Civic learning is imperative for a healthy democracy.

Civic Learning and Institutional Transformation

Civic learning can be facilitated by a wide range of formal and nonformal pedagogies and teaching strategies. These can include traditional forms such as lectures and discussions as well as active methods through problem solving, exercises, informal small groups, simulations, case studies, role plays, and other approaches, all of which can be conceived and practiced with civic learning in mind.

Recent years have witnessed increasing interest in service learning and other particular forms of community-based learning as a central component of the active learning approach to democratic education at the undergraduate level. Such pedagogies broaden the learning and teaching process, expand the arena for learning beyond the formal classroom, and can contribute to institutional transformation. They integrate classroom texts with experiences in community work outside the classroom and, in so doing, broaden the outcomes of undergraduate education.[11] But they are far from the whole story and are not the exclusive means of facilitating civic learning.

Democratic education, as the larger philosophical context for civic learning, has four dimensions. One of these dimensions lies outside our present discussion, namely, direct political engagement. Another, service learning, is a part of our current discussion of civic engagement. The other two dimensions are critical to this narrative. First, democratic pedagogy opens up the classroom by including the student not only as the acquirer of knowledge but also as its producer. By thoroughly immersing the student within the everyday realities of community-based learning, democratic pedagogy nurtures the reflective process, and the student is asked to discover the larger social meanings embedded in these often parochial and sometimes prosaic settings. Students must uncover the full force of the macroinstitutions that set the agenda for the immediate community circumstances. They must identify the relationships that are often disguised in the ordinary and discover in its large significance what famed sociologist C. Wright Mills once described as the linkage between "public issues and private troubles."[12]

This process of making meaning can utilize various innovative teaching tools, such as dialogical journals in which students compare and contrast the interplay between their field experiences and the course texts. Opening the classroom to discussion of field experiences, no matter how mundane, for class interrogation provides important reflection for students. Often community members are invited into the classroom, in person or electronically, for further analytic conversations. Some teachers also employ biographical and autobiographical pairings as a means to foster connections, contrasts, and context. Our observation is that conventional classroom teaching, often based largely on knowledge acquisition solely garnered by textual analysis, comes up short when compared with rigorous textual analysis that includes a generous and responsible deployment of community-based learning programs.

Democratic education not only includes such pedagogical practices but also has transformative potential for reconciling professional education and liberal education through a reconceptualization of the relationship between work and democracy.

Long estranged, these two seemingly separate realms can be linked when the learning has a civic purpose. As Sullivan argues, we return professional education to democratic practice when we reunite theory and practice within the curricular experience. When professional work is conceptualized as a reciprocal relationship between a particular profession and its publics, we introduce a civic relationship that goes beyond a market relationship.[13]

Linking work and democracy adds a civic dimension to applied and professional education. When applied and professional learning become reflective practice, it opens the possibility for increasing their integration with the vast intellectual resources available in the liberal arts and for transforming civic engagement into civic learning. Learning of this type has the potential to prepare civic professionals who value the responsibility of addressing the needs of the communities they serve.

Constructing the Civic Institution

Civic learning can help transform undergraduate education and the educational institution of which it is part.[14] While each institution is distinct and there is no single blueprint, it is possible to identify several broad design elements.

Leadership

Educational transformation requires institutional leadership with the ability to unite diverse groups around a common purpose. Because of the special culture of colleges and universities, leadership should not be confused with authority, namely, the ability to compel behavior, nor should it be confused with power and the capability to shape it. Instead, leadership in higher institutions is ideally transformative leadership that can transcend station or rank and originate within any level, and across levels, of the campus community. Transformative leadership is required at multiple levels: administrative, faculty, staff, and trustee. Indeed, effective leadership for civic learning in higher education will likely require the ability to address issues arising from faculty members of diverse types, in addition to senior and midrange administration and governing boards.[15]

Programs and Resources

Leadership begins with a comprehensive vision of undergraduate education that includes the role of civic learning. A transformative program must encompass three critical elements: (1) a multidiscipline-based curriculum that spans the undergraduate experience, (2) a coordinated cocurricular civic engagement program, and (3) meaningful service partnerships with local and/or global communities. Each of these in turn will build on the others as faculty, administrative staff, and community partners are brought into a meaningful relationship, aligning engaged service with community impact and civic learning. Faculty members more fully understand community programs, and they begin to identify community-oriented research projects. Students will be part of action research agendas that directly benefit community partners. Further, community actors, who normally work in parallel, will now form intracommunity partnerships, sharing resources, writing grants in common, and accessing the sustainable assets of the community.

Faculty members from diverse disciplines can find common cause in unifying their teaching and research projects in relation to a particular civic purpose or project. Learning communities, course clusters restricted to enrollment by common student cohorts, provide a curricular architecture enabling disciplinary and civic synergies that mutually advance teaching, service, and community priorities. As demonstrated at Wagner College, a comprehensive four-year curricular program will more likely position students as civic learners.

A cocurricular civic engagement program coupled with a robust undergraduate curriculum can offer genuine leadership opportunities for students. Reconceptualizing leadership as part of civic engagement and public service allows institutions to reclaim student leadership as a core responsibility of the student affairs staff. Within the domain of the cocurricular, residential education, and student activities, the conjunction of leadership and service allows students to own the civic agenda and, in so doing, identify and engage with their community partners; this, in turn, can enable them to link with fellow student organizations. In this way, the civic agenda becomes the "curriculum" for the student affairs professionals, helping them better align student development, personal wellness, and psychological well-being. In addition, the respective administrative offices will develop a common agenda, share resources accordingly, and enhance their professional development. The focus on assessment and outcomes drives further improvement in the areas of student development, residential life, student activities, health services, and athletics. New campus partnerships are likely to emerge.

Finally, community college partnerships elevate the entire institutional commitment to civic learning. A genuine partnership transcends the traditional extractive relationships of well-intended college research and service programs, where the community is reduced to a learning laboratory for the convenience of higher education. A mutual relationship is built on ongoing dialogue and active participation, often found in joint steering and advisory committees. Learning and community outcomes will be clarified. A commitment to comprehensive and ongoing assessments is necessary for a successful partnership. The ultimate goal is for students to develop meaningful civic learning and for the community partnerships to realize a genuine impact on mutually agreed upon outcomes. For the college or university, these partnerships move them closer to identifying, supporting, and documenting their stated civic mission. Long-term success is a function of a university's efficiency in aligning its sustainable assets with the needs and assets of the community. If the institution is overextended, all good intentions will likely evaporate in the face of institutional contingencies. Examples of success may include the effective integration of professional programs, such as teacher education, allied health, and engineering, that are linked closely with these partnerships. Business administration, the performing arts, medical education, and other programs with significant experiential learning requirements are likely prospects for this type of integration of institutional assets with community needs.

Infrastructure and Resources

For a successful transformative program, institutional leaders should make strategic investments in faculty development and civic engagement leadership. Recentering the institution around a comprehensive civic program should allow for reconceptualizing positions in student affairs, academic administration, and basic infrastructure. Tufts University received a substantial grant to establish an entire college of citizenship and public service in a research university.[16] Wagner College was able to achieve this realignment with modest investments, all financed by net revenue increases from greater student retention as well as position realignment and reliance on student peer leadership roles.

Leadership and professional development are critical elements for success, affordability, and sustainability. More than foundation grants, fundamental change begins with educational work, with pedagogical innovation and faculty development, and with administrative leaders able to adjust the performance and reward systems needed to encourage and support faculty leaders in civic engagement. Assessment protocols need to be funded and incorporated into strategic decision making on every level. In the end, civic learning must become a primary educational priority. All successes will flow from this essential change.

Looking to the Future

Liberal education can be viewed as a form of critical inquiry and reflective practice connected to democratic practice. At the college and university levels, it has potential benefits for students, for the institutions in which they participate, and for the democracy of which they are a part. Institutions differ in their degree of commitment to liberal education, civic learning, and civic engagement itself. But despite differences, some institutions are strong in their commitment, and others have greater potential to strengthen this purpose.

At present, the gap between the civic potential and the reality of higher education is severe. About one-third of young people do not complete high school and are unlikely to benefit from higher education. Those who do attend colleges and universities find themselves in a highly stratified system, composed of institutions that use their reputations and resources to compete fiercely for the most qualified applicants. As a whole, the sector segregates the most academically successful students from the rest, graduates only about 59 percent of undergraduates within six years (with noncompleters unequally distributed across institutions), and reproduces socioeconomic inequalities to a greater degree than in the past.[17] Meanwhile, the cost of higher education continues to rise, exacerbating the discrepancies.[18]

Education is perceived as a "positional good": To hold a more prestigious degree puts you ahead of the competition in the job market. What makes a degree prestigious is its reputation, as ranked by *U.S. News & World Report* and others. To date, parents and students have been willing to pay for prestigious degrees even if they are not convinced that the educational experiences are intrinsically valuable or have civic benefits. To be sure, some colleges offer thoughtful and innovative liberal arts curricula because of the commitments of their faculty and academic leaders—or in order to compete for students with strongly civic interests (or both). But overall, despite excellent examples of programming at some institutions, liberal education and civic education risk being viewed as niche markets provided, for the most part, to students who have already developed civic commitments by age eighteen. These are the young people who need such an education least.

Changes in youth culture, public priorities, or policy could shift those incentives. Several promising changes are on the horizon, although benign outcomes are still far from assured.

Center for Information and Research on Civic Learning and Engagement (CIRCLE) studies suggest it is possible that young people will demand more and better civic opportunities. Today's younger generation—often named the Millennials—demonstrates high rates of community service in high school and voted at near-record levels in the presidential election of 2010. Surveys show them generally idealistic, enthusiastic about diversity, and interested in public service—although not government careers—at least relative to their immediate predecessors.[19] To the extent that their priorities shape the market, they may reward colleges and universities that provide democratic education.

Already, the Millennials are the most diverse cohort in history. Young people may decide it is crucial to learn to collaborate with people different from themselves, in which case they should seek liberal education with a democratic spirit. On the other hand, before reaching college age, they navigate educational systems that are highly stratified by socioeconomic status, more racially segregated than thirty years ago, and designed to reward individual academic achievement. If we expect students to demand collaborative, democratic experiences in college, we must hope that they change their expectations. One obstacle is interpersonal trust. The proportion of young Americans who say they generally trust other people is the lowest since surveys began to ask about trust in the 1960s. People who deeply distrust their fellow citizens would benefit from democratic education, but they may not seek it.

The period when we come of age influences our behavior and attitudes as citizens because early experiences are formative.[20] Most of the popular and scholarly books published about the Millennials appeared between 1997 and 2007. They focus on the Internet, prosperity, and war as formative experiences. But for the *next* cohort reaching college age, the Great Recession will surely be formative. Much will depend on how they rate the performance of major institutions, including the national government, in these hard times. The Greatest Generation of the 1930s mostly concluded that the government was on their side; they then participated and trusted at high rates for the rest of their lives. A similar outcome is hardly foreordained this time around. Despite survey evidence that young people were idealistic and tolerant as of 2008, a retreat from public life and democratic values certainly remains possible.

One major change that has already occurred is the shift of many aspects of life online. College students—by virtue of their young age and their relatively high socioeconomic status—are among the heaviest users of online tools. It is risky to predict the civic consequences of this shift because the tools and the way they are used keep changing rapidly. For instance, five years ago, the topic of online citizenship was dominated by concerns about anonymity and rootlessness. But now Facebook is the most prominent tool, and it is used mainly by people who know one another.

A deeper change is from civic engagement as the province of institutions (with budgets, leaders, and rules of admission) to civic engagement as a set of à la carte choices. The newspaper industry, for example, laments the "unbundling" of news products. Many Americans used to purchase one newspaper that combined international and local news, serious issues and fluff, editorials, letters, comics, sports scores, want ads, and classifieds. People who wanted classifieds and sports were forced to subsidize serious journalism. Now those products can be obtained separately online, and most people are choosing not to pay journalists. Daily newspaper readership dropped in half from 1972 to 2006, according to the General Social Survey.[21] In the same period, according to the American National Election Studies, the proportion of people who said they regularly followed the news fell from 36.5 percent to just 26 percent. These declines were steeper for young people, only 11 percent of whom said they regularly followed the news in 2008.[22]

Much more than the newspaper has been unbundled over the last century. We have unbundled political parties into collections of entrepreneurial politicians and discrete ballot initiatives. We have unbundled careers by losing most of the unionized jobs and secure, lifelong positions. We have unbundled religion by creating a proliferation of faith-based networks, organizations, and self-help groups that are separate from congregations. We have unbundled civil society by moving from demanding membership organizations to loose networks. Colleges and universities are under pressure to unbundle their services by selling education in separate pieces, as is common in the private for-profit sector, which enrolled more than three million students in 2008–2009.[23] Clay Shirky argues that the Internet makes it possible to organize most kinds of collective action without organizations at all, so we should see that happen widely.[24]

The consequences for people who have civic skills and motivations are beneficial: They have more opportunities to engage in a world with literally millions of political blogs, e-mail lists, and Facebook pages. But people without such advantages can easily be left out; and we have lost the means to subsidize certain important public goods, such as professional journalism and civic associations that are capable of recruiting youth. It is possible that we will learn to use distributed social networks to recruit, motivate, and educate all young people at low cost. But the trend today is toward deeper gaps between the superengaged and the completely alienated.

When independent institutions in a competitive market fail to provide a public good, one strategy is for government to offer different incentives. In this case, civically oriented liberal education is a public good that is undersupplied, and the government could encourage more of it.

With the passage of the Edward M. Kennedy Serve America Act in 2009, the budget of the federal Corporation for National and Community Service is on course to triple. The corporation influences civic engagement by providing full-time service positions, by funding service learning in colleges as well as K–12 schools, and even by officially measuring America's annual "civic health" (in partnership with the Census and the National Conference on Citizenship). The corporation's impact on higher education depends on the policies it chooses to adopt. For example, it has never established learning objectives for its grantees. If it did so, and if the objectives were wise, the impact could be helpful. Also, how stringently the corporation prevents its grantees from participating in "politics" will affect civic engagement on campuses. The corporation must prevent grantees from undertaking *partisan* activities, but that leaves a lot of room to decide which political activities are allowable. Students should be encouraged to identify the root causes of public problems and to seek policy changes as well as directly serve others.

Community colleges are receiving more interest from policy makers because of the populations they serve and their relatively high return on investment. They have potential for civic engagement because of their community roots but would need considerably more support before they could provide high-quality liberal arts/civic education for most of their nearly twelve million students.

At the precollege level, federal and state education policies now emphasize standards and accountability in reading, math, and science. Although CIRCLE's research disputes the claim that federal policy has caused civic education to shrink, civics certainly has not been a national priority.[25] There is little evidence that priorities will change, but policy makers could decide that civic education is a route to more advanced academic skills. If they choose to support K–12 civic education because of its academic and psychosocial benefits, higher education will have new opportunities to assist with teacher training, research, and other support for K–12 schools.

Civic engagement is a result of not only individual experiences (such as educational opportunities in school or college) but also grand events in national and international politics. For example, the same schools and families that produced rather conventional engaged citizens around 1958 were producing cultural and political radicals one decade later.

The future of American politics—not just the formal system of elections and legislation but also the broader political climate—is impossible to predict. But it will not be static. One possibility is a shift to political and procedural reform and civic renewal, as in the Progressive Era. Other possibilities are much darker. Higher education has an important role in steering change toward deliberative, equitable, and democratic directions.

This final section has described structural obstacles to civic education and liberal education at the college level, obstacles that will require large-scale shifts in public priorities and public policies to remedy. Yet it remains true—and important—that significant numbers of colleges and universities have found success by voluntarily committing themselves to combinations of civic and liberal education, informed by ethical commitments to their own communities. They provide the examples from which a larger movement must be built.

Notes

1. Thomas Ehrlich, *Civic Responsibility and Higher Education* (Phoenix: Oryx Press, 2000).

2. Barry Checkoway, "Dilemmas of Civic Renewal at the University of Michigan," in *Public Work and the Academy: An Academic Administrator's Guide to Civic Engagement and Service-Learning*, ed. Mark Langseth, William M. Plater, and Scott Dillon (Bolton, MA: Anker, 2004).

3. Association of American Colleges and Universities, "Liberal Education," www.aacu.org/resources/liberaleducation.

4. Harry C. Boyte and Nancy N. Kari, *Building America: The Democratic Promise of Public Work* (Philadelphia: Temple University Press, 1996).

5. Checkoway, "Dilemmas of Civic Renewal."

6. Ehrlich, *Civic Responsibility*.

7. Harold Pashler, Mark McDaniel, Doug Rohrer, and Robert Bjork, "Learning Styles: Concepts and Evidence," *Psychological Science in the Public Interest* 9, no. 3 (2009): 105–19.

8. Allan Bloom, *The Closing of the American Mind* (New York: Simon and Schuster, 1987).

9. Donald A. Schon, *The Reflective Practitioner: How Professionals Think in Action* (New York: Basic Books, 1984).

10. Anne Colby, Thomas Ehrlich, Elizabeth Beaumont, Jason Stephens, and Lee S. Shulman, *Educating Citizens: Preparing America's Undergraduates for Lives of Moral and Civic Responsibility* (San Francisco: Jossey-Bass, 2007).

11. Bruce W. Speck and Sherry L. Hoppe, *Service-Learning: History, Theory, and Issues* (Westport, CT: Praeger, 2004); Jean R. Strait and Marybeth Lima, eds., *The Future of Service Learning* (Sterling, VA: Stylus, 2009).

12. C. Wright Mills, *The Sociological Imagination* (1959; repr., Oxford: Oxford University Press, 2000), 18.

13. William A. Sullivan, *Work and Integrity: The Crisis and Promise of Professionalism in America* (New York: HarperCollins, 1995). See also chapter 6 in this volume.

14. Ehrlich, *Civic Responsibility*; Colby et al., *Educating Citizens*; Anne Colby, Elizabeth Beaumont, Thomas Ehrlich, and Josh Corngold, *Educating for Democracy: Preparing Undergraduates for Responsible Political Engagement* (San Francisco: Jossey-Bass, 2007).

15. Checkoway, "Dilemmas of Civic Renewal."

16. Robert M. Hollister, Molly Mead, and Nancy Wilson, "Infusing Active Citizenship throughout a Research University: The Tisch College of Citizenship and Public Service at Tufts University," *Metropolitan Universities Journal* 17, no. 3 (2006): 38–54.

17. Alexander W. Astin and Leticia Oseguera, "The Declining 'Equity' of American Higher Education," *Review of Higher Education* 27, no. 3 (2004): 321–41.

18. Laura G. Knapp, Janice E. Kelly-Reid, and Scott A Ginder, *Postsecondary Institutions and Price of Attendance in the United States: Fall 2009 and Degrees and Other Awards Conferred: 2008–09, and 12-Month Enrollment 2008–09* (Washington, DC: National Center for Education Statistics, 2010), 4.

19. Morley Winograd and Michael D. Hais, *Millennial Makeover: MySpace, YouTube, and the Future of American Politics* (New Brunswick, NJ: Rutgers University Press, 2008); Abby Kiesa, Alexander P. Orlowski, Peter Levine, Deborah Both, Emily Hoban Kirby, Mark Hugo Lopez, and Karlo Barrios Marcelo, *Millennials Talk Politics: A Study of College Student Political Participation* (College Park, MD: Center for Information and Research on Civic Learning and Engagement, 2007).

20. Karl Mannheim, "The Problem of Generations," in *Essays on the Sociology of Knowledge*, ed. Paul Kecskemeti (New York: Oxford University Press, 1952).

21. National Opinion Research Center at the University of Chicago, *General Social Survey 1972–2006*, analyzed by Peter Levine.

22. *American National Election Studies*, analyzed by Peter Levine.

23. Knapp, Kelly-Reid, and Ginder, *Postsecondary Institutions*, 18.

24. Clay Shirky, *Here Comes Everybody: The Power of Organizing without Organizations* (New York: Penguin, 2008).

25. Peter Levine, Mark Hugo Lopez, and Karlo Barrios Marcelo, *Getting Narrower at the Base: The American Curriculum after NCLB* (College Park, MD: Center for Information and Research on Civic Learning and Engagement, 2008).

6

Evoking Wholeness

To Renew the Ideal of the Educated Person

Theodore E. Long

"We educate the whole person." That claim expresses a widespread ideal among colleges and universities in the United States, especially residential liberal arts colleges. It suggests that baccalaureate education has a larger purpose than simply transmitting knowledge, namely, the multi-dimensional formation of persons for full and meaningful lives beyond the academy. What that ideal means and exactly how it is realized, however, are rarely explained, as if its meaning were clear to all and its ac-complishment a foregone conclusion.[1] By taking it for granted, however, we educators have left its realization at best uneven and often neglected. If we believe that developing "the whole person" is important, we need to focus on it and create a systematic, assessable educational approach to realizing its possibilities. Doing so, however, will require a different mode of thinking about higher learning and a redesign of the educational enterprise, for our current practice is not well suited to fulfill the dream we espouse.

In what follows, I sketch some major elements of a renewed educa-tional emphasis on evoking wholeness in our students. This is not so much the beginning of a conversation, which others have already initi-ated, as an effort to center thinking, map the terrain, and clear a path for more extensive and systematic work ahead. The discussion is intention-ally broad in scope and focused primarily on substantive analytic issues, not matters of process or practice. I first reframe the concept of whole-ness, and then the main body of the chapter elaborates its major features and shows how they might be evoked educationally. I conclude with some comments about the liberally educated person for the twenty-first century.

Reframing the Idea of Wholeness

An exegesis of the gauzy rhetoric of mission statements, viewbooks, and catalogs would expose several assumptions about the education of the whole person that are rarely articulated. First, students are composed of multiple dimensions (e.g., mind, body, and spirit, or intellectual, social, ethical, and aesthetic), and the educational program addresses each of them in some way. Second, higher education finishes, extends, or elaborates upon these naturally occurring traits, functioning as an agent of a natural maturation process rather than developing traits distinctive in kind. Third, the formal academic curriculum primarily develops the intellectual side of persons; most education related to the other dimensions takes place outside the classroom in the cocurriculum.

It has long been clear from personal testimony and research on college effects that cocurricular experiences can make a substantial impact on students, often cited as among the most important and memorable of their college careers.[2] Historically, such student development was primarily generated informally and idiosyncratically through life experience in the array of cocurricular activities, organized or not. As Harvard dean Archie Epps often observed, students participated in an "invisible curriculum" in which they learned a great deal, but without design or guided instruction, and not always to their benefit. It has been difficult for students to sort out what they have actually learned from the power and intensity of their experiences. To the extent they can do so, it is not easy to discern how much of their learning is actually part of natural maturation as opposed to some higher learning that would not have otherwise occurred.

Over the past generation, colleges and universities have started to build intentional programs to focus and intensify cocurricular learning and to identify methods to make it more productive. Those welcome initiatives have brought whole-person education into the sunlight, insisting that it deserves just as much serious educational attention as the formal curriculum, perhaps even enhancing academic learning in the process. So we are developing in higher education today what I would call a *curriculum and pedagogy of the whole person* that seeks to make good on the promise so many colleges make to their students.[3]

Even so, the prevalent view among faculty is that educating the whole person should remain sequestered in the cocurriculum. Faculty often raise questions of purpose and priority about investments in efforts they consider tangential to the primary educational mission of the academy, from athletics to civic engagement. As a result, eager reformers may lack willing partners or meet active resistance in their efforts to advance whole-person education. As Richard Keeling has aptly noted, colleges are organized in vertical silos, and whole-person education actually cuts across them horizontally.[4] Our challenge is to find a way to bring those horizontal processes into organizational practice, but we cannot do that without reframing the idea of whole-person education in a way that can gain allegiance of both faculty and student affairs professionals.

I believe we can do so by moving away from the traditional viewpoint about educating the whole person in two ways.[5] First, we should refocus whole-person education on what is distinctively "higher" about what students learn, and I believe the idea of *evoking wholeness* outlined in this chapter is a distinctive, transformative contribution higher education can make to student development. Unlike the traditional ideal, which concentrates on honing the common features of personhood students *bring* to higher education, the new ideal of wholeness defines a set of specific educational *outcomes* we want students to achieve. An education for wholeness seeks to develop genuinely new capacities and outlooks that flow specifically from *higher* learning. Students will continue to develop along the multiple dimensions of personhood, and colleges can certainly assist in that maturation, but that is not the primary calling of higher education. What we seek instead is to evoke in our students a higher order of personhood, one that becomes whole, or integral, in some meaningful sense by virtue of the higher educational experience.

Second, we cannot sequester an education for wholeness in the cocurriculum. It must also be *grounded in the academic program*, a compelling expression of the curriculum itself. Knowledge developed through formal study lies at the heart of the academic enterprise, and it engages many critical dimensions of the whole person we presume to educate. The academic curriculum is also the one common feature of higher education across the country and around the world, so academic learning must contribute in some significant way to an education for wholeness for it to be complete and authentic. An education for wholeness must certainly go beyond the curriculum, but no effort to evoke wholeness can have integrity without a strong academic component. In addition, there must be strong ligaments linking academic programs to the cocurriculum to ensure that the learning process itself is as well integrated as the outcomes we seek. Evoking wholeness is itself a holistic process that musters its greatest impact across the entire array of educational experiences a college or university provides.

Major Elements of Wholeness

In part I, Don Harward identifies three major dimensions of liberal learning: the epistemological, the psychosocial ("eudaemonic"), and the civic.

Because they express the primary aspects of the persons we educate, those three dimensions provide a compelling framework for classifying the elements of wholeness we hope to evoke in our students. Along each dimension, I suggest three primary learning outcomes that are genuine expressions of wholeness *and* that mark a distinctively higher, collegiate level of learning. Along each dimension, the first outcome describes a *type of knowledge and understanding* that higher education can nurture. A second outcome in each set identifies the *higher-order capacity or skill* that higher education can elicit. Finally, the third element in each category defines an *ethic* we hope students will embrace in that dimension of life. There may well be more such outcomes, but these nine at least display oft-noted features of the educated person that are integrated coherently within and across the three dimensions.

Epistemic Wholeness

When we talk about what college students learn, our ordinary referent is the epistemological dimension, where we focus on developing breadth and depth of subject-matter knowledge. Often neglected, however, is the development of the *knowing person,* or what kind of knowers our students become. Mastery of higher-order subject matter is integral to higher learning, but so is becoming one who knows in the particular way that higher learning evokes. When higher education is successful, students go beyond earlier modes of knowing to develop (1) a coherent worldview, (2) the capacity for judgment, and (3) intellectual honesty.

Worldview

Students learn many things before coming to college; indeed, they often know more things about the world than their teachers. But rarely have they organized their knowledge of discrete things into any coherent understanding of the relationship of those things, how they fit together or influence one another. The vocation of higher education is to help students put the pieces together in a coherent and well-considered worldview so they can understand how the world works, establish core analytic principles of their own, and address the big questions of life.[6] It is important to note that in addition to systematizing discrete knowledge, a worldview involves definitions of value, primacy, and beauty, so it taps multiple dimensions of knowing that grow out of academic and cocurricular experience alike. Philosophers, artists, scientists, coaches, chaplains, counselors, and even facilities workers all can contribute to helping students build a worldview.

Judgment

Academically, first-year students seem fixated on learning the correct answers rather than exploring uncertainties. Socially, they want to know exactly where they stand with others to guide their behavior rather than navigate each situation on its own. In both realms, the new student lacks a fully developed capacity for judgment, which involves weighing the facts and circumstances and settling on a balanced conclusion or a prudent course of action in an uncertain and complex situation. Academically, judgment is perhaps the premier higher-order skill of reason, and as students benefit from good instruction, we see over time the blossoming of that capacity in their response to questions, their papers, and their dialogue on increasingly difficult issues. Likewise, we often see new students who make harmful blunders in social judgment and then build and demonstrate impressive social and emotional maturity. Such development of judgment clearly marks a person who has benefitted from a higher education.

Intellectual Honesty

I have chosen this term to describe the multiple dimensions of what we might understand as an epistemic ethic. Fundamentally, intellectual honesty entails seriousness about truth seeking and accountability to norms of truthfulness about the world, as well as self and others.[7] It first obliges us to do our best to discern what is true, recognizing that we cannot expect to grasp the full truth, and correspondingly, to acknowledge the limits of our understanding. The academic norm against plagiarism then amplifies that obligation by insisting that we acknowledge others' contributions to knowledge and that we not falsely claim as our own what others have created or developed. Finally, to be intellectually honest is to be a realist about the world and ourselves, to "confront the brutal facts," even when they run counter to our own assumptions or beliefs.[8] Academic instruction has long insisted on this principle, but one can readily see its applicability to life beyond the classroom in developing and using knowledge about all aspects of life with others.

Psychosocial (Eudaemonic) Wholeness

Today, psychosocial wholeness is often framed in terms of wellness—the healthy development of body, mind, life habits, and social skills—for the sake of both personal maturation and academic success. Noting the increasing lack of wellness among students today and its adverse effect on learning, early efforts of the Bringing Theory to Practice Project endeavored to refocus the academy on strengthening collegiate programs of psycho-social development and reconnecting well-being with academic success.[9] These are well-placed and needed efforts, but they retain the traditional assumption that the psychosocial contribution of collegiate education is to refine and elaborate the basic features of personhood. We must now reach further to identify the genuine contribution of higher education, academic and cocurricular, to personal development. Three higher-order aspects of wholeness are particularly noteworthy in that regard: (1) life meaning and purpose, (2) self-guidance, and (3) personal integrity.

Life Meaning and Purpose

What am I here for? What should I do with my life? In what can I find fulfillment? How do I make a contribution? These are the kinds of questions that collegiate education enables students to address coherently and systematically. Academically, students go beyond their taken-for-granted assumptions to examine classical answers to such questions and to form both a viewpoint about their adequacy and a consolidation of the most compelling elements for themselves. In preparing for a career, they should now go beyond saying, "I want to be a _____," as younger students often do, to determine why they want to do such work and how it will be meaningful to themselves and others. In relationships, they now should build on affinity and attraction to develop a sense of what is important to them in selecting friends and partners. In college, life meaning and purpose are therefore not given as something natural; they are rather considered and chosen, becoming "mine" in the fullest sense, filling out the students' sense of possibility and direction.

Self-Guidance

Prominent among academic aspirations is the goal of developing independent, lifelong learners out of students who start by wanting to know what will be on the test. But there is much more to self-guidance, which involves the capacity to steer oneself effectively through all the aspects of life. Self-guided persons are able to envision possibilities and set direction, to translate those visions into effective action to reach goals, to reflect on and assess one's own actions, to exercise personal discipline and self-correction, and to adjust one's own behavior to that of others. This capacity should be distinguished from being willful or selfish, as many new students are, because it is not simply motivation, desire, or self-regard that is required to be self-directed. What collegiate education fosters is both an internal cybernetic guidance system to navigate the world and a coherent sense of personal responsibility for the active management of one's life affairs and the consequences of one's own actions.

Integrity

Personal integrity is a collegiate ideal emphasized both in academic and in cocurricular programs, but too often it is simply taken as part of a code to be enforced rather than an educational outcome to be fostered. As Stephen Carter understands integrity, it involves three steps: "1) *discerning* what is right and what is wrong; 2) *acting* on what you have discerned, even at personal cost; and 3) *saying openly* that you are acting on your understanding of right from wrong."[10] Integrity therefore requires more than following a rule book, and higher education goes beyond that to help students discern what is right and wrong in particular situations, not just in general; to construct action as an expression of reasoned discernment, not just personal pleasure or pain; and to treat oneself as being accountable, not only for acting thusly but also for providing a morally coherent account of why one acted that way. This is the second great contribution that higher education can make to ethical development.

Civic Wholeness

In recent years, the ideal of civic engagement has become a prominent feature of collegiate education—not just service projects but also active involvement in the activities of the public square. Historically and philosophically, developing citizens has always been seen as an important aspect of higher education, but recently, educators have become much more intentional about citizenship education.[11] In AAC&U's renewed conception of liberal education, one of the focal learning outcomes is "civic knowledge and engagement—local and global," a central aspect of learning for personal and social responsibility.[12] There are many dimensions to civic education, and in a global age, education for civic wholeness is more complex and challenging than ever. Nonetheless, there are three specific civic aspects of persons that collegiate education is especially well positioned to foster, and they are applicable to most all dimensions of citizenship: (a) cosmopolitanism, (2) commitment to a common good, and (3) civility.

Cosmopolitanism

This term has recently been associated with issues of globalization, where it is certainly central, but its relevance is not limited to that context.

Cosmopolitanism involves a general capacity of persons to reach beyond social boundaries and engage people who are different from themselves in a way that effectively bridges diverse communities.[13] Appiah thinks of cosmopolitans as people who can navigate a "world of strangers" peacefully and affirmatively, the capacity for which rests on a sense of "obligation to others" by virtue of their humanity, and embrace the particularity of others, which he describes as "taking seriously the value . . . of particular human lives."[14] In its academic dimension, a baccalaureate education that introduces students to new social worlds and fosters an appreciation for them naturally drives in the direction of cosmopolitanism. Engaging others from different backgrounds in a learning environment, the quintessential experience of undergraduates even in the classroom, establishes higher education as the premier institution for learning to navigate difference effectively. That suggests that homogeneity and the tight bonding of similar persons is inimical to genuine higher education, which is designed not only to confront students with difference but also to nurture their capacity to appreciate and navigate it.

Commitment to a Common Good

The point of developing this orientation in students is not, as some worry, to inculcate a singular point of view about public policies or what the common good includes, with all the contention that implies. It is rather to guide students beyond their own personal concerns and self-interest toward the ideal and challenge of building communities that work for all participants. The *civitas* in question may range from the family to the globe, but in every case, it is higher education's vocation to nourish students' capacity and commitment to address public issues from the point of view of what is best for the community as a whole. The more diverse the community, of course, the more difficult it will be to discern and to realize that ideal, but one minimal baseline commitment would seem to be fundamental: to support human flourishing, individually and collectively, an ideal that aligns self-regard with collective interests. In that context, we seek to educate persons who center their lives on making life better for all, not just themselves.

Civility

Like cosmopolitanism, civility combines both a capacity and an ideal. Civility's competence is to participate effectively in the life of the public square in ways consistent with democratic discourse; its hope is to do so in a way that respects others engaged in public discourse and action, honoring their common humanity and citizenship. The special gift of civil discourse is therefore to confront differences of viewpoint and interest with a graceful and affirming counterpoint that discerns common elements and seeks productive ways to reconcile honest and deeply held differences. As "the sum of the many sacrifices we are called to make for the sake of living together," civility constitutes a public morality that holds communities together, especially when they are quite diverse.[15] The ethos of colleges and universities has long been built on this principle, perhaps uniquely among societal institutions, and it is even more important today as public discourse becomes increasingly coarse and caustic. It should not be difficult to see that its cultivation is built into academic dialogue and has a critical role to play in cocurricular life as well.

Evoking Wholeness

Educating the whole person in those nine dimensions is not a didactic process so much as it is a process of socialization.[16] Instead of filling persons up with knowledge, it involves drawing out their human capacity for wholeness in new ways. Rather than being marked by a threshold of achievement, it is much more an ongoing process of development and elaboration of personal capacities. It is therefore proper to characterize the education of the whole person as one of evoking wholeness, in which students do not simply *acquire* an education in the way they purchase a product or receive a gift; they actually *become* someone who exemplifies certain distinctive personal qualities, the qualities of an educated person.

For too long, we have accepted whatever wholeness students develop in college simply as a happy by-product of the learning setting, especially in residential colleges, where the greatest array of resources for whole-person education are typically mobilized. We have not been as intentional or systematic as we might in designing pedagogies and executing processes of learning specifically toward the objective of socializing persons for wholeness. When we do so, we will discover that evoking wholeness requires both academic and cocurricular educators to adopt some new approaches to (1) institutional alignment and coordination, (2) curriculum and pedagogy, (3) advising, and (4) assessment.

Institutional Alignment and Coordination

For whole-person education to succeed for all students, the entire institution must be mobilized for that purpose. Doing so may require significant change in the way colleges and universities organize the delivery of their programs, for it requires careful alignment and coordination of (1) educational goals and objectives, (2) curriculum and cocurriculum, and (3) theory and practice.

To become anything more than ad hoc or occasional, the major elements of wholeness must be framed explicitly as part of institution-wide learning goals. We cannot claim to educate the whole person unless we are intentional about and accountable for that objective across the entire institution. Further, all educational programs of the institution must also embed those same objectives in their goals and objectives. It is important to affirm that whole-person education itself must be *wholistic* in the institutional sense of being part of the entire educational program—not just core curriculum, not just residential life, but everything.

The second alignment critical to whole-person education is that between theory and practice. Professional studies programs often engage students in practice but often are not focused on the whole person. Liberal studies programs frequently address aspects of the whole person but often fail to connect to practice. Cocurricular programs are noteworthy for emphasizing practice but too often neglect theory. The education of whole persons, however, depends both on understanding that is rooted in theory and on practice that enables students to test those principles and to make them real in their lives. To achieve wholeness, for example, students cannot merely study worldviews; they have to build one for themselves. They cannot simply admire historical figures who are self-guided; they have to develop a practical method of guiding themselves. Bringing theory and practice together in both curriculum and cocurriculum is a large challenge, but it is critical to successful whole-person education.

The achievement of aligned goals and objectives entails an alignment of educational effort between curriculum and cocurriculum. Educational idealism notwithstanding, however, this has been contested territory as faculty and student affairs professionals have each claimed exclusive authority in one sphere and resisted encroachments from the other. Moreover, the conception and role of a cocurriculum vary considerably according to the residential character and community culture of the institution, so even at its best, the significance of this alignment will vary by institutional type. For those where cocurriculum is or can be robust, a new approach to realizing this critical alignment is required. Rather than claiming authority and educational roles on the basis of organizational position, we have the opportunity to coordinate educational effort on the basis of mutual accountability to student learning goals for whole persons, where all parties have both educational interest and some special expertise.

Curriculum and Pedagogy

This is an appropriate point to reiterate the importance of the academic dimension of whole-person education, which must have the capacity to deliver some level of whole-person outcomes on its own, whatever the character of an institution's cocurricular program. Where a robust cocurriculum is available to students, academic learning should also provide a strong foundation for a partnership that can deliver even more powerful whole-person outcomes. Thus, academic leaders and faculty must take educational responsibility for some of what has previously sequestered in student affairs. At the same time, student affairs professionals must adopt some of the important curricular and pedagogical tools that faculty routinely employ if they are to maximize their effectiveness in whole-person education.

The need to create new approaches to curriculum and pedagogy becomes manifest when institutions are well aligned for whole-person education. With regard to curriculum, the minimum requirement for the academic program is to *integrate* whole-person learning goals into the formal curriculum. For epistemic goals, that may simply involve making explicit what is implicit, but integrating eudaemonic and civic learning goals is a more substantial task, for they are often not even implicit in academic programs today, and curricular elements will have to be created anew. In the cocurriculum, the first challenge is not so much to integrate whole-person elements into programs as to *create* formal curricula to educate the whole person, for much cocurricular learning remains ad hoc and unsystematic, even if it is often powerful. It needs to be formalized and disciplined to ensure the widespread achievement of whole-person outcomes. In addition, just as academic learning tends to neglect psychosocial and civic goals, cocurricular learning often lacks any focused attention on epistemic learning, which remains fundamental to whole-person education, even in the cocurriculum.

Developing a pedagogy expressly for whole-person education is a second educational challenge. Considered a socialization process, whole-person education involves the formation of knowledge about the nine aspects of wholeness, skill sufficient to put them into practice, and a commitment to doing so. Because higher education is a secondary, consensual form of socialization that builds on the deep, primary qualities developed through compulsory engagement with parents, tutelage for wholeness relies primarily on an affirmative, experiential pedagogy combining elements from both academic and cocurricular pedagogies but replicating neither exactly. Knowledge of the elements of wholeness is built most effectively through case studies, in which students learn not just patterns of what has gone before but also examples they can link to their own experience. In complementary fashion, the skills of wholeness are best nurtured through coaching in experiential settings where students confront challenging life situations, some academic and some not. Commitment to living in wholeness, while sometimes enforced by sanctions for violating academic and community rules, is primarily fostered by student engagement with multiple role models who can demonstrate in their daily lives what it means to live a life of wholeness.

Advising

Student advising is a pivotal site for mentoring students toward whole-person outcomes, but it is rarely exploited for that purpose to any significant degree. That possibility is usually overshadowed by registration timetables and the competing demands faced by faculty and staff. Those realities only accentuate the fundamental emptiness of our idea of academic advising, which is conceived not as an educational act devoted primarily to learning but as a bureaucratic one of processing people through a system. Where there is serious educational advising, it tends to focus on the best students, to whom faculty are attracted, or the worst, who need to make up academic deficits, so most students miss out on that opportunity. Likewise, some educational advising does involve aspects of wholeness, but to the extent that wholeness is not formally incorporated in a curriculum or pedagogy, it does not arise naturally in the dialogue of faculty and students.

There are four important steps we can take to enhance advising for whole-person education. First, organize advising as an aspect of whole-person education by establishing an *advising protocol* for advisors and students that defines how advising is linked to the whole-person curriculum and how it can be used productively for whole-person development. Second, require students to produce *assessable learning products* from their advising relationship that express what they have learned regarding whole-person education in the process. Third, *deploy all faculty and professional staff* as advisors / mentors as a defined part of their workload. Finally, create *advising/mentoring partnerships* among advisors with different types of experience and expertise to ensure that students get multidimensional mentoring. Achieving such systematic attention to advising will certainly require some realignments, but the effort would benefit more general academic dialogue as much as whole-person education, and it could inspire some significant innovations in educational delivery that would profit the entire educational enterprise.

Assessment

The assessment of learning outcomes has gained great momentum over the past decade, but sadly, whole-person learning outcomes have not ordinarily been included in that effort. So the most important innovation we must undertake in assessment at this time is to include whole-person learning outcomes as a central topic of assessment. For many, whole-person outcomes are not readily subject to assessment because they are qualitative, even ineffable, rather than quantitative and directly measurable. Social science has demonstrated, however, that every human phenomenon can be measured and assessed in some way, even though the methods of assessment must vary according to the nature of the phenomenon, and the knowledge produced has different levels of precision and completeness. As Jim Collins has observed, saying we cannot measure such outcomes "is simply a lack of discipline." If we are serious about whole-person education, "what matters is not finding the perfect indicator, but settling upon a *consistent and intelligent* method of assessing your output results, and then tracking your trajectory with rigor."[17]

Consistent with the previous discussion of whole-person pedagogy, it is important to devise assessment instruments that are well aligned with the nature of the desired outcomes and how they are produced. Whole-person outcomes are not associated singularly with any specific major program, the core curriculum, or any one aspect of the cocurriculum, so they can only be assessed cumulatively across the student's total educational experience. That fact suggests a simple pretest/posttest model for assessing such learning, but because whole-person education is also developmental, there is good reason to assess whole-person learning periodically, perhaps annually, so the developmental process itself can be understood, and assessment can be used as part of the learning process itself, not just an up or down measure after learning is completed. Finally, in light of the learning involved in whole-person education, it is important that we not try to wedge whole-person learning into an artificially precise measurement framework but rather utilize qualitative measures based upon students' active demonstration of their capacities in the nine areas identified earlier.

The Ideal of the Educated Person in Higher Education

Since higher education became a mass phenomenon in the United States, people have taken an educated person to be someone who "has gotten an education," as if education is a consumer good not integrally connected to the person but merely possessed. The ideal embedded in that conception is *getting* the product, to finally possess it as a badge that qualifies the graduate for certain occupational and social opportunities. That narrow conception of what it means to be educated has eclipsed a more historic ideal of education as a transformational experience in which colleges actually educate the person to become someone who can lead a fulfilling life of wholeness, not just display a badge of ownership. The time is right to renew this historic ideal of the educated person by concentrating intentionally on evoking the distinctive attributes of wholeness appropriate to higher education.

That historic conception of educating the person was originally associated with small liberal arts colleges as a naturally occurring aspect of the educational experience. In the era of mass education, however, that ideal foundered as interest in professional studies came to overshadow liberal arts, as close faculty-student relationships became increasingly difficult to sustain, as close residential communities gave way to universities as small cities, as faculty specialists concentrated more on their disciplines than on students as persons, and as the cocurriculum claimed the task of building personal skills independent of academic preparation.

Fortunately, those conditions are no longer barriers to the achievement of whole-person education. Thanks to the fine work of the Association of American Colleges and Universities and other associations and national projects, the historic ideal of the educated person has been reconstituted in a conception of liberal education for the twenty-first century that includes whole-person educational outcomes, that drives liberal education into all the disciplines, and that ties liberal education to practice and engagement with experience in the world.[18] By framing a specific set of liberal learning outcomes within a context and culture of educating the whole person, the institution can make explicit what once was implicit and can demonstrate that intentional design of curricula and pedagogy, coupled with rigorous assessment, can make liberal education possible—even in large universities.

The burden of this chapter has been to analyze and articulate more extensively the whole-person dimensions of the liberally educated person that can guide transformative education for baccalaureate students in all institutions. The key to that achievement is to realize once more that whole-person education is *anchored* in academic learning and *extended* into experiential learning associated with the intellectual disciplines and with experience beyond the classroom. That will not occur by trying to import and assimilate all the dimensions of whole-person education from the cocurriculum into the academic program. Instead, it will become possible when we see that the general conception of whole-person learning includes what faculty already can deliver through their disciplines and through their scholarly and professional norms. As they embrace and expose those possibilities in their own work, we will make whole-person education available to everyone and magnify its impact by partnerships across the different sectors of our colleges and universities. Then we will realize the full possibilities and power of baccalaureate education to evoke the multiple dimensions of what it means to be an educated person in the twenty-first century. And as we transform our students' lives in that way, they will in turn transform our world in ways we can only imagine.

Notes

1. Thomas Christenson, "Educating the Whole Person" (unpublished manuscript, 2010).

2. Richard J. Light, *Making the Most of College: Students Speak Their Minds* (Cambridge, MA: Harvard University Press, 2001); Ernest T. Pascarella and Patrick T. Terenzini, *How College Affects Students: A Third Decade of Research*, vol. 2 (San Francisco: Jossey-Bass, 2005).

3. Stanley Fish, among others, has recently argued against the efforts to build a systematic program of whole-person education in colleges and universities. He suggests it is not our job and we can't do it well, so we should not do it at all. Derek Bok has offered a persuasive rebuttal to this point of view, and I would add only two points for emphasis. First, the evidence of significant college effects on students, even without intentional design for whole-person education, implies an ethical responsibility on our part to ensure that students get the best outcomes higher education can foster. Second, higher education provides the best institutional occasion, context, and resources for developing certain socially valuable capacities; few other institutions can make such a difference. Stanley Fish, *Save the World on Your Own Time* (New York: Oxford University Press, 2008); Derek Bok, *Our Underachieving Colleges: A Candid Look at How Much Students Learn and Why They Should Be Learning More* (Princeton, NJ: Princeton University Press, 2006).

4. Richard P. Keeling, "Creating a Culture for 'Campus Change for Learning'" (paper presented at the Presidential Leadership Coalition of the Bringing Theory to Practice Project, Georgetown University, Washington, DC, November 10–11, 2008).

5. I came to these conclusions in dialogue with Richard Hersh and Richard Keeling about their valuable and stimulating work on transformational education for the whole student, and I am grateful both for their thoughtful work, which provoked me to think anew about whole-person education, and for their generous intellectual engagement, which enabled me to sharpen my own thinking. Richard H. Hersh, Matt Bundick, Richard Keeling, Corey Keyes, Amy Kurpius, Richard Shavelson, Daniel Silverman, and Lynn Swaner, "A Well-Rounded Education for a Flat World" (paper sponsored by the S. Engelhard Center: College Outcomes Project, presented at the Leadership Coalition: President's Symposium, Washington, DC, November 10–11, 2008).

6. Anthony T. Kronman, *Education's End: Why Our Colleges and Universities Have Given Up on the Meaning of Life* (New Haven, CT: Yale University Press, 2007).

7. Sissela Bok, *Exploring Happiness: From Aristotle to Brain Science* (New Haven, CT: Yale University Press, 2010).

8. Jim Collins, *Good to Great and the Social Sectors: Why Business Thinking Is Not the Answer* (New York: HarperCollins, 2005).

9. Association of American Colleges and Universities, "Bringing Theory to Practice Project", www.aacu.org/bringing_theory.

10. Stephen L. Carter, *Integrity* (New York: Basic Books, 1996).

11. A. Bartlett Giamatti, *A Free and Ordered Space: The Real World of the University* (New York: Norton, 1988); Martha C. Nussbaum, *Cultivating Humanity: A Classical Defense of Reform in Liberal Education* (Cambridge, MA: Harvard University Press, 1997).

12. Association of American Colleges and Universities, "Liberal Education and America's Promise," www.aacu.org/leap.

13. Robert D. Putnam, *Bowling Alone: The Collapse and Revival of American Community* (New York: Simon and Schuster, 2000).

14. Kwame Anthony Appiah, *Cosmopolitanism: Ethics in a World of Strangers* (New York: Norton, 2006).

15. Stephen L. Carter, *Civility: Manners, Morals, and the Etiquette of Democracy* (New York: Basic Books, 1998).

16. Theodore E. Long and Jeffrey K. Hadden, "A Reconceptualization of Socialization," *Sociological Theory* 3, no. 1 (1985): 39–49.

17. Collins, *Good to Great*, 9.

18. Association of American Colleges and Universities, "Liberal Education and America's Promise."

7

Knowledge and Judgment in Practice as the Twin Aims of Learning

William M. Sullivan

What is the future of liberal learning? This most distinctive of American educational traditions is both an object of concern and often overlooked amid the changing academic landscape. The academy has moved toward an ever more central position in contemporary society, propelled by long-running connections between academic research with industry and government and its growing role in the preparation of personnel for the labor market. As higher education has moved ever closer to a universal rather than elite constituency, for many college has come to mean chiefly a route to the more desirable positions in the workforce. This idea has been urged on the public not only by business leaders and the mass media but also by political leaders of both major parties.

Such an educational program is inadequate to prepare students for a world grown increasingly intertwined yet precarious. Students need the contributions of the tradition of liberal education to enable them to make sense of the world and discern their place in it. Fortunately, a number of developments in the world of higher education are converging on a rethinking of liberal learning. A central dimension of these new currents is the rediscovery of liberal learning's concern with wise judgment and responsible engagement as necessary complements to broad knowledge and intellectual rigor. This chapter outlines the key issues involved in this new direction and draws out some of its implications for undergraduate education and for faculty purpose and identity as well.

The Challenge of Articulating a Vision of Liberal Learning for Today

These developments have changed the balance between what colleges and universities have most prized historically—the disciplines of the sciences, the humanities, and the social sciences—and the growing demand for the "practical arts" of business, engineering, technology, and the health professions.[1] The growing tendency to organize undergraduate education around instrumental, often specifically economic, purposes poses a serious threat to the future, and even the survival, of the tradition of liberal learning. Within the academy, however, this instrumental conception of educational purpose does not go unchallenged. When it is questioned it is most often by academic champions of critical thinking. Typically, such advocates of critical thinking argue that college exists to instill in students the distanced intellectual stance typical of the sciences and other analytical modes of thought embodied in the intellectual disciplines. This is advanced as a higher goal than the utilitarian aim of workforce training, and its advocates sometimes connect critical thinking with developing reflective citizens. These aims are presented, justifiably, as genuine benefits to both individuals and the larger society.

These two conceptions of education's purpose suggest two clashing agendas. *Agenda* is here used as a metaphor to get behind the abstract language of policy objectives and outcomes to articulate the ways in which education is pictured and enacted in actual courses of study and ways of teaching. To talk of an agenda means focusing attention on how a particular set of educational experiences reveals the things that are actually valued in a college experience. The metaphor of an agenda also connotes an effort to be clear about what institutions and their staffs are "up to" in their choice of educational content, the architecture of the curriculum and cocurriculum, and their practices of teaching and assessment.[2]

The instrumental agenda emphasizes the occupational outcomes of the college degree, often stressing practical skills over conceptual thinking and formal knowledge. Its opponents emphasize mastery of theoretical knowledge and conceptual capacities of the kind embodied in the arts and sciences disciplines.[3] The latter has tended toward an identification of liberal education with induction into a disparate set of increasingly specialized disciplines. On the other hand, the former, despite its sometimes defensive stance within the academic setting, seeks to make college a more direct and effective preparation for entry into job and career. Neither of these agendas has proved congenial to the traditional aspirations of liberal education, so reinventing liberal learning for our times must also include a reshaping of the role and identities of faculty as well as curriculum and pedagogy.

While the instrumental agenda can, at its most extreme, stress standardized routines and rigid educational programs, it is perhaps less obvious that today's academic disciplines typically also fall short of the broad intellectual, moral, and civic purposes once espoused by higher education.[4] What seems particularly lacking in many institutions is serious effort to provide an integration of students' educational experiences with the orientation and resources necessary for the ethical application of knowledge as individuals, as workers, and as citizens and participants in civil society. In any case, it is also striking that neither the instrumental nor the critical thinking approach seems very effective in engaging the energies and aspirations of many of the students who pass through higher education, as documented by many studies that show a pattern of large-scale disengagement and underachievement.[5] Other research, however, shows that this generation of students is concerned not only with the economic benefits of their education but also, to an increasing degree, with how they can make sense of their lives and live them well.[6]

The instrumental and critical thinking agendas often contend, and sometimes intersect, within national debates about the point and value of higher education. But the notion that higher education's purpose could be practical without being simply utilitarian and be intellectual without remaining detached is heard less often. Yet, one of the defining commitments of the tradition of liberal education has been just such a purpose: one that is practical in that it aims to enable students to engage with their lives, but open to critical exploration, and, most significantly, an engagement motivated by a response to values that transcend the individual. This is the idea of liberal education as preparation for a life of significance and responsibility.

Reclaiming Higher Education's Orphaned Aims

In the face of these challenges and rival agendas, American higher education is witnessing a number of efforts to articulate the goals of liberal education so as to reinvent liberal learning for our times. These developments are perhaps not quite a movement, though they do exhibit common features. Perhaps most importantly, such efforts reject the adequacy of either utility or critical thinking as exhaustive descriptions of the aims of higher education. In different ways, these emerging developments seek to reclaim what have been called the "orphaned aims" of liberal education, particularly joining concern with knowledge to students' development as persons and their engagement with larger values.[7] That is, they are attempting to articulate in new ways the traditional aim of enabling students to make sense of the world and find a meaningful place in it.[8] These include a new attention to the exploration of large, orienting questions about the world and human identity, about meaning and life purpose, all of which have been central concerns of the tradition of liberal education.[9]

Along with concern for imparting knowledge and developing intellectual capacity, these new currents also seek to affirm the importance of students' development as persons as well as minds. This turn toward educating the whole student is based upon more than ideals of uplift. It can draw upon a significant body of research. This work shows that even the economic and cognitive benefits sought by advocates of the instrumental and critical thinking agendas depend in significant degree upon students' development as persons, particularly their cultivation of curiosity about the world, self-understanding, and engagement with serious, long-term purposes.[10] While these new approaches to liberal learning give attention to questions of occupational choice and preparation, they seek to integrate all these aims by engagement with larger values and responsible participation in the life of our times. The growing movement for educating for civic responsibility and public service provides examples of how this can be done.[11]

It is this attention to students' development as persons, along with explicit preparation for using their knowledge and skills to engage responsibly with their lives, that distinguishes this movement for renewal in liberal education. These goals do indeed articulate aims that have been orphaned with the development of a university torn between disciplinary learning and instrumental training. Especially when contrasted with the more common conceptions of higher education as primarily concerned with either providing economic advantage to students or instilling in them habits of critical thinking, the turn toward a fuller agenda represents a movement of revitalization. It is seeking nothing less than to renew the academy's educational mission in its most important sense.

Rethinking Liberal Learning as Three Fundamental Shifts in Perspective

The reinvention of liberal learning for our times can be brought about by three fundamental shifts in perspective:

1. From an instrumental to a developmental understanding of the college experience
2. From a consumerist to a participatory understanding of learning
3. From an individualist focus to a social ecology of learning

First Shift: From an Instrumental to a Developmental Understanding of the College Experience

The underlying discovery, or rediscovery, is that college is a formative experience. There is abundant evidence that the time spent as students has profound effects on sense of world and self as well as on larger purpose. Furthermore, it is also clear that the influences within the undergraduate experience are multiple and operate in a variety of settings, ranging from the classroom to cocurricular activities to work experience and social life with peers. Where these influences converge toward common aims and values that support responsible learning, the overall educational effect is strong and positive. Where students experience fragmented and conflicting influences, the effects are correspondingly confused and contradictory.[12]

This means that college study is never simply neutral in its effects. It necessarily has formative, developmental impacts on those who undertake it. This realization undercuts the familiar metaphor of higher education as simply a way to acquire instruments for personal advancement. This imagines knowledge and intellectual skills as value-neutral resources from which students can choose what they wish. This instrumental understanding often describes higher education as a kind of market in which student-consumers (often along with their parents) shop for desirable tools and goods. There is, of course, truth in this picture. But it is seriously incomplete and misleading. What it overlooks is how educational choices affect the identities, chances, and purposes of those who make them. Because the student-as-customer metaphor underestimates the latent impacts college necessarily has on students, it can provide no help to student-consumers for understanding what their "purchase" is doing to, as well as for, them, in either positive or negative ways. This is really flying blind when trying to launch one's life course.

But for the renewal of liberal learning, this discovery has great positive value. If the totality of college experience is formative in shaping students' development as learners and as persons, then it becomes feasible to imagine a more intentional aim at those great educational goals college catalogs often espouse. Awareness of the formative effects of the overall environment is the first step. It renders the undergraduate experience more transparent to all involved. There remains the practical challenge of investigating those effects to discern how the educational mission might be made more effective. This shift in perspective enables educators to aim more concretely at an education that develops the abilities and commitments the institution wishes to promote.

Since the effects tend to be holistic, their accomplishment requires co-ordination and cooperation among the various parts of the undergraduate experience. This realization entails a need for considered action. To effect positive educational outcomes, there needs to be mutual agreement about the educational mission among faculty in different areas. But the effects will remain limited if the conversation and consensus remain only among faculty. They must expand to involve student life personnel, academic support staff, and all others involved in providing the college experience. The shift toward a formative understanding of undergraduate education therefore changes the game. It places new responsibilities and demands upon academic leadership. But it also holds out new levels of achievement for those institutions able to grasp the opportunity.

Second Shift: From a Consumerist to a Participatory Understanding of Learning

The second major change in perspective has been aided by advances in the understanding of learning. The great realization has been that learning is necessarily an active process of self-development rather than a simple transfer of information. Learning is less like consumption of a commodity and more like developing a skill or an expertise. Learning theorists argue that expertise is best developed through learning by doing. Indeed, modern learning theory suggests that even theoretical knowledge and analytical skills are learned more effectively when, rather than being taught in isolation, students are able to learn concepts and methods through employing them to understand actual contexts of living and experiences. Studies of the development of expertise from a wide range of fields, from athletes to musicians to artists and scientists, have uncovered common patterns that have direct implications for learning in college. Acquiring expertise in any area requires experience in emulating models of competent practice, response to feedback on that practice, and recurrent attention to the goals as well as the actions and understandings (such as the rules) that constitute the activities of that area of activity, whether it is athletic, artistic, professional, or academic.[13]

This more interactive understanding of learning complements and reinforces the conception of higher education as an ongoing developmental process that shapes the perception, imagination, and identity of all who undergo it. This shift in perspective holds two great potential benefits for revitalizing liberal learning: It can help educators become more self-aware and intentional about how their own activities contribute to larger educational goals, and it also suggests the possibility and importance of leading students to become more self-aware about their own development.

These implications of the discovery of the primacy of active learning also directly support the aims of the new movement for liberal education. Moving toward competence and expertise in any academic area begins with mastering procedures for describing particular events and objects in general concepts. This is analytical thinking. It remains the core focus of higher education. However, while college courses typically ask students to solve prestructured problems by applying analytical methods, the development of expertise—and the maturation of intellectual capacities—requires going further. Achieving these ends demands learning how to think with and through concepts in complex and unstructured situations: to learn how to make sense of ambiguous situations and to formulate problems as well as solve problems already given.

These are the kinds of cognitive capacities needed for flexible and resilient performance, not only in the arts and sciences but also in professional and civic life. In principle, liberal learning connects the aim of knowing about the world with the need to take up a stance within the world. This means "knowing that" must be linked to "knowing how," that the theoretical and the contemplative exist in interplay with the active and the practical attitudes. Too often, however, the arts and sciences provide too little teaching and active learning that can promote this development. So, part of the shift in perspective needed to reinvent liberal learning is a shift in pedagogy to foreground those forms of teaching and learning that contribute directly toward the development of intellectual sophistication and responsible engagement.

Decades of research have made clear what some of these teaching practices are and, at least in part, why they are effective. Examples include participation in courses that link various disciplines and points of view around big questions that matter for students and the world; experiential learning that involves direct experience with issues, sometimes in social service, and concepts under study and guided reflection on such experience; taking part in research along with faculty; learning to work together with other learners to both solve problems and better understand other points of view; and the intensive use of writing as a medium for exploring experience and constructing knowledge.

These teaching practices all involve putting concepts to use in contexts that approximate actual life situations, whether in scholarly, research, or practical contexts, allowing theoretical knowledge and experience to mutually influence each other. They also provide more intensive interaction between students and faculty and with peers than is typical, along with more intensive attention to forms of thinking and communicating. Such practices also directly encourage self-awareness within the context of cooperating as well as competing with other students. Such pedagogies can be shown to have high impact on both student engagement in learning and on student achievement, reversing the overall trends toward underachievement. Not least important, these pedagogies have proven even more beneficial for first-generation college students and those from underrepresented groups.[14]

Third Shift: From an Individualist Focus to a Social Ecology of Learning

The hidden soil nurturing this flourishing of personal development in liberal education is the set of practices and social bonds that sustain a community of learning. This social ecology is often taken for granted or simply ignored by both the instrumental and the critical thinking agendas, focused as they are on stimulating individual achievement, often in explicitly competitive contexts. Yet, recognizing the formative nature of college education directs attention to the importance of aligning the various aspects of campus life, including the academic core but reaching beyond it as well. This third shift, toward greater awareness of the role of an institution's social ecology in fostering student development, is also supported by a significant body of research on how learning occurs.

This research demonstrates that social bonds provide the indispensable basis for individual action, including learning and achievement.[15] Effective learning in schools or colleges depends upon networks of communication organized around shared norms and expectations of reciprocity. Such relationships encourage mutual respect and the trust that grows out of shared purpose. In fact, social bonds centered on a common valuing of learning are key factors in enabling individual development. (For example, it is by supporting the value of learning and by weaving it into the norms of household life that parents who have not experienced formal education themselves can still provide crucial support for their children's achievement.) The dependence of individual flourishing upon such networks of relationships is clear in organizations ranging from armies and team athletics to scientific and business groups. But it is also the case in both schools and higher education. Rather than mere "instruments" at the disposal of individual actors, the networks of relationships that sustain and enforce concern with learning constitute patterns of meaning through which individuals come to define themselves and find motivation to persevere and achieve.

This insight sheds more light on the first shift in perspective, from an instrumental to a developmental understanding of higher education. Individual intellectual growth depends upon participation in communities that value and support learning. When the pedagogical practices in use contribute to and strengthen the norms and networks that sustain these communities of learning, the outcome is student growth along a number of dimensions. This is because intellectual growth is intertwined with moral development: For instance, achieving greater competence depends upon capacities for persistence and resilience in the face of difficulty. And these traits of character have been shown to be grounded in developing a sense of larger purpose and meaning.[16] Participating in communities of learning oriented toward important life goals is a crucial resource for enabling such development to unfold.[17]

However, the educational practices of today's universities and colleges often do too little to activate these potentials. They typically direct students' attention toward mastering procedures for describing particular events and objects in terms of general concepts far more than toward learning how to bring such skills to bear on questions of moment in social and personal life. Analytical thinking is important, but a nearly exclusive focus on analysis in abstraction from life fails to utilize the high-impact practices that foster the growth of informed and responsible thinkers or citizens. The relation of training in analytical thinking to students' struggles for meaning and orientation in the world, let alone ethical judgment, is all too rarely given curricular attention or pedagogical emphasis.

Linking "Knowing What" with "Knowing How": The Key Role of Practical Reasoning

A recast liberal education, one that reunites the orphaned aims with instruction in the disciplines, must go beyond the purely analytical to provide students with experience and guidance in using theoretical knowledge and analytical tools to engage in deliberation and action. Thus, the emerging model of liberal learning needs to become centered upon teaching a wider conception of thinking, one that includes the "knowing how" rooted in the disciplines of practice as well as the "knowing that" of the analytical fields. That is to say that the teaching and learning practices must be aligned with the goals of liberal learning and be strongly rooted in communities of learning in synchrony with these ends. Achieving this kind of educational community is not just a project of restructuring the curricular architecture, of subjects and methods. It is also at its heart a matter of the faculty as a community of learning and practice—a community that today must expand to include the personnel on the "other side" of campus, in student life. They, too, are important educators, and their participation will be crucial to the long-term success of efforts to reorient liberal education.

Given the disparate starting points of today's faculty—especially when including both the arts and sciences and the professional fields such as law, engineering, business, nursing, or medicine—what could provide a common meeting point from which mutual understanding and eventual collaboration might develop? There is a strong candidate for this role of mediating discourse: traditional practical reasoning. Practical reasoning designates a form of cognition that goes beyond reflection to deliberate and decide upon the best course of action within a particular situation. Its aim is a reflective decision to act in a certain way in light of one's sense of purpose given the particular circumstances of the present. Therefore, practical reasoning demands that individuals understand the proper aims of the activity in which they are engaged as well as the context of that activity. It also requires perceiving the different purposes and perspectives of other participants in the situation and the capacity to balance conflicting perspectives while aiming at an outcome that seems best for these persons, in this situation, at this time. Such thinking is characteristic of professional judgment as well as being the key capacity of citizens and statesmen.

It is probably no coincidence that practices for teaching practical reasoning have been more developed in professional fields such as nursing and medicine, where it is essential that students learn to "do" as well as "know," than in the arts and sciences disciplines. As Lee Shulman has pointed out, in professional education, where students must learn to put knowledge to use in the service of others, the unit of study is often the case. A case is a unique situation, one that cannot be solved simply through the application of formula. It must first be understood and classified as "a case of" before analytical thinking can even begin. And the student must take an active part in this effort to interpret the situation. Because it involves the use of analogy and comparison, such interpretive activity opens the way toward reflection on the strengths and limits of various methods but also toward self-awareness on the part of the learner of abilities and weaknesses. Finally, in professional practice and training, such reflection is usually a group process, a search for clarity through debate that must end in practical judgment: to resolve the case in this way or that. Shulman argues that such pedagogy is needed to enrich and energize the liberal arts and sciences, making ideas come alive by linking them to the needs of the world and demands for action.[18]

Bringing Together Professional and Liberal Learning

If this is so, then a fully developed vision of liberal learning—one that is formative and developmental in purpose, focused on active pedagogies, and self-consciously engaged in cultivating communities that sustain networks of learning—cannot afford to neglect the contributions of the professional fields. Students typically study in these areas today for instrumental reasons and because the professions hold open the potential for both a respectable life and a meaningful way to contribute to the larger world. In this way, students are already engaged in moving between the liberal arts and sciences and the professions. What students most need in order to do this well is to learn to configure and use knowledge so as to enable them to make sense of the world and find a meaningful place in it. For this, collaboration between the liberal arts disciplines and the practical fields is essential. The good news is that such collaboration is possible as well as needed.[19]

Consider some examples drawn from a research seminar convened by the Carnegie Foundation for the Advancement of Teaching that intentionally brought together educators from professional fields as well as liberal arts disciplines.[20] The intent was to examine how a common focus on teaching students to reason in context might provide a means for bridging the often deep campus divides between the arts and sciences and the professional programs. Entitled A Life of the Mind for Practice, the seminar included teachers of the liberal arts side by side with faculty from medicine, law, education, and engineering. Imagine an engineer at the beginning of her career. A recent graduate, she is skilled in the analytic techniques she learned in her engineering program. But she finds herself working on an international project for the first time, collaborating with engineers from other nations who define their work differently than she does. How can these engineers work together, in a way that meets the various needs of the client, the employer, and the engineers themselves? In one engineering course that has been designed explicitly to address these concerns, students supplement the analytic skills learned in their engineering courses with knowledge drawn from the humanities and social sciences about how the engineering profession and its history differ across nations. Through assignments that require students to imagine the work of engineers in other societies and its ramifications for their own conduct, and vice versa, the course introduces students to important knowledge and skills—drawn from both the liberal arts and the engineering profession—for an increasingly global professional world and workplace.

Or consider another course, this time one that links the sciences with humanities, but does so by focusing on the practical concerns of personal, family, and civic life. Human biology provides students with an introduction to some of the key findings of the contemporary life sciences. But the course gets its significance from questions about the human import of these scientific discoveries. Rapidly advancing biological knowledge—think of genomics, for instance—is increasingly important to the ability to act well as voter and citizen, and even as a member of one's family. Think of the expanding range of decisions that has sprung up in the face of serious or terminal illness and end-of-life care. As advances in biological science and medical technology have extended life, they have also increased the burden of judgment and decision upon both health care professionals—which some of the students in the course will become—and families. How, then, do we think about these matters so as to be able to act well in a context where there is real disagreement about the basis for judgment?

These questions arise from the students' actual or anticipated practical involvements and commitments as responsible participants in society. In that sense, they have an intrinsic civic dimension. Finally, though, they are questions that stimulate the practical imagination. Among the several dimensions of personal identity, it is the practical imagination that proposes what we can make of our lives and the things we may hope for, individually and together. The scope of the practical imagination either expands or contracts students' capacities to engage with their lives in resourceful, reflective ways. It was Aristotle, one of history's great educators, who said that the institutions of a city need to be aligned in order to shape its citizens' acquisition of knowledge, skill, and character so they would care about their community and be able to contribute to its welfare. Schools, like his Lyceum, should be organized to concentrate this formative process. The effort to provide wider and more integrated horizons for students' practical imaginings remains the purpose of the reconceived liberal learning embodied in courses such as those described.

The faculty members gathered in the Life of the Mind for Practice seminar found surprising resonance across the divide between professional and liberal arts. That is, they found common ground and common cause around a specific pedagogical intention. All wanted to provide students with more than formal knowledge and analytical skill, important as these are in college education. They also aimed to provide students with opportunities to bring this knowledge and skill together in pursuit of important practical purposes that contribute to the life of the world. On this theme, the professional school faculty found they had a good deal to teach. That is because professional education must provide space for aspiring professionals to learn how to think like professionals in making judgments of importance amid the uncertain conditions of practical experience. (This often goes against the academic grain of professional schools, so that clinical teaching often acquires a certain stigma of an "impure" activity compared with the exposition of theoretical knowledge.)

In courses such as these, in both the liberal arts and sciences and in professional fields, students learn to frame their thinking through interplay of theoretical knowledge drawn from the academic disciplines and their particular loyalties as citizens; as possible future engineers, nurses, physicians, or pharmacists; and as persons with responsibilities for others. Through such experiences, students can explicitly learn how to move fluidly between the distanced, external stance of analytical thinking—the third-person point of view typical of most academic thinking—and the first- and second-person points of view that are internal to acting with others in a situation.

This is practical reasoning: the back-and-forth between general knowledge and the challenges and responsibilities that come with particular situations, an ongoing process of reflection whose end is the formation of habits of critical judgment for action. The pedagogical vehicles for teaching this movement between viewpoints span the professional and the arts and sciences disciplines: the case study, as already noted, but also the literary and historical exploration of character and response to challenge; the simulation; and participation and reflection upon actual involvements in the world in various forms of experiential learning. But their common feature is recognition that in practical reasoning it is always the involved stance, the point of view integral to purposeful human activity, that provides the ground and the goal for critical, analytical reasoning.

Knowing Why and Knowing When:
Fostering Practical Wisdom

The professional teaching practices that are of value for rethinking liberal learning, however, are principally those that are organized to develop just this kind of engaged, or practical, reasoning. This kind of reasoning involves "knowing how" to make knowledge relevant to actual persons in uncertain situations. But it also necessitates engaging with questions of purpose and value: "knowing why" some decision is right and, indeed, "knowing when" such-and-such an intervention is appropriate.

Unlike purely technical judgment, which employs methods to achieve pregiven ends, practical judgment involves the blending of formal knowledge with the concrete and value-laden dimensions of the situations of professional work. The pedagogies of professional education, then, necessarily involve a directly moral dimension: They must teach students what the profession stands for; they must seek to be persuasive advocates for the profession's highest standards of practice. By necessity, this is unapologetically formative education with public responsibility in view.

A more integrated form of liberal education provides a way to address a large problem confronting our culture, perplexing and frustrating individuals and institutions. On the one hand, progress in academic disciplines is like the division of labor that underlies economic growth: By focusing on a single criterion, it is possible to become progressively better at attaining it. On the other hand, where what matters is integration among several goals—as in professional practice and in civic life—decisions often cannot be broken down into single-goal issues; the several goals must be blended, and compromised, with other goals. In such situations—and most of life, especially civic life—the premium is on holistic practical judgment.

Such judgment can also be described using the traditional term *practical wisdom*. Unlike simply wielding an instrument or following the rules, practical wisdom requires an active understanding of the deeper purposes of social practices. Achieving the ends of such practices of marriage as well as medicine, of education as well as civic activism, requires a kind of reasoning that is appropriate to the practice involved. This is true of the professions and the arts as well as business and government. In recent work, Barry Schwartz and Kenneth Sharpe have powerfully recovered a venerable insight: that practical wisdom is the end of education. Drawing upon contemporary cognitive psychology as well as sociology and classical philosophy, Schwartz and Sharpe show how holistic practical judgment—perceiving a situation correctly so as to engage with it in the right spirit, making possible insightful deliberation and purposeful action—can be developed, but also undercut, through different ways of organizing both education and work.[21] This work underscores the importance to liberal learning of the shifts in perspective discussed earlier.

Important as professional education can be to the development of these capacities in students, it is the possibility of developing a holistic understanding of the world through study of the arts and sciences that makes liberal learning indispensable. Judgment has to be informed by both disciplined knowledge and trained experience. The ability to ask questions, investigate complexity without being overwhelmed, and keep refined judgment through participation in communities of practice is necessary for successful development of expertise in any art, craft, or profession. But as we have seen, this is far from the typical outcome of higher education.[22] What the liberal arts at their best can contribute to this purpose is more than tools or disciplines. The arts and sciences also contain surprising power, not only to provoke insight but also to enchant and beguile both teachers and learners toward wider horizons for living and deeper engagements with the world.

These considerations also suggest the need to articulate a new sense of identity for faculty. In their capacity as guides in the realm of liberal learning, they function as more than the disciplinary specialists that college and university faculty have aspired to become over the past century. There is an analogy here to the work of physicians. Just as in their clinical judgment, physicians must learn to deploy general knowledge in the service of practical judgments of what is important for the healing of particular patients in specific situations. Liberal arts teaching requires a similar kind of practical wisdom. As a recent study of medical practice concluded, medicine is "more than a science." It is a complex practice of healing in which "diagnosis and treatment are intensively science-using activities," though not "in and of themselves, science."[23]

In an analogous way, liberal arts teaching of the kind discussed in this chapter is not an "application" of disciplinary knowledge. Nor is it identical to induction into particular fields, whether professional or among the arts and sciences, as is typical of introductory courses in many fields. These are all versions of the educator as disciplinary specialist. Rather, genuine liberal education entails a different understanding of the liberal arts teacher as an intensively discipline-using educator whose aim is not so much specialized knowledge as the fostering of practical wisdom. Such a self-understanding is probably already widespread in the ranks of liberal arts faculties, among those who feel a calling to this kind of work. But it goes against the grain of the academy's more fashionable model of disciplinary specialist. If a genuine reinvention of liberal education is to succeed, it will require that this alternative faculty identity become public, recognized, supported, and advanced.

Notes

1. Steven Brint, "The Rise of the 'Practical Arts,'" in *The Future of the City of Intellect: The Changing American University*, ed. Steven Brint (Palo Alto, CA: Stanford University Press, 2002), 231–59; Patricia Gumport, "Universities and Knowledge: Restructuring the City of Intellect," in *The Future of the City of Intellect*, 47–81.

2. William M. Sullivan and Matthew S. Rosin, *A New Agenda for Higher Education: Shaping a Life of the Mind for Practice* (San Francisco: Jossey-Bass, 2008), 95.

3. For documentation and an elaboration of the educational practices and values at stake in this contrast, see W. Richard Scott and John W. Meyer, "The Rise of Training Programs in Firms and Agencies," in *Research in Organizational Behavior*, ed. Lawrence L. Cummings and B.M. Staw (Greenwich, CT: JAI Press, 1991), 297–326.

4. See, for example, the historical discussions in Douglas Sloan, "Harmony, Chaos, and Consensus: The American College Curriculum," *Teachers College Record* 73, no. 2 (1971): 221–52, esp. 246–47, and Julie Reuben, *The Making of the Modern University: Intellectual Transformation and the Marginalization of Morality* (Chicago: University of Chicago Press, 1996).

5. Derek Bok, *Our Underachieving Colleges* (Princeton, NJ: Princeton University Press, 2007), esp. 86–101; George D. Kuh, Ty Cruce, Rick Shoup, Jillian Kinzie, and Robert M. Gonyea, "Unmasking the Effects of Student Engagement on College Grades and Persistence," *Journal of Higher Education* 79, no. 5 (2008): 540–63.

6. Larry Braskamp, Lois Calian Trautvetter, and Kelly Ward, *Putting Students First: How Colleges Develop Students Purposefully* (Bolton, MA: Anker, 2006).

7. Donald W. Harward, "Engaged Learning and the Core Purposes of Liberal Education," *Liberal Education* 93, no. 1 (Winter 2007): 6–15, www.aacu.org/

liberaleducation/le-wi07/documents/le-wi07_Harward.pdf. This article reports on how the formerly orphaned aims of liberal education have been consciously brought together in the work of the Bringing Theory to Practice network, developed and led over the past decade by Donald Harward.

8. For a discussion of the range of new approaches, see "Symposium on Effective Practice," *Liberal Education* 95, no. 4 (Fall 2009), 6–45.

9. The efforts of national philanthropic institutions have also pushed this development ahead: The Teagle Foundation has promoted a wide-ranging series of experiments in introducing the "Big Questions" into a variety of curricular areas. Over a decade, the Lilly Endowment has supported the intensive development of campus programs in church-affiliated colleges and universities aimed at enabling students to consider questions of life purpose and values while pursuing undergraduate studies in a wide range of subject matters, including both the arts and sciences and the professional fields. The Lilly Endowment, "Program for the Theological Exploration of Vocation," www.ptev.org; W. Robert Connor, "Big Questions?" Teagle Essays (revised October 13, 2005), www.teaglefoundation .org/learning/essays/20051011.aspx.

10. The ongoing work of the Liberal Education and America's Promise (LEAP) initiative of the Association of American Colleges and Universities (www.aacu .org/leap) exemplifies this integrated approach: National Leadership Council for Liberal Education and America's Promise, *College Learning for the New Global Century: A Report from the National Leadership Council for Liberal Education and America's Promise* (Washington, DC: Association of American Colleges and Universities, 2007).

11. Ann Colby, Thomas Ehrlich, Elizabeth Beaumont, and Jason Stephens, *Educating Citizens: Preparing America's Undergraduates for Lives of Moral and Civic Responsibility* (San Francisco: Jossey-Bass, 2003).

12. Ernest T. Pascarella and Patrick T. Terenzini, *How College Affects Students: A Third Decade of Research*, vol. 2 (San Francisco: Jossey-Bass, 2005), esp. 629.

13. John D. Bransford, Ann L. Brown, and Rodney R. Cocking, *How People Learn: Brain, Mind, Experience and School* (Washington, DC: National Academies Press, 1999); Charles Bereiter and Martin Scardamalia, *Surpassing Ourselves: An Inquiry into the Nature and Implications of Expertise* (Chicago: Open Court, 1993).

14. George D. Kuh, *High-Impact Educational Practices: What They Are, Who Has Access to Them, and Why They Matter* (Washington, DC: Association of American Colleges and Universities, 2008).

15. The classic study is by James S. Coleman and Thomas Hoffer, *Public and Private High Schools: The Impact of Communities* (New York: Basic Books, 1987). The concept of "social capital" that Coleman used to describe these networks of norms and reciprocal relationships has been developed and expanded by other scholars showing its importance for many dimensions of personal and social development, notably Robert D. Putnam, *Bowling Alone: The Collapse and Revival of American Community* (New York: Simon and Schuster, 2000), esp. 296–305.

16. William Damon, *Path to Purpose: How Young People Find Their Calling in Life* (New York: Free Press, 2008).

17. Anne Colby and William M. Sullivan, "Strengthening the Foundations of Students' Excellence, Integrity, and Social Contribution," *Liberal Education* 95, no. 1 (Winter 2009): 22–29.

18. Lee S. Shulman, "Professing the Liberal Arts," in *Education and Democracy: Re-imagining Liberal Learning in America*, ed. Robert Orrill (New York: College Entrance Examination Board, 1997), 151–73.

19. The following section excerpts material that is used with permission from *Liberal Education* 96, no. 3 (Summer 2010).

20. This work is described in more detail in Sullivan and Rosin, *A New Agenda*.

21. Barry Schwartz and Kenneth Sharpe, "Practical Wisdom: Aristotle Meets Positive Psychology," *Journal of Happiness Studies* 7, no. 3 (2006): 377–95. See also their *Practical Wisdom: The Right Way to Do the Right Thing* (New York: Riverhead Books of Penguin Press, 2010).

22. See the discussions by Bereiter and Scardamalia, *Surpassing Ourselves*, and Damon, *Path to Purpose*.

23. Katherine Montgomery, *How Doctors Think: Clinical Judgment and the Practice of Medicine* (New York: Oxford University Press, 2005), 46, 52.

8

Assessment and Evaluative Studies as Change Agents in the Academy

Ashley P. Finley

The complex and incremental nature of institutional transformation in higher education means—almost by definition—that change cannot be attributed to a singular event, finding, or artifact. The markers of change will be slow to emerge. The leaders may change. The progression toward evolution may falter, decline, and even stagnate. Shifts in language, policy, and attitudes that are the building blocks of long-term transformation may be visible mostly in hindsight. These characteristics of change are not new; they are the hallmarks of transformation that underlie nearly every successful social movement from suffrage, to civil rights, to gay rights. Similarly, the educational movements of the twenty-first century are equally radical for institutions. They are exemplified by the paradigmatic, structural, and cultural shifts to more fully and cohesively integrate the foundations of a liberal education; the movement from an orientation that is teaching centered to one that is learning centered; the recognition to fulfill the institution's civic mission by preparing students to be full participants in a democracy. Yet, if change is slow, inevitably nonlinear, and the routes toward the goal numerous, how can we be sure we're on the right track once the institutional journey has been undertaken? The answer, in a word, is assessment.

Not all social movements are sustained, and far fewer reach the kind of radical outcome exemplified by change as enduring as, for instance, a constitutional amendment or the racial integration of America's public schools. What defines the difference between a successful movement that leads to substantial social, political, or cultural change and one that merely brings people together for a time and then fades away? Social theories on collective action have suggested that the efficacy and sustainability of social movements over time tend to successfully combine three key elements. The first is that social actors in the movement share a common view of what the *problem* is. This understanding is central to agreeing on strategies for change, agenda setting, and selecting leadership. The second element of a successful social movement is that participants have a common understanding of what the *solution* to the problem is. Without consensus on a solution, precious resources, time, and energy can be squandered trying to effect change that does not have wide compliance or necessary input. The final element for success is simple: *resources*. Social movements are built on the premise that many people can make a difference. But those people need a place to meet, to communicate, perhaps even a way to compensate for lost wages or time away from family. Even at a time when various forms of virtual communication have eased some burdens of time and space, nothing can fully eradicate the resource-intensive process of bringing people together.

The powerful lesson for campuses in their own efforts toward transformational change is not only that they need these elements but also that assessment is at the heart of each of them. It is through assessment that we can look critically beyond highly visible institutional problems to what may be more systemic issues. What if the problem defined as "retention" is not about enticing students to stay with glamorous living amenities, but really about the lack of curricular cohesion that fails to fully engage students in their learning and within the larger networks that provide them access to a community—at the campus, local, national, and global levels? Additionally, it is through the use of assessment that common (and even commonsense) solutions to problems such as retention can be effectively evaluated. Because institutions are dynamic, assessment is essential for evaluating solutions over time and understanding where to adjust, revise, or scrap them altogether. And it is through assessment that we can more fully gauge the resources necessary to effect change.

Concerns for resources predominantly fall into two major categories: the ones we must find and those we must make better use of. Assessment can enhance our ability to mobilize resources in either category and help us recognize the difference between the two. For example, assessment can help balance the focus on resource expenditures to consider not just basic implementation costs but also implementation review—assuring budgeted resources do not fall to waste.

The challenge is to develop the ideas of a successful social movement into a campus-level framework for the more effective use of assessment across the institution. How assessment can be used to target problems of institutional gaps between the strategic plan and curriculum design; how campus mapping models (different from curriculum maps) strategically outline solutions across campus silos to effect holistic change; and how resource assessment is positioned in connection with curricular goals are each matters of attention.

Assessing for the Problem

Much has been written about the approaches for assessing programs, such as first-year programs, learning communities, capstone experiences, and writing-intensive courses. And there are existing strategies for curriculum assessment (e.g., curriculum mapping, assessment of student portfolios). There are also approaches for institutional assessment (i.e., national surveys such as the National Survey of Student Engagement [NSSE]; institutional markers such as retention, persistence, and graduation; and standardized skills-based tests such as the Collegiate Learning Assessment [CLA] and Collegiate Assessment of Academic Proficiency [CAAP]). It is telling that there is very little alignment across these methods of assessment at the program, curricular, or institutional levels. For example, more than 80 percent of a representative sample of campuses reported using student portfolios to evaluate programmatic outcomes, while less than 10 percent of campuses reported using portfolios for institutional-level assessment.[1] Similarly, about 65 percent of campuses indicated they used student interviews for program assessment, whereas student interviews were used by less than 20 percent of campuses for institutional assessment.[2] Is this because desired outcomes at the program and institutional levels are too disparate to employ common assessments? Are the student voices and perspectives mined from interview data more relevant to the assessment of programmatic success than institutional success?

Differences in the methods of assessment on a single campus say something about how few outcomes are shared across postsecondary institutions. They also say something about the visibility of students at one level and not at another. But most critically, they say something about the missed opportunity to capitalize on the essential utility of effective assessment—a storytelling device. The challenge for those on campuses undertaking institutional change is to first ask and answer the following question: What is the story we want to tell about student learning at this institution?

Institutional problems are often defined by the need to redress specific institutional foci. The common issues are retention, persistence, and a pending or just-passed accreditation review. Any of these alone, and certainly all in combination, make for worthy objectives. But these foci require input and evidence from program-based and curricular-level assessment to provide an empirical foundation for decision making. To capitalize on the relationship between institutional goals related to retention and persistence, for example, faculty and administrators alike need to ask hard questions about what they are doing to encourage students to stay. Though little can be done about students who leave due to financial constraint or family obligations, more intentional efforts can be applied to the students who leave to find an institution that is a "better fit," "more challenging," or "friendlier."

While retention is often measured by how many first-year students enter their sophomore year, the necessary assessment of students' engagement in learning and the practices that facilitate their engagement must be a multiyear strategy. To engage in this assessment strategy means considering that the college experience comprises multiple parts that together form the collective volume of student learning at an institution. The narrative pieces from the first-year experience, to the general education curriculum, through the major, must be connected to fully capture the depth of cognitive development, learning attainment, and expectations for future growth. When an institution sets out to tell a story, assessment becomes the narrator.

A good story also needs transitions, the connective elements that link parts of the story together. In higher education, these connective elements are the effective learning practices that most engage students, challenge them to engage big questions, encourage their connectedness to peers and faculty, and foster their involvement in the community. A breadth of research indicates practices such as learning communities, service learning, first-year programs, and undergraduate research are all connected with higher retention, persistence, and graduation rates.[3] Yet when we undertake assessment of courses or programs that apply these practices, data on the learning outcomes associated with these practices are rarely scaled up to more fully inform evidence for outcomes at the institutional level. Similarly, assessment must also work backward from the institutional level to the course level in order to identify the critical gaps in the curriculum where effective practices and associated data on outcomes may be missing.

Thus, the real question regarding institutional change and assessment is: What story could institutions begin to tell if they were to more carefully connect the dots of assessment across the institution—from course-level outcomes to the institutional level? "There are many techniques for assessing goals, but the key is to find learning-related goals in common."[4] For many campuses, this is the essence of the problem in their movement toward change—to clarify the intent of assessment across campus, frame these intents in learning-oriented goals, and allow these goals to be informed by the mission and cultural history of the institution.

Assessing for the Solution

So if a common understanding of the institutional problem is the need to coherently connect assessment across multiple years of the student learning experience, what then is the solution? For assessment to tell a story about student learning, narration must be facilitated across various dimensions. Thus, the solution should connect a broad view of institutional assessment with a ground-level perspective on student work, interactions with peers and faculty, cognitive development, and learning outcomes attainment. The most effective way to frame assessment in this way is to remember that, not unlike a story, the pathway toward outcomes attainment has a beginning, a middle, and an end. The solution must therefore include plans for assessment at each of these stages to ensure a logical progression toward long-term outcomes. Second, assessment plans should consider that students, faculty, student affairs personnel, and administrators may share some common outcomes but not others and that the strategies and resources needed for reaching those outcomes will likely vary by the roles, duties, and responsibilities across these constituencies.

One of the most helpful solutions for charting assessment in this manner is to construct a logic model. Logic models are an evaluation tool widely used across various sectors of public life, from nonprofit organizations, to national funding bodies, to government agencies. "A logic model is a systematic and visual way to present and share your understanding of the relationships among the resources you have to operate your program, the activities you plan, and the changes or results you hope to achieve."[5] Aptly named, logic models are an effective assessment device precisely because their construction demands that the rationale for integrating program elements, connections between those elements, and the linkages to the intended outcomes all *make logical sense*. "[L]ogic models should depict, in a common sense manner, the relationship between the underlying rationale and the elements of evaluation, which include resources, activities, objectives, indicators, impacts (i.e. short-term impacts), and long-term outcomes of a program."[6]

Logic models facilitate the process of effecting institutional change in three major regards. First, the methodology for constructing the logic models—starting with the end outcomes and working backward toward resources—takes a high level of communication across various constituencies. Quite often the process of making the model is in itself considered to be as important as the actual execution of the steps. This is because in working through the step-by-step sequencing of the model, those constructing the model (i.e., faculty, student affairs staff, and administrators) must explicate their thinking at every stage. "By describing the characteristics of our programs that communicate relevance, quality, and impact, we foster buy-in from our stakeholders and audience. By including these characteristics within the various elements of the logic model, we communicate to others why our programs are important to them."[7]

In addition to facilitating communication and dialogue across change agents, an equally important impact of logic models is to simplify and clarify the intended outcomes and the progression of steps necessary for reaching them. Because of this, logic models should not be loaded with complicated details or presented in tiny font to accommodate every idea. The merit of the template is to force concision. Details will emerge within subsequent conversations when specific steps of the model are ready to be engaged. For the purposes of an institutional overview, the end result of the logic model should be an accessible, user-friendly schematic that can be easily shown and discussed.

Finally, once a logic model has been developed, it becomes an invaluable tool for envisioning the role of an integrated and intentional plan for assessment. This is not only because the outcomes have been clearly identified but also because each step toward meeting those outcomes has also been clarified. Assessment, therefore, must happen at every part of the model—not just at the end when it is time to assess outcomes. Often, even the most well-intentioned campuses focus on the curricular inputs needed for change, identify some of the relevant outcomes, but forget about the steps that must happen in between to connect these two pieces. There is an implicit assumption that if certain elements have been identified, activities arranged, and actors coordinated, evidence of outcomes will simply emerge. In actuality, this is far from the reality. Change takes careful construction. Without identifying the intervening mechanisms of the plan, the final analysis of outcomes will likely be confounding, if not altogether inconclusive. What follows are the descriptive steps of a logic model for institutional change.

Starting at the End: Identifying and Differentiating Outcomes

Though logic models can differ, they are often viewed in an "if . . . then" format, where plans for change are causally sequenced in a way that maps their logical flow from beginning to end.[8] In this basic format, logic models consist of four primary parts: inputs, activities/processes, outputs, and outcomes (see figure 8.1). However, the order in which the model is actually developed begins with first identifying the outcomes being sought and then working backward through the various parts of the model so that the final step is identifying inputs (resources needed for change). The rationale for backward modeling is to encourage model developers to focus on the outcomes they seek rather than the outcomes they end up with. "Starting with the inputs tends to foster a defense of the status quo rather than create a forum for new ideas or concepts. . . . In such a reversed process, we ask ourselves 'what needs to be done?' rather than 'what is being done?'"[9]

Beginning with outcomes, campuses need to conceive of the short-term, intermediate, and long-term goals or effects being sought. Long-term outcomes are those that may take years to be fully assessed. These outcomes tend to reflect large-scale cultural shifts (e.g., the institutional shift of moving from a teaching-centered to a learning-centered environment). Intermediate and short-term goals can be assessed in shorter periods of time, but these outcomes are necessary markers needed to indicate advancement toward long-term goals. For example, the long-term effectuation of a learning-centered environment might rest upon the achievement of intermediate outcomes, such as increased retention and changes in the faculty reward structure, that more fully recognize the scholarship of teaching and learning. In turn, these intermediate outcomes may rest upon the achievement of short-term outcomes related to the attainment of specified learning outcomes among students (including students from underrepresented groups) and greater engagement in the scholarship of teaching and learning among faculty.

It is important to remember that even though a well-designed logic model will include an inclusive list of desired outcomes, not all programs—curricular or cocurricular—must meet every outcome. A key strength of logic models is that they expose the most effective routes for reaching intended outcomes. Foundational programs, such as general education curricula, will likely be connected to most, if not all, outcomes. General education courses establish the foundational learning experiences and skills development that can be linked over time with more complex experiences through major and concentration areas and cocurricular opportunities. Other campus programs, however, such as study abroad, may best achieve a subset of institutional outcomes. Another subset of outcomes may be reached through writing across the curriculum programs, civic engagement work, or student affairs programming.

Additionally, the outcomes of logic models can represent multiple areas of campus life—outcomes at the student, faculty, student affairs, and institutional levels can all be included. Most effective is when model developers step back and examine the overlap across the desired outcomes in each of these areas. This enables a campuswide vision for the collectively shared and distributed responsibility for reaching institutional goals and outcomes—a view suggesting that students do not receive their degree from a single entity on campus but from the *whole* institution. Thus, the

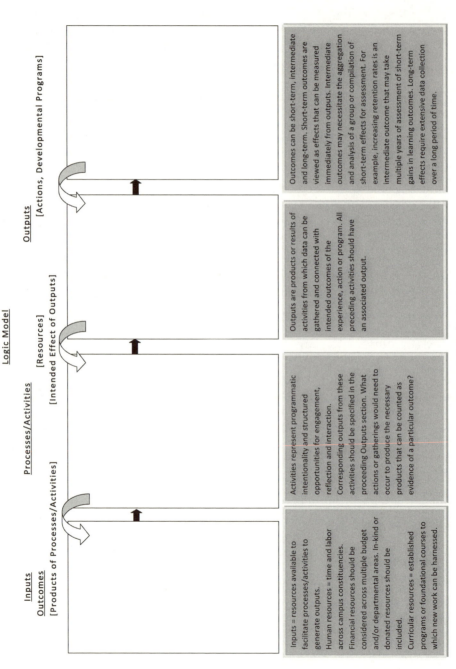

Figure 8.1. Logic Model.

use of logic models to identify and assess outcomes provides a holistic picture of student learning and development on campus, a way to account for the unique contributions of institutional mission and culture, faculty and staff, and community context.

Ascertaining the Signals of Change: Outputs

The second component of logic models is the outputs. Outputs are the products of student, faculty, and student affairs work resulting from certain activities or processes.[10] Outputs can also be characterized as quantifiable evidence to indicate outcomes are being achieved. Outputs of institutional change may consist of student papers, number of collaborative projects, and hours of community interaction or civic engagement. At the faculty level, outputs may consist of number of hours spent with students in out-of-classroom learning exercises or community engagement activities, as well as number of published articles on the scholarship of teaching and learning.

Creating Pathways to Indicators: Activities and Processes

The third component of logic models is the activities and processes. These are the actions that need to be taken to produce the desired or indicated outputs.[11] In executing institutional change, campus leaders need to identify the action steps related to organization, coordination, and communication needed to produce the intended outputs at the student, faculty, and institutional levels. For example, to reach the intended outputs for faculty and students, institutions may want to focus efforts of communication and organization around orientation activities (both for new students and faculty) and faculty development. Further, if, for example, an output involves increasing the number of contact hours or collaborative projects involving students' engagement in the community, activities or processes need to be pinpointed that enable students to meet and work with community partners to foster the production of such outputs. Similar considerations need to be extended to other areas of campus life that play equally critical roles in facilitating outcomes, such as activities related to student affairs and advising.

Assessing for Resources and Identifying Inputs

Finally, all logic models must account for inputs—the resources necessary to initiate all intended activities or processes. Broadly, resources can be conceptualized as time, money, and infrastructure. Specifically, these may be broken down into curricular inputs (e.g., the number of courses offered, the physical or technological space needed for learning), faculty time, budgetary allotments, and staff needs. Inputs related to increasing civic engagement on campus, for instance, must be attentive to logistical costs, as in costs for transportation, meals, additional faculty time, and coordination with class schedules.

Just as social movements require sufficient resources to achieve societal transformation, so too do the change processes of effecting institutional transformation. Resources in higher education will likely always be a topic of discussion. Tuition hikes, federal grant monies, faculty salaries, and buildings—the ones being built and the ones that *should* be built— usually dominate the discussion. But assessing for resources takes the discussion in a different direction. Resources are the first box in the logic model. They are the engine. Assessment facilitates the evaluation of two primary types of resources: the resources we have and the resources we need to find. With institutional outcomes carefully mapped and the processes for reaching these established via the logic model, there are multiple strategies for the assessment of resources of both types.

Because logic models illustrate the ways in which outcomes can be connected across multiple programs and sectors of campus, these models can also demonstrate the alignment of resources across these areas. When focusing assessment on the inputs section of the logic model, campuses should consider where resources may be overlapping. For example, attention to civic engagement efforts across student and academic affairs may provide an opportunity to share costs in transportation, programming, and planning time. Better coordination among faculty and residential life staff and student affairs professionals can help facilitate civic engagement experiences outside the classroom while easing burdens on faculty time and enhancing residential programming. Assessing for resources also means using results to not only tell us about outcomes but also illuminate the programs that are more or less effective in meeting these outcomes. Assessment at the institutional level should entail some attention to basic program evaluation. Programs that consistently do not produce compelling results (or any results because they are not being evaluated) should be eliminated or modified to liberate resources for more successful programs that have a track record of accountability.

Coupled with looking closely at alignment of resources for redundancies and opportunities to share resources, institutions should assess forms of ongoing institutional assessment that have strong budget lines and provide useful data sources. By doing so, institutions can more fully exploit resources allocated for institutional assessment to gather additional meaningful data related to student learning. For example, deeper analysis of NSSE data can be a useful resource for taking a closer look at particular outcomes associated with "deep learning," perspective taking, and civic engagement.[12] Additionally, course evaluations represent one of the most common, and commonly underused, embedded forms of institutional assessment. In their most traditional form, course evaluations are assessments of teaching (e.g., "Would you recommend this professor to a friend?"; "The instructor was organized"). Far less often, but more helpful to institutional goals, they can be assessments of student learning (e.g., "As a result of course material or discussions, I sought additional materials outside of class"; "This course encouraged me to examine a perspective from another viewpoint"; "This course encouraged me to reflect on previously held viewpoints or attitudes"). Even a selective retooling of course evaluations would be a more fruitful use of existing resources for the assessment of institutional goals.

Another method of effective resource assessment is through careful management of the institution's "assessment capital"—the willingness of campus constituents to help and participate in various forms of assessment during the year. This is done through the coordination of assessment efforts to strategically account for the timing of survey administrations, the data being collected, and who is being asked to participate. The consequence of overexpending assessment capital is that a culture of assessment is replaced by a culture of oversurveying, a key symptom of which is low response rates. Greater accountability of survey administrations helps discourage redundancies in survey topics, oversurveying of particular populations of students, and an even distribution of administrations during the academic year. Both of these steps, for students and faculty, will help ease survey fatigue. Once there is greater coordination across surveys, campuses can go a step further by being more creative in sampling techniques. Students are too often surveyed as a population, either as an entire student body or as a cohort within a particular class year (e.g., all first-year students). Institutions would be better served by employing random sampling techniques; selecting only a random portion of available students would still produce a representative and statistically viable sample, and a new sample of students could be chosen for subsequent administrations. Thus, each survey would draw from a new, or less frequently surveyed, pool of students and faculty. The hope is that by decreasing the frequency with which students and faculty are solicited for participation, survey fatigue will also decrease. Ultimately, through the careful management of assessment capital, institutions can begin to develop a culture of assessment by first demonstrating to students and faculty that their time and voices are valued.

Final Thoughts

Achieving institutional change is not easy or fast, but it is also not impossible. The mechanisms of what have long guided the success of social movements may provide helpful solace to those institutions embarking on the journey. Being able to identify the problem, a viable solution, and the resources to get there must be part of the overarching framework for change. But beneath these theoretical underpinnings is the practical guidance of a logic model to pull the vision at ten thousand feet down to the classroom level, the residence hall, and the common areas of campus life. Every strategy for change needs both of these: the overarching vision and the plan for execution.

Moreover, fundamental for both vision and execution is the purposeful integration of meaningful, outcomes-based assessment. This is the means through which to connect the problem to the solution and to interrogate the availability of necessary resources. And within the practical structure of the logic model, assessment becomes the strategy for telling the story of how change will occur. Working backward, campuses can find the narrative voice of assessment to talk about the outcomes, outputs, activities, and inputs that will guide the change mechanisms. Furthermore, the unifying intent of this model is to allow the story of institutional change to be shared across campus as each stage of assessment is implemented and developed. Through engaging in dialogue, multiple campus constituencies are invited to establish expectations and perspective for success at the next stage.

The vitality of this strategy lies squarely on the foundations of what social movements are—a collective of people working toward a common goal. And the ability of a logic model to foster communication is a crucial component of this collective work. Without dialogue, without simplification to facilitate shared understanding, without agreeing that it will take everyone's efforts to reach the end point—change cannot happen. Assessment is not the answer to institutional change—it is simply the collective means toward it.

Notes

1. George Kuh and Stanley Ikenberry, *More Than You Think, Less Than We Need: Learning Outcomes Assessment in American Higher Education* (Champaign, IL: National Institute for Learning Outcomes Assessment, 2009), 3.

2. Kuh and Ikenberry, *More Than You Think*.

3. Jayne E. Brownell and Lynn E. Swaner, *Five High-Impact Practices: Research on Learning Outcomes, Completion, and Quality* (Washington, DC: Association of American Colleges and Universities, 2010).

4. Thomas Angelo, "Doing Assessment as if Learning Matters Most," *AAHE Bulletin* 51 (May 2009): 5.

5. W.K. Kellogg Foundation, *Logic Model Development Guide* (Battle Creek, MI: W.K. Kellogg Foundation, 2004), 1.

6. Ralph Renger and Alison Titcomb, "A Three-Step Approach to Teaching Logic Models," *American Journal of Evaluation* 23, no. 4 (2002): 493–503.

7. Paul McCawley, *The Logic Model for Program Planning and Evaluation* (Moscow: University of Idaho Extension, 1997), 2, www.uiweb.uidaho.edu/extension/LogicModel.pdf.

8. See Kellogg Foundation, *Logic Model Development Guide*; P.H. Rossi, M.W. Lipsey, and H.E. Freeman, *Evaluation: A Systematic Approach*, 7th ed. (Thousand Oaks, CA: Sage, 2004).

9. McCawley, *Logic Model for Program Planning and Evaluation*, 1.

10. See Kellogg Foundation, *Logic Model Development Guide*. See also Barry Isaacs, Cinda Clark, Susana Correia, and John Flannery, "Utility of Logic Models to Plan Quality of Life Outcome Evaluations," *Journal of Policy and Practice in Intellectual Disabilities* 6, no. 1 (2009): 52–61.

11. Kellogg Foundation, *Logic Model Development Guide*.

12. National Survey of Student Engagement, "Creating Scales and Scalelets," http://nsse.iub.edu/_/?cid=368.

9

Fostering Faculty Leadership for Sustainable Change in the Academy

Adrianna J. Kezar and Alice (Jill) N. Reich

Promise: Jan has been at Midwestern Liberal Arts College for five years and is excited to integrate service learning into her biology course. In graduate school she and some fellow students created a field-based experience that she wants to replicate as part of her teaching. Because of Jan's interest in new methods of teaching, her dean sent her to a conference about service learning. She worries about the time commitment as her colleagues have emphasized the importance of research for tenure and promotion, but she has met several other faculty members on campus through the center for teaching and learning who have already included it in their courses and have offered to share best practices and advice with her. She wants more people in her department to think about the role of service learning and has recently brought it up in curriculum discussions. Because of her vocalness, she has been put on a committee that is working on changes. Jan has been chatting with other like-minded colleagues across campus for tips about how to navigate the curriculum committee and achieve her goals. She is really thankful that she became connected to the center for teaching and learning network.

Perils: Don is a sociology faculty member at a large, urban public institution and has been there for fifteen years. He has been interested in getting students more involved in voting and political participation. He has spoken to colleagues over the years, mostly senior, but they do not see the importance of his ideas. In fact, they are often fairly hostile. When Don mentions the issue to his chair, she says, "You know it is always like that with faculty. They just resist new ideas." Younger colleagues have come in with an interest, but he does not want to burden them until they get tenure. He feels really isolated and talks to the dean about his passion for citizenship education. His dean says he is really busy dealing with the declining state budget and cutting costs, but perhaps they can talk next fall. Don is beginning to feel the pinch of extra administrative work now that the campus has increased the number of non-tenure-track faculty. He decides to shelve his ideas, hoping for a better time.

Faculty as the Necessary Agents of Sustainable Change in the Academy

These two narratives foreshadow the theme of this chapter: that faculty leadership, a necessary component of successful academic change, is at a time of both promise and peril. Careful attention and creative intervention are needed to capitalize on the promise and overcome the perils currently in play. But before we dig deeper into this theme, it is important to understand why faculty leadership has become a prominent ingredient in contemporary calls for change in the academy.

Several recent national studies exploring institutional change and transformation have documented faculty leadership as a key ingredient for success.[1] The largest study of institutional transformation and change in higher education demonstrated that shared leadership among the various stakeholders (administration, faculty, and staff) on campus is necessary for creating buy-in and ownership, enthusiasm, and energy for momentum.[2] It is essential for creating a vision connected to implementation practicalities and for the shift in values that must permeate the organization. Deep and sustained change requires persistent and substantive faculty involvement.

Moreover, while showing the importance of multilevel leadership or shared responsibility for change, these studies point in particular to the importance of faculty leaders who play a variety of key roles.[3] For example, faculty leaders can be cultural influencers, shifting faculty values and perspectives, particularly in disciplines that have become ossified and with colleagues resistant to change. These faculty leaders serve as political influencers, winning over colleagues to the change even when concrete institutional rewards are unavailable. And often they are the academic entrepreneurs who garner the revenues or grants to support change and forge partnerships. Too often today we think of these change activities as part of administrative work rather than activities led by the faculty. Yet studies of change describe complex and very large institutions of higher education with dual authority structures where faculty have delegated authority because of their expertise and knowledge about teaching and learning. This dual authority structure requires shared leadership.

While faculty are needed agents in change, within many institutions they have felt pressured because of increased workloads and changing incentives around research and teaching to abdicate authority to administrators. Furthermore, studies of faculty leadership demonstrate there has been little infrastructure in place to support skill development for faculty to be leaders. Typically, faculty do not learn leadership skills in graduate school; in fact, much of their training and social structures work against the type of skills necessary to be a good leader, skills such as vision development, networking, politics, and relationship building. Once they become faculty, they can continue to work quite autonomously, so it is easy to forget the value and necessity of working with others, essential ingredients for creating change. Thus, both organizational pressures and individual skill and motivation have created challenges for fostering faculty leadership. But the literature on faculty leadership indicates there is more focus on the need for individual development than on recognition of organizational constraints. In spite of our earlier history and traditions of shared governance, higher education today is trailing behind other sectors, such as business, that have for several decades recognized that meaningful change requires ownership and involvement from stakeholders throughout the organization.[4]

In this chapter, we explore some of the complexities involved in building the faculty leadership necessary for the kind of deep, sustainable change discussed in this book. We divide these complexities into two parts: (1) the perils of engaging faculty and (2) the promise of engaging faculty. This approach is unique in moving beyond the focus of most recent research that has identified and documented the key role of faculty leaders, examined how faculty and the administration need to work together in a shared or multilevel leadership process, and described some ways to build the skills needed among faculty. These contributions, while important, have ignored and hence not capitalized on the context in which faculty leadership already takes place. In order to effectively capitalize on existing forms of faculty leadership, we need to understand the current state of the academy and how this affects the possibilities for leadership. We will delineate new strategies for fostering the skills that are necessary components of leadership and propose new ways to overcome the organizational obstacles now facing faculty seeking to lead change on their campuses. The past focus on faculty skill development is less relevant because faculty are increasingly learning leadership skills as part of inter- and multidisciplinary research and teaching projects, and their interest in and commitment to becoming change agents is fostered by their involvement in engaged learning. More important now is to delineate how leadership skills are being learned, to expand these skills and foster their use across a range of situations, and to overcome the obstacles that prevent effective leadership among the current generation of faculty.

Our audience is academic administrators and policy makers who make decisions that impact campuses; faculty (both tenure-track and non-tenure-track) who may be interested in leading campus change; and staff who are often looking for partners in creating change. In short, our thesis is that the type of engaged and transformative learning environment proposed in this book not only requires but also builds faculty leaders. It is a timely topic because the new generation of faculty has many individuals passionate about this kind of learning for their students and themselves. But the current academic context and structures work such that faculty have few opportunities to take advantage of their commitment. Only with awareness of these conditions can we hope to reverse these trends, thereby fostering the leadership necessary for developing and sustaining the transformative learning environment we seek.

The Perils of Faculty Leadership: Glass Half Empty

Historically, faculty leave graduate school with no leadership training and enter a socialization system on campus that, at best, informally provides some of them with knowledge about how to lead. Few empirical studies exist, but conventional wisdom suggests that faculty have typically developed skills as leaders through the socialization that takes place during the tenure process and through involvement in shared governance on campus. Traditionally, tenure-track junior faculty are mentored by more senior-tenured faculty who explain the institutional structure, politics, key issues on campus, and committees central to making a difference. Through this socialization process, junior faculty are introduced to shared governance processes such as a Faculty Senate, committee structures, ad hoc groups, and other aspects of governance with which faculty are expected to be involved as they become associate and full professors. Through the concept of shared governance, faculty are expected to play a leadership role by providing their voices on key issues that are important to the institution. In these ways, faculty begin to identify as leaders as they learn about the informal processes (relationships that should be developed or networks to join) and skills (politics) needed to make a change.

While it is debatable whether or not consistent mentoring occurs on many campuses, whether socialization processes are strong across different institutional types, or whether shared governance is more an ideal than a reality, there is a sense that in the past these structures played some role in fostering leadership among at least some faculty at some institutions. And although there have long been few visible incentives or concrete rewards for leadership, it was considered an expectation of the profession once one had achieved a certain status. While not perfect, this system of socialization and shared governance could be relied on to produce faculty leaders. To be sure, some campuses did a better job than others.

Unfortunately, even this tenuous system (tenure, socialization and shared governance, professional norms for expecting and naming leaders) of fostering faculty leadership has been in decline over the last twenty years. In some sectors, such as community colleges, the change started much earlier as large student enrollments, reduced funding, and external pressures forced institutions to hire increasing numbers of part-time faculty, to move away from a predominantly tenure-track faculty, to proceed toward unionization, and to lose shared governance structures. These same factors are now occurring across the entire academy. The number of non-tenure-track faculty has risen at all institutional types, presently representing two-thirds of our nation's faculty. Not just two-year institutions but the majority of four-year institutions are now staffed predominantly by non-tenure-track faculty who are not socialized to campus culture, receive little if any orientation, and are not thought of by themselves or others as potential leaders.[5] Thus, most often they are not included in shared governance activities and typically have few expectations about campus leadership.[6] If the current trends in hiring non-tenure-track faculty (three out of four appointments) continue, then tenured faculty will become a marginal part of our higher education institutions, perhaps existing only within elite research universities or liberal arts colleges or within a few select departments. We also know that non-tenure-track faculty, particularly part time, use less engaging pedagogies, focus less on diversity, and spend less time with students.[7]

Increasingly, the tenure-track faculty who remain find themselves involved less with overall institutional affairs and more with local or departmental decision making. In general, they have less of a voice in the overall institution, its planning, and its development.[8] Faculty find themselves increasingly as "managed professionals," with the administration making the major decisions for the institution and the faculty having less and less input into the overall work environment.[9] Academic values are increasingly being short shrifted for more corporate or bureaucratic values of the administration.[10] In a national study, Schuster and Finkelstein reported that faculty feel as if they have less influence now than they did in previous decades.[11] At the same time as they are reporting a decline in the broader mechanisms of shared governance, they report more work in service and local administration (paperwork, accountability and assessment, admissions, scheduling). These dual-authority paths may be exacerbated by the uneven distribution of tenure- to non-tenure-track faculty further limiting their time and ability to be involved in leadership and broader change efforts. You may be lucky enough to be on a campus with fewer non-tenure-track faculties, a more robust tenure system, and healthy shared governance processes. Unfortunately, if past trends continue, it may be slowly eroding without your knowledge, as many campuses have shifted their workforces in the last ten years with little awareness by faculty.[12]

As if this were not a difficult enough system to navigate, faculty have long argued that institutional and professional rewards are mostly for publishing. More recently, public attention on teaching and student learning has begun to build emphasis in this area as well. But few, if any, rewards for being involved in campus leadership exist. Moreover, the pressure to publish has intensified over the last three decades. Schuster and Finkelstein found that publication standards for tenure are more than triple what they were in the 1970s.[13] Campuses (except for community colleges and some undergraduate institutions) increasingly place significant weight on publications for tenure and promotion and place virtually no weight on other criteria. Not only are service and leadership short shrifted, but the overwhelming publication requirements can focus faculty efforts at the assistant and associate level exclusively on publication. Moreover, with increasing public attention on student learning, the implications for service are further compromised.[14]

In addition, faculty report increasing stress due to heavier workloads compared with earlier decades. In recent years, faculty have been asked to try new pedagogies and retool their teaching on an ongoing basis, to integrate new technologies into their classrooms, and to assess their teaching and student learning.[15] The dramatic increase in knowledge production in some fields makes further demands on faculty time—just keeping up with regular advances in one's field can become all consuming.[16] Because of all these increasing demands, the work week for faculty is increasing, requiring ever more hours to complete a regular workload. As women have entered the professoriate, and they do in ever-increasing numbers, they have to manage the double burden of household responsibilities and work. Even the most recent data show that these burdens are generally not shared by their spouses, including care for elderly parents.[17]

Why focus on all these barriers and challenges? Without an awareness of them, we cannot foster change by creating the kinds of support needed for faculty to be successful leaders. If the challenges are not recognized, it is even more likely that faculty will burn out and relinquish leadership roles in the future. Alas, we cannot offer a quick "silver bullet" solution, but we believe that faculty stakeholders can together build solutions. We must change our mind-set about faculty life, recognizing that being in the academy is much different than it was just a generation ago. We must build faculty leaders who understand the constraints yet find within them new, efficient, effective, and sustainable solutions for our campuses.

The Promises of Faculty Leadership: Glass Half Full

While many of the changes in the academy create a difficult environment for developing leadership, other shifts can be used to foster faculty leadership. There are at present several factors that can support the change we seek. These include changing demographics, faculty retirements, interdisciplinary teaching and research, and new paradigms for teaching and learning. In short, there is a cadre of faculty with a vision and commitment for change who are already in clusters and networks, positioned to work collectively, and who often already have leadership skills.

Numerous studies document that the diversification of faculty results in more women and underrepresented minorities in higher education institutions.[18] These are just the people who tend to experiment with new and innovative pedagogy such as service learning, collaborative learning, and the like.[19] Research reveals varying reasons for the relationship between gender/race and use of innovative pedagogies, including an interest in changing power relationships in the classroom, the importance of helping one's community, and/or recognition of needing to work with a variety of individual learning styles among an increasingly diverse student body. No matter the reason, the trend results are the same: These new faculty are more likely to engage in practices that create the type of learning environment proposed in this book. Gappa, Austin, and Trice found that new faculty have such a deep passion for these issues (service, citizenship, community-university partnerships) that they are drawn into just the kind of work that ultimately builds the leadership skills that can then be used to create the desired change.[20]

At the same time, graduate students are being introduced to new paradigms related to research and knowledge production. In more recent years, action research, critical theory, community-based research, and even interpretive research approaches have required greater connections with communities outside of the academy for the creation of knowledge. All these approaches encourage faculty to become engaged with their research topics in ways that are connected and holistic, breaking away from the narrow, more objective stance toward their area of study, their students, and the communities they research. Both of these trends—new demographics and socialization to new paradigms—create a group of faculty who are mastering leadership skills as a part of carrying out their research agenda and becoming successful teachers. Among the new professoriate are many who are well poised to be leaders with the vision for and commitment to the kind of change espoused in this book.

Change such as we seek requires a critical mass to make a sustained difference. Another trend that bodes well for this shift is the mass retirement of faculty we are experiencing. Approximately 50 percent of the faculty retired between 2001 and 2010; this was the most massive turnover of faculty in the history of higher education.[21] While numbers were smaller than predicted because of the economic recession and lack of a mandatory retirement age, a huge shift has nonetheless taken place and is still in progress in some institutions. The faculty who were part of the significant expansion of the higher education system in the 1960s and 1970s are now retiring. And because these retirements are occurring in a wave, rather than slowly over time, many campuses are experiencing clusters of hires within departments and schools. This trend represents an opportunity for the new hires clustered in groups to create a new value system and to support the new vision they have for teaching and research. While this may not be occurring in every case, it represents an untapped source of leadership that, when recognized, can be fostered and utilized.

Not only are a new commitment and vision in place for leading this change, but the very skills necessary to implement this change are being learned through the processes many of these faculty bring to their teaching and research. Increasingly, graduate students are being introduced to community-based and inter- and multidisciplinary research. The kinds of community-based, inter- and multidisciplinary work described in this book require that faculty work in groups and teams. The skills needed to work effectively in these groups require faculty to grow in ways that help them be leaders. They learn how to work effectively in a collective endeavor toward a desired outcome, a key ingredient for any change agent. They are learning communication skills; relationship building; and the politics of working in teams and groups within larger units, organizations, and communities. A typical barrier preventing faculty from learning to be effective change agents is that they have difficulty moving a change beyond their department or local unit because they do not understand how to communicate with a broad range of people. However, civic engagement and community-based work bring faculty into contact with individuals in other departments and units in and outside of the academy. All these skills are helping to train and socialize faculty in important capacities on which campuses can build and change. Thus, at the same time that faculties are increasingly structured in ways that can work against their leading institutional change, we have a great opportunity to enhance faculty leadership for sustained change. A critical mass of new faculty with a passion, vision, and commitment for engaged learning, who think about research and teaching in more connected ways, are gaining leadership skills through their work and creating a sustaining system for desired change. As they advance their teaching and research agenda, they are simultaneously learning to be leaders.

The promise outlined in this section is generally ignored as a source of leadership in the academy, and so it remains an untapped potential for institutions and individuals interested in creating a more engaged learning environment. We are not suggesting that all new faculty are committed to engaged learning or have the kinds of teaching and interdisciplinary research agenda that help them develop leadership skills, but we are proposing that these are increasing trends that, when recognized and fostered, can be leveraged to foster the very change agents the new system requires.

What Can Be Done to Enable Leadership in this Context of Perils and Promise?

Faculty involved in engaged pedagogies and/or community-based, interdisciplinary research are at the same time developing leadership skills, although neither they nor their colleagues usually recognize or label this as such. This recognition is a great place to begin. Faculty development can be offered that demonstrates the skills learned through interdisciplinary research, and pedagogies fostering civic engagement are transferable to leadership and creating change. This approach to faculty development is likely to provide a more effective way to attract faculty into leadership programs. For example, there may be more interest among faculty to learn new pedagogies known for enhancing student learning and/or to become involved in community-based interdisciplinary research groups because these are directions of increasing federal funding.[22] Faculty often do not perceive of themselves as leaders so will not pursue faculty development with that label. Campuses would do better to offer faculty development programs related to immediate interests of faculty—teaching and/or research—and then to make the connection to how these skills can also be used to become a leader or change agent on campus.

With this foundation, administrators and faculty change agents can next identify and connect faculty with common interests in these innovative pedagogies, faculty who are often spread out and unaware of each other. Through these connections, faculty with a commitment to engaged learning consolidate their knowledge and network their connections to make these pedagogies more effective and more efficient to implement. Faculty can share strategies for overcoming pressures they may experience from colleagues who do not share their enthusiasm for new pedagogies or research paradigms. In this way, their passion and interests are expanded rather than stamped out, and opportunities to build a critical mass of engaged faculty on campus are fostered. Strategic hiring and connecting interested faculty will also create the collective will and enthusiasm needed to face the obstacles mentioned earlier.

But the issues are multidimensional and so too must be the solutions. The promise for change cannot be fully realized only by growing faculty leadership through faculty development, cluster hiring, and networks. Formal structures within the academy must also be addressed directly. We review the key practices and policies campuses can use to combat these obstacles and highlight how these approaches address challenges such as the rising standards for tenure and promotion or the increase in contingent

Table 9.1 Policies, Practices, and Values Supporting Faculty Leadership and Barriers They Address

Policy, Practice, or Value	Barriers Addressed
Department/School Level	
Supportive individuals	Rising publications standards Socialization as a faculty member—lacking leadership skills Expansion of faculty role Fear of speaking up before tenure and promotion
Autonomy and flexibility in role	Rising publications standards Rise of contingent faculty Expansion of faculty role
Supporting faculty to go to conferences	Socialization as a faculty member—lacking leadership skills Rising publications standards
Campuswide	
Collegiality and campus networks	Socialization as a faculty member—lacking leadership skills Rising publications standards Academic capitalism Fear of speaking up before tenure and promotion
Policies for contingent faculty	Rise of contingent faculty
Campuses that see questioning as healthy	Fear of speaking up before tenure and promotion Lack of shared governance

and part-time faculty.[23] Table 9.1 summarizes how each approach to fostering faculty leadership addresses barriers or hindrances.

Help Faculty Build Off-Campus Networks

Faculty can be assisted in becoming change agents by attending professional conferences focused on topics such as citizenship, diversity, innovations in teaching and learning, civic engagement, or community partnerships. These conferences and the stories and demonstrations they provide help faculty foster a vision, create a network of like-minded people, strengthen leadership skills, and garner insight into the ways they might approach change on their own campus. Conferences assist them to build the leadership skills they lack, refine the skills they are developing, and save time by learning about key strategies and models to follow. In this way, faculty can still play a leadership role even as workload increases and demands for publications rise. Departments and schools that make such opportunities available for faculty through additional funding or by letting faculty know about these opportunities foster greater leadership. These conferences socialize faculty to leadership, introduce leadership skills, and connect faculty to people who can help them learn shortcuts for facilitating their leadership efforts, leaving time for research and additional teaching responsibilities.

Foster Collegiality and Campus Networks

Campus collegiality and mentoring networks are another way to address rising workloads because they link faculty to networks that provide information about how to increase productivity and efficiency. Administrators can foster faculty leadership at home by creating connections among people and by valuing collegiality. Through these networks, early-career faculty not only learn valuable leadership skills but also make important connections to faculty who can advocate on their behalf during the tenure and promotion process. On some campuses, centers for teaching and learning offer symposia and workshops, while on other campuses, centers for community partnerships offer ongoing structures for community-based teaching and research. There is also a variety of smaller ways to do this, many involving small amounts of funding or even none at all. Faculty are often eager to organize events, bring in speakers, foster important discussions, and exchange ideas, especially when these tasks are shared with colleagues and the outcomes benefit all. These events can serve many direct goals for enhancing teaching and research and at the same time create networks that foster faculty leadership aimed at desired change.

For example, a college might sponsor faculty learning communities to cultivate faculty networks and promote collaboration on different themes each year (e.g., civic engagement pedagogies, community-based research programs, or learning-centered communities). Faculty selected for the program meet several times throughout the academic year to discuss the topic, identify individual and collaborative projects related to the theme, receive funding to travel to related conferences, and present their projects to the campus community at the end of the year, thereby building a sustainable system for growth and change. Another often missed opportunity for building faculty connections is to consider campus spaces. Placing like-minded faculty offices near one another and creating common spaces on campus for people to meet and socialize over lunch can be an unnoticed but strategic step.

These kinds of campus support structures link faculty to networks that optimize their productivity and efficiency. In a sense, today's faculty need instant relationships built for them rather than their taking the time to organically develop these relationships themselves. At the same time, when faculty have a base of support across campus, they feel more confident playing a leadership role.

Role Flexibility: Count Leadership as Service or Teaching

Another important strategy for assisting faculty in pursuing leadership opportunities is to find ways for leadership to be visibly valued by the institution. Faculty find it especially difficult in pretenure years to exercise leadership for organizational change as well as meet other teaching, research, and service requirements. Department chairs or deans can facilitate change by recognizing leadership in those areas that count toward tenure and promotion requirements. While acknowledging leadership in service seems intuitive, institutional administrators can go further by substituting leadership for teaching or acknowledging it within the faculty member's teaching responsibilities. For example, faculty engaged with their students in community-based research can be awarded a teaching credit for advancing student research in the field (perhaps a laboratory credit). Or faculty who teach a course that places students in community-based work could be allocated more than one course credit in recognition of their leadership and interdisciplinary efforts. These steps to include leadership as part of the faculty role demonstrate the institution's value of this work.

Develop Policies for Including Non-Tenure-Track Faculty in Governance

Given the increasing trend toward non-tenure-track positions among faculty, it is essential to consider ways to involve these faculty members in all aspects of institutional life. Contracts for non-tenure-track faculty typically focus only on the number of courses to be taught in a specific semester. Little attention is given to the retention of such faculty across time or to their interests and potential to contribute more broadly to the institution. Typically, non-tenure-track faculty receive little mentoring, no annual reviews, and little substantive feedback on their work.[24] In order to capitalize on the talent and expertise of this very large and growing population, campuses must create more specific guidelines, policies, and practices for their inclusion in all aspects of faculty work life. Faculty contracts need to be altered to include specifics about expectations for teaching and student learning, service, and when appropriate, research. This articulation needs to be followed by invitations to join a Faculty Senate, committees, department meetings, and other governing bodies that develop relevant policies and approaches. While some institutions may choose not to give non-tenure-track faculty equal voting rights, ensuring that they participate in some manner is important for developing collegiality and campus leadership. Also, although non-tenure-track faculty are often interested in participating in community-based work in their teaching and research, they are often excluded from professional development where these opportunities and skills can be identified and fostered. Just like their tenured colleagues, non-tenure-track faculty should be encouraged to utilize new pedagogies and then helped to access them; to participate in professional development; and especially on campuses where their participation occurs over several years, to engage in research and other professional growth activities.[25]

Final Thoughts

Community-based teaching and research offer significant promise for enhanced student access and learning, create new knowledge, and allow higher education to contribute to our communities.[26] This kind of learning and research represents a new way of thinking and acting for many campuses, a way of being that is best initiated, fostered, and sustained by shared governance within which faculty, both tenured and nontenured, play a key leadership role.

In taking this stance, it is tempting to focus only on the promise of faculty leadership as we seek to capitalize on how it can change the learning environment. However, we began this chapter by articulating the perils of the academy because it is important for administrators and other leaders to be aware of the context in which we work. We must understand the generational changes that have taken place in who the faculty is and what faculty life is like if we want to be successful in fostering faculty leadership. We must know the impact that changes related to cost savings and flexibility (e.g., rise of non-tenure-track faculty) are having on our learning environment and students. Lessons from the research university campuses that shifted to large numbers of non-tenure-track faculty ring clear. Many of these decisions were not intentional choices but simply institutional drifts most often characterized by lack of planning or thought. They were the result of the pressures around costs and revenues in the midst of decentralized hiring processes, departmental autonomy, lack of a cohesive faculty staffing plan, and no administrative hiring guidelines.

At a time when the public is clamoring for meaning in higher education, connections to their colleges and universities, and cost-effective learning, it is important for campus leaders to weigh the costs and benefits of their decisions. Campuses need to recognize and capitalize on the untapped potential of faculty who desire to use new pedagogies and research paradigms, who have a vision for change, who are developing leadership skills, and who think about their work in connected and community-based ways. In the future, let both Jan's and Don's efforts be successful.

Notes

1. Peter D. Eckel and Adrianna Kezar, *Taking the Reins: Institutional Transformation in Higher Education* (Westport, CT: American Council on Education and Praeger, 2003); Adrianna Kezar, Rozanna Carducci, and Melissa Contreras-McGavin, *Rethinking the "L" Word in Higher Education: The Revolution on Research in Leadership* (San Francisco: Jossey-Bass, 2006).

2. Eckel and Kezar, *Taking the Reins*.

3. Studies of change caution, though, that simply fostering faculty leadership without support from the top is often problematic. Studies of science, technology, engineering, and math (STEM) initiatives that supported individual faculty leaders but did not focus on top-down support of leadership were not as successful as efforts that created multilevel leadership within their environment, because faculty struggled to get needed resources, supportive processes such as change in rewards, and a sense of priority that comes from those in positions of authority; see University of Maryland, *Change and Sustainability in Higher Education (CASHE): Final Report* (College Park: University of Maryland, 2010). Recent change initia-

tives funded by the National Science Foundation, such as the ADVANCE grants, encourage multilevel leadership where the administration provides support for the change process, and faculty leadership is fostered to help bring more women and minorities into the STEM disciplines. This book recognizes the importance of both top-down and bottom-up leadership, but in this chapter we focus on how to *foster* faculty leadership, a topic mostly ignored in the leadership literature within higher education.

4. Bernard M. Bass, *The Bass Handbook of Leadership: Theory, Research, and Managerial Applications*, 4th ed. (New York: Free Press, 2009); Craig L. Pearce and Jay A. Conger, *Shared Leadership: Reframing the Hows and Whys of Leadership* (Thousand Oaks, CA: Sage, 2003); Peter M. Senge, Art Kleiner, Charlotte Roberts, Rick Ross, and Bryan Smith, *The Fifth Discipline Fieldbook: Strategies and Tools for Building a Learning Organization* (New York: Doubleday, 1990).

5. Jack H. Schuster and Martin J. Finkelstein, *The American Faculty: The Restructuring of Academic Work and Careers* (Baltimore: Johns Hopkins University Press, 2006).

6. Roger G. Baldwin and Jay L. Chronister, *Teaching without Tenure: Policies and Practices for a New Era* (Baltimore: Johns Hopkins University Press, 2001); Judith M. Gappa, Ann E. Austin, and Andrea G. Trice, *Rethinking Faculty Work: Higher Education's Strategic Imperative* (San Francisco: Jossey-Bass, 2007); Jean Waltman and Louise August, *Making the Best of Both Worlds: Findings from a National Institution-Level Survey on Non-Tenure Track Faculty* (Ann Arbor, MI: Center for the Education of Women, 2007).

7. Paul D. Umbach, "How Effective Are They? Exploring the Impact of Non-Tenure Track Faculty on Undergraduate Education," *The Review of Higher Education* 30, no. 2 (2007): 91–123; Paul D. Umbach, "The Effects of Part-Time Faculty Appointments on Instructional Techniques and Commitment to Teaching" (paper presented at the thirty-third annual conference of the Association for the Study of Higher Education, Jacksonville, FL, 2008).

8. Schuster and Finkelstein, *The American Faculty*.

9. Gary Rhoades, *Managed Professionals: Unionized Faculty and Restructuring Academic Labor* (Albany: State University of New York Press, 1998).

10. Sheila Slaughter and Gary Rhoades, *Academic Capitalism and the New Economy: Markets, State, and Higher Education* (Baltimore: Johns Hopkins University Press, 2004).

11. Schuster and Finkelstein, *The American Faculty*.

12. Mary Burgan, *Whatever Happened to the Faculty? Drift and Decision in Higher Education* (Baltimore: Johns Hopkins University Press, 2006).

13. Schuster and Finkelstein, *The American Faculty*.

14. Gappa, Austin, and Trice, *Rethinking Faculty Work*.

15. Gappa, Austin, and Trice, *Rethinking Faculty Work*; Schuster and Finkelstein, *The American Faculty*.

16. Mary Deane Sorcinelli, Ann E. Austin, Pamela L. Eddy, and Andrea L. Beach, *Creating the Future of Faculty Development: Learning from the Past, Understanding the Present* (Bolton, MA: Anker, 2006).

17. Schuster and Finkelstein, *The American Faculty*.

18. Ibid.

19. KerryAnn O'Meara, Aimee LaPointe Terosky, and Anna Neumann, *Faculty Careers and Work Lives: A Professional Growth Perspective*, ASHE Higher Education Report 34, no. 3 (San Francisco: Jossey-Bass, 2008).

20. Yet faculty are aware that these commitments per se are likely not rewarded in the tenure and promotion process. We need to recognize that at some institutions, faculty members who assume leadership for change may be putting their careers at risk. The best approach to building these skills and leading the change is to align this work with recognized and credible academic goals. See Gappa, Austin, and Trice, *Rethinking Faculty Work*.

21. Schuster and Finkelstein, *The American Faculty*.

22. James M. Conway, Elise L. Amel, and Daniel P. Gerwien, "Teaching and Learning in the Social Context: A Meta-Analysis of Service Learning's Effects on Academic, Personal, Social and Citizenship Outcomes," *Teaching of Psychology* 36, no. 4 (2009): 233–45.

23. For a full review of these policies and practices, see Adrianna Kezar and Jaime Lester, "Supporting Faculty Grassroots Leadership," *Research in Higher Education* 50, no. 7 (2009): 715–40.

24. Baldwin and Chronister, *Teaching without Tenure*.

25. For more details about including non-tenure-track faculty in governance, see Baldwin and Chronister, *Teaching without Tenure*, and Adrianna Kezar, Jaime Lester, and Gregory Anderson, "Lacking Courage, Corporate Sellout, Not a Real Faculty Member: Challenging Stereotypes of Non-Tenure Track Faculty That Prevent Effective Governance," *Thought and Action* 22 (Fall 2006): 121–32.

26. Christine M. Cress, Cathy Burack, Dwight E. Giles Jr., Julie Elkins, and Margaret Carnes Stevens, *A Promising Connection: Increasing College Access and Success through Civic Engagement* (Boston: Campus Compact, 2010).

10

Threshold Concepts of Teaching and Learning that Transform Faculty Practice (and the Limits of Individual Change)

Kenneth R. Bain and Randall J. Bass

The Lightbulb Problem

How many ideas does it take to change a professor's teaching practices? How many professors have to change in order to improve student learning across a curriculum? Faculty-centered pedagogical change has guided curriculum transformation for the past thirty years, at least since "the age of the faculty developer" of the 1980s met the "age of the learner" in the 1990s.[1] Teaching centers and faculty development efforts have largely pivoted on the evangelical belief that if you can get professors to change the way they conceptualize the relationship between their teaching and student learning, then their course designs and teaching practices will change—and student learning will improve. This paradigm of individual change implies a theory of overall curriculum transformation that is premised on the eventual mass conversion of the faculty—or at least enough to get to a tipping point—to change the curriculum and the very culture of higher education. It has been a reasonable and mostly all-consuming hypothesis.

We are both directors of centers for teaching and learning who have been working within this paradigm of individual change for a long time (about fifty years combined, mostly in research universities). We have seen the effectiveness of this approach and have learned a great deal about how and when this approach is effective, and we spend most of this chapter exploring what we have found to be the most effective concepts and approaches at the heart of the faculty change strategy. We divide our discussion into two related parts: (1) approaches that start with research and theory about learning and (2) strategies that start with expert thinking and disciplinary practices. Both belong to the learning paradigm and are learning-centered approaches; and both, in different ways, open up a spectrum of learning that moves beyond the cognitive to include the fullness of what we think of as *embodied* approaches to learning (our variant term for what is more widely called engaged learning).[2] Although not the only ways to go about effective faculty development, these are, we believe, emblematic of approaches that characterize the best of the current state of the faculty change paradigm.

However, we want to conclude then by asking, are they enough to transform the academy? If the goal is to put transformative learning at the center of higher education, will that ever be achievable through strategies that depend on enough professors having a lightbulb moment about student learning? By framing the question this way, we adamantly do not mean to villainize or pathologize faculty attitudes and practices. Of course, there is resistance on every campus. But we believe that the limits of the faculty change model are likely rooted more in the system of higher education and the way environmental pressures ultimately trump individual traits and motivations. Yet, in addition to the considerable pragmatic environmental factors, we wonder also if there is not something intrinsic to the *learning* paradigm itself that points beyond the faculty change paradigm. Is there perhaps a fundamental incongruence between change strategies focused on individual faculty (and often bounded courses) and approaches to teaching and learning that in their very core concepts lead beyond individual courses to programmatic goals, beyond the formal curriculum to cocurricular and experiential learning, and beyond a narrow gage of cognitive development to a more integrative embrace of affect and metacognition? If so, then a turn to a more structural approach to change is inevitable. However, such a shift should be guided by the best principles, or *threshold concepts*, that have driven the faculty change model over the past thirty years. This is what we want to explore before returning to the question of limits of individual change.

Threshold Concepts of Teaching and Learning

In order to explore this set of questions about what it takes for faculty to see their teaching—and student learning—differently, we want to co-opt the idea of threshold concepts. Threshold concepts are typically employed as a means for analyzing the relationship between the epistemologies of their disciplines (or interdisciplines) and strategies for making those essential ways of thinking visible and accessible to their students.[3] According to the original essay by Meyer and Land, a threshold concept can be considered as akin to a portal, opening up a new and previously inaccessible way of thinking about something. It represents a transformed way of understanding, or interpreting, or viewing something without which the learner cannot progress. As a consequence of comprehending a threshold concept there may thus be a transformed internal view of subject matter, subject landscape, or even world view. This transformation may be sudden or it may be protracted over a considerable period of time, with the transition to understanding proving troublesome. Such a transformed view or landscape may represent how people "think" in a particular discipline, or how they perceive, apprehend, or experience particular phenomena within that discipline (or more generally). It might, of course, be argued, in a critical sense, that such transformed understanding leads to a privileged or dominant view and therefore a contestable way of understanding something.[4]

Although later in this chapter we talk about threshold concepts as a way of conceptualizing how students encounter disciplinary knowledge in courses, here we want to turn the idea of threshold concepts onto the subject of teaching and learning, and faculty change, itself. That is, we want to use threshold concepts in a more self-reflexive way and ask: What are the fundamental, integrative concepts at the heart of transformative pedagogy? What is it that faculty need to understand about teaching and learning in order to have a "transformed view" of the pedagogical landscape? Just as teaching designs in any given discipline should be tailored to helping students negotiate these thresholds, we believe the heart of faculty change has to begin with methods that help faculty approach these thresholds. Are there a few threshold concepts of teaching as a practice that are responsive to transformative student learning?

Consider the three great questions of teaching: What do I want my students to learn? How will I create an environment where they are most likely to learn that? How will they and I know whether or not they have achieved? Coming out of traditional graduate programs, most faculty are pretty well prepared for the first question, a little bit prepared for the third, but not well prepared at all for the second. If there are threshold concepts for teaching, then recognizing that second question as worthy of ongoing inquiry is certainly the first important threshold concept: recognizing the complexity of what Lee Shulman named "pedagogical content knowledge," the body of knowledge that helps teachers understand the best ways to organize, adapt, and represent knowledge in a given domain. Pedagogical content knowledge constitutes the boundary zone between our knowledge about learning and the constructs and practices of any given discipline or profession. It implies dissolution of the artificial division between content and ways to teach content; and it stands as the first order of threshold concepts about teaching and learning. It also opens the door to both approaches to faculty change we want to address: theory-driven approaches (connecting research on human learning to student learning) and practice-driven approaches (connecting disciplinary episte-mologies and expert *practice* to student learning).

Approaches Driven by Learning Theory and Research

In 1996, the Searle Center for Teaching Excellence at Northwestern University initiated a year-long program to help both junior and senior faculty members explore the research and theoretical literature on human learning and incorporate some of the implications of that literature into their teaching practices. Four years ago, the Research Academy for University Learning (RAUL) at Montclair State University initiated its own considerably expanded version of that program, called the Engaged Teaching Fellows Program. For the 2010–2011 academic year, more than sixty Montclair faculty members sought admission into the program, and twenty-four were selected to participate, half tenured and half within their first five years on the faculty. In late August 2010, the participants met for three full days of highly interactive workshops and discussions, with follow-up sessions scheduled for November, January, and March. Between the formal sessions, the fellows maintained Internet contact with each other and with the director of RAUL while working on the revision of a single course.

While the faculty participants explored a variety of ideas from the research and theoretical literature, three fundamental concepts (or threshold concepts) stood at the heart of their explorations and subsequent course revisions: (1) Humans construct knowledge rather than receive it. (2) Extrinsic rewards such as grades can have the effect of reducing interest and the likelihood that students will take a deep rather than a strategic or surface approach to their learning. (3) Major social forces such as what Claude Steele calls stereotype threat can shape the learning and academic performance of students.[5] Let's explore each of these ideas briefly and see how they changed traditional approaches to teaching and learning.

One of the prevailing notions about teaching and learning in many disciplines is the implicit assumption that if people encounter the key facts of any area of study, they will learn. Thus, teaching in those traditional classrooms often consisted of the delivery of information, which students were expected to transcribe into their notes, subsequently study and memorize, and reproduce on an examination (or in some cases, merely recognize a correct answer on a multiple-choice examination). Over the last fifty years, a variety of research and theoretical work has produced a different model of learning that calls for greatly different pedagogical practices.

In that revised model, humans construct a sense of reality and then use those constructions to understand new sensory input. Students do not arrive in class as blank slates ready to absorb whatever the professor may say. Rather, they arrive with an array of mental models of the world, and they use those models to understand everything they encounter, including the lectures they hear, the textbooks they read, and any experiments they may do. Thus, their preexisting models will often have more influence on their ultimate understanding than will anything they encounter in the course. In physics, that may mean students arrive with a pre-Newtonian concept of motion and leave with that same idea, and the difference between the top students and those who score lower is largely determined by how many formulas they can memorize rather than any conceptual understanding. In history, students often arrive with the notion that all societies in all of time operate pretty much the way they think their own world works, and they will take those ideas and try to wrap fifth-century Greece or nineteenth-century United States around them.

Natural Critical Learning Environments

After an exploration of this initial concept and the research and theoretical literature that supports it, faculty members in the Engaged Teaching Fellows Program begin to devise learning environments (what the program calls natural critical learning environments) that will challenge existing constructions.[6] In broad terms, this means identifying the key paradigms that students are likely to bring to the study of the subject and creating compelling intellectual challenges to those concepts. This process often means faculty members will be exploring ways to put their students in situations in which their existing models will not work, an environment that the program calls "expectation failures." All faculty design their teaching in some form to do this implicitly, and we build on their current practices. What we emphasize in the program is how course designs might more deliberately take into account the prior conceptions students bring to a course, and how faculty might do more to elicit those conceptions and make use of them in setting the agenda for the course; this also allows us to discuss how creating a natural critical learning environment depends on the alignment of many aspects of course design, including thinking about how course elements might work together or at cross-purposes.

One of these elements that can work at cross-purposes is assessment and grading, the extrinsic system of rewards and punishments that has considerable influence on how students approach learning. Beginning in a series of studies in Europe in the 1970s, researchers identified three broad approaches that university students take to learning. Some students take what the literature calls a surface approach, simply trying to replicate everything they encounter. Within such an approach, students memorize, regurgitate on an examination or paper, and then purge their minds. Others take a strategic approach, driven largely by the desire for higher grades. Such students seldom become risk takers, fearful that any extra intellectual explorations will jeopardize their grade point averages, and they seldom become adaptive in their expertise, able to transfer their knowledge to novel conditions. Only those who take a deep approach are likely to learn conceptually. Learners who take a surface approach are often driven by fear, expediency, and the desire simply to survive the academic experience; strategic learners, although they value learning, are often driven by recognition for their successes (in the form of higher grades). Only the learners who are more likely to take a deeper approach, so the research and theoretical literature suggest, will pursue the meaning behind the text and think about implications and applications of ideas.

Participants in the Engaged Teaching Fellows Program encounter this literature as well as the research literature on extrinsic and intrinsic motivation. That literature explores the positive and negative effects extrinsic rewards can have on fundamental interest, including the finding that if humans feel manipulated by an extrinsic reward, often their intrinsic interest will decrease. The fellows explore that literature and the possible influences that grades and appeals to grades can have on interest and on the kinds of approaches students are likely to take to their studies. How might assessment and grades be used in order to increase the chances that students will take a deep approach to their learning? Such questions lead the fellows to consider the implications of the following: Are humans most likely to take a deep approach to their learning when they are trying to answer questions or solve problems that each individual learner regards as important, intriguing, or just beautiful? If so, how do we reform a traditional educational environment in which learners are seldom in charge of the questions? How could the use of grades be better integrated with the conditions that might lead to a deeper approach to learning? Perhaps the key threshold concept here for faculty is that grades can be a driver for a deeper approach but only under certain conditions, conditions that may require rethinking of certain pedagogical practices, such as making more use of formative assessment; allowing independent goal setting; raising the challenge level of performance assessments (and supporting that higher bar); and making more room for questioning, uncertainty, and risk taking.

Finally, the fellows explore a body of literature that began to emerge in the 1980s and 1990s about the influence of social forces on the learning of university students. Much of that consideration focuses on a phenomenon that psychologists Claude Steele and Joshua Aronson dubbed *stereotype threat* and *stereotype vulnerability*. Steele, Aronson, and now a whole host of others have found that anyone who is a member of a social group about which there is a widespread negative social stereotype will likely feel the sting of that social notion even if he or she personally rejects that stereotype.[7] The research the fellows explore suggests that such an influence occurs because, at minimum, the targets of the negative image resent, sometimes on a subconscious level, that anyone might think of them in terms of that negative stereotype. As fellows in the program begin to explore the implications of that research, they also begin to consider these central questions: Who is learning within my class and who is not, and are there demographic patterns in that learning that stem from broader social forces such as stereotype threat? If so, how can an educator respond to those forces?

The Promising Syllabus

The upshot of all these considerations (and the exploration of other ideas from the research and theoretical literature) is the creation of something the program calls a *promising syllabus*, which is more than the pieces of paper distributed to students on the first day of class—it is a whole new way of conceptualizing and organizing a class. The contours of that kind of revolutionary syllabus first began to appear in the study of university teachers who were having enormous success in fostering deep approaches to learning.[8] In broad terms, it contains three parts: (1) the promise[9] or invitation, usually conveyed in a story that raises a central and compelling question; (2) an explanation of what the students will be doing that will help them achieve that promise, accept that invitation; and (3) the beginning of a conversation between teacher and students about how both will come to understand the nature and the progress of the students' learning.

The emphasis of this approach is on intrinsic appeals, on giving students a strong sense of control over their own education, on raising questions or problems that will capture the students' interests. With that syllabus, the fellows attempt to create their own version of a natural critical learning environment, weighing the implications of the research and theoretical literature.[10] Many of those new courses will contain some of the changes already implied as well as incorporate experiences for students that go outside the classroom and include elements of service learning or fieldwork, opportunities for students to explore questions and problems in both an academic and extracurricular setting.

The threshold concepts implied in this process have impact on three significant areas of faculty practice: planning, execution, and evaluation. Faculty begin their planning not with questions about what they will do or "cover" in the course, but with explorations of what paradigms students are likely to bring to the course and how the course might challenge those paradigms, helping students see the problems they face in believing whatever they may believe. The planning deliberately attempts to foster deep approaches to learning rather than the vague notion of "learning the material," and it raises important epistemological questions about the nature of knowing within any discipline and across disciplines.

It also means that faculty must often move outside their own disciplines in preparing the class, recognizing that most disciplines and most graduate programs do not provide the scholar with any research-based insights into what conditions are most likely to foster certain intellectual outcomes. In some cases, that approach simply means, for example, that faculty abandon the notion that students must be marched up Bloom's taxonomy of cognitive abilities (whether faculty are familiar with Bloom's famous taxonomy or not), learning to recall the material before they can ever analyze, synthesize, and evaluate. In place of that notion emerges an integrative rather than a linear approach to learning in which students become engaged in mastering all levels of cognitive activity simultaneously.

As fellows begin to consider questions of evaluation, they focus increasingly on formative evaluation, on helping students improve their work long before any summative judgments (the final grade) are made about their efforts. Such an approach to evaluation also means faculty plan activities to help students understand and adopt the criteria of the class and discipline as they attempt to join a new community of knowledgeable peers. It means they help students develop the ability to judge their own work and move as much as possible, and for as many students as possible, from extrinsic to intrinsic motivation.

Part of that reconsideration of evaluation means, of course, that faculty rethink how they might bring students into the grading process. In the course of doing so, they consider several broad questions about grades: What does the grade represent in terms of intellectual, physical, emotional, professional, or any other kind of ability? (What can the A student do that the B student cannot do?) Does the grade represent where students are in reference to a standard, each other, or themselves? What are the implications for the learning environment in answering this question? Does the grade represent where students are in their abilities at the end of the class, or is it a compilation of where they have been during the course of the term?

Classes that invite students to an enterprise that is "bigger than the class itself," to something that has immediate significance outside the confines of the course, seem to have the greatest influence on both students' approaches to the learning and their satisfaction with their learning and the educational experience. Although it is impossible to generalize, in such classes, students are more likely to take a deeper approach to their studies by becoming engrossed in the pursuit of big questions and projects. Retention rates are higher in those classes, but more important, students are more likely to understand conceptually, to think about implications and applications, and the entire experience is likely to have a sustained, substantial, and positive influence on how they will subsequently think, act, and feel.

Approaches Driven by Expert Thinking and Disciplinary Practice

The deep learning approaches just described speak to a way of thinking about teaching that echoes the exhortation from Michael Wesch that "We are not teaching subjects, but subjectivities."[11] Creating critical learning environments that emphasize teaching "subjectivities" rather than subjects is not intended to diminish the importance of content but to return content to the larger context of form and process where it originated: in the fullness of thought and action, belonging to fields of knowledge and communities of committed practitioners. This is an important bridge between the center of universities (core practices around epistemic knowledge) and the periphery (the experimental and cocurricular-engaged learning practices that often draw on more reflective and affective pedagogies).

This has been the promise and effect of an approach to classroom inquiry that begins with faculty looking at their own disciplinary practices as what we might call the *practices of expertise*. This stream of thinking also has its grounding in research and theory, including work on cognitive apprenticeship and research on expertise (exploring differences between experts and novices, as well as expert and nonexpert practitioners). Although this approach is informed by theory, as a faculty development approach it focuses more on faculty disciplinary practice. In 2000, the Center for New Designs in Learning and Scholarship at Georgetown University started a national project known as the Visible Knowledge Project, with an emphasis on studying the impact of new technologies on student learning, primarily in the humanities. The approach that follows evolved from this work and has streamed with several other influential projects and approaches.[12]

Exploring the practices of expertise helps mediate conversations with faculty about two-way processes for making thinking and learning visible, just as the Engaged Teaching Fellows Program helps faculty better understand how students bring into the classroom their "mental models of the world." Faculty in a practice-driven model focus on how to make their goals and mental maps of their disciplines and teaching structures more explicit and operational in their designs. To do this they need to understand that expert practice, based on expert knowledge, is quite diverse in nature, including formal and informal knowledge, experiential knowledge, and self-regulating knowledge. One of the problems with expert knowledge is that much of it becomes habitual and therefore tacit in the teaching process and thus requires effort to reclaim in ways that allow faculty to break down their own mental actions into smaller tasks as part of the instructional process. When faculty participate in processes that help them slow down and look closely at what they are expecting of students and how those tasks often compress many different features of thinking and knowing, they are better able to recognize what it takes to design a sequence of tasks that approximates expert thinking—albeit, of course, not at expert levels of performance. (Here, *expert thinking* means the models we use to guide our instruction of novices and the cultivation of their intellectual development in a domain.)

As with the Engaged Teaching Fellows Program, this process also tends naturally to lead to a focus on formative stages of learning, what we call in the Visible Knowledge Project *intermediate thinking processes*.[13] Before you can work with faculty on course designs that address intermediate processes, the faculty have to find value in making student thinking visible at key moments that are not high-stakes assessments. Such low-stakes and intermediate assessments come in many forms, including a recent flourishing of interest in various forms of reflection and analysis that students might use to document their own learning processes.[14] For faculty already engaged with certain forms of pedagogies (those using certain digital and social media, as in the Visible Knowledge Project, or community-based learning or service learning courses), the focus on visible intermediate thinking and self-reflection arises naturally. This is not so for all faculty. This is where an approach that begins with the nature of disciplinary knowledge and expert practice becomes a meaningful point of entry.

Thresholds and Bottlenecks

The first of these points of entry brings us back to *threshold concepts*. Threshold concept theory posits that at the core of every discipline, a few key concepts represent fundamental ways of thinking and practicing in that field. Threshold concepts are distinguished from other building block concepts by their *integrative* nature: "A threshold concept is thus seen as something distinct within what university teachers would typically describe as 'core concepts.' A core concept is a conceptual 'building block' that progresses understanding of the subject; it has to be understood but it does not necessarily lead to a qualitatively different view of subject matter."[15] Examples of threshold concepts that emerged through the original research in 2003 include "opportunity cost" in economics, "limit" in mathematics, and "signification" in literary and cultural studies. The naming of a single concept or idea as a threshold concept belies the broader valence of the term that unfolds through the threshold concept literature. Sometimes threshold concepts are explicit in instruction but require a lot of practice and application within authentic settings in order to truly understand how to *think with* a particular concept. In other cases, threshold concepts are more implicit, such as the concept that "historical thinking is constituted by the construction of an interpretation of the past based on multiple sources." In this sense, threshold concepts are not merely concepts to be memorized but are more like signature intellectual moves in a domain.

Threshold concepts also share the key feature of frequently representing what David Perkins called *troublesome knowledge* (in that they may run counter to students' lived experience or values, or the concept may just be counterintuitive in the context of everyday life). The idea that students can take a protracted amount of time to grasp threshold concepts—and that students will vary in their ability to cross the threshold—is a critical dimension of the usefulness of threshold concepts as a component of curricular improvement. They help faculty attend to what critical disciplinary concepts and ways of thinking look like from the students' experience and provide a bridge between the teacher's (expert practitioner) and the students' (novice learners) experience.

When you get faculty thinking about threshold concepts—especially their troublesome nature—in their fields, they begin to look differently at how threshold concepts often require some period of time for grasping, and consequently that some students will take more time than others to pass through the threshold. Similarly, students can appear to have a grasp on threshold concepts, but it may turn out that their understanding is only mimicry or at least very thin. One consequence of taking threshold concepts seriously is to recognize that one does not acquire them by merely listening or learning passively; the more authentic and active the learning context for acquiring threshold concepts, the more likely that performance of knowledge will be a better representation of enduring understanding.

The troublesome nature of threshold concepts—and the protracted nature by which students pass through them—is what gives thresholds the quality more of a passageway than a door. Meyer and Land use the term *liminality* to refer to this in-between state while students are engaging and absorbing the threshold concept.[16] The notion of troublesome knowledge and liminality has numerous implications for faculty development and pedagogical design, not the least of which is to help faculty think about whether they are making all the intermediate steps for understanding explicit and available to students as part of their struggle to understand. When you work with faculty around threshold concepts, they are able to think about both variation in student learning and the troublesome nature of a discipline's core concepts together. This can be a key shift for faculty, to connect those "key paradigms" and "compelling intellectual challenges" of their disciplines to a more systematic way of understanding student struggles through the threshold, struggles that might otherwise be written off as bad student behavior or poor preparation. It also provides a different way of approaching what the Engaged Teaching Fellows Program called *expectation failures*, by understanding the constructs that "put their students in situations in which their existing models will not work" as intrinsic to what it means to *think with* the threshold concepts of a discipline.

Not all difficulties with learning are due to the troublesome nature of threshold concepts. Students can encounter a wide range of "instructional bottlenecks." This is an important component of a similar project at the University of Indiana called Decoding the Disciplines, which has developed a multistep process for helping faculty think about the tacit knowledge of the fields that underlie their ways of knowing and working. This process includes identifying "instructional bottlenecks," which they define as tasks that are difficult or troublesome for students, and then identifying "the steps the expert would go through to accomplish the task the students have not done well at. This is a difficult process for experts to do, because much of their knowledge operates so tacitly, they are not aware of possessing knowledge inaccessible to their students."[17] Once a professor identifies a bottleneck and engages in the hard work of thinking through all the steps of expert practice entailed in the activity, then it is possible to think systematically about (1) how those steps get modeled, (2) how students have the opportunity to practice the steps, and (3) how they can receive feedback on their practice. As students (and faculty) slow down to accommodate each stage of these processes, faculty also need to ensure they are finding ways to keep students motivated to see the connection between particular tasks and larger ideas.

At Georgetown we have combined these two approaches into a faculty development initiative called the Bottlenecks and Thresholds Initiative.[18] There is a natural compatibility between threshold concepts and instructional bottleneck approaches. We believe this is a particularly rich marriage of the two approaches, primarily because threshold concept theory lacks a pedagogical design or faculty development element; similarly, the instructional bottleneck approach—being strong in design and development—can break down difficult intellectual activities into smaller manageable parts without losing sight of the more complex integrative picture.

Embodied Learning

Bottlenecks, thresholds, and the broader approach of thinking about expert thinking are all effective ways to help faculty see a fuller range of *learning* (beyond cognition) through the lens of disciplinary practice. Even on a pragmatic level, the Decoding the Disciplines project talks about at least three different categories of bottlenecks: *practical* bottlenecks (e.g., students don't know how to read selectively or actively), matters of *understanding* (e.g., students may not understand how to deal with multiple perspectives); or *affective* (e.g., they lack emotional engagement in the subject or let their values unselfconsciously shape their ability to be critical or analytical). Most importantly, though, these approaches that help faculty think about the knowledge they are trying to teach are fundamentally and ultimately about *practice*, about what David Perkins would call a "flexible performance capability" with knowledge, about what can be done with knowledge and in what settings. And once faculty shift from thinking about knowledge as content to knowledge as practice, they move out of the territory, as John Seely Brown puts it, from "learning about" to "learning-to-be."[19]

This larger context of knowledge, of learning to be, belongs not typically (or exclusively) to classrooms but to experience and communities of practice. In the right faculty development context, focus on disciplinary thinking can lead to what we came to call in the Visible Knowledge Project *embodied pedagogies*, learning strategies and course designs that engage affective as well as cognitive dimensions, not merely through the role of emotion, but through personal significance, motivation, creativity and intuition, through expressions of self-identity and subjectivity, all as the foundation of intellectual engagement. In this context, working with embodied pedagogies can help faculty think about teaching their courses with two core ideas: (1) the importance of self-knowledge and experience as a primary means of bridging the identity of learners with disciplinary knowledge and (2) the significance of emotion and embodied cognition in intellectual development for the whole spectrum of expert development—as crucial in initial engagement of novice learning as it is with more advanced stages of integrated understanding.

For faculty, the challenge is not only to make room for emotional engagement but also to model how to engage emotion in cognitive and critical thinking. Faculty who recognize the importance of affect and personal development in embodied pedagogies develop instructional and assessment tools to accommodate these fuller dimensions of learning, rethinking how knowledge construction is connected to self-construction, cognition to affect, and knowing to not knowing and uncertainty.

When faculty confront practice-focused and knowledge-focused approaches to embodied pedagogies, a much wider range of participation is possible in transformative education programs. This, for example, has been the case with the curriculum infusion programs implemented at Georgetown, where faculty across the curriculum create short modules around mental health and wellness that are organically connected to the intellectual content of the course.[20]

The threshold shift here is not only about helping students connect life and learning; it implies a revaluing of reflective and integrative thinking as a cornerstone of transformative education inside and across disciplines. If theories of active learning (and natural critical learning environments) imply movement between thinking and doing, or theory and experience, embodied learning approaches add a third element to theory and experience: reflection. Here, reflection is intimately tied to metacognition and helping students be reflective and adaptive with their knowledge. Yet it is probably not possible to teach students to be metacognitive: that ability arises from experience. But the implication for course design and student learning is that we can do more to create the kind of experiences that are more likely to give rise to metacognition and to create occasions and give guidance for students to be reflective and make meaningful connections about their learning, over time, and among all the elements of their education.

These approaches also give faculty a wider pedagogical lexicon by which to think about multiple forms of assessment (formative and summative) that help bridge curricular learning to cocurricular learning and wider experience. They can inform the development of integrative, reflective writing that accompanies traditional assignments or connect learning experiences to a larger narrative of learning; they can inform new approaches to using digital tools and social media to help faculty design classrooms as intellectual communities; and they can help create intellectual and pedagogical bridges between traditional classroom designs and the kind of learning that characterizes high-impact practices.

The Limits of Individual Change

As effective as these approaches are with faculty and as beneficial as they are to students, the question persists: Are they enough to transform an institution or higher education? Is it reasonable to hope that effective faculty change strategies, supported by internal funding for faculty developers and centers for teaching, and buttressed by changing reward structures, would lead to new structures and priorities? Our experience cautions us to believe that this model can only take us so far (and has). Competing influences in the higher education environment are fierce. And in many institutional types, it is unlikely that the reward structures will change very much, if at all. It may be that another powerful threshold concept of *institutional* change is accepting the limits of *faculty* change as a transformational strategy. If not just the faculty change paradigm, then what else?

One way to think of complementary (not alternative) strategies to faculty change is what we think of as the "least/most strategy." That is, rather than always asking how we can get faculty to change the ways they teach or address student learning, we might ask a different question: Where are the places that an institution can put the least amount of new resources to get the most impact? We can imagine targeting this question at several different levels. First, are there ways to develop course-modification strategies that do not require major course redesigns but have substantial payoff in impact on student learning? This is what we have found at Georgetown, for example, in our curriculum infusion programs, where faculty create short modules connecting students' lives with their learning in ways that are intrinsic to the course's intellectual material. The heart of curriculum infusion's success has been encouraging each faculty member to implement the model in ways that are grounded in who they are and integrated with how they already teach. And although professors participating in curriculum infusion programs come already equipped with the threshold impulse to help students make this connection, they need not have had a series of other threshold insights in order to implement the change. The program is effective because it in essence fixes a broken circuit that exists in the academy—in the location of the classroom. Faculty want to enable students to see the personal relevance of course material but often don't know how (and don't want to give up much time or content); students want to make those connections but rarely have a way of doing so without needed structure and scaffolding.

The key point is that in order to make curriculum infusion work, we have made a calculation about where to make the investment for change—and it is not primarily in changing faculty, per se, but in creating an environment that allows faculty to *step into* (and out of) a program that has a life of its own. The least/most principle is at work here because we have invested primarily in building a model, supporting a cross-campus team to execute the model through work with faculty, providing modest stipends to faculty and student health providers to participate, and building a community that has a structural identity beyond any individuals. From the perspective of course design, the short curriculum infusion modules represent very modest modifications for a relatively high payoff in impact.

Not all improvements in student learning can work this way. Nor will a targeted program such as curriculum infusion transform an institution or even the nature of student learning by itself. But the least/most principle might also be applied at the next order of magnitude in thinking about the curriculum. That is, where might an institution make a *differential invest- ment* in a few key model courses that have high influence on students and that, through their centrality in the curriculum, become models of what can and should be done with the student experience? On the one hand, this shifts the focus of change from faculty to students: If we invested more heavily in transforming students as learners early in their college careers, might they be better prepared to make the most of—and perhaps agitate for a certain kind of learning—a whole range of learning environments, active, passive, surface, strategic, and deep?

But it also shifts the way we think structurally about differential in- vestment in the curriculum—and where centers for teaching and other faculty development efforts might invest their time. What would it look like to transform courses such that faculty who choose to teach them adapt their teaching strategies to fit those course structures (and thereby perhaps undergo many of the same changes in practice and perspective on student learning that traditional faculty development processes imply), but the transformed curricular structures are not embodied in the professors but in the enduring course practice, which is not dependent on who is teach- ing it?

In other words, what would it look like to make an investment in trans- forming *courses* that in turn might transform *faculty* rather than investing in changing faculty, hoping in turn they will transform their courses? Such course-focused differential investments have some models, of course, such as the pioneering Studio Physics courses at Rensselaer Polytechnic Institute and subsequently at MIT, or the implementation of universal course design at the University of Kansas along principles of cognitive apprenticeship, and many others. And some emerging electronic portfolio practices are also working to this effect, where faculty can modify some of their teaching practices in light of a larger architecture for student learning that transcends the level of the individual course. But ePortfolio practices are as yet rarely central to an institution's core curricular practices, nor are they typically understood as a different way of comprehending faculty change.

More importantly, we have only begun to imagine how such course investments could carry the full range of embodied learning dimensions implied in the theory-driven and practice-driven approaches we have dis- cussed. At Montclair, for example, the Research Academy for University

Learning has been engaged in an effort, with the support of a grant from the Creative Campus Initiative, to work with Peak Performances, the folks who bring visiting performing and visual artists to campus, to form and guide an interdisciplinary team of a dozen or fewer faculty members who are building a course on creative thought. That team is employing all the major conclusions drawn from more than a quarter century of research and theory on university learning and how best to cultivate it. It is also employing the best practices of twentieth-century classes on creative thought, including a highly successful course developed by Paul Baker, and adding to those experiences the insights of recent research and theory.[21] This effort to fashion a new course is intended to create an institutionalized context for something that will transform the learning experience of students and might itself lead to a later effort with a team of faculty members to build, for example, a course on scientific thinking that similarly draws on holistic and integrative principles of learning.

Such collaboratively designed courses would be research based and evince the key thresholds of teaching and learning we have discussed as a matter of structure and practice, without necessarily requiring the faculty who teach them to re-create the same journey of discovery around the key thresholds, one professor at a time. These kinds of courses, and other examples we have discussed, also require institutional investment in the kinds of facilitative scaffolding that will sustain them—in centers for teaching and other modest targeted investments that keep partners across academic, student affairs, and other spheres engaged in connecting, by design, the periphery to the center.

It may also be the case that these kinds of change strategies—focused on course and program structures and less on faculty change—are the logical consequences of the threshold concepts intrinsic to the learning paradigm: that designing for transformational learning inevitably takes us beyond the boundaries of the individual course or even the formal curriculum. Perhaps it is inevitable that once we all start to design for the integrative nature of threshold concepts, or recognize the linkages among prior knowledge and personal and intellectual development and the dynamics of social learning, that the path to curricular change can no longer exclusively run through individual faculty development and faculty change but must take a more structural approach. Such a shift might be the logical and necessary consequence of thinking beyond courses to programs, beyond discrete knowledge domains to integrative approaches to learning and transformative education.

Will the thoughtful implementation of a wider repertoire of change strategies transform the academy? We can only hope. But we do believe that our best chance is to see with clear eyes both what has worked so effectively to transform teaching and learning on our campuses and why by itself it will likely never be enough.

Notes

1. Mary Deane Sorcinelli, Ann E. Austin, Pamela L. Eddy, and Andrea L. Beach, *Creating the Future of Faculty Development: Learning from the Past, Understanding the Present* (Bolton, MA: Anker, 2006).

2. Our use of *embodied pedagogies* shares a great deal with the term *engaged learning* (a much more common term), which has taken on a wide range of meanings, from merely active learning to civic engagement. For the most part, the terms could be interchangeable; we use the term *embodied* here to emphasize learning that includes but goes beyond cognition to fold in sensory as well as emotional engagement, and knowledge as "experienced through the body as well as the mind." For an earlier elaboration of embodied learning, see Randy Bass and Bret Eynon, "Capturing the Visible Evidence of Invisible Learning," *Academic Commons*, January 7, 2009, www.academiccommons.org/commons/essay/capturing-visible-evidence-invisible-learning.

3. Jan H.F. Meyer and Ray Land, *Threshold Concepts and Troublesome Knowledge: Linkages to Ways of Thinking and Practising within the Disciplines*, Enhancing Teaching-Learning Environments in Undergraduate Courses Project, Occasional Papers Series (Edinburgh: University of Edinburgh, Coventry and Durham, 2003); "Threshold Concepts and Troublesome Knowledge (2): Epistemological Considerations and a Conceptual Framework for Teaching and Learning," *Higher Education* 49 (2005): 373–88; Ray Land, Jan H.F. Meyer, and Jan Smith, eds., *Threshold Concepts within the Disciplines* (Rotterdam, the Netherlands: Sense Publishers, 2008).

4. Meyer and Land, *Threshold Concepts and Troublesome Knowledge*, 1.

5. Claude M. Steele and Joshua Aronson, "Stereotype Threat and the Intellectual Test Performance of African-Americans," *Journal of Personality and Social Psychology* 69, no. 5 (1995): 797–811, www.ncbi.nlm.nih.gov/pubmed/7473032.

6. Ken Bain, *What the Best College Teachers Do* (Cambridge, MA: Harvard University Press, 2004).

7. In addition to the work cited earlier, see some of the recent work on stereotype threat: Joshua Aronson, Michael J. Lustina, Catherine Good, Kelli Keough, Claude M. Steele, and Joseph Brown, "When White Men Can't Do Math: Necessary and Sufficient Factors in Stereotype Threat," *Journal of Experimental Social Psychology* 35, no. 1 (1999): 29–46; Jean-Claude Croizet and Theresa Claire, "Extending the Concept of Stereotype Threat to Social Class: The Intellectual Underperformance of Students from Low Socioeconomic Backgrounds," *Personality and Social Psychology Bulletin* 24, no. 6 (1998): 588; Steven J. Spencer, Claude M. Steele, and Diane M. Quinn, "Stereotype Threat and Women's Math Performance," *Journal of Experimental Social Psychology* 35, no. 1 (1999): 4–28; Claude M. Steele and Joshua Aronson, "Stereotype Threat and the Intellectual Test Performance

of African Americans," *Journal of Personality and Social Psychology* 69, no. 5 (1995): 797–811; Claude M. Steele, Steven J. Spencer, and Joshua Aronson, "Contending with Group Image: The Psychology of Stereotype and Social Identity Threat," *Advances in Experimental Social Psychology* 34 (2002): 379–440.

8. Bain, *What the Best College Teachers Do*.

9. In this case, a promise means an opportunity, as in a "promising situation," rather than a guarantee.

10. Ken Bain, "Understanding Great Teaching," *Peer Review* 11, no. 2 (2009): 9–12.

11. Michael Wesch, "From Knowledgeable to Knowledge-able: Learning in New Media Environments," in "New Media Technologies and the Scholarship of Teaching and Learning," ed. Randy Bass, special issue, *Academic Commons*, January 2009.

12. Two prior related projects include the Peer Review of Teaching Project, led by Dan Bernstein (University of Kansas), and the Course Portfolio Project, led jointly by Pat Hutchings and Lee Shulman (Carnegie Foundation for the Advancement of Teaching). Both projects focused on faculty practice and close examinations of student work and performance.

13. The term comes from Sam Wineburg; see his *Historical Thinking and Other Unnatural Acts* (Philadelphia: Temple University Press, 2001).

14. This is especially true of the crucial role of reflection in the growing range of ePortfolio practices. See, for example, Kathleen Blake Yancey, "Reflection and Electronic Portfolios," in *Electronic Portfolios 2.0: Emergent Research on Implementation and Impact,* ed. Darren Cambridge, Barbara Cambridge, and Kathleen B. Yancey (Sterling, VA: Stylus, 2009).

15. Meyer and Land, *Threshold Concepts and Troublesome Knowledge*, 1.

16. Meyer and Land, *Threshold Concepts and Troublesome Knowledge*, 10.

17. David Pace and Joan Middendorf, "Decoding the Disciplines: Helping Students Learn Disciplinary Ways of Thinking," *New Directions for Teaching and Learning,* no. 98 (Summer 2004); Leah Shopkow, "What Decoding the Disciplines Can Offer Threshold Concepts" (paper presented at the second Threshold Concepts across the Curriculum Conference, Kingston, Ontario, June 2008), 3.

18. See http://cndls.georgetown.edu/bottlenecks-and-thresholds.

19. John S. Brown, "Minds on Fire: Open Education, the Long Tail, and Learning 2.0," *EDUCAUSE Review* 43, no. 1 (January/February 2008): 16–32.

20. See the case study by Joan Riley and Mindy McWilliams on Georgetown's curriculum infusion initiative in this volume.

21. Robert Flynn and Eugene McKinney, eds., *Paul Baker and the Integration of Abilities* (College Station: Texas A&M University Press, 2003).

11

Financing Change

Priorities, Resources, and Community Involvement

Kent John Chabotar

At a time of economic uncertainly and financial turmoil, efforts to bring about transformative change are especially difficult.

- Concerns for short-term survival dominate decisions. Incremental fixes to save money in academic programs and administrative services are emphasized over real strategic thinking in which priorities are reconsidered and reset.
- When the budget is barely balanced and financial equilibrium is elusive, the ability and willingness to identify new resources for long-term change soon dissipate.
- Change involves key stakeholders on and off campus who may be highly skeptical, very anxious, and unfamiliar with institutional governance.

Resetting Priorities

More often than not, financial concerns drive institutional decisions about change and almost everything else. Colleges and universities quickly realize they cannot attain long-term transformational change merely by adding more students or programs, by cutting costs and staff of existing departments and programs, or even by selective outsourcing from admissions to facilities. Moreover, transformational change cannot simply be another add-on priority but usually involves reconsideration and resetting of current priorities before change can be realistically undertaken. By substituting transformational change for one or more priorities, attention focuses on change as well as the redeployment of resources. How can colleges and universities deal with this process most effectively?

Use of Strategic Thinking

Undoubtedly, resetting priorities is much easier if an institution has a mission or strategic vision that sets goals for instruction, research, and service. The board can state this vision in a formal plan with a mission statement, continuing and specific objectives, and definite programs and assignments of responsibility. It can also be organic—developing and changing over time and supplemented by periodic statements of intermediate-term academic or administrative milestones. Such clear ends for the institution, whether formal or informal, are essential ingredients for deciding which priorities make the most sense for the future.

Functional Analysis

At the most general level, priorities can be listed by function: instruction, research, academic support (e.g., library, instructional technology), student services, and institutional support. Unless transformational change is included among the priorities, this often leads to labeling instruction as the "core business" and a top priority and institutional support as far less important.

For example, when I became the vice president and treasurer at Bowdoin College, President Robert Edwards had clear priorities as he established a budget committee to work with us to restore financial equilibrium. The committee was also to work within the budget principles that President Edwards gave the budget committee when it was established. These were to expend a higher proportion of the budget on the academic program and less on administrative overhead; protect tenured or tenure-track faculty positions; and link tuition and fee increases to the increase in the consumer price index. This led to the elimination of seventy positions, almost all of them from the administrative and support staff. The downside was that faculty did not fully appreciate how dependent much of their teaching and research was on administrative support. My analogy then and now is that a faculty member is akin to an aircraft carrier needing the help of destroyers and supply ships (or computing centers and academic support programs) in order to perform most effectively.

Program Analysis

Still, true priority setting has to occur within and not merely between functions. Within institutional support, for example, you can set priorities for human resources, finance, and other administrative units. Employee training might be ranked higher than new employee orientation. The most difficult but ultimately most valuable priority setting occurs within instruction and the academic program. Guilford College, College of Saint Benedict, and Saint John's University are among the colleges studying how to prioritize faculty hiring and academic programs in order to make the best use of resources.[1]

Departments and majors can be rated on criteria such as relevance to the mission, internal and external demand for the program, and finances. Consider potential, too. Programs may rate more highly if the college allocated more resources to them. The result may include "flagship departments" and majors to which we make financial commitments as well as lower-ranked programs that can be trimmed or eliminated to free up resources for transformational change. When the Guilford faculty approved the academic prioritization process, they sought to determine which programs

- are strong across the board and for which resources should be maintained or increased;
- have a small number of weaknesses that might be addressed with additional resources, or whose strengths are not sufficient given the resources already committed to them; and
- are weak in multiple areas and would require significantly more resources, and should therefore be considered for consolidation or termination.

Not all academic program prioritization processes are as methodical. Plunging state revenue has compelled many public universities to cut programs to save money, sometimes with scant faculty participation. In 2010, Florida State University planned to suspend or terminate ten undergraduate majors and three graduate-level programs, which led to layoffs of sixty-two faculty members, of whom twenty-one were tenured. The fourteen universities in the Pennsylvania state system of higher education were ordered to consider for consolidation or suspension any program with fewer than thirty graduates during a five-year period.[2]

Financial Models

Such models forecast revenues and expenses for five or more years to detect future implications of current decisions. They reveal how even small percentage increases compound quickly over time. The model can cover the entire budget or just parts related to transformational change. If the institution, for example, decides to pursue adult education, the model can study issues such as relationships between financial aid and net tuition, long-term costs of new programs specifically designed for adults, and the effects of new students on student-to-teacher ratios and average class size.

The model can confirm or discourage the institution's ambitions before precious resources are committed. Forecasting assumptions must be clear and convincing (e.g., inflation, fund-raising expectations, levels of state appropriations, and formula funding). Other characteristics of an effective model include simplicity, complete coverage of important issues for the decision maker, easy to control in terms of the model's outputs being predictable given selected inputs, stable by not producing ridiculous answers, adaptive to the data needs of the decision maker, and easy to communicate to a wide range of constituencies.

Future Perfect is an Excel-based financial modeling tool that allows the institution to create its own "dashboard" of strategic indicators and include the one-time effects of special projects such as a new building or capital campaign.[3] The user can see the effects of changing any variable such as enrollment, fees, and staffing on future budgets and the increases in operating and total net assets. The model also includes these changes in revised statements of activity and financial position. The user can decide which spreadsheets, tables, and graphs are reported to the president or chancellor, financial officers, governing board, and other constituencies.

Budget Flexibility

Budgets with the flexibility to encourage initiative and respond to unanticipated changes are a necessary element for sound budgeting. Flexibility can be served by setting aside funds for one-time expenses, such as travel or equipment, and encouraging departments with new ideas to apply for them. Such funds might be seed money for transformational change. Another idea is to prepare alternative budgets—with different details or justifications as the "official" budget—that can be used if revenues or expenses fluctuate markedly and unexpectedly. At Guilford College, we budget initially based on a "worse case" scenario on enrollment but also plan to add back funds if the "better case" scenario is closer to actual results.

Budget flexibility is served by "sensitivity analysis," or the calculation of the fiscal effects of small changes on major budget drivers. For example, what are the effects on the budget of 1 percent increases or decreases in student fees (net of financial aid), endowment spending, faculty and staff salary pools, and departmental operating budgets? One way to achieve consensus on a campus budget advisory committee is to give each member a list of these 1 percent changes and ask them to find increased revenues and/or decreased costs sufficient to balance the budget. That not only helps to achieve the goal but also educates the committee and community about how complex a budget is.

Identify New Resources

Essentially, the aforementioned "growth by substitution" cuts the expenses of one priority to fund the change priority. What new resources may also be obtained to support change?

Higher Enrollment

Enrollment growth is no panacea. As a short-term measure, more students can boost revenue if financial aid is controlled and related increases in faculty and staff are contained. When Guilford increased its enrollment by 45 percent in five years, the good news was administrative and support staff increased only 25 percent. The bad news was that the faculty grew by 60 percent, which undoubtedly reduced average class size and improved course discussions but mitigated the financial benefit of enrollment growth. New academic programs are not an economical way to attract more students, especially if the lack of resources diminishes course quality, advising, programming, and placement in graduate schools or jobs.

Unless the institution is 100 percent tuition dependent, we lose money on every student we enroll. Gifts, state aid, endowment earnings, and other revenue balance the budget. In addition, a college or university with excess capacity and empty classroom seats can grow less expensively—and apply the savings to transformational change—than if new capital costs for classrooms and offices must be incurred.

Public universities such as the University of Michigan and the University of Virginia have earned more money by attracting out-of-state students and charging them in excess of $30,000 a year in tuition. Other states, including Massachusetts and Wisconsin, are trying similar strategies, with more sure to follow. The problem is that too many states may be chasing the same relatively economically advantaged out-of-state students.[4] Kent State recruits more students by "a revenue-sharing model which rewards departments for enrollment gains by returning 100 percent of growth dollars initially and then gradually shifting the dollars to the general fund."[5]

Increased Tuition and Fees

For most colleges and universities, student fees provide most of the revenue. This includes many prestigious public universities that draw as much or more from tuition and fees as they do from state appropriations. That being said, we saw nationally in 2010–2011 very small increases in tuition and fees in both private and public sectors, lower than in previous years. Published tuition and fees at nonprofit private colleges and universities increased by 4.5 percent for 2010–2011. This is the second smallest increase in thirty-seven years, following the 4.3 percent increase reported in FY 2009–2010. Published tuition and fees for 2010 increased by 7.9 percent at public universities, 6 percent at two-year public colleges, and 5.1 percent at for-profit institutions.[6]

These increases are not as important as what the institution actually earns in net tuition after deducting the costs of financial aid.

- Inflation-adjusted net tuition and fees at nonprofit private institutions actually declined by 11.2 percent over the past five years, from $12,750 in 2005–2006 to $11,320 in 2010–2011.
- In 2010–2011, full-time students at nonprofit private colleges received an estimated average of approximately $16,000 in grant aid from all sources and federal tax benefits.[7]

Colleges and universities that can make the "value proposition" to students and families that education is an investment justified by postgraduation outcomes will have less of a financial aid burden than those competing solely on cost. Part of these savings can be used to support transformational change. Conversely, change can also boost or even create the value proposition, permit higher fees, lower the financial aid discount, and essentially pay for itself. Kent State University charged higher prices for its financial engineering masters program, one of only forty in the world.[8]

Targeted Fund-Raising

In this economy, fund-raising may seem an unlikely source of new resources for change. According to findings of the annual Voluntary Support of Education survey, private giving to American colleges fell 12 percent in 2008–2009, the steepest decline in the survey's fifty-year history.[9] In 2009–2010, donations to the nation's largest charities dropped 11 percent, a decline that was the worst in the two decades since the *Chronicle of Higher Education* started its Philanthropy 400 ranking of the organizations that raise the most from private sources.[10]

Targeted fund-raising may be more promising. Institutions raise more money when they are able to make the case that donors can add to excellence and serve their passions rather than come to a financial rescue. It also helps if the college or university has a concrete change strategy that donors can support with a restricted gift, especially if it improves the quality or efficiency of the academic program.

Higher Taxes

Taxes and state appropriations are an uncertain and declining proportion of the budgets of public colleges and universities. Although state higher education funding has increased over time, its share of state funds has decreased in recent years. Higher education's share peaked at 13.1 percent in FY 1997–1998. It was 11.3 percent in FY 2008–2009 and 11.9 percent in FY 2009–2010.[11]

Trying to reverse this trend, some states are considering tax increases earmarked for higher education. Table 11.1 shows the options proposed by a strategic planning committee as a means of raising additional revenue for higher education in Colorado.[12]

Taxes support not only public higher education but, in some states, private colleges and universities too. For example, in North Carolina, private institutions receive $1,350 in need-based grant aid and $1,850 in merit-based aid for each in-state resident enrolled. At Guilford College alone, these funds amounted to $3.2 million in FY 2010–2011 and could be used for both routine and transformational uses of financial aid. For example, *merit* can be defined beyond traditional measures of academic quality to attract new types of students.

Increased Endowment Spending

More spending from endowment may also be an unlikely support for change. A NACUBO-Commonfund survey disclosed that 27 percent of

Table 11.1 Summary of Possible Revenue Streams to Fund Higher Education

Proposal	Amount
Restore income and sales tax rates to 5.0% and 3.0%, respectively	$445 million
Expand sales tax to specific services	$550 million
Implement 1.0% surcharge on extraction	$150 million
Implement a 4.0 mill levy statewide	$350 million
Implement a 4.0 mill levy in counties where an institution of higher education is located	$240 million

institutions planned to reduce endowment spending in FY 2008–2009.[13] Carleton and Spelman were among the colleges to reduce endowment spending so as not to liquidate too many assets when the market was at a low point, or what I call a "buy high, sell low" fallacy.[14] Others considered increasing their spending rates to generate more budget support. Nationally, the NACUBO-Commonfund survey found that in fiscal year 2008–2009, 54 percent of colleges and universities increased their actual spending even as the value of their endowments declined.[15]

Endowment can support change by earmarking a portion of the annual spending, or endowment spending can increase by whatever amount the change effort needs for a fixed period. For example, 0.25 percent might be added to the standard 5 percent spending rate for five years. The hope is that the change the endowment supports pays for itself through long-term benefits to academic reputation, net student fee income, and fund-raising.

Increased Debt Financing

Long-term debt in the form of bonds is often incurred for new buildings and major renovations that may be related to transformational change. For the 654 institutions that reported long-term debt at the end of FY 2008–2009 in the NACUBO-Commonfund survey, average debt increased from $109 million to almost $168 million (54 percent).[16] It is easier to support debt with a transformational change that adds enrollment or revenue from new sources that can be deployed for debt repayment.

More Grants

Foundations and government agencies may be financially supportive. Among the most popular sources of grants in higher education are the National Science Foundation (NSF), U.S. Department of Education (DOE), Fund for the Improvement of Postsecondary Education (FIPSE), U.S. Department of State (DOS), Mellon Foundation, Walmart Foundation, and Lumina Foundation. The extent to which and the ways in which they award grants for innovation depend on many factors, including the following:

- Funder's long-term and annual priorities
- Innovativeness and feasibility of the proposal
- Conversations with the funder to gauge interest and ways to focus the proposal
- Organization's credibility in completing grants on time, on budget, and with expected results

- Evidence the grant will lead to sustained organizational improvement and not a one-time benefit

Even a cursory search will often uncover a variety of programs relevant to the contemplated change. For example, if a college or university wants to improve its international perspectives in recruitment or curriculum, it could turn to a variety of governmental funders. Here are four:

- *NSF Partnerships for International Research and Education (PIRE)*: PIRE enables U.S. higher education institutions to establish collaborative relationships with international groups or institutions in order to stimulate new knowledge and promote the development of a globally engaged U.S. scientific and engineering workforce.
- *DOE Faculty Research Abroad*: This program provides grants to higher education institutions to fund faculty to maintain and improve their studies and language skills by conducting research abroad for periods of three to twelve months.
- *FIPSE Program for North American Mobility in Higher Education*: FIPSE runs collaboratively among the United States, Mexico, and Canada. This program funds consortia in support of a student-centered North American dimension to disciplines that complement existing exchange programs.
- *DOS Fulbright International Education Administrators Program*: This program offers annual seminars in Japan, Korea, and Germany designed to introduce participants to the society, culture, and higher education systems in these countries. The seminars include campus visits, meetings with foreign colleagues and government officials, attendance at cultural events, and briefings on education.[17]

Other Sources

Increasingly, colleges and universities, especially publicly funded state schools and those with small endowments, are turning to alternative revenue streams to make ends meet.

New graduate programs in selected areas can be profitable. New England College added a masters in management with a health care specialization and an MFA program in poetry, which combined online work with two ten-day on-campus sessions. In 2003, the first year that New England College offered a graduate program, it generated $1 million in revenue. In the 2008–2009 academic year, the graduate programs were budgeted to earn $5 million.[18]

Some colleges and universities are real estate developers. Many institutions already do this by owning student residence halls and apartments. However, institutions are finding that their property is in demand for uses beyond the academic program and student life. For example, the California State University system allowed professional soccer to build a 27,000-seat stadium at the system's Dominguez Hills campus. The university shares revenues from rent, parking, and the box office.[19] Another real estate venture involves leasing office space in new academic buildings to government and nonprofit organizations.

Neighbors and community groups are often concerned about the noise and effects on housing prices when colleges and universities expand their real estate holdings. Public officials are reluctant to see too much property become tax exempt. Institutions should be proactive in explaining their plans and safeguards in small group meetings, zoning hearings, and the media. To the extent possible, incorporating reasonable suggestions into final plans may not only assuage some concerns but also increase trust for future projects.

In *Diversifying Campus Revenue Streams: Opportunities and Risks*, James C. Hearn summarized a range of new revenue possibilities, including the following:

- Instruction, including online programming and niche-oriented non-degree programming
- Research and analysis, including technology transfer initiatives, business incubators, and e-commerce initiatives
- Pricing, including differentiated pricing and user fees
- Financial decision making and management, including venture capital investment as well as participation in arbitrage and options markets
- Human resources, including compensation incentives for entrepreneurship and retirement/rehiring incentives for faculty
- Franchising, licensing, sponsorship, and partnering arrangements with third parties, including logo-bearing clothing, tours and camps, and event sponsorships
- Auxiliary enterprises, facilities, and real estate, including on-campus debit cards, facility rentals, and alumni services[20]

Involve Key Stakeholders

Change is hard, especially if it has been achieved at the expense of your program or passion. If critics cannot get you on the decision, they will get you on the process. It is preferable to get the facts out rather than allow trustees, faculty members, and others to speculate and be led by their own fears to think and act precipitously. Top administrators not only should be open with information but also should solicit feedback and advice.

Education

Stakeholders need to be educated about the need for change, its benefits and challenges, and the larger environment in which the institution finds itself. This can be done with student and administrative newsletters, open meetings, and use of an intranet. At Bowdoin College and Guilford College, I led all-campus, case-based workshops on strategy and financial issues. Be sure that trustees favor the change before going public. Trustees hate surprises, and their support can help win over others.

Organization

If you do not have a widely representative institutional budget or planning committee, consider starting one now. It can be a sounding board for administration and trustees in analyzing the situation and obtaining solutions. It can also portend reactions on campus to your information and proposals. The Strategic Long-Range Planning (SLRP) Committee at Guilford College has managed to produce two comprehensive plans that cover a decade. At Bowdoin, then-president Edwards established a Strategic Planning Task Force that served a similar purpose. As he wrote:

> The Strategic Planning Task Force, as a whole, will conduct its work at a fairly broad conceptual level. Because of the College's basic health, it will not undertake a fundamental examination of its purposes and mission; instead, it will identify Bowdoin's broad strengths and the intentional themes that it should emphasize, strengthen, and protect against financial erosion. It will necessarily be a 'learning' group—looking at the College in relationship to world and national economic and educational changes.[21]

Process

Strategic plans do not just happen. Neither do budgets. Until a decade or so ago, many viewed budgeting as a technical exercise of completing worksheets and waiting for allocations from the finance office. The perceived and actual importance of the budgeting process has risen markedly, with much more competition for scarce resources and a recognition that budgets often dictate priorities more effectively than strategic plans. A campus community is more likely to understand and support transformational changes envisioned by a plan and budget they helped develop. The plan and budget may also be better informed and more accurately reflect campus realities. The predominant view will be that these documents are fair because the process was.[22]

In a participative process, a committee *recommends* to the president or chancellor, who may then decide to recommend the plan or budget to the board or legislature or to amend or reject it without consulting the committee again. (Public colleges and universities usually have another intermediate level of review at the system office or state agency.) Additionally, the president or chancellor may impose goals or constraints. For example, the committee may be expected to develop a budget that is balanced, spends no more than 5 percent of the endowment's lagging market value, invests at least $2 million to reduce deferred maintenance, and assumes no growth in enrollment or employment.

The committee should be representative of the principal campus constituencies: faculty, administrative staff, support staff, and students. Support staff (e.g., secretaries, facilities and dining service workers) should participate because they are aware of, experienced in, and often disproportionately affected by cutbacks. If possible, members should be elected or at least nominated by their respective constituencies, not appointed. Election or nomination provides greater legitimacy and visibility for the individual and the process.

Meetings characterize both consultative and participative approaches. These meetings may be "all-campus" at a small college or "all-school" at a large university. Participants should not only hear progress reports but also have an opportunity to speak. The committee might solicit reactions to planning or budgeting options under consideration. Use e-mail and the campus intranet to convey this information. Posting a draft on the institution's Web site and soliciting opinions via a conference board or chat room on the campus intranet can be very effective. Consider holding focus groups or individual meetings with off-campus stakeholders whenever contemplated academic or physical changes affect them.

Quaker Principles

As the first non-Quaker chief executive since Guilford College was founded as a boarding school in 1837, I needed to learn about Quaker principles and practices and how to apply them in my new role. While only 10 percent of our employees and students formally describe themselves as Quaker, and the community includes many faiths, we strive to maintain the traditions of our history. At Guilford College, we rely on principles from our Quaker heritage to make decisions, including the strategic plan, academic program prioritization, and the annual budget.

- The "sense of the meeting" is equivalent to a decision but is not handled like the typical motion. It arises out of a sense that the truth of a "best" solution exists if we enter discussion with open minds and a willingness to be led by others, even if a proposal is already under consideration. Although there might be informal ballots, or a show of hands, to see where people stand during the discussion, we believe a formal vote negates the power of the whole group and may lessen the sense of responsibility of the minority.
- Consensus does not necessarily occur, but there is "substantial unity" about what to do. People either endorse the proposal or, if opposed, agree to "stand aside" and not prevent consensus. This principle prevents a majority opinion from dominating the meeting and decision because anyone in opposition can refuse to stand aside, prevent consensus, and defeat the proposal.
- "Moments of silence" open and close many meetings, classes, and events. These moments allow meeting participants to transition from what they were just doing to focus (or "center") on the purpose of the meeting. Even thirty seconds of silence improves meeting participation and productivity.[23]

Talking about transformational change is easy. Actually doing it is hard. Financing decisions are among the most important determinants of whether change will succeed or fail. These decisions involve careful analyses of, and choices among, alternative levels of revenue and costs. They also call for being transparent with the data and inclusive of stakeholder views. In this case, the means are keys to achievement of the desired ends.

Notes

1. Robert C. Dickeson and Stanley O. Ikenberry, *Prioritizing Academic Programs and Services* (San Francisco: Jossey-Bass, 2010).

2. David Glenn and Peter Schmidt, "Disappearing Disciplines: Degree Programs Fight for Their Lives," *Chronicle of Higher Education*, March 28, 2010, http://chronicle.com/article/Disappearing-Disciplines-/64850/.

3. The PFM Group, "PFM Future Perfect," https://fm.pfm.com/default.aspx/ctrl/Default/nodeID/f131f62f-67ad-4e5a-9885-01f6268f4620.

4. Paul Fain, "At Public Universities: Less for More," *New York Times*, October 26, 2009, www.nytimes.com/2009/11/01/education/edlife/01public-t.html.

5. Carol A. Cartwright, "Financial Opportunities in the Public University Sector," www.tiaa-crefinstitute.org/pdf/programs/Slides110106_cartwright.pdf.

6. National Association of Independent Colleges and Universities, "Private College Tuition Increases 4.5 Percent for 2010–11; Institutional Student Aid

Up 6.8 Percent," news release, June 29, 2010, www.naicu.edu/news_room/ private-college-tuition-increases-45-percent-for-2010-11-institutional-student-aid-up-68-percent.

7. National Association of Independent Colleges and Universities, "Private College Tuition Increases 4.5 Percent for 2010–11."

8. Cartwright, "Financial Opportunities in the Public University Sector."

9. Council for Aid to Education, "Contribution to Colleges and Universities Down 11.9 Percent to $27.85 Billion: Greatest Decline Ever Recorded," news release, February 3, 2010, www.cae.org/content/pdf/VSE_2009_Press_Relsease .pdf.

10. Noelle Barton and Holly Hall, "Top Fund Raisers in 'Philanthropy 400' Saw Steep Drop in Donations Last Year," *Chronicle of Higher Education*, October 18, 2010, http://chronicle.com/article/Top-Fund-Raisers-in/125009.

11. National Association of State Budget Officers, "A New Funding Paradigm for Higher Education," www.nasbo.org/LinkClick.aspx?fileticket=MEqFX1WtTP Y%3D&tabid=38.

12. Colorado Department of Higher Education, "Summary of Possible Revenue Streams to Fund Higher Education," July 7, 2010, http://highered.colorado .gov/Publications/General/StrategicPlanning/Meetings/Resources/Sustain/ Sustain_100723_Possible_Revenue_Streams.pdf.

13. National Association of College and University Budget Officers-Commonfund, *2009 NACUBO-Commonfund Study of Endowment Results* (2009).

14. Kenneth E. Redd, "Surviving a Wild Ride," *Business Officer*, November 2009, www.nacubo.org/Business_Officer_Magazine/Magazine_Archives/ November_2009/Surviving_a_Wild_Ride.html.

15. NACUBO-Commonfund, *2009 Study of Endowment Results*.

16. Ibid.

17. J. Van de Water, Madeleine Green, and Kim Koch, *International Partnerships: Guidelines for Colleges and Universities* (Washington, DC: American Council on Education, 2008), www.acenet.edu/Content/NavigationMenu/ProgramsServices/cii/ AppendixC_editKK_Final_UpdatedMay09.pdf.

18. Francesca Di Meglio, "Colleges Explore Alternative Revenue Streams," *Business Week*, August 7, 2008, www.businessweek.com/bschools/content/aug2008/ bs2008087_167724.htm.

19. Meglio, "Colleges Explore Alternative Revenue Streams."

20. James C. Hearn, *Diversifying Campus Revenue Streams: Opportunities and Risks* (Washington, DC: American Council on Education, 2003).

21. Robert H. Edwards, an internal Bowdoin College memorandum.

22. Kent John Chabotar, "Managing Participative Budgeting in Higher Education," *Change* 27, no. 5 (September/October 1995): 21–29.

23. Kent John Chabotar, "Using Quaker Principles to Budget in Tough Times," *Inside Higher Ed*, February 10, 2009, www.insidehighered.com/views/2009/02/10/ chabotar.

PART III

IMPLICATIONS LIKELY TO FOLLOW FROM SUSTAINED TRANSFORMATIVE CHANGES

12

International Perspectives on Liberal Education

An Assessment in Two Parts

Richard A. Detweiler (Part A) and Jerzy Axer (Part B)

PART A:
INTERNATIONAL INSIGHTS ON
THE ESSENCE OF THE LIBERAL ARTS[1]

In recent years liberal arts education—a distinctly American approach to higher education—has generated substantial interest in many nations.[2] While there are undoubtedly many reasons for this interest in an American-style approach to education, a commonly expressed theme by educators outside the United States is that "people from our countries who went away to college in the U.S. came back different, and changed in valuable ways that benefit our societies."[3]

At the same time, in U.S. society there are renewed questions about the value of liberal education and whether the study of the liberal arts is practical and useful. The national enthusiasm for measurable learning outcomes as applied to precollegiate education is resulting in increasing U.S. federal and state governmental demands that similar measures be applied to higher education; the movement toward high-stakes testing conveys a growing conviction that learning can be documented by facts that are accumulated in student heads rather than in the development of a way of thinking and acting. These views differ sharply from a liberal arts conception of what it means to be educated.

The purpose of this chapter is to explore the essence of liberal arts education by comparing its development and application in the United States with how it is viewed and used in other countries. There is certainly no shortage of books, articles, and speeches on the subject of liberal arts education—its history, philosophy, assumptions, purpose, and content. In the United States, few topics generate more lengthy and heartfelt discussions by college faculty than the question of what must be included in liberal arts graduation requirements; it is not unusual for modifications in such requirements to take years of contentious discussion before there is agreement on change.

Are there cultural and social assumptions built into our thinking about the liberal arts that, if we understood them more clearly, might help educators inside and outside the United States focus their work more clearly on their desired educational outcomes? Is it possible that those of us committed to liberal arts education—in the United States and other nations—knowingly or unknowingly impose American values in ways that counter the nature of liberal arts education itself? What aspects of this form of education should be duplicated in nations or societies that do not share the American historical, social, and cultural context?

Emulating the historian Alexis de Tocqueville, who taught us more than 150 years ago that the perspectives of a thoughtful foreigner can yield substantial insight into otherwise unseen cultural assumptions and values, the liberal arts will be viewed from the perspective of those who developed it in its current form in the United States as well as from two distinctively different perspectives. These alternate perspectives include a report on the thinking of educators from Muslim-majority nations regarding American-style liberal arts education and a consideration of the development of higher education in Poland (briefly summarized in part A of the chapter and developed in full and intriguing detail by Jerzy Axer in part B).

The Roots of Liberal Arts Education

While there are many volumes on the history of higher education, the selective history provided here—one focusing on ideas that originated in Western Europe and subsequently extended across the Atlantic—is designed to establish the context for the subsequent perspective assessment of American-style liberal arts education.[4]

Classical Roots: The Development of Rulers

A relatively formalized approach to a "higher education"—one intended for the elite as ruling individuals as contrasted with an education in trades—is well known to have originated in classical Greece as represented in the works of Socrates and Plato as well as others. Classical thinking about education was reified much later into the seven classical subjects in the fifth century by Martianus Capella, a resident of a North African

Roman province. He was the "founder of the trivium and quadrivium in mediaeval education" who defined the liberal arts as the study of logic, grammar, dialectic rhetoric, geometry, arithmetic, astronomy, and music.[5] His framework proved to be one of lasting impact: European higher education institutions were founded in the eleventh and twelfth centuries in Italy (University of Bologna), France (University of Paris), and England (University of Oxford), with his liberal arts at their core. While the typical founding roots of institutions in this era were either in law (e.g., Bologna) or theology (e.g., Paris), the first course of study typically focused on Capella's trivium and quadrivium, with advanced degrees following in theology, law, or medicine.

It was several hundred years later when "the shapers of the Renaissance turned to Cicero's educational philosophy for inspiration and adaptation"—seeing a broad *education* (contrasted with training for a profession) as essential for a free people.[6] This development not only shaped the Renaissance but also shaped liberal arts education as it developed much later in what was to become the United States, and even later, in Poland.[7]

Pre-Revolution American Roots: Creating a Leadership Elite

The story of American higher education begins during the colonial period in the 1600s and 1700s. As a British colony, the approach taken was based on the educational model of Oxford and Cambridge at that time. Most often founded by various Protestant denominations, these institutions were designed to bring civilization to a newly developing land. Rudolph describes the founding of higher education as follows:

> Approximately a hundred Cambridge men and a third as many Oxford men emigrated to New England before 1646; among them were the founders of Harvard, the fathers of the first generation of Harvard students. Their purposes were complex, but among other things, they intended to re-create a little bit of old England in America. . . . Of course a religious commonwealth required an educated clergy, but it also needed leaders disciplined by knowledge and learning, it needed followers disciplined by leaders, it needed order.[8]

To become a leader, as people thought about it at that time, required a curriculum heavily (though not entirely) classical, one that placed an emphasis on the major languages of instruction and scholarly discourse (Latin, Greek, and Hebrew), with course work in rhetoric, philosophy, ethics, math, and a variety of courses we would now label as science (e.g., physics) and social science (e.g., economics and sociology).

Without question, this education was designed for the elite. One need only read an excerpt from a Harvard commencement address in the 1670s. The speaker asserted that, if it were not for a Harvard education, the "everyday person" might be in charge: "The ruling class would have been subjected to mechanics, cobblers, and tailors; . . . the laws would not have been made by *senatus consulta* [decree] . . . but plebiscites, appeals to base passions, and revolutionary ramblings."[9]

Of course the period leading up to and following the American Revolutionary War of 1776 required a fundamental reframing of higher education from being purely elitist to being necessary for a representative democracy. While still elite in character (not all people were allowed to become leaders or citizens), the education of a far broader and more representative cross-section of citizens began to be seen as essential. This change in thinking is evidenced in the many dozens of liberal arts colleges founded in the late 1700s and early 1800s. For example, clergyman John Christopher Hartwick (the founder of Hartwick College), who was both a Lutheran clergyman and a utopian, believed the society developing in the Americas could be made better through higher education. In support of this belief, he made a bequest to create a "seminarium"—ultimately founded in 1797—that would be committed to "enabling, preparing, and qualifying proper Persons . . . in Learning or Knowledge of the Instrumental Literature such as generally are taught in the American Colledges [*sic*]."[10]

Western European Roots: Serving the Nation-State

During this same era when such colleges were being founded in the United States, a singularly profound development sent higher education in Europe along a path that both separated it from classical education and provided a challenge that helped shape liberal arts education into its modern form in the United States. The founding of Humboldt University in Germany in 1810 was that development—an educational approach that later became characterized as the research-oriented, technical/professional model of higher education. According to Taylor, Humboldt's approach, based on Kant's thinking, was "designed to serve the needs of emerging nation-states."[11] Specifically, it was designed to "provide educated bureaucrats for the state, and second, to conduct research whose goal was the production of new knowledge."[12] In short, the modern research university was created, with a focus on research as well as professional and technical education, and the study of classical subjects as a part of higher education was left behind. This model was widely adopted by European universities, and with the dominant global role of European nations in the century following, it was also adopted virtually worldwide. Except, that is, in the United States.

Post-Revolution American-Style Liberal Arts Education: The Inquiring Citizen

By the early 1800s, the Cambridge/Oxford approach to higher education in the United States was being threatened: It needed to adapt to the thinking of people in a democratic republic in which citizenship was no longer to be trusted to a small elite, and the value and usefulness of the liberal arts approach was being challenged by the growing reputation of Humboldtian universities in Europe. The leading professors of the era worked at European institutions, which educated people for professional purposes; interest in the liberal arts was waning.

In response to these challenges, the *Yale Report of 1828* was written by Yale faculty members as a defense of the liberal arts.[13] It is quite remarkable that this document, written more than 180 years ago, became a lasting template that recognizably describes liberal arts education as it is practiced in the United States today. While the number of purely undergraduate liberal arts institutions is now a small part of American higher education, the study of liberal arts—both in purpose and content—is a significant part of virtually every undergraduate degree program in the United States, whether offered by the large state institution, the research university, or the liberal arts college. *The Yale Report* gives tremendous insight into these dynamics of the time:

> The Universities on the continent of Europe, especially in Germany, have of late gained the notice and respect of men of information in this country. . . . But we doubt whether they are models to be copied in every feature, by our American colleges. We hope at least, that this college may be spared the mortification of a ludicrous attempt to imitate them. . . . The students come to the universities in Germany at a more advanced age, and with much higher preparatory attainments, than to the colleges in this country. . . . The pupils, when they enter the university, are advanced nearly or quite as far, in literature if not in science, as our students are when graduated.[14]

What, then, should a liberal arts education be? While the Humboldt approach was designed to serve the state through the development of an elite, the authors of *The Yale Report* stated that a liberal education was intended to develop engaged and informed citizens; while the Humboldt approach was intended to develop expertise, the liberal education approach was intended to develop the inquiring mind; and while the

Humboldt approach focused on the lecture hall or laboratory, the liberal education approach focused on the creation of a learning community. In the process of reacting against the Humboldt model, the Yale faculty gave a clear elaboration of American-style liberal arts education, which is summarized here in three parts: its purpose, its content, and it context.

Purpose: Develop Informed and Engaged Citizens

The Yale Report describes education's citizenship purpose as particularly significant, with a contrast of the U.S. context and the European ("Eastern") one:

> Our republican form of government renders it highly important that great numbers should enjoy the advantage of a thorough education. On the Eastern continent, the few who are destined to particular departments in political life, may be educated for the purpose, while the mass of the people are left in comparative ignorance. But in this country, where offices are accessible to all who are qualified for them, superior intellectual attainments ought not to be confined to any description of persons. Merchants, manufacturers, and farmers, as well as professional gentlemen, take their places in our public councils. A thorough education ought therefore to be extended to all these classes. It is not sufficient that they be men of sound judgment, who can decide correctly, and give a silent vote, on great national questions. Their influence upon the minds of others is needed; an influence to be produced by extent of knowledge, and the force of eloquence. Ought the speaking in our deliberative assemblies to be confined to a single profession? If it is knowledge, which gives us the command of physical agents and instruments, much more is it that which enables us to control the combinations of moral and political machinery.[15]

In contrast to European elitism, education in the United States is *necessary* for every person—an education required for a representative form of democratic government to work.

Content: Develop the Inquiring Mind

What should every man study?[16] A liberal education should develop the thinking person—the inquiring mind. This is accomplished, according to *The Yale Report*, by developing "the *discipline* and the *furniture* of the mind; expanding its powers, and storing it with knowledge."[17] Quoting Cicero, areas of study must be broad: "*Est enim scientia comprehendenda rerum plurimarum, sine qua verborum volubilitas inanis atque irridenda est.* [Without knowledge of many things, copiousness of words is meaningless and even absurd.]" A liberal education should develop "a solid *foundation* in literature and science" and is "not designed to include *professional* studies . . . , is not to teach that which is peculiar to any one of the professions; but to lay the foundation which is common to them all."[18]

Context: Live-In Community

The third characteristic of a liberal education described in *The Yale Report* follows:

> A most important feature in the colleges of this country is, that the students are generally of an age which requires, that a substitute be provided for parental superintendence. When removed from under the roof of their parents, and exposed to the untried scenes of temptation, it is necessary that some faithful and affectionate guardian take them by the hand, and guide their steps. . . . The parental character of college government, requires that the students should be so collected together, as to constitute one family; that the intercourse between them and their instructers [*sic*] may be frequent and familiar.[19]

While the notion of a residential college, then, is very much a part of the American model, it is also clear that the notion of "family"—close relationships among faculty and students as contrasted with the distant Humboldtian expert—was also seen as essential to the American approach to higher education.

These attributes of a liberal arts education remain fully recognizable today. The Association of American Colleges and Universities (AAC&U)—the preeminent organization for liberal education in the United States—definitively describes liberal education for the twenty-first century as "intellectual and personal development," "a necessity for all students," and "essential for success in a global economy and for informed citizenship."[20] Further, the vast majority of American institutions of all types expend considerable resources on the development and maintenance of an educational community, including some combination of residence halls, cocurricular programming, residential colleges within large universities, sports and athletic programs, and student life facilities and staffs.

This linkage between intellectual capacities and citizen involvement is not unexpected. Bruce Kimball, in his book *Orators and Philosophers*, notes that there have long existed two different liberal arts traditions. One of these traditions emphasizes the importance of learning an analytic mode of inquiry (which he calls "artes liberales"), and the other emphasizes the development of the competencies necessary for effective citizenship (which he calls "the liberal-free ideal").[21] The artes liberales (thinking) tradition includes open-mindedness, freedom to search for the truth, and tolerance of diversity of views, whereas the liberal-free ideal (citizenship) tradition includes leadership, virtues or character, and embracing truth for its own sake. These traditions are not in conflict; they are seen as two components of the same tradition. As such, they represent different frames of reference for thinking about, designing, and implementing liberal arts curricula.

As currently practiced in the United States, the purpose (informed and engaged citizens) and context (an emphasis on community) remain largely unchanged. The content of a liberal arts education is now nearly invariably defined as some combination of study in breadth (through general education or core requirements) plus study in depth (through a major).

In conclusion, liberal arts education as it exists in the United States today was shaped by the particular history of this nation, representing in a post-Revolutionary era the values of a people who were working to evolve a successful democratic republic. That these are generally believed to be laudable values, and that the educational purpose is good, is not the question. The question is whether, or how, these values should be applied in nations that do not share this history or these cultural values. Is there an essence of the liberal arts that is applicable in many contexts—an approach to education that has a profound and recognizable impact on people and their abilities to contribute to their own societies?

Different Perspectives on American-Style Liberal Arts Education

To give insight into the answer to this question, perspectives from two different contexts are considered: one by educators from Muslim-majority nations, the other from Eastern Europe. These examples are not meant in any way to be representative of the many perspectives on the liberal arts from around the world; they are presented as valuable contrasts in that they describe the thinking of educators who have been particularly deep and reflective thinkers about American-style liberal education.

A Perspective by Educators from Muslim-Majority Nations

Higher education has a long and deep history in the Muslim world. Indeed, the first institutions we would likely recognize as universities originated in the Islamic world 1200 years ago in Morocco (Al Karaouine) and Egypt (Al Azhar), founded when their science, medicine, and math were far ahead of Europe. It was only when Arabic works, as well as ancient Greek works, were translated into European languages that European institutions were subsequently founded.

American-style liberal arts institutions also have a lengthy history in Muslim-majority nations; for example, Forman Christian College in Pakistan was founded in 1865, the American University of Beirut was founded in 1866, and the American University in Cairo was founded in 1919. While these institutions, and many others, were founded by missionaries, as were most liberal arts colleges in the United States, like most American colleges they were from the outset centrally committed to serving local and national needs and are now largely or entirely secular.

The interest in American-style education has expanded far beyond the early missionary-founded institutions, with a large number of state as well as private institutions in Muslim-majority nations seeking to provide a higher education of the highest possible quality and value. This may seem an odd development at this time in history when relations between the United States and Muslim countries are at a particularly low point, but the quality and impact of American higher education remain highly regarded.

The historical and social context within which higher education is developing in these nations is very different from the conditions that resulted in American-style liberal education. Virtually all these nations have been dominated by an external (Western European) colonial power in their relatively recent history, and in many cases their national borders have been created by the actions of these same powers. How is liberal education being adapted to this context?

At a meeting in Istanbul including fifteen educational leaders from Muslim-majority nations, participants explored the reasons for the growing number of locally originated American-style liberal arts–oriented undergraduate colleges and universities in Muslim-majority countries.[22] In these discussions, common liberal arts phrases were used just as they frequently are in the United States—catchphrases easily dispensed without great depth of consideration (e.g., the development of critical thinking, study in breadth plus depth, education of the whole person). Of real significance was the discussion of how American-style liberal arts education was adapted in ways that are culturally and socially appropriate to Muslim-majority nations, resulting in an educational experience very different from both the American context and from the approaches typically used in these nations.[23] For the sake of comparison, the same three categories used in the description of American liberal education are used here.

Purpose: Educate Change Agents

A broad education is profoundly important for creating agents of societal change. These agents may be leading intellects who challenge accepted or acceptable thinking, people who will question the assumptions of a society (being societally "subversive"), or individuals who will lead change within their societies. At the same time there is concern that the degree of challenge be appropriate for the context within which the change agents are operating, seeking to create constructive involvement and not societal instability. For example, Saudi Arabia's Effat University is "committed to constructive engagement with the whole of human culture" and "will strive to impart international humanistic Islamic values to its students and prepare them to be effective members of their respective institutions and useful contributors to their societies without being either narrow-minded or possessed with a liberalism that leads to (societal) dissolution."[24]

Content: Develop People Intellectually, Personally, and Socially

Developing and supporting the development of intellect is essential, and scholarship in its broadest definition is highly valued. Intellectual development is accomplished by teaching people how to formulate questions, think about the implications of knowledge, and be open to new ways of thinking—fundamentally different from just "asking questions" or "learning facts." Equally, education involves not only cognitive development but also the more complete development of the whole person; education will have little long-term impact if one does not place an emphasis on the social, personal, and maturational development of the student.

Context: Flattened Hierarchy

Respect for students is role-modeled in every context. Student thinking is valued; if a student says something that is flawed, it is not just rejected but is used as the beginning place for educational growth. Faculty are not seen merely as experts who deliver academic content but as individuals who are also constant learners, whose capabilities and effectiveness can be grown and developed through intentional efforts.

It is fascinating to note that, while there is virtually nothing in the previous descriptions that is contrary to liberal education as conceived in the United States, it is hard to imagine that an American institution could be found that would have, or think to list, this same set of priorities. This affirms the notion that the liberal arts have, at their essence, some set of common purposes that are then interpreted in ways that are historically and culturally determined. Before exploring this idea more fully, let's consider another perspective on the liberal arts.

A Perspective from Eastern Europe

The Polish experience, which continues to evolve as an educational experiment, is fully and eloquently described by Jerzy Axer in the second part of this chapter; what is described here is a very brief summary of some of the differences in perspective he describes between the American and this particular Eastern European context.

The Polish experience provides a particularly compelling perspective from which to view, and disambiguate, ideas about "American-style" and "liberal arts" education. Although Poland is a European country, its history has resulted in the dominant influences on its higher education being substantially different from those that were key in the development of higher education in Western Europe and the United States: Poland's earliest higher education developments (before the end of the eighteenth century) focused exclusively on Cicero's conceptualization; it missed the development of the national Humboldt-style research university, which only arrived at the time of World War I while the country was under foreign occupation; and from the end of World War II until 1989, higher education was shaped by an externally imposed authoritarian government.

Purpose: Autonomy and Freedom

Freedom is the supreme value, and individuals (and educational institutions) must be free of political or social pressure, imposed restraints, and repressive or totalitarian authority. To be effective as an individual and citizen, it is necessary to understand and defend one's own freedom and learn to rebel against any rule or action that threatens freedom.

Content: Classical Studies

Classical studies are the catalyst of education for autonomy and freedom because of their emphasis on the development of an analytic mode of thinking. Civic responsibility, because it connotes responsibilities imposed by foreign and totalitarian governments, cannot directly be part of liberal education.

Context: Choice

In consultation with tutors, students design individual curricula by selecting classes from among all those the university offers; students and tutors are jointly responsible for obtaining a broad, general, and interdisciplinary education. Care is taken to assure that moral equilibrium (avoiding the sense that some people are superior to others) occurs.

As with the example from Muslim-majority nations, there is nothing overtly problematic about this description of the liberal arts; it seems reasonable enough. But the Polish emphasis on freedom—as a cultural and an educational value—is at a far higher level than it is in the United States, where the emphasis is seen largely in the context of partisan politics. As a result, educational practice and policy in Poland include an inherently critical stance against political and social pressure, as well as suspicion of such ideas as "serving society."

What Is Liberal Arts Education?

A comparison of the views of the liberal arts from the three different cultural contexts included in this chapter is fascinating. Americans tend to see liberal education and citizenship as inherently linked; from a Polish perspective they must, for historical reasons, be carefully separated; and in the view of educators from Muslim-majority nations, there is a necessary tension between stability and change. Whereas Americans tend to be self-conscious in asserting that education must be value free, educators in Poland openly adopt the values of Cicero as the basis of a liberal arts education, and educators from Muslim-majority nations make an explicit link to Islamic values. For example, Effat University sees the values of Islam (reading as a divine act) and liberal education as integral to one another:

> Effat University believes that the future of the nation lies in the divine act of reading as expressed in the Holy Quran. The verb IQRA, "read," transformed a nation which favored the oral transmission of culture and the lyrical expression of ideas into a nation that produced a formidable number of written manuscripts. Effat University maintains that its future prospects reside in reviving this important part of the divine inspiration, reading, and in increasing comprehensive human knowledge in order to provide the nation with an infusion of new blood and guide it towards enlightenment.[25]

The "community" dimension of liberal arts education is also interestingly nuance based on the national context: In the United States this is a highly desired attribute, and the emphasis on community service and volunteerism is particularly valued. In Poland—and apparently in other nations with more recent experience with communist or totalitarian governments—"community" and "service" mean doing what you are told to do by government or political officials; this must be opposed because it is contrary to the central value placed on personal autonomy and freedom. And in the context of the educators from Muslim-majority nations, one neither wants to passively comply with societal expectations nor oppose them too strongly—one wants to create change without threatening social stability because the impact of instability is, based on decades of experience, so negative.

The particular purpose of liberal education seems to be dependent on the social, cultural, and historical needs of a nation: to be a more effective contributor to society (the United States), a constructive agent of change (Muslim-majority nations), or a thoughtful proponent of autonomy and freedom (Poland). How this is accomplished also varies, with educational approaches including an emphasis on the study of the classics (Poland), breadth of study (the United States), or personal/social development as well as intellectual development (Muslim-majority nations). Finally, the educational context is also differently emphasized, including community (the United States), the development of a flattened hierarchy among students and faculty (Muslim-majority nations), or the importance of choice (Poland).

Are there essential attributes of a liberal arts education that underlie these cultural differences—at least insofar as this limited analysis is concerned? For *purpose*, the higher ultimate goal is to better the human condition in its broadest sense, but one must learn to be discerning in what one chooses to do. To merely say "be a responsible citizen" or "become involved" allows a person to serve interests that may not be for the larger good. In the description of what it means to be a change agent was the notion that one must learn to be thoughtful about choices—to learn to act in ways that will improve society rather than acquiescing to expectations or demands.

For *content*, learning as a nonspecialist to ask good questions, to be open to new or different ideas, and to be analytic in how one thinks appear to be common features. What one studies in particular seems less important than the notion that the goal of liberal learning should not be specific professional or technical expertise but should, as stated in *The Yale Report*, focus on the foundations that underlie all professions.

Finally, *context* varies greatly by culture; the common theme may be some degree of egalitarianism—the conviction that people, regardless of role, should be valued.

As noted earlier, there is nothing in these descriptions that would be antithetical to the liberal arts advocate in the United States. But it is interesting to consider how a curriculum, perhaps stripped of some cultural (or habitual) assumptions, would be designed if the common features were the guide. Rather than arguing about which courses should be included in a general education requirement, or whether study in a particular academic department should be required, might one begin considering a clearer focus on the discipline of critical learning and thinking and on the implications of choices for the progress of humanity?

This description of essential attributes of the liberal arts as gained from international perspectives should also cause American educators to ask important, though perhaps not socially acceptable, questions. Does the typical American college's requirement of "study in breadth plus depth" really accomplish central liberal arts learning goals? Is a college's liberal arts curriculum evolving in part from the agenda of academic departments concerned with maintaining their own enrollments and position? If so, is it being distorted as much as a curriculum shaped by the dictates of government policy? As educators, should we engage in more thoughtful, and vocal, opposition to the types of simple learning outcomes that seem to be of increasing interest to our regulators? Is it important to head off greater government intervention into the way we do our work? Do we need to encourage more critically constructive thinking about our nation and its actions? When encouraging service and community involvement, do we need to assure that students entering such work are actively considering the ways in which the institutions they are supporting are furthering or inhibiting human advancement as opposed to less-just political or social goals?

Further, U.S. public skepticism about the value of the liberal arts, and the (unfounded) belief that in a time of economic stress a professional undergraduate degree is the best route to employment, has resulted in many colleges scrambling to add professional programs and certifications to attract students. Instead of bowing to this societal pressure, should we not be courageous change agents who take serious steps to change our society's direction?

Last, while American academics are quick to laud their objectivity and value neutrality, a simple lesson of this analysis is that we are all influenced by our own cultures. Perhaps we should, as the educators at Effat University did, make the effort to identify the ways in which our institutions' educational goals are influenced by both values and culture; for if we do not take the time to do this, we will lose the long-term impact that our form of education is supposed to have on shaping individuals and societies in ways that further human progress.

To conclude, we can do no better than to quote two historians of an earlier era—Will and Ariel Durant—people who eloquently (though in dated, gendered terms) describe what should be our highest calling as liberal arts educators:

> Consider education not as the painful accumulation of facts and dates and reigns, nor merely the necessary preparation of the individual to

earn his keep in the world, but as the transmission of our mental, moral, technical, and aesthetic heritage as fully as possible, for the enlargement of man's understanding, control, embellishment, and enjoyment of life. . . . If progress is real despite our whining, it is not because we are born any healthier, better, or wiser than infants were in the past, but because we are born to a richer heritage, born on a higher level of that pedestal which the accumulation of knowledge and art raises as the ground and support of our being. The heritage rises, and man rises in proportion as he receives it. . . . If a man is fortunate he will, before he dies, gather up as much as he can of his civilized heritage and pass it on to his children. And to his final breath he will be grateful for this inexhaustible legacy, knowing that it is our nourishing mother and our lasting life.[26]

PART B:
INTERNATIONAL PERSPECTIVES ON LIBERAL EDUCATION: POLISH CASE EXAMPLE[27]

Correlating the idea of general education with education for leadership in a republican civil society, so important for liberal arts education, goes much further back than the idea of universities. My own life and experience have been such that I have an especially clear perception and a particularly personal outlook on that part of tradition originating from the teaching and political experience of Marcus Tullius Cicero.

I first came in contact with *De oratore* as a university student—early enough to experience a sense of initiation. This work attempts to organize the reflections of several generations on the nature of human communication in the republican system and on the importance of that communication for strengthening the freedom of the individual and for organizing a community of free people. If it is a textbook, it is one only in the sense that it indicates a road, it investigates the essence of social debate, of conversations that enable people to reach the core of their views, while also getting them accustomed to sharing these views with their fellow citizens as well as commanding them to pass on the records of such conversations to future generations.

It is Cicero's premise that in order to raise free people (*cives reipublicae*), you have to equip them with the broadest possible education, and only this is worthy of citizens. It will help them with their personal careers, but above all it will make them capable of understanding and defending their own freedom. They will not be helpless when faced with anything new; they will not have to fear changes and any challenges unforeseen by their teachers. Greater drama is added to any reading of *De oratore* when you realize it is a sui generis memoir written by a citizen of the republic, an artist and intellectual, who lived at a time of major political change: The Roman republic was on the wane, while at the same time Rome was achieving the position of the sole superpower imposing a new order throughout the Mediterranean world.

In terms of immediate political success, Cicero failed dismally—he paid with his life for his commitment to defending the republic. On the other hand, though, he managed to process the experience of the aristocratic republic into a new model for educating future generations that would be living in a completely different world.

His idea was to replace the traditional system of educating the elite, through oral transfer of knowledge and role models, with a written treatise preserving the essence of the oral tradition for times when the continuity of the republican experience would be broken. *De oratore* is written in the form of a "seminar cycle" taught by Cicero's deceased teachers who had been killed in successive waves of political purging. The author has his teachers discuss the sum of human knowledge, the transfer of which is subordinated to a supreme objective that forms the core of republican ethics. This is human freedom of self-fulfillment, aspiring to expand one's *dignitas* and *auctoritas* (importance and prestige) while upholding the good of the community of which one is a member (*bonum reipublicae*). The kind of dialogue that organizes the structure of *De oratore* is the essence of the Roman tradition of civic debate: partners who respect one another reaching shared conclusions by working out a compromise.

Cicero's hands and his head were nailed to the speaker's platform (rostrum) in the Forum, the same one from which he had pronounced his views, as a sign that new times had arrived. But his essentially revolutionary idea for education reform—opposing Greek rhetoric and its teaching of practical effectiveness in action, in favor of education in the artes liberales (arts worthy of free people)—survived and had a huge impact on European culture. It was the Ciceronian tradition that Quintilian used over a century after the death of *De oratore*'s author to design his new model of education for the elite; later, Erasmus of Rotterdam served as a mediator between Cicero and Quintilian on the one hand and Renaissance humanism on the other. It is the Ciceronian faith in education's being superior to instruction that lies at the foundation of the liberal arts education idea.[28]

I was not aware of all this forty years ago as a participant in the seminars of my mentor, Professor Kazimierz Kumaniecki; I thought I was studying to be an expert, a professional classical philologist, while the seminar itself fascinated me as a form of training in textual criticism. The influence of this powerful book didn't manifest itself until much later.

While initially I had thought about classical studies in terms of a refuge from the totalitarian reality, an ecological niche enabling me to maintain a degree of private intellectual independence, I paradoxically became—I understand that today—the best example of how powerful liberal arts education can be in transforming an egotistical individual seeking to escape from society into someone who wants to change the social reality.

Poland had a long tradition of special respect for, or even a cult of, Cicero. The source of this can be traced back to the tradition of what we call the First Republic (the Polish-Lithuanian Commonwealth, which existed in the sixteenth to eighteenth centuries), whose political nation built an original republican political system. This was a Renaissance republic of nobles; in its heyday it effectively implemented civic ideas modeled (at least in a self-interpretation of the noble nation) on the Roman concept of *cives reipublicae*. In this structure, the actual sovereign was not a king but the nation of nobility, meaning that 10 percent of the population was enjoying developed civil liberties in a parliamentary system (with local preelections).

In this context, and differently from what was happening in Western Europe at this time, Cicero also became a teacher of parliamentary political practice, while his republican language constituted the fundamental fabric of public dispute.[29] This was also when a peculiar way of thinking about freedom (*libertas*) developed in Poland, in which freedom was seen as the supreme value, giving citizens the right to rebel against any rule that threatened this freedom (including their own monarch). "Nos Poloni ad libertatem sumus nati, aliae nationes servitutem pati possunt" ("We Poles are born to freedom, other nations may live in bondage"), people would say, paraphrasing Cicero's distinction between being a citizen of the Roman republic and living in a different country or system.

This saturation of Polish public discourse with Ciceronian republican diction, unique when compared with the rest of Europe, needs to be seen as the reason for the enthusiasm with which people such as Kazimierz Pułaski and Tadeusz Kościuszko, representing very different social views, adopted the American idea of a sovereign nation and took part in the War of Independence.[30] This concept of freedom survived the downfall of the Polish-Lithuanian Commonwealth and its partitioning by its neighbors, becoming the foundation for building a new identity for the elites of a nation without statehood in the nineteenth century. Republican freedom—in the absence of institutions where it could be practiced—became intertwined with messianic, Romantic ideas of the nation's martyrdom and resurrection. Being later a part of the program of different political patriotic movements, it remained a major component of Polish mentality also under communist rule in the years 1945–1989.

This is why I found it easy in the 1960s, in my youth, to see *De oratore* as a book about the Polish fate, about the fate of the Polish intelligentsia, about the duty of being faithful to tradition and passing it on to future generations. It also offered encouragement to treat teaching like a mission. This mission could be fulfilled only if you acted against the system, or at least in spite of the system. Educating people to be good citizens did not mean preparing them to be part of the country's official political life as it was then, but educating them to become a "citizen of the republic of independent spirit" that existed only in dreams and was supposed to emerge after the current system collapsed in the distant future, certainly not within our lifetime.

This conviction that education consists in raising people to be faithful to the past for the benefit of a distant future, in constant opposition to existing governments trying to destroy remembrance of the past in order to control the present, was very much alive at the university where I was educated.

The academic milieu, restricted in its freedom by the existing political system and deprived of autonomy but preserving its memory, enthusiastically greeted the birth of the Solidarity social movement in 1980 and hastily began rebuilding its self-governance and seeking new forms of operation. Martial law imposed on December 13, 1981, marked the start of a decade during which—a paradox—for the very first time, the academic community began planning an alternative concept of the university to the existing one, that of a really autonomous university. The opportunity to create this kind of university came in 1990.

A return to the source became our motto once the communist system in Poland collapsed and universities gained the opportunity to share in developing their own missions. What source could we have had in mind at that point? This was in no way obvious. Contrary to Western Europe, Poland had no strong tradition or its own form of the Humboldtian university. The simple reason was that when this model emerged and flourished in the nineteenth century, the Polish nation-state did not exist, and its past and future territory, split among the partitioning powers, included operating German, Russian, and Austrian universities founded to develop knowledge but primarily to educate officials for what—from the Polish people's viewpoint—were the occupying empires. So to what "source" were we to return?

It was not until the short period of independence from 1918 to 1939 that national Polish universities modeled on the Humboldtian idea began to develop. In this sense, it was a short-lived tradition. After World War II, universities were taken over by the totalitarian authorities and adjusted to suit the new political system. In essence, universities in communist Poland were a degenerated form of Humboldtian university, serving the interests of a nonsovereign country and not guaranteeing freedom of research. This was precisely the kind of university we rebelled against. The return to the source had to involve searching for something deeper down. What lay deeper down, in fact, was the layer I mentioned earlier, the layer that included the tradition of classical education and the gentry nation's mythical freedom from the times of the Polish-Lithuanian Commonwealth.

The first law on higher education passed in independent Poland in 1990 was a good reflection of the essence of our dreams and aspirations. It provided for establishing strong university autonomy and a supra-university representation with decision-making capabilities, in the form of a main council, elected by the academic milieu. That law enabled the academic community to develop civic activity, creating a kind of corporate republic of scholars and students. In this sense, intentionally or not, it drew upon the beginnings of the university idea as well as the Polish republican tradition. Even though higher education as a whole was state-run and financed from taxpayers' money, the government practically withdrew from interfering with it for more than ten years.

In these circumstances, it was possible to establish and develop the very experiments it has been my pleasure to head and which I will outline here. We had no extensive knowledge on the Western European university system, and only a semi-mythical idea as to the American system. To a great extent, we tried to work out our own system.

What guided us was the idea of universities free from any government political pressure, concentrated mainly on their mission to liberate individuals from the totalitarian system's legacy, encouraging them to be active and responsible and to reveal instead of conceal their desires and needs. Our aim was to break free of imposed restraints in favor of restraints intentionally chosen and accepted by teachers and students in their desire to renew the university community protected by its autonomy from future claims by authorities.

In this context, in the community where I was active it was also possible to put forward the seemingly outdated idea that classical studies should be made the catalyst of this renewal, an idea obviously influenced by my own education.[31]

This starting point for the reform, a paradox at a time when classical studies were being marginalized in the West, gained enough acceptance within the University of Warsaw (UW) for its rector to task me in 1992 with setting up new, model, "genuine" humanities studies affiliated with the research unit I headed: the Centre for Studies on the Classical Tradition in Poland and East-Central Europe (OBTA). That was how the Collegium of Interdepartmental Individual Studies in the Humanities (MISH) came into being. It was a system of learning and not a university unit. Within a few years, all the University of Warsaw's humanities and social sciences departments joined the project, forming a kind of confederation. It enabled a group of students, those who passed a special qualification procedure, to obtain BA- and MA-level degrees in a mode hitherto unknown in Poland: They were guaranteed tutor supervision, and with their tutors could design individual curricula by selecting classes from among all those the university offered; they were held jointly responsible for their choices; and apart from professional training, they were obligated to obtain a broad, general, and interdisciplinary education.

As we saw it, this form of studying was supposed to work as a catalyst of general change—the entire university was supposed to transform into a MISH, and the MISH as such would close down. This did not happen. The evolution of the whole system of higher education ultimately took a different direction. On the one hand, university-level schooling developed on a mass scale, with student numbers growing severalfold as the standard of schooling deteriorated accordingly, and on the other, after a long period of doing nothing, the government administration began showing an inclination for running, controlling, and unifying things. Consecutive amendments to the relevant laws (in 2001 and 2005) began restricting university autonomy, instead reintroducing a system of central control over this sector—treated as a sector of the economy—by the government. I outline the reasons for this later.

Before this happened, though, the MISH UW had won significant prestige nationally. Structures modeled upon it were established at all the leading universities, bringing together the best professors and students, the most inquiring minds who were prepared to take a risk. They accounted for a very small number of students (less than 1 percent at the UW) but were the pride of every university rector.

We knew nothing about the idea of liberal arts education at the time, and this lack of knowledge caused me to react so spontaneously when Dr. Nick Farnham from the Christian A. Johnson Endeavor Foundation in New York invited me to Budapest in 1996 to a meeting between educators from Central and Eastern Europe and American partners to discuss this very idea.

My spontaneous reaction was rather like the behavior of Monsieur Jourdain when he suddenly realized he spoke in prose (it is a quotation from my speech opening this conference).[32] However, this meeting did give us a sense of partnership with the Americans that we have never lost since. We had the extreme good fortune of winning the support of the American community, which believed it was essential to revive the spirit of liberal education in America and was prepared to trust in the efforts being made at the eastern edges of Europe to develop a local model of liberal education.

By the way, we did not know that parallel to our own experiments, work was progressing, in regular consultation with U.S. partners and with the support of the U.S. Embassy in Poland, to develop a nationwide system of public evaluation and accreditation of courses at the leading universities. This was when (1995–1997) the University Accreditation Commission (UKA) was appointed, a body modeled on the accreditation procedures applied in the United States, in the belief that the academic community was capable of producing and following very high professional and moral standards, without any interference from the government.

We imagined that society would take over the system of higher education from the government, and a far-reaching diversification of this system would occur. That was why we attached great importance to the leading universities' autonomous actions while failing to appreciate the possibility of resistance from the central bureaucracy.

The next level to which my colleagues and I took our activity was to transfer the MISH concept (a structure based on a confederation of departments within a research university) to interuniversity relations. As a result, the Artes Liberales Academy (AAL) was formed in 1999. This system enabled students to build their individual courses with the help of two tutors from two different universities, to compose their curricula from classes offered by the seven participating universities. We treated this concept like a laboratory, enabling us to take advantage of the enthusiasm and readiness for reform shown by prestigious academic communities from all over Poland as we practiced our civic activity skills.

The Artes Liberales Academy also served as support for courses modeled on the University of Warsaw's Collegium MISH, organized at other universities. It was managed by a council enjoying extensive prerogatives and composed of representatives of the rectors of all the cooperating universities. Accreditation was provided by the aforementioned republican community-based University Accreditation Commission (in 2002).

Out of a genuine sense of obligation to expand the democratic relations in academic space to countries of the former Soviet Union, eastwards of Poland, and believing that just as we had received assistance from the West, we should now provide it to others, we set up the East-Central European School in the Humanities (MSH) in 1996. It continues to operate to this day, supported and developed by the same community that created the MISH and AAL, training faculty from Ukraine, Belarus, and Russia who are working to change the relations at their universities in the spirit of democratization and autonomy. Thanks to this structure, we have also managed to transfer the MISH idea to several universities in Ukraine (Lviv, Kiev, and Uman) and Russia (Rostov-on-Don).

During this most favorable period in our activity, I was always aware that American liberal education had developed in very different circumstances and that we had to be very careful not to transplant various institutional and organizational forms, even if they worked very well in the United States, to the very different conditions of Poland and Eastern Europe. You can adopt the spirit but not the letter. I concluded that our situation was a little like the early development stage of liberal education in America—that is, we could develop our freedom because our way was not blocked by any respected, rigid national university model. Everything was still pliable, and everything still seemed possible.

As I mentioned earlier, the circumstances in which we operated began to change at the start of the twenty-first century. The government bureaucracy began striving very hard to regain control over higher education, to centralize decision making, to curb university autonomy, and to create uniform official programs and systems of control. This was quite easy because the weakness of civic structures within society enabled the government to play the role of the representative of interest of external social environment toward the egotistical, as they called it, corporate concept of the autonomous university. Taking advantage of Poland's joining the Bologna Process (1999) and then Poland's EU accession (2004), the government used the argument that universities should open up to society.

In actual fact, however, what happened was a kind of recolonization of higher education by the education bureaucracy. It is a global trend that Frank Furedi diagnosed so insightfully in his book *Where Have All the Intellectuals Gone?*[33] This process in Poland was facilitated by the conformism of part of the academic community, who were more afraid of radical change and genuine participation in public life at their own risk than of the familiar game of cops and robbers played with political authorities applying economic pressure and legal constraints.

Meanwhile, for circles that believed in renewal stemming from genuine grassroots activity among the academic community, the resulting situation was a complete paradox. On the one hand, there was the downside related to the fact that within an autonomous university, our formula had won the acceptance of the best students, professors, and enlightened rectors, but their influence on the system decreased as autonomy lessened. On the upside, the situation reactivated one of the traditional sources of our activity—resistance to rules and dictates imposed from the outside, in other words an attitude of subversive activity as part of the mission of liberal arts education à la polonaise.

In these circumstances, without abandoning existing forms of activity, we decided to concentrate on building a separate structure within the University of Warsaw, as the best Polish research university, that would confer its own BA, MA, and in future also PhD degrees, with the intention of treating this experiment as a laboratory of liberal arts education in Polish conditions in 2008–2009.

We called the new unit the Collegium Artes Liberales (College of Liberal Arts and Sciences), fully aware that it would be largely different from an American liberal arts college, particularly in not being a residential unit and not running just BA but also graduate courses. We believed, however, that this formula would help us preserve and promote the fundamental and immutable values of liberal arts education, particularly those that are a part of the American artes liberales tradition (emphasizing the analytic mode of thinking). We realized it would be much harder to develop the other component of that tradition: the liberal-free ideal (emphasizing the development of effective citizenship).[34] Our main objective was to prove that the increasingly likely prospect of undergraduate education's being marginalized at Polish research universities, and leading faculty's becoming concentrated on the graduate level (a process also known from the United States), was the wrong road to take.[35]

The collegium cooperates very closely with the MISH, serving to integrate students and faculty. We are making the collegium's core curriculum available to all MISH students. Thus, our collegium was devised as a microuniversity, preserving and developing the republican civic academic community that had emerged in the 1990s. Now it is threatened in the new system due to the gradual introduction of a new form of the European Humboldtian university. This is how the Commission of the European Communities—supported by the bureaucracy of national governments—is transforming the results of implementing the Bologna Process, which goes against the original Bologna Declaration.[36]

I can say with full conviction that we owe a great deal to our partnership with American educators. The role of the Christian A. Johnson Endeavor Foundation, and personally its president Julie J. Kidd, is impossible to overestimate. From 2000 we have received its financial support for our efforts, it being fully understood that we do not intend to copy any U.S. model but plan to develop original solutions. As part of this support, I have also received invaluable advice from people such as Nick Farnham, Adam Yarmolinsky (a tree in his memory grows in the garden of our collegium), Julie J. Kidd herself, and Don Harward.[37] His deep commitment to rethinking everything we are doing has been hard not to appreciate as well. It helped us properly develop the collegium's concept in 2006, and now, in 2010, it gives us a clear idea of the goals and methods of our activity up to 2016, when the first PhD degrees will be conferred by the collegium.

All these contacts have fully confirmed that an artes liberales education should be founded on experience repeated in a given society for generations. The American experience is different from the European, and the Polish experience is similar to the American in that it includes a love of freedom and the lack of a tradition of enlightened absolutism. However, on the contrary to the Americans, exactly from the end of the eighteenth century, in collective and individual life alike, we could not practice forms of civic engagement generated by ourselves, instead having to focus on combating and rejecting the model of civic activity imposed by foreign empires or a totalitarian system.

This is what poses the greatest problem when it comes to developing the part of the liberal education idea that assumes the creation of a community on the one hand, and on the other—perhaps more importantly—educates people for leadership and at the same time for citizenship.

In Poland, you have to move very carefully in that whole space the Americans call effective citizenship. Things that are obvious in America—that society the way it is, despite all its faults, ensures individuals proper conditions for development and for serving that society—are not obvious in the Polish reality, and especially in Polish ideas about that reality. The problem is exacerbated by an extreme deficit of trust typical of postcommunist societies.

This can lead to pathologies. It is worth noting that given the lack of willingness and possibilities to implement liberal education in a residential environment replacing parental superintendence, our students are embedded in a mass of "normal" fellow students and find it too easy to be successful in terms of evaluation and advancement in internal hierarchies and political youth groups, which threatens their moral equilibrium. They could get the erroneous impression that they are special and better and thus start treating liberal education as a privilege that should be rationed.[38]

Again, I see the antidote to this in drawing on the Polish tradition, on the idea of the republican autonomy of the university as a whole and the contribution of liberal arts students to such a republic. This is starting to work; for several years now, MISH students have been winning the UW student government elections (testifying to the power of liberal education as education for leadership) and learning to serve the whole community.

It is also important to realize that in Polish society, where a relatively strong role is played by the Roman Catholic Church, knowledge of the Bible is poorly internalized. At the same time, the language of values was compromised under communism by the newspeak of the totalitarian state. Communities that teach in the spirit of liberal arts have to find their own language, restoring words and notions related to moral and social values to their genuine meaning, and slowly rebuild the sphere of trust between teacher and student, individual and community.[39]

Another thing we need to remember is that in America today, education has been turned more and more into a private good, which students buy because they can earn more money if they have an education. In Europe and in Poland, education is considered a public good. In the markets of the post-Soviet space, it is largely not the quality of education but having a certificate to show for it that is important. Thus, liberal arts education is in opposition to a university's short-term economic interests (requiring a great deal of work while being available for free under the constitution), while on the other hand the degrees obtained by students educated in this mode are new on the market, so their holders risk much more than the graduates of traditional departments.

The necessary condition for freedom of liberal education to take hold in Poland is, in my opinion, the internal self-organization of autonomous universities, giving them the right to introduce innovations, even if they are partly supported by taxpayer funds.[40] Autonomy has to serve as the foundation of a revival of mutual trust between the university and the social environment the university is meant to serve. Only university autonomy offers a chance for the development of liberal education, education whose very nature involves opposition to repressive social and political authority, education that in Poland can seek support only within the traditional love of freedom. In these circumstances, we can also be hopeful that students and professors introducing liberal education to Poland will be less likely to succumb to any temptation to treat this idea as "libertarian" rather than "communitarian."

We feel honored that our American partners have come to perceive some aspects of our activity as useful case examples in rethinking their education system.[41] I realize this usefulness could be limited, and only practice will show if we are able to repay our debt at least to some small extent.

Notes

1. Thanks is expressed to Jerzy Axer for stimulating discussions on this topic and to Carol Detweiler and Gregory Wegner for their formative comments on drafts of this chapter.

2. Steven Kobloick and Stephen Graubard, eds., *Distinctly American: The Residential Liberal Arts College* (New Brunswick, NJ: Transaction Publishers, 2000).

3. Richard A. Detweiler, "Lessons from Middle East 'de Tocquevilles,'" *Inside Higher Ed*, October 30, 2006, www.insidehighered.com/views/2006/10/30/

detweiler. This sentiment has been expressed in personal conversations I've had with the leaders of more than a dozen American-style institutions in various world regions.

4. In this chapter we are knowingly omitting a consideration of the development of higher education in the Muslim world as well as in Asia. The omission is not from lack of appreciation of the long and important history represented, nor of the influence of Islamic scholars on the development of higher education in Europe, but because the theme of this chapter relates to liberal education as it has evolved in a more contemporary context.

5. William Stahl, "To a Better Understanding of Martianus Capella," *Speculum* 40, no. 1 (January 1965): 102–15.

6. Ethyle Wolfe, "Cicero's 'De Oratore' and the Liberal Arts Tradition in America," *The Classical World* 88, no. 6 (1995): 459–71.

7. See Axer's elaboration of Cicero and his impact in part B of this chapter.

8. Frederick Rudolph, *The American College and University: A History* (New York: Knopf, 1962), 4, 7.

9. Samuel Eliot Morison, *The Founding of Harvard College* (Cambridge, MA: Harvard University Press, 1935), 250.

10. Henry Hardy Heins, *Throughout All the Years: The Bicentennial Story of Hartwick in America, 1746–1946* (Oneonta, NY: The Board of Trustees of Hartwick College, 1946).

11. Mark C. Taylor, *Crisis on Campus* (New York: Knopf, 2010), 18.

12. Taylor, *Crisis on Campus*.

13. Committee of the Corporation and the Academical Faculty, *Reports on the Course of Instruction in Yale College* (New Haven, CT: Hezekian Howe, 1828), www.yale.edu/yale300/collectiblesandpublications/specialdocuments/Historical_Documents/1828_curriculum.pdf.

14. Committee of the Corporation and the Academical Faculty, *Reports on the Course of Instruction*, 21.

15. Committee of the Corporation and the Academical Faculty, *Reports on the Course of Instruction*, 29.

16. "Man" is true quite literally—at that time higher education for women was uncommon, and women did not have a vote.

17. Committee of the Corporation and the Academical Faculty, *Reports on the Course of Instruction*, 7.

18. Committee of the Corporation and the Academical Faculty, *Reports on the Course of Instruction*, 10, 14.

19. Committee of the Corporation and the Academical Faculty, *Reports on the Course of Instruction*, 9.

20. Association of American Colleges and Universities, "What Is Liberal Education?" www.aacu.org/leap/what_is_liberal_education.cfm.

21. Bruce A. Kimball, *Orators and Philosophers: A History of the Idea of Liberal Education* (New York: College Entrance Examination Board, 1995).

22. This meeting was convened in 2007 by the Hollings Center for International Dialogue. The basic purpose of the meeting was to explore whether there was

potential for development of productive relationships between independent universities in Muslim countries and in the United States. The meeting was held under Chatham House Rule, meaning that while the general content of the conversations could be disclosed, comments could not be attributed to any person.

23. The ideas expressed here are based on my understanding of the perspectives of the fifteen educators who were a part of these discussions; these should not be interpreted as representing the thinking of all educators from these or other nations.

24. Effat University, "About Effat," www.effatuniversity.edu.sa/index .php?option=com_content&task=view&id=19&Itemid=101; Effat University, "Our Core Values," www.effatuniversity.edu.sa/index.php?option=com_content &task=view&id=482&Itemid=550.

25. Effat University, "Our Core Values."

26. Will Durant and Ariel Durant, *The Lessons of History* (New York: Simon and Schuster, 1968), 101–2.

27. I am much obliged to Richard Detweiler, with whom I had a very stimulating discussion on liberal education. I consider my text to be an illustrative example based on my personal experience compared with his more general and objective analysis. These reflections are the effect of my discussions with the colleagues who, together with me, developed the projects in the spirit of liberal arts education in Poland, especially Professor Jan Kieniewicz, cofounder of the Institute for Interdisciplinary Studies "Artes Liberales"; Professor Marek Wąsowicz and Professor Andrzej Tymowski, co-initiators of the Collegium Artes Liberales idea; Professor Piotr Wilczek, the Collegium's director; and Professor Robert Sucharski, co-organizer of the East-Central European School in the Humanities.

28. Jerzy Axer, "A Latin Lesson, or Words on Freedom," in *Autonomia uniwersytetu. Jej przyjaciele i wrogowie* [The autonomy of the university: Its enemies and friends], ed. Jan Kieniewicz (Warsaw: FIAL, 2007), 181–89.

29. Jerzy Axer, "W krzywym zwierciadle tradycji antycznej [Fairground mirror of the classical tradition]," in *Retoryka i polityka. Dwudziestolecie polskiej transformacji* [Rhetoric and politic: Twenty years of Polish transformation], ed. Marek Czyżewski (Warsaw: Wyd. Akademickie i Profesjonalne, 2010), 37–43.

30. Jerzy Axer, "Da Pułaski a Kościuszko. Cicerone nella tradizione repubblicana dei protagonisti polacchi della rivoluzione americana," *Ciceroniana. Nuova* 8 (1994): 53–62.

31. Jerzy Axer, "How the Classical Tradition Can Serve to Promote Liberal Education in the Twenty-First Century: The East-Central Europe Case Example," *Kritika & Kontext* 3, no. 1 (1998): 113–16.

32. Jerzy Axer, "What Is Liberal Education? Can It Support Both Freedom and Equality? Is It for Everybody?" *Kritika & Kontext* 2, no. 4 (1997): 116–18.

33. Frank Furedi, *Where Have All the Intellectuals Gone? Confronting 21st Century Philistinism* (New York: Continuum, 2006).

34. See Richard Detweiler's discussion in this chapter under "Context: Live-In Community."

35. Stanley Katz, "Liberal Education on the Ropes," *Chronicle of Higher Education*, April 1, 2005, B6; cf. Jerzy Axer, "Acceptance Speech," Fifth Award Presentation

of Hannah Arendt Prize, in *Hannah Arendt Prize 1999* (Vienna: Institut für Wissenschaften vom Menschen, 2000), 29–32.

36. Voldemar Tomusk, "The Garbage of the Garbage: The Second-Level Sub-Optimal Policy Process in European Higher Education" (revised version of a paper presented at the colloquium "L'européanisation et la professionnalisation de l'enseignement supérieur, quelles convergences?" Université Paris Descartes, January 14–15, 2010).

37. The Christian A. Johnson Endeavor Foundation office, especially S. Kassouf, was extremely helpful and involved.

38. As Donald Harward aptly observed during his visit to the collegium in May 2010.

39. Donald W. Harward, Elisabeth Minnich, Jerzy Axer, and Marek Wąsowicz, "Republican Virtues and the University. Panel Discussion," in *Autonomia Uniwersytetu*, 137–52.

40. Jerzy Axer, "Autonomia uniwersytetu i innowacyjność [University autonomy and innovative self-organization]," *Nauka* 2 (2010): 7–10. The activity of our milieu was successful and resulted in changes in the new law on higher education, which was successfully voted in our parliament in January 2011. The minister accepted amendments proposed by me that open new possibilities to develop structures such as Collegium MISH and Collegium Artes Liberales at the University of Warsaw.

41. Donald W. Harward, "Why the Effort to Establish Liberal Education in East-Central Europe Might Prove Interesting for American Educators," in *Autonomia Uniwersytetu*, 123–36; Donald W. Harward, "Remarks at the Core of What You and We Are About in Support of Liberal Education," in *Debaty IBI AL* [Debates IBI AL], ed. Jan Kieniewicz et al., vol. 2 (Warsaw: IBI AL, 2011).

13

Implications of Transformative Change in Higher Education for Secondary Education

A Dialogue

Daniel Tad Roach and Michael V. McGill

Higher education has become a commodity, a credentialing process that trains up workers for the demands of the economy, according to any number of sources. Although a direct link may be impossible to establish, meanwhile, research describes a college and university environment in which students are too often disengaged, depressed, and abusive, where they cede to minimal expectations and withdraw from involvement for the general good.

How can these institutions engage students in significant learning, making them more aware of purposes beyond themselves, and "prepare them intellectually and emotionally for a future of choice?" (as was posed in part I). The proposal is to transform these institutions so they offer young men and women a more holistic educational experience that constitutes a culture for learning.

Recall Donald Harward's observations in part I about the meaning of transformative change in the academy:

Transformative (institutional) change will mean at least the following:

- "Shifting the paradigm" from teaching to learning and then fully attending to whether learning occurs
- Prioritizing pedagogies of engagement, connecting knowledge and discovery to judgment and practice
- Rejecting the operative myth of Cartesian dualism and structuring what we offer to students with the realization that they are whole persons with intellectual, emotive, and civic dimensions
- Reenvisioning and reordering reward structures for faculty and staff that align with our core purposes
- Addressing the socialization patterns that currently dominate the preparation of our faculties and academic leadership, as we define for

ourselves and for our institutions the meaning of being a "teacher/scholar"

- Deepening the contexts for learning and for strengthening what faculty can do best by practices and support systems
- Recognizing that not all learning occurs in the classroom and that not all teaching occurs by faculty
- Most importantly, restructuring priorities, resources, and practices, including the financial, so that changes are brought from the periphery to the center of the institution, and to what it delivers, and to what its publics then expect

McGill: What elements of these assumptions resonate especially for elementary and secondary school educators?

Roach: The world of secondary education has been affected by the same cultural and educational patterns identified in the world of colleges and universities. That shouldn't be surprising.

We obviously look to that world for both educational and strategic reasons. We in the schools have a deep interest and commitment to preparing students for success and engagement as undergraduates; we evaluate and assess our own effectiveness through an analysis of how well our students compete both in the college admissions process and in their work as undergraduates.

At the same time, a number of related factors conspire to reduce the ambition and spirit of secondary education. As we face economic dislocation and recession, it's inevitable that parents and students will see their investment in private secondary schooling as one that should lead to tangible return: admission to college and access ultimately to the world of the professions. It's easy in this environment to create strategic academics that honor and pursue only individualistic achievement, but the results of such approaches are disturbing both to individual students and to society as a whole.

If we shift the paradigm from individualistic achievement and competition to one that honors collaboration and engagement committed to the public good, we will succeed in developing new and exciting educational approaches and schools.

McGill: The utilitarian ethic is a major issue. Over the last forty years, we've heard increasingly about the importance of education, but the concern has been almost exclusively to increase economic productivity. Elementary and secondary education also seem to be seen increasingly as a commodity that's bought and sold in bottom-line terms. If the objective of the system is to turn out "a product" that will "succeed" in these terms, it'll be hard to develop new and exciting approaches, particularly ones that aren't just unconventional but also bold.

For high-performance public schools, the problem is similar to what you describe in independent schooling: Parents move to town so their kids can have a first-rate education. But what does that mean, and why pursue that kind of experience? Is it a fast track to the good life? Is it about illumination, self-discovery, and service? Families sometimes want one of those objectives, sometimes the other, and sometimes both. These different ends aren't always in conflict, but it's certainly not hard to find contradictions.

For example, Scarsdale High School decided four years ago to move away from Advanced Placement to what we call Advanced Topics courses so teachers could worry less about covering content for AP tests and offer students more opportunities for in-depth exploration and reflection. Program evaluations show the revised courses are deeper and richer than before, as we'd hoped, but the transition was bumpy. Many parents resisted because of fears about college admission and college credits, and it took over a year just to decide to move ahead. And in the larger picture, the actual change wasn't revolutionary to start with. The politics, not the education, were the problem. The specific issue may have been particular to Scarsdale, but these kinds of tensions arise with some regularity.

The situation can be even more fraught in our more troubled public institutions, but for different reasons. For instance, a central premise of the current school reform movement is that we have to close an "achievement gap" between poor, often minority, children and more affluent youngsters. But since the utilitarian definition of *achievement* is reductive—doing well on standardized tests—many schools that serve low-income kids are using instructional approaches (e.g., scripted teaching or straight-out test prep) that are apt to leave their graduates with an education that's both grim in process and mediocre in result. That's not going to help either the individual or the society realize its potential.

Roach: We make a fatal mistake if we don't challenge and engage students with the essential questions facing our country and the world. Even students who comply and accept a teacher-dominated classroom and a regimen of high-stakes standardized tests will arrive at college unable to think, problem-solve, or create. Those students who find such teaching and educational practices boring, disconnected, and fragmented will drop out of the educational world as quickly as they can.

McGill: That's the problem my friends in urban education describe. When children are smaller and relatively compliant, many of them will go along with uninspiring curriculum and routine teaching, even if they don't find meaning in what they're doing. Problems start to become more evident as they reach the middle grades. Students are undergoing the pressures and struggles of early adolescence, and little in their experience tells them that what they're doing in school has a point to it. Why hang in there?

We see a lot less of that kind of open disaffection in high-performance schools; because families and peers have a strong ethic of achievement, kids will play the school game longer. Then, if they're lucky, they'll happen to get a great teacher somewhere in school or college. But absent an education that's structured more systematically to capture and intrigue and inspire, and given the kind of problems Don Harward describes in undergraduate education, that's far from a sure bet. So what's the upshot?

I was talking recently with one of my nephew's friends who's a business major at one of our state universities. I don't know how typical he was, but I was unsettled by how unengaged he was in his classes and by how generally incurious he seemed about anything except skiing or how much money he could make when he got a job. It felt like such a waste for him and, ultimately, like such a real loss for society. Multiply the individual case many times, and it's a serious concern for our democracy.

But let me go back to something you said earlier. You were talking about "strategic academics" and contrasting that kind of education with one that "honors collaboration and engagement committed to the public good."

Roach: I think we have to embrace and pursue transformational learning practices. But we're blocked to the possibilities of reform and imagination by three historic movements: the inertia and fear of change at the secondary level; the pressure and high stakes of competitive college admissions; and the anxiety and focus of parents. Only the colleges can help us redefine the meaning, purpose, and character of authentic education.

In particular, the implications of college admissions anxiety inevitably distort the moral and ethical development so central to the secondary school experience. As failure of any kind becomes unacceptable, as students adopt a belief not in education but in transcripts and test scores, the very notion of academic engagement, intellectual exploration, and collective learning becomes alien to them.

Unfortunately, highly competitive college admission hasn't led to progressive and transformational approaches to curriculum development, teaching techniques, or assessments. Rather, the process, intensified and, to a degree, distorted by the media, has paradoxically moved secondary schools to think cautiously and strategically about education.

Rather than thinking creatively and imaginatively about ways to engage and inspire twenty-first-century students, secondary schools have to a large degree locked in commitments to the Advanced Placement program and in many cases embraced grade inflation as a way of protecting their college admissions competitiveness. As students face fierce and arduous competition for precious places among a set number of prestigious schools, they adopt an approach to education that is anxious, strategic, and ultimately dangerous to their health, moral and ethical development, and identity. Private secondary school students turn to alcohol and drugs with the same kind of intensity and emptiness we see on college campuses, and issues of depression, anxiety, and eating disorders now inevitably frame a year in the academy.

McGill: This is true in public education as well, although I do wonder about the degree to which these kinds of destructive behaviors can be traced back to specific events or processes such as college admission; kids in lower-performance schools have many of the same problems.

Still, the broad point is well taken; the absence of larger purpose cannot help any young person become a full human being. Neither are students likely to develop as fully as people or citizens when mechanical goals—getting good grades or getting into college—take the place of ones with authentic meaning. In this connection, many people have heard of the 1983 report *A Nation at Risk*, but probably one of the most interesting commissioned reports nobody has heard of is *The Education of Adolescents*, published seven years earlier, in 1976.[1]

The report noted that while most adolescents were in the workforce in the early 1900s, by midcentury the large majority were being warehoused more or less anonymously in large school buildings where the population was all pretty much the same age. Young people had been isolated both from work that had evident purpose and from a normal demographic that included the adults who'd once mentored them on the job, in the fields, or in the home. Nobody should have been surprised, the report said, when alienation and anomie resulted.

The panel that wrote the report recommended replacing the then-comprehensive high school with a comprehensive *education* that would be provided in centers throughout the community. Specifically, the school day would be reduced to two to four hours for instruction in liberal academic studies. In the remaining time, students would participate in educational programs or work in new community arts centers or career education centers, depending on their interests and aptitudes. Also, everyone would be involved in some kind of meaningful, mentored work in community government.

Of course, the report barely saw the light of day before it was buried. It was way too radical. Thirty-some years on, though, the basic principles—connecting intellectual inquiry with experience and reintegrating young people into something more like a real community—continue to be relevant. Also, the report still challenges us to rethink many of the specifics we take for granted in today's schools: the physical location of learning and the nature of adult mentoring, for instance.

Roach: The secondary school should commit itself to the development of transformational teacher-apprentice models to prepare students for authentic work and engagement.

McGill: It's a tricky proposition. Once we moved beyond old models of vocational training to the idea of real-world experiences that teach broader thinking skills and problem solving, things got a lot more complicated—and interesting. We want to share the benefits of liberal learning, and we want that learning to be grounded in real experiences that give it heft in students' lives. There are lots of implicit tensions in that bargain, but I agree that it's important to pursue.

Roach: We also have to challenge students to take responsibility for the culture, intellectual engagement, and graciousness of their schools by giving them voice, ownership, and positions of leadership.

McGill: Several of us were discussing the academic parallel to that principle today. We're involved in a directed districtwide effort to enhance students' thinking skills and their capacity to solve "insoluble" questions: global warming or ethnic conflict, for instance. To move ahead, we need to involve them more directly. For example, we need to learn what work they find interesting and what kinds of teaching help them understand how to deal with nonstandard problems of the sort that have no single answer.

Roach: In the early 1980s, Ted Sizer returned from a one-year visit to private and public high schools across the country and argued that he found overwhelming patterns of student boredom and docility in classrooms dominated by teacher talk and rote learning. As Sizer reimagined the American high school in books such as *Horace's Compromise* and *Horace's School*, he developed core principles to help schools deepen their historic performance and commitment to exemplary learning.[2]

Sizer argued that the philosophy of "less is more" would enable teachers and students to develop deep and authentic understanding and mastery of essential skills and habits of mind. Therefore, he emphasized depth and quality of learning, thinking, analyzing, and calculating instead of coverage of large amounts of material. He moved the focus from a teacher-centered classroom to one in which the student was the scholar, the performer. The goal, Sizer said, was for the students to be able to teach themselves.

Second, Sizer argued that schools could ignite student learning, curiosity, and passion through the use of essential questions, ones that required reflection, study, and deep thinking. Such questions would help students begin to do the authentic work of historians, scientists, and mathematicians. They'd also help students understand the exciting nature of the scholarly conversations and arguments that lead to debate, innovation, and creativity.

Third, Sizer argued that student work should be public demonstrations of mastery. He called such displays exhibitions, and he argued that teachers should plan their courses backward: By specifying what ultimate exhibition of mastery would look like, teachers would design syllabi, assessments, and readings that specifically prepare students for the display of such habits of mind at the end of a semester. Exhibitions honor the conversations that take place between a student and a teacher as they both work to move toward student exhibition of mastery.

Finally, Sizer argued that the teacher's role should be that of a coach, a guide, a facilitator of learning. The metaphor of coaching emphasized that students achieve mastery and learn by practice, by rehearsal, by revision, by self-assessment.

These approaches celebrate and enact the great tradition of public and private school teaching. Through them, we make the case that transformational education is tied to a civic and public good; we make the case that quality education is a response to a country and world in need of creativity, reform, imagination, and development.

If we do this work well, students will arrive as undergraduates ready to take full advantages of the culture and opportunities affirmed by the principles of the Bringing Theory to Practice Project—principles I've come to see as important and central to effective reform in the ten years I've worked with them.

McGill: One of Ted Sizer's most significant contributions was his interest in professional and institutional growth. I remember his quoting Ralph Tyler, one of the last of the original progressive educators. Tyler said that, first and last, progressivism "was about the conversation among teachers; it was always about the conversation." Ted understood that teaching becomes deeper and more powerful primarily through a process of sharing self-aware, reflective practice. The same is true of entire schools. Deep, lasting improvement is organic.

In contrast, strategic plans, data-driven education, templates for reform, and the other manifestations of recent organizational change theory are blunt instruments. Impose them on a school or school district without regard for the people, the culture, or the conditions, and the consequences are unpredictable and often undesirable. On the other hand, when these approaches are understood as tools, not as blanket solutions, they can be more useful.

My grandfather was a carpenter. When I was little, I thought his cherrywood toolbox was a wonderful, mysterious treasury. It was about two feet wide by three feet long, and inside were chisels and wood planes and files of all descriptions. Some he'd made himself. I imagine him in an internal conversation about which would be best for the rough or the fine work at hand.

If the people who work with kids—teachers, school heads, and I'd like to include school superintendents along with them—can engage in serious conversations about the tools they have at hand, there's a good chance they'll find intelligent ways to use or adapt these theoretical constructs to improve their craft and the quality of learning in their schools. Or they'll discard the tools they have for ones they invent, ones that are better.

Things being what they are today, though, public schools are too often defined and driven by people who don't have experience in or a feel for what they're trying to repair. These people have a lot of power and a bully pulpit; their narrative is simple and easy for the public to understand. We're talking now about corporate leaders, distant state bureaucracies, and a press that's remarkably unquestioning and trusting of both.

The narrative assumes these people understand the carpenters' craft better than the carpenters. And in many cases, they're uninterested in history, experience, or research that might cause them to question their own certainties. They're requiring the craftspeople to use a saw here or a hammer there—"and don't ask questions." It's not the best way to do the fine work of whole-school improvement, let alone of nurturing individual minds and spirits.

Roach: I think Sizer described the essence of academic culture when he said that schools should be places of "unanxious expectation"—in other words, places where teachers set standards high but express an expectation, an eagerness, to help students achieve mastery.

McGill: Culture and the relationships that are part of it are so much of what makes a school great. You need individual teachers with a deep foundation in academic content, who care for young people, who are self-reflective, and who take pleasure from each day's small academic victories. But it's collective energy—the culture and the relationships—that enables the whole institution to change lives for the better so that the influence on individual students isn't just random or idiosyncratic. An aggregation of superstars who work with kids doesn't have the same impact as a strong faculty where teachers collaborate and build on each others' efforts.

Roach: I worry that one of the greatest challenges facing secondary schools today is our collective unwillingness to engage, fully engage, the hearts and minds of our students in authentic work. The best secondary schools aren't the ones that revel in the course competition of this new era; rather, the best ones develop and refine their programs according to the principles I described before.

More broadly, they also have a clear sense of mission. They prepare students for engaged and responsible leadership and participation in the work of the democracy and the world. They prepare students to develop the intellectual and critical thinking skills not only to join the essential conversations and debates that animate our disciplines but also to join the work and conversations that take place in politics, civic affairs, and the media.

We need to eloquently and passionately explain the mission, purpose, and philosophy of transformational education.

McGill: The point about explicit mission is particularly important on the public side. It's partly a political and partly an educational necessity. Citizens deserve a more thoughtful exploration of the issues surrounding school reform, especially given the power of the corporate/bureaucratic narrative. Ideally, we'd reflect deeply on why we have public schools and what we expect them to achieve. Among other things, that would give us a better starting point for discussions about where we go from here.

Currently, many people still see elementary and secondary schools as training grounds where children learn "the basics" until they get ready for the big stuff later on. And large numbers of American schoolchildren are memorizing, practicing skills in rote form, feeding back what they're told, and spending valuable class time getting ready for standardized tests. It's going to be hard to get beyond relatively low-grade learning without some shared higher vision of purpose and some wider understanding of the kind of education that will realize it.

If we want tomorrow's citizens to solve the problems our democracy faces, today's students need to engage fully with important content, ideas, and experiences. There's ample evidence that high school students and even small children can do that and still develop essential skills. In fact, I'd argue that they're more likely to develop those skills when they're also involved in the interesting, significant questions human beings wrestle with.

Roach: The danger of fostering an educational system that rewards memorization, rote learning, strategic thinking, and standardized testing is that we as a culture unwittingly indicate that school is not about creativity, critical thinking skills, and the use of writing and the scientific method for the pursuit of thought, reflection, and creativity. Rather, it's a place for ideas, concepts, and themes that have no relevance, no connection, no meaning. The danger of locking students away from commentary, analysis, protest, and engagement in the authentic questions of our time is that they'll be unprepared for the world of work and civic engagement.

For example, if we teach writing to conform to the requirements of a standardized test that asks a barren and empty question and requires a twenty-minute essay, we suggest that it's a game, a skill to be mastered for a requirement. In fact, writing isn't an obstacle to be surmounted—it isn't a barren exploration of a five-paragraph structure; it is a way of thinking, exploring, debating, arguing, clarifying, creating, refining, and enacting. But because we often accept the contortions of a testing culture, we lose the essential dynamism of the art of writing.

Perhaps this is why professional lawyers, doctors, businesspeople, and journalists shake their heads today and tell me that many of the best and the brightest undergraduates and graduate school students do not know how to write, how to problem-solve, how to create, and how to collaborate.

McGill: The point about dynamism, what I'd call engagement, is particularly important. I mentioned our work on thinking and nonstandard problem solving. While we recognize that people in and outside of school have to think well about topics that may not enchant them, one of Scarsdale's operating premises is that students are more apt to probe and reflect deeply when they're working in areas that capture their interest. As a result, we're trying to build in more opportunities for inquiry research starting in the very earliest grades.

I tell what I think is a very neat story about a fifth grader who got interested in the significance of the Battle of Iwo Jima because his mother was reading *Flags of Our Fathers*. Among other things, he started an e-mail correspondence with a former Marine who happened to live in New Orleans, and then the student wrote and filmed a podcast describing his research. It ended with his holding up a bag of volcanic beach sand the Marine had sent him. It was impressive . . . and very moving.

Roach: Let me give you an example of student work that captures the excitement and transformation of authentic learning. The assignment asked students to respond thoughtfully to Charles Blow's recent *New York Times* essay attacking private schools as places where racism, intolerance, and harassment thrived.[3] Here is an excerpt from a St. Andrew's senior's response—the student addresses Mr. Blow directly:

> Your central claim, that boys in private schools are more likely to discriminate against those who vary from social "norms," could not be more accurate. Generally, my private school friends, particularly those from the all-boys' school, fit cleanly into the cookie-cutter pattern of the elitist youth. They all have more money than the vast majority of the country. They all come from two-parent homes. They all belong to various, exclusive country clubs. Most importantly, however, they all solely associate with each other.
>
> Throughout my years before high school, I was blindly complicit to acts of discrimination that I now abhor. Whether it was a snide remark made in passing or the public mockery of someone outside our group, these acts of intolerance were both disgusting and frequent. While at the time, I thought of these violations as nothing more than harmless jokes, I have come to understand through living in a more accepting, diverse community that these seemingly small comments act as the foundation for a larger sense of intolerance and hatred.
>
> However, I would like to offer one critique of your otherwise accurate depiction of the state of acceptance among private school boys. You draw a distinct connection between the common intolerance and the fact that these boys are "chosen" when they are admitted into their various schools.
>
> You say that simply by being chosen, these boys gain an inherent sense of elitism and exclusivity. You argue that the mere act of being accepted into a private school will inherently lead to a sense of entitlement within the boy and his family. This argument, however, leaves no room for a progressive, countercultural school to exist. Having attended four vastly different private schools, I can personally attest to the fact that not all private schools were created equal.
>
> Quite simply, it is the duty of the school to destroy any sense of entitlement that might be fostered by the admissions process. If a school sets a standard of diversity, acceptance, understanding, and tolerance then its students will emulate these values. If, however, a school turns its nose up at the chance for diversity and a wide range

of backgrounds amongst its students, then the students will likewise follow its lead.

The prose is sharp, coherent, and compelling; the tone is gracious, thoughtful, serious, and balanced. The writer accurately depicts Blow's central claim and responds to that argument in a fair and judicious manner. He graciously agrees and disagrees: He establishes an important contrast in the approaches of different schools. He humbly admits to his complicity in words of intolerance and manners and spirit and shows how young people move from ignorance to perception.

A less seasoned, less versatile, and less experienced writer, one not skilled in the art of authentic work, might be tempted to engage not in analysis and argument but in defensive, angry, and inappropriate responses. The essay works because in its expression, tone, and substance, the writer believes deeply and enacts gracefully the purpose of writing.

This essay brought me out of my seat, for not only was the writing articulate, balanced, mature, and sophisticated, the essay was authentic, as deserving of publication and national conversation as anything in the *Times*.

Yet such writing has limited applicability in American classrooms or no place in the world of standardized testing, unless one seeks, as St. Andrew's does, to both develop authentic learning opportunities and to identify an outlier test, the CWRA, that honors students by giving them an essential question and time to develop a coherent essay.

McGill: What the two assignments—research on the significance of Iwo Jima and the response to the *Times*—have in common is that both center on interesting questions that very clearly engage these two learners. In its own way, each one also invites the learner to see relationships between ideas and real-world experience: the fifth grader and the U.S. Marine, the St. Andrew's student and Mr. Blow. Neither of these students is merely memorizing nor parroting information. Both have to appreciate different perspectives, evaluate the relative value of information, construct an argument, and make a case in a persuasive way—the elementary schooler in writing and orally, the senior high student in writing alone.

Roach: Here's how we look at the issue of authentic learning. It's the process we follow when we pose, consider, and debate essential questions that face scholars in their fields and leaders in their positions of responsibility and influence. In the words of writer and college professor Gerald Graff, it means entering the legitimate and compelling conversations that animate our lives as students and citizens. Too often, Graff argues, life in the academy or college is completely disassociated from the essential debates and arguments of both our times and our disciplines.[4] Too often, we see the life of the mind as distant from the life of the citizen, the reformer, the activist.

Of course, the word *authentic* suggests there is also a form of learning that isn't genuine, real, or transformational. The opposite of authentic learning is learning that is not learning at all—it may be learning that is teacher talk parroted back in an exam blue book; it may be learning that is desperately and strategically geared to please the teacher and secure the coveted grade. Authentic learning frees us, liberates us to be independent, creative, and resourceful citizens of the world. Rote learning, passive learning, and strategic learning all lead to paralysis, emptiness, and despair, not only for the individual but for the community as well. The stakes are that high.

The greatest problem facing American schools today is the education establishment's refusal to take the minds of high school students seriously. At our so-called best, we are willing to drill, to threaten, and to intimidate teachers to teach to high-stakes tests, or to comprehensively cover material, but we are unwilling to free teachers, students, and schools to pursue a form of learning that will activate students' minds, ownership, and sense of responsibility in the world of today. At our worst, we ignore standards completely and fail to prepare students for engaged and enlightened participation in our democracy.

McGill: The obstacles to the kind of education you're describing are pretty daunting. Peel back layers of the onion, starting with what I called the corporate narrative. People in power have found a powerful way to describe "the problem" of America's schools and to prescribe "the answer" of high-stakes tests and other "get tough" measures. But from the start, their narrative goes off track with the flawed idea that everyone shares one problem and that there must be a single solution.

The analysis also ignores many of the most significant roadblocks to authentic learning. In public education, there's the problem of diffuse mission I mentioned before. As a people, we want our schools to achieve many different things, ones often related only marginally to the life of the mind, character development, or lives of contribution. We are interested in schools doing everything from getting kids to pass state tests to producing good linebackers. Also, by definition, public school governance is politicized, and the politics easily turn unproductive.

And that's before you even get to educational issues. If SAT scores are a legitimate yardstick, for example, the nation's public school teacher corps still comes from the bottom third of each graduating college class—although that measure may seem a little inappropriate, given the topic of this discussion. Anyhow, unlike some of their counterparts in Europe and Asia, teachers in the United States probably aren't among our more able graduates to start with. Many have little or no experience of an "authentic" education themselves, and we do relatively little to help them develop their abilities as they mature.

Until we invest in attracting a consistently promising teaching force to the field, as well as in helping teachers enhance their craft throughout long careers, so they *can* transform lives, the quality and character of learning will vary widely. That reality potentially takes us down a road that Don Harward has alluded to: selective incentives and other measures intended to drive teaching and school culture toward more transformative practice. I am not going there right now, though, if only because of the scale of the problem; in the United States today, we lose hundreds of thousands of teachers every year through retirement or resignation. With our current resourcing, we can't even replace those departures with people who are both smart and liberally educated, let alone with highly skilled teachers who can offer students a transformational experience.

This could sound reasonably hopeless, I know, and I'd like to wind up on a more positive note; I'm an optimist about public education because I have to be. So what of the future?

Roach: A great democracy needs and deserves great schools and colleges, institutions that are bold, assertive, and creative enough to invigorate our citizens, our democracy, and our world. Our mission statements promise such thinking, but we often settle for conventional answers and predictable results. I do not hear or feel a sense of urgency or creativity that would push education to respond powerfully to twenty-first-century needs. Instead, I see a country paralyzed, unable to act to combat global warming, nuclear proliferation, economic dislocation, and educational paralysis. I think the answer to our paralysis lies in a different way of thinking about schools and colleges in America—a different way of thinking about learning.

I envision an American high school that commits itself completely to the cultivation of authentic learning and civic engagement and leadership. Such a school would thrive as a place where the intellectual and student life of the school directly addressed the most compelling issues facing our democracy and world. It would graduate students who see their education as a source of intellectual, moral, spiritual, and civic awakening. It would serve as a direct response to a democracy in need of creativity, engagement, and hope. Such a school would celebrate and enact the potential and reality of the global world, encouraging and providing language immersion and international study experiences.

McGill: A fate devoutly to be wished. Over a century and a half ago, Horace Mann said the public school was the greatest invention in the history of mankind. The idea of public education was a promise: to bring a diverse people together; to empower each one to think and act effectively; to enable everyone to learn from unlike others; to inspire all to strive for the common good; and to bind them together in one nation. Today, we readily accept the cliché that the process of schooling should end up with "No Child Left Behind." But both the idea of public education and this ideal are in doubt.

Ironically, many of America's great independent schools do a better job today of approaching that ideal than many public institutions. They offer a clarity of mission that's uncommon in the politically charged world of public schooling, for example. Often, they're also more ethnically and racially, if not economically, diverse. The charter school movement is essentially an effort to mimic these strengths in a quasi-public setting.

At one level, voucher schools, charter schools, and other alternatives to traditional public schools are an interesting and potentially useful experiment. In fact, I'd argue that for public schools, a demonstrated record of success or a demonstration of special promise should be a path to similar deregulation, a way to ease the straitjacket of high-stakes tests and other impediments to the more meaningful, transformative learning you've described, Tad.

The darker side of these experiments is that they leave behind the children in the 97 percent of other schools that are still regular public institutions. As students depart to attend a charter school or home school, those left behind are increasingly apt to be the alienated and disenfranchised, those lacking home support, those with special needs. And as money, building space, and other resources go to the more motivated, upwardly mobile families who choose charter schooling, the huge majority of left-behinds lose again. That's not how to realize the idea or the ideal of public education.

The vast number of America's children are now and will be in the public system for the foreseeable future. Our common destiny depends on an act of public will. People invest themselves and their resources—human or material—in things they believe in; college alumni give money to the annual fund because their education changed their lives. So we, the people, first of all must rededicate ourselves to the idea of public education, a commitment that requires national, state, and local leaders who have the vision and the courage to call us all to higher cause.

Notes

1. The National Commission on Excellence in Education, *A Nation at Risk: The Imperative for Educational Reform* (April 1983), http://reagan.procon.org/sourcefiles/a-nation-at-risk-reagan-april-1983.pdf; John Henry Martin, *The Education of Adolescents* (Washington, DC: National Panel on High School and Adolescent Education, 1976).

2. Theodore R. Sizer, *Horace's Compromise: The Dilemma of the American High School* (New York: Houghton Mifflin, 1984); Theodore R. Sizer, *Horace's School: Redesigning the American High School* (New York: Houghton Mifflin, 1992).

3. Charles Blow, "Private School Civility Gap," *New York Times*, October 29, 2010.

4. Gerald Graff, *Clueless in Academe: How Schooling Obscures the Life of the Mind* (New Haven, CT: Yale University Press, 2003).

14

Do Disciplines Change? Would Flipping the Curriculum Right-Side Up Lead to Change?

Thomas Bender

Do disciplines change? Yes and no. The professional institutions that sustain scholarship, mainly research universities and graduate schools within them, change slowly. Such change as occurs is quite limited. The basic structure and organization of colleges, universities, and disciplinary associations have not changed since the 1920s, nor have the requirements for doctoral degrees. Yet the content of the disciplines has been transformed again and again. Noting the distinction between structure and content provides some analytic purchase on the ways graduate training and disciplinary professionalism limit transformative changes in the structure and educational practices of higher education more generally. But it also clarifies opportunities for change. The distinction also makes clear the persisting capacity of these structures to facilitate the advance of research. In fact, it may well be that the impressive eventfulness of knowledge production is grounded in *la longue durée* of uneventfulness that characterizes structure.[1] It is possible, however, to work with that structure if we reorder the relation between disciplinary knowledge and liberal learning. After discussing something of the recent history of academic disciplines, graduate education, and the relation of research to teaching, I offer some proposals to this end.

If the structure of professionalism has been stable, there has been a subtle but extremely important change in professional identity of faculty, particularly those employed at research universities since World War II. The change has not affected every professor, but overall there has been a major shift in the center of gravity among the professoriate. I noticed this change in the course of examining a shelf of books on the American academic professions and universities published in the 1940s in NYU's Bobst Library. I was searching for statistics on the employment of scholars in the humanities. I failed to locate a good run of statistics, but in paging through the introductions of the books I pulled from the shelves, I was struck by the unself-conscious description of the subjects of these books, that is to say, the professors. In a variety of phrasings, it was clear that professors were "educators." Their careers were as teachers, some of whom also did research. That was their professional identity. They taught, identifying with teaching primarily, with scholarship an added appeal of the profession for many but not all.

This identity would change during the extraordinary postwar transformation of American higher education, now sometimes wistfully characterized as "the golden age" of higher education.[2] The story is familiar. Postwar enrollments increased dramatically, and federal funding commenced—overwhelmingly directed to research rather than teaching. New demand for PhDs was voracious; the graduate schools could not supply the numbers needed, and ABDs routinely obtained appointments. The precise data on the expansion of higher education are striking, and they illustrate in a powerful way the changing identity of the professoriate. Between 1940 and 1990, enrollment increased by a factor of ten, federal funds by a factor of twenty-five, and—note this—the average teaching load of faculty was reduced by half.[3] During these boom years the identity of the higher education faculties changed—quietly but consequentially. If in the 1940s the faculties were made up of teachers, some of whom undertook research, the professoriate of 1990 and beyond has been increasingly constituted by researchers who taught, perhaps as little as possible.

This shift is evident in a phrasing one hears in the halls of our colleges and universities: "Between my teaching and my committee responsibilities, I have no time for *my work.*" This said, it must also be noted that the teaching that *is* done today is on the whole vastly more creative and effective. More than a tight narrative presented by lecture and textbook, today's teaching in history—and the humanities more generally—uses a combination of diverse readings and more complex lectures/discussions to present the humanities as interpretive disciplines, and there is an emphasis on development of the sort of critical thinking that is at the heart of a liberal arts education.

What role, if any, did the graduate schools of arts and sciences and the professional disciplinary associations play in these developments? I can speak most knowledgeably about the discipline of history. The story there is mixed. But one can say with assurance that in its early years, the American Historical Association took a serious, even proprietary interest in the history curriculum in high schools and colleges. In 1892, soon after its formation, the American Historical Association organized the Committee of Ten, a distinguished group of historians including Woodrow Wilson, then of Princeton, and chaired by Charles Kendall Adams of the University of Wisconsin, which established what is still more or less the history curriculum for seventh grade through high school, with a notion that the college curriculum, for the few students who then went on to college, would build upon that.[4] They thought of this work as "civic education." Moses Coit Tyler of Cornell, the first occupant of a chair in American history, explained to Herbert Baxter Adams, who established German-style doctoral education in history at Johns Hopkins, that his "interest in our past" is "chiefly derived from my interest in our own present and future; and I teach American history not so much to make historians as to make citizens and good leaders for the State and Nation. . . . I try to generate and preserve in myself and my pupils such an anxiety for the truth that we shall prefer it even to national traditions or the idolatries of party."[5]

While the phrase "civic education" may suggest something less robust and inclusive than the whole of the "liberal arts," it is important to keep in mind that the "humanistic education" of the Florentine Renaissance, the root of Anglo-American liberal education, was oriented very much to prepare republican citizens.[6] Until the 1940s, the American Historical Association cooperated with various foundations and educational associations (including the National Council for the Social Studies) to reform both K–12 and college curricula and teaching methods. Along with the Mississippi Valley Historical Association (now the Organization of American Historians), they supported the development of various initiatives in what is now called "public history."[7] Then came the academic boom years, and university historians took what has been called the "long walk" away from education in the schools.[8] That act weakened their identity as educators, and it sharpened the distinction between college-level and high school teachers. But it implied more: a distinction between those who taught and those who did research in higher education as well. By 1960, the audience for the disciplines became almost exclusively fellow specialists; teaching was oriented toward a different audience, being at one with the general public.

These distinctions had consequences a half century later. Public officials, academic historians, and educators responded to a call for national standards first enunciated by President George H.W. Bush at the National Governors' Conference in 1989 and embraced by Governor Bill Clinton of Arkansas, the chair of the conference. Lynn Cheney, chair of the National Endowment for the Humanities, was on board too. She made a major grant for the development of such standards in history to Charlotte Crabtree, director of UCLA's National Center for History in the Schools, and her colleague in the history department, Gary Nash.[9] The standards that emerged represented current scholarship in the discipline, particularly the development of social history, which expanded the story from the celebration of presidents and other elite figures to lives and impacts of the whole of the population, including workers, women, African Americans, and various ethnic groups. Nor did the standards and suggested pedagogical exercises hesitate to address that part of the American story marked by violence and injustices to workers and, especially, people of color.

Cheney then turned against the standards project and became a leading critic. She had previously praised the project as the best grant she ever made, but she moved to the right with the Republican sweep in the November 1994 Congressional elections, probably to avoid being outflanked on the right by Newt Gingrich. In January 1995, before the report was officially released, she attacked it in the pages of the *Wall Street Journal*. In response, the Senate voted 99 to 0 to condemn the National History Standards. Diane Feinstein, a well-educated and liberal Senator, complained that this was not the kind of history she had been taught at Stanford. That is probably correct. The lesson to be learned from this incident is that the research machine of history had lost contact with its larger public. The impact of the 1960s, from the civil rights movement to feminism, hastened the profession's embrace of social history, which transformed the American story, not only expanding the historical actors in the national story but also recognizing the importance of struggle to the expansion of the rights of citizenship.

The fruits of a narrow professionalism defined by specialists writing for other specialists came home to roost. The Senators and many others, including parents, were surprised and shocked to see the results of a revolution in historical scholarship about which they knew nothing.[10] Many had unthinkingly assumed, an assumption based on a previous generation of textbooks, that American history's contribution to liberal learning was a celebration of elites and was focused mainly on the activities of white males.[11] The extraordinary disciplinary growth and professionalization that occurred in the postwar years allowed a turning inward by practitioners. The larger public—the schools, the general education classes in colleges, and the reading public—had become marginal to the disciplinary definition of professional audiences. This eroded the capacity of historians to contribute liberal education as envisioned at that time.

For the disciplines to play a central role in liberal learning, they must consider the concerns of the larger public and do so in a language the public shares and with methods that are sufficiently transparent to allow the public to understand the derivation of the conclusions. And most important of all, the liberal arts disciplines ought to address—again, at least some of the time—issues that matter to the public. The disciplines could present their work in a way that will enable the public to understand the importance of what might seem to be (or actually be) an esoteric body of knowledge.

Analytic virtuosity is rewarded more than description of the world. Of course, there are philosophical as well as practical arguments against a demand that disciplines mirror or fully represent the world. Still, there is a reasonable expectation that disciplines can provide useful representations and understandings of oneself and of the world or that part of the world that is the discipline's focus, whether it is the economy, political life, or the arts. The contemporary university, philosopher Alasdair MacIntyre has written, is not engaging the right questions, those pertinent to "plain persons." We humans, he insists, desire to know and need to know "what power in the natural and social world" we need to "take account" of. We have specialists answering specialist questions, but no one is "speaking of the relationship between the disciplines. . . . How should the findings among these disciplines contribute to our understanding of ourselves and of our place in nature?"[12] Indeed, that is the aim of the liberal arts, yet much of higher education works against that goal.

In the wake of the Great Recession of 2009 and continuing, the discipline of economics has been criticized for its supposed limited connection to the real world. This critique is not new. In fact, in 1991 it was strongly articulated by economists themselves (with statistical as well as discursive evidence). The American Economic Association surveyed faculty and graduate students in all the doctoral-granting economics departments ranked by the National Research Council. The results revealed widespread concern about the narrowness of instruction and the unworldliness of what was taught. The graduate schools were "too preoccupied with formalism and technique to the exclusion of studying real world problems and issues." Fixing that would require a reduction of the emphasis on formalist approaches and would invite a style of analysis that blended "theoretical, empirical, and institutional research."[13]

Not surprisingly, the most outspoken critics of the doctoral programs were the faculty of top-ranked liberal arts colleges. They complained of "the increasingly technical focus of graduate training in economics."[14] In 1995, one of those critics, William J. Barber of Wesleyan University, elaborated a critique in *Daedalus*, the journal of the American Academy of Arts and Sciences. He complained that the history of economic thought—central to any liberal arts approach to economics—was being abandoned in the leading doctoral programs.[15] The discipline defined its work increasingly as "problem-solving" in general, mostly deploying mathematical means.[16] Most striking, even astonishing, a survey of graduate students at the six top-ranked economics departments revealed that a very large proportion (68 percent) of them believed that "having a thorough knowledge of the economy" was "unimportant."[17] If liberal learning involves a fund of knowledge, some understanding of self and the social and natural world around us, then this belief, very much the product of doctoral education, means something very important is wanting in the most advanced education our society offers.[18]

Philosophy has moved in the same direction. In fact, no U.S. humanities discipline moved farther in this direction than philosophy, which in its Anglo-American version has been in hot pursuit of the status of "science" since World War II. The philosopher Alasdair MacIntyre, who declined to join that race, believes that too many important questions, the ones central to liberal learning, do not get asked in contemporary philosophy. "What is it to live life well? What is it to live life badly?"[19] The request is not to know how one should think about such a question, which analytical philosophers are prepared to discuss, but rather what does it mean, or at least seem to mean?

If the university is a grab bag of disciplines and subdisciplines, as MacIntyre thinks it is, who will explore the relations between disciplines, that domain of knowledge that Richard Rorty identified as "incommensurable"? These conjunctures are precisely the ones Rorty invites us to deploy to constitute the "conversation of mankind," without the pretense of seeking universal truth.[20] Philosophy, MacIntyre points out, used to occupy this space. "In what," he asks now, "does the unity of a human being exist? And how should the findings of . . . [the] disciplines contribute to any understanding of ourselves and of our place in nature"?[21]

The humanities and social science disciplines have of late disdained the notion of synthetic knowledge—sometimes on postmodern principle, sometimes for lack of interest—favoring instead a variety of alternatives, including formal, analytical, and technical invention as well as theory, identity politics, or a vision of total command of a particular subarea of a discipline. All these are pertinent to current methodologies, which are foundational for disciplinary research. But they obviously fail as approaches to liberal learning.

We are rightly suspicious of singularity, universalism, and wholes, but a cosmopolitan pluralism, not disciplinary silos, is the answer. Disciplines are merely tools: means, not ends. The self-referential and tautological definition of economics attributed to Jacob Viner is pertinent to all disciplines as organized in graduate schools: "economics is what economists do."[22] That is like saying a hammer hammers—leaving aside its limited but vital usefulness as a tool in making homes to live in. As tools, disciplines provide the *means* to expand our knowledge, but they do not alone constitute that knowledge.

Oddly enough, proposals for reform, few and far between as they be, nonetheless tend to come from the most senior and accomplished

disciplinary leaders. Such issues are often the stuff of presidential addresses to disciplinary associations. They are also a constant concern of
the executive directors of the various disciplinary associations. They often
push for the creation of committees, commissions, and reports on the discipline, often addressing the relation of doctoral training to the discipline's
role in liberal education. These commissions are often led by significant
figures in the discipline, but their reports are seldom read by department
chairs, and even more rarely are they the subject of a department meeting.[23] And foundations, more than deans, are likely to promote and fund
such discussions.

One recent example is the Teagle Foundation. Under the leadership of
its recently retired president, Robert Connor, the foundation took up the
challenge of examining and improving the relationship of the disciplines
to a liberal arts curriculum. White papers were developed for the fields of
biochemistry and molecular biology, classics, economics, history, and religion. Across the reports (all available on the Teagle Foundation's website)
was a consensus that doctoral training narrows the intellect and leaves
new PhDs ill-equipped to teach broad courses. The reports also reported
(uncritically) a common assumption that I believe is a false binary: narrow
(deep) and synthetic (superficial). All binaries are problematic, and this
one is no exception. And one could make the opposite argument: Narrowness is superficial, and broad is deep. To defend my reversal I would cite
John Dewey, who argued that the larger and richer the context, the greater
one's grasp of meaning is likely to be.[24]

The report the National History Center's working group presented
to the Teagle Foundation, titled "The History Major and Undergraduate
Liberal Education" (2008), points in these directions, taking AAC&U's
definition of liberal learning, which specifies an education that "empowers individuals with broad knowledge and transferable skills, and a strong
sense of value, ethics, and civic engagement." History teaching seeks, according to the report, to produce "the capacity to sift through masses of
information and determine what matters, and a capacity for closely reading various texts. Each of these is crucial in contemporary society, where
anyone with internet access and a bit of curiosity is likely to confront
information overload." History, in contrast to many disciplines, is content
heavy. Its methods are far from esoteric and quite close to what one seeks
in liberal learning generally—"critical thinking, clarity of expression in
speaking and writing, reading comprehension, quantitative literacy, the
ability to organize facts and ideas, argumentation, and the like." In addition, history "places a premium on the capacity for synthesis." At its best,
history provides references for the life experiences the students' futures
may hold.[25] These observations seem to be pointing in just the right direction. Few historians would disagree with them, but few would consider

taking up the departmental challenge of adjusting their curriculum—self-consciously—toward these ends. Nor does any doctoral program, according to a recent survey of all 157 doctoral programs in history undertaken by the American Historical Association, seek to prepare their doctoral students to teach in this fashion.[26]

Neither do they bring to the attention of future scholars and teachers Ernest L. Boyer's *Scholarship Reconsidered: The Priorities of the Professoriate* (1990).[27] In this important book, Boyer argues that scholarship comes in many forms, not simply the monograph in the humanities and the refereed articles in the social and hard sciences. Works of synthesis and textbooks and other teaching materials ought to be considered as well. Except for the faculty in the major research universities (one hundred or so institutions), there is little reason to evaluate faculty on the single category of original research as a mark of achievement or professional excellence. For the many other hundreds of four-year institutions, there are multiple indicators of the liveliness of mind and intellectual engagement with the literature and ideas of the discipline essential to college teachers. Is it a fear of the supposed erosion of standards that forces the singular measure of publication, something that often gives unwarranted credit for mediocre scholarship so long as it is bound between covers?

Are there other measures more pertinent for identifying the talent necessary for first-rate teaching? Of course there are. Of the three best undergraduate teachers I had, one was a publishing scholar, one never completed his PhD dissertation (but the university was smart enough to keep him on till retirement), and the third waited until retirement to publish his first book. Books and articles are easy to count; they are something deans and presidents can present in graph form to assure the trustees, parents, rating magazines, and themselves. Of course there will be and ought to be faculty committed to research as well as teaching. They will do research out of love of research and because they may have a special talent for it. That is where path-breaking research comes from. Such passion and particular talent for research and writing are obviously likely to result in both better and more significant articles and books than those produced simply because of a barely relevant requirement. Those who do excellent scholarly work should be rewarded for that, but so should those who in other ways, more suitable to their passions and interests, improve the education of the liberal arts college.

The liberal arts core is a twentieth-century invention within American higher education. Beginning with Columbia University after World War I, reinvented and reenforced by the University of Chicago in the 1930s, it was given a new and more modest structure by Harvard University. Refusing the label "liberal arts," for its supposed elitism thought inappropriate to a democratic society, they called the curriculum General Education in a Free Society, and it was widely replicated, persisting at Harvard and elsewhere until the 1970s. It was held together by the assumption that there was a coherent "Western civilization" distinguished by its record of invention and nourishment of freedom and universal values, an achievement supposed to have been most fully realized in the United States.

Without the glue of a progressive story of Western civilization, punctuated by the beginnings of civilization in ancient Greece and Rome, its recovery in the Renaissance, its expansion in the Enlightenment, and, presumably, its flowering in the postwar free world, this notion of a liberal core, even if still required, lost its capacity to inspire or hold together the elements of a liberal education. And at a practical level, faculty no longer had the breadth of knowledge (and, perhaps, vision) to deliver the synthesis implied in "Western civilization." In fact, even at the point that Harvard published the Red Book outlining the liberal arts core, it had been hollowed out. As Julie A. Reuben pointed out in *The History of the American University: Intellectual Transformation and the Marginalization of Morality*, with the secularization of the university early in the twentieth century, the edifice was cracking.[28]

Even as the authors of the Red Book proceeded with their recommendations, they realized that disciplinary developments were a serious challenge to the curriculum they were proposing. The report pointed out that "one of the subtlest and most prevalent effects of specialism has been that . . . subjects have tended to be conceived and taught with an eye . . . to their own internal logic rather than their larger usefulness to students."[29] Academics did not want to teach civics. While the report assigned to the philosophy department the task of teaching "the place of human aspiration and ideals in the total scheme of things," the discipline was resisting that sort of philosophizing and was just then turning in on itself, embracing the donnish analytical movement.[30]

For a generation, these tensions and misfits in the program of liberal learning were overcome by a persistent belief that Western civilization was, in fact, a liberal and humane universal in the making. Confidence in this civilizational story was shaken by the (belated) recognition in the 1960s and 1970s of empire, racism, sexism, economic inequality, injustice, and violence at home and abroad. Within academe in the 1980s and 1990s, Western civilization and the Enlightenment in particular were undercut by a cluster of intellectual movements collectively labeled postmodernism.

We are still there. But early in the twenty-first century, a more inclusive metanarrative seems to be emerging across the disciplines and in popular thought: a unified globe. The language of globalization in the 1990s may have been little more than a neoliberal ideology celebrating the market, but there was in fact an unprecedented level of global connectedness and mutual influence. Here is the potential of cosmopolitan glue—as distinguished from a universalist one—for the liberal arts. If there is to be a foundation for the liberal arts going forward, it must be global and cosmopolitan.

On the basis of the argument about the narrowing and turning inward to disciplines, we must ask where one will find the teachers. Any solution must acknowledge the rigidity and narrowness of graduate training and the professional commitment of faculty to the notion of tight disciplines. Change there is not likely, at least not soon. But one can change the structure of the university in a way that can make that limitation an asset instead of a problem. The option is to accept the institutional rigidity we cannot change and take advantage of the intellectual creativity and innovation that occurs within disciplinary paradigms. We need to put that creativity to work in a different structure that will maximize the value of the disciplines.

Disciplines provide students with unparalleled intellectual tools. We need to enable students to acquire those tools early on, and then we need to provide them with a setting to bring those tools into the world, a world of multidisciplinarity and collaboration—a bit of real world within the academy.

Basically, I think we must question present assumptions about the college curriculum and the sequence of learning experiences that make the most of the intellectual resources available in our institutions of higher education. I think we must turn those assumptions upside down, or downside up. We need to restructure the curriculum so that it emphasizes disciplinary formation at the beginning, saving the particular focus on liberal learning for later in the collegiate career once students have adequate tools for creative and rigorous thinking. And the curriculum should be worldly, experiential, and collaborative—all essential for practice in civic life, the original aim of what we call the liberal arts or liberal learning. This reorganization will take advantage of the narrowness and methodological strengths of the disciplines, and it will prepare students for the challenge of liberal learning and collaborative thinking about actual real-life problems.

I do not intend here to sketch out the curriculum this implies; it would be different in different institutions. But the point is to encourage disciplinary learning from the first year. No general requirements are necessary save for expository writing, foreign language training, and mathematical literacy. President Eliot was correct when he instituted the elective system at Harvard 150 years ago: Student interest is the teacher's best ally. Whether well grounded or not, the vast majority of students dislike the synthetic courses that are usually part of the liberal arts requirements. Let them select majors upon arrival, allowing those not yet sure to sample a variety of options and require those who are sure to explore at least one other option. By their third year, students would be reasonably well grounded in their disciplinary choice and perhaps more than one. (This does not preclude a reasonable selection of electives.) But in the third year, there is a pedagogical interest in encouraging an opening up, taking courses—introductory or advanced depending on preparation by way of earlier elective courses—in various fields of the sciences, arts and humanities, and social sciences.

Some would argue that students are not ready to take disciplinary courses before taking broad liberal education courses. This is utterly implausible. Many students do take disciplinary courses; at some schools a smattering of them constitute the liberal education requirement. More important, however, disciplinary knowledge is easier to learn than multi- or interdisciplinary knowledge. Within an established paradigm, the material is put into a coherent package. Introduction to disciplines early and thoroughly gives students the equipment to think, to criticize, to innovate. The incommensurable, which is the stuff of multidisciplinary courses, must be addressed, like life, with no fixed method, no set theories, no models. This is when liberal thinking, not disciplinary thinking, is needed. And it can best be learned at the end, not the beginning, of the college experience.

In the final year, students would bring this fairly well crystallized intellectual equipment and a substantial fund of specialized knowledge into conversation with other people trained differently, in different disciplines. This experience will produce two kinds of growth: The first, which is rather simple, is additive, new knowledge; the second is knowledge that is the product of a self-reflexivity compelled by contact with radically different modes of thinking and verification.

How might this happen? All or most of students' work should be collaborative, in workshops that include representation from each of the usual divisions—humanities and arts, social sciences, and natural sciences. These workshops could equal two courses or even a full-semester course load, and they would have real-life issues for which knowledge, policy formulations, and possible plans for action would be developed. The focus for each workshop would invite collaboration among all three divisions. The workshops would be global in their dimensions, with challenges in two or more regions of the world, where ideas about the challenges are circulating among two or more regions of the world, and where there are indications of transregional causes.

If the groups have twenty students, there should perhaps be at least three from each division, with one responsible faculty member who has access to two consulting faculty from the other two divisions. Some obvious examples of issues to be explored are the environment, health (especially pandemics such as HIV/AIDS), inequality, energy, nutrition, democracy and public life, war and peace, markets and democracy, support for the arts, literacy, gender and equality, translation, Internet rights, immigration and citizenship, and "the color line."

Admittedly, such a reorganization of the collegiate curriculum would be a major revolution in educational strategy—and in the definition of liberal learning, a definition that restores the civic component that was present at its beginning half a millennium ago. It combines expertise and collaboration, which is surely to be the hallmark of the future, and it is framed in terms of a self-consciously global framework, also an inevitable aspect of the future. And toward that end it is likely to inculcate, ever so naturally, a cosmopolitan approach to intellectual work and an alternative to the binary of localism and universalism. Perhaps it will approximate what the philosopher Anthony Appiah calls "rooted cosmopolitanism," which in his definition combines acceptance of connections across cultural difference while still believing in one's own identity and deepest values.[31]

Notes

1. Here I play on the famous but quite different division deployed by Fernand Braudel in *The Mediterranean and the Mediterranean World in the Age of Phillippe II*, trans. Sian Reynolds (orig. ed. 1949; 2 vols.; New York: Harper and Row, 1972).

2. See Thomas Bender, "Politics, Intellect, and the American University," *Daedalus* 126, no. 1 (Winter 1997): 1–38; Louis Menand, "The Marketplace of Ideas," ACLS Occasional Paper, no. 49 (New York: American Council of Learned Societies, 2001).

3. Clark Kerr, *The Uses of the University*, 4th ed. (Cambridge, MA: Harvard University Press, 1995), 142.

4. See Robert Orrill and Linn Shapiro, "From Bold Beginnings to an Uncertain Future: The Discipline of History and History Education," *The American Historical Review* 110, no. 3 (June 2005), 727–51; Ian R. Tyrrell, *Historians in Public: The Practice of American History, 1890–1970* (Chicago: University of Chicago Press, 2005), chaps. 1, 2, 3, 7; Gary Nash, Charlotte Crabtree, and Ross Dunn, *History on Trial: Culture Wars and the Teaching of the Past* (New York: Knopf, 2000).

5. Moses Coit Tyler, letter to Herbert Baxter Adams, quoted in Bert James Lowenberg, *American History in American Thought* (New York: Simon and Schuster, 1972), 393.

6. See Quentin Skinner, *The Foundations of Modern Political Thought*, 2 vols. (Cambridge: Cambridge University Press, 1978).

7. See Tyrrell, *Historians in Public*, esp. chaps. 9–12.

8. Nash, Crabtree, and Dunn, *History on Trial*. See also Orrill and Shapiro, "From Bold Beginnings to an Uncertain Future."

9. The story is told in Nash, Crabtree, and Dunn, *History on Trial*.

10. Nash, Crabtree, and Dunn, *History on Trial*.

11. For a neoconservative reaction by a major historian, see Gertrude Himmelfarb, *The New History and the Old* (Cambridge, MA: Harvard University Press, 1987).

12. Alasdair MacIntyre, *God, Philosophy, Universities: A Selective History of the Catholic Philosophical Tradition* (London: Continuum, 2009).

13. W. Lee Hansen, "The Education and Training of Economics Doctorates: Major Findings of the Executive Secretary of the American Economic Association's Commission on Graduate Education in Economics," *Journal of Economic Literature* 29, no. 3 (1991): 1086.

14. Hansen, "The Education and Training of Economics Doctorates," 1081.

15. William James remarked that any discipline becomes a liberal or humanistic discipline if taught historically, which he thought possible for all fields.

16. Think Steven D. Levitt and Stephen L. Dubner, *Freakonomics: A Rogue Economist Explores the Hidden Side of Everything* (New York: William Morrow, 2005).

17. William B. Barber, "Reconfigurations in American Academic Economics: A General Practitioner's Perspective," *Daedalus* 126, no. 1 (Winter 1997): 96.

18. That this is not what draws students to graduate school but is rather learned there, see Chris Golde and Timothy M. Dore, *At Cross Purposes: What the Experiences of Today's Doctoral Students Reveals about Doctoral Education* (Philadelphia: Pew Charitable Trusts, 2001).

19. Quoted in Thomas S. Hibbs, "Stanley Cavell's Philosophical Improvisations," *Chronicle of Higher Education*, October 15, 2010, B7.

20. See mostly the last chapter of Richard Rorty, *Philosophy and the Mirror of Nature* (Princeton, NJ: Princeton University Press, 1979).

21. MacIntyre, *God, Philosophy, Universities*, 175.

22. For the quotation and acknowledgment that no one has documented the attribution, see Hansen, "The Education and Training of Economics Doctorates," 1054n.

23. The American Historical Association (AHA) has sponsored a pamphlet by Michael J. Galgano, "Liberal Learning and the History Major" (2008), of which 1,170 copies were distributed free or at modest cost; another with collaboration between the AHA's National History Center and the Teagle Foundation, Stanley N. Katz, and James Grossman, "The History Major and Undergraduate Education" (2008), distributed 1,278, again free or at modest cost. Whether these are high or low numbers—I think them quite low—there has certainly been no "buzz" in the profession about either, nor was there much of a crowd (fifty or so in a convention that drew nearly ten thousand participants) when the latter one was presented in a panel discussion at the annual convention of the AHA.

24. John Dewey, "How We Think," in *The Middle Works*, ed. Jo Ann Boydston (Carbondale: Southern Illinois University Press, 1976), 6:272.

25. Katz and Grossman, "The History Major and Undergraduate Liberal Education," 1, 2, 5–7.

26. Thomas Bender, Colin Palmer, Philip M. Katz, and the AHA Committee on Graduate Education, *The Education of Historians for the Twenty-First Century* (Urbana: University of Illinois Press, 2004).

27. Ernest L. Boyer, *Scholarship Reconsidered: The Priorities of the Professoriate* (New York: Carnegie Foundation for the Advancement of Teaching, 1990).

28. Julie A. Reuben, *The Making of the Modern University: Intellectual Transformation and the Marginalization of Morality* (Chicago: University of Chicago Press, 1996).

29. James Bryant Conant, *General Education for a Free Society* (Cambridge, MA: Harvard University Press, 1945), 74.

30. Conant, *General Education for a Free Society*, 71.

31. Kwame Anthony Appiah, *Cosmopolitanism: Ethics in a World of Strangers* (New York: Norton, 2006).

15

Liberal Education and the Policy Landscape

Carol Geary Schneider and Debra Humphreys

> We want one class of persons to have a liberal education, and we
> want another class of persons, a very much larger class of neces-
> sity in every society, to forgo the privileges of a liberal education.[1]
>
> —Woodrow Wilson, 1909

> [T]rends in postsecondary education are moving in a very differ-
> ent direction. Not that there has been a policy debate about deny-
> ing liberal education to some fraction of the college population.
> Rather, . . . liberal education [has been marginalized], moving it
> off the policy and public radar screen altogether.[2]
>
> —Carol Geary Schneider, 2005

Taken together, the chapters in this book sketch the contours of an exciting emerging vision for twenty-first-century educational excellence. They
document the many ways in which American colleges and universities
are reinventing liberal education for today's students and challenges.
Collectively, they detail a new approach to institutional change and curricular design that is focused not on whether students have accumulated
a sufficient number of credits in arts and sciences disciplines, the so-called
liberal arts, but, instead, on what students know and actually can do with
their liberal education, both in relation to the wider world and in relation
to their own life goals.

By adapting the traditions and strengths of American liberal education to twenty-first-century contexts and challenges, the most innovative
colleges and universities in the country are charting a new course that,
if applied more widely, could provide the majority of today's college

students with better preparation not only for professional success but also for the larger project of navigating a complex, fast-changing economy and exercising responsible judgment in their roles as citizens and thoughtful people.

Thanks in no small part to the leadership of faculty and academic administrators who see the value of a liberal education, there is a new intentionality on hundreds of campuses about a set of learning outcomes that are emerging as the key benchmarks for educational quality in the twenty-first century. Adapting the enduring goals of liberal education to the needs of a more globally interconnected society, these outcomes encompass broad knowledge of the wider world in all its interdependent complexities, including science, cultures, and society and the study of cross-cultural encounters and global interdependence. The essential outcomes also include a host of intellectual and practical proficiencies, such as written and oral communication skills, information literacy skills, and the ability to solve complex problems in diverse teams. Finally, these twenty-first-century liberal education outcomes include personal and social responsibility and civic knowledge as well as a sophisticated set of *integrative* capacities that enable college graduates to apply knowledge to real-world problems.

The Association of American Colleges and Universities describes the full set of these essential learning outcomes in its 2007 report *College Learning for the New Global Century*.[3] Colleges and universities in all sectors of higher education are developing curricular designs and educational practices to enable more students to acquire this broad set of learning outcomes and to assess their achievement of them. The most important challenge we face in fostering transformative learning is not the absence of good teaching and learning strategies or the absence of good curricular designs. Examples of good teaching and exciting integrative curricula can be found on many college campuses and in every sector of higher education.[4]

If one stayed only in the pace-setting colleges, universities, and innovative programs where faculty take seriously the challenge of helping students achieve a twenty-first-century liberal education, one easily could assume that we stand at the dawn of a new age of educational excellence—if we could muster enough resources to get the job done for all our students.

Unhappily, however, when we look beyond these islands of innovation and move into the realm of public policy and discourse, we find a very different landscape. Looking at higher education as a whole, we confront a state of affairs—endemic within our enterprise, but largely invisible to the public and to policy leaders—in which only *some* students benefit from the advantages of a strong, horizon-expanding liberal education, while millions of others, typically underserved students from low-income and minority communities, are steered toward narrow training and significantly less empowering goals for their own learning.

At institutions with a strong commitment to the liberal arts and sciences, the majority of students will take a course of study that probes global developments, diversity and interdependence, the arts and humanities, social and cultural contexts, and the workings of science, as a discrete enterprise and in relation to the larger society. These forms of study—and the modes of inquiry that undergird them—build the societal insight and intellectual capacities that students need to navigate the global community, a fast-changing economy, and the complexities of their own lives.

But when students enroll in so-called career and technical programs, they get only a hint, or nothing at all, of this broader education. They will learn concepts and skills they need for a first job, or a specific job, but they will not develop the breadth of knowledge and adaptive capacities that give them the versatility to navigate the rapid pace of change across the economy. And, of course, students enrolled in narrowly designed curricula miss out on the richness that a liberal education brings to personal and civic life—the parts of higher education that prepare us for life, not just to make a living.

These inequities occur both within institutions and across all sectors, public and private, large and small, two year and four year. They are sobering in and of themselves, but more sobering still is the fact that policy makers have no interest in ensuring or expanding access to the benefits of a liberal education.

It is not the case that policy makers are indifferent to higher education altogether—it is, rather, quite the contrary! At the federal level, the state level, in regulatory bodies and in legislatures, as well as in many foundations, policy makers are decidedly interested in "fixing" higher education and expanding student success. Prevailing notions of the problems that need to be "fixed," however, are indifferent to the larger aims or life-enhancing outcomes of a liberal education as the present volume envisions them.

In policy circles, higher education is all about the economy. Reading the evidence that the economy needs more workers with postsecondary education, policy leaders and legislators are determined to get more students into—and through—some form of postsecondary education. But, as we will see in this chapter, policy leaders have not spent much time asking what kind of learning today's innovation-fueled economy requires and rewards. Overlooking the core point that a knowledge economy needs broadly educated people who can respond rapidly and constructively to new developments, policy makers at all levels have made job skills and short-term training a priority while overlooking the importance of the very outcomes a liberal education develops.

If we—that is to say, those who recognize the value of liberal education to individuals and our society writ large—want to change this state of affairs, we will need to both engage and enlarge policy makers' and the public's understanding of what students need from a contemporary college education and why. We also will need to amend the prevailing public and policy views of what is "wrong" with higher education, of what needs to be "fixed," and what broad-based solutions might look like.

In the remainder of this chapter, we examine the prevailing disconnects between the values of liberal education and current policy priorities as well as what we can do to remove these disconnects. In the final part of the chapter, we focus especially on the current dialogue about student success and how that policy dialogue can—and should—be reframed to include a strong focus on the quality of learning. The battle to make liberal education a resource for our entire society and all our students is far from lost, but it will take both creativity and long-term determination to make liberal education what it surely was a half century ago: a widely shared policy and educational priority, as the Truman commission report of 1947 made clear.[5]

Higher Education and Current Policy Priorities

Colleges and universities are now far more in the spotlight than ever before in national discussions about public policy and the state of our nation. The economy is, of course, the main driver because, in sum, it is demanding more. In the influential recent report *Help Wanted*, Anthony Carnevale and his colleagues note that "By 2018, the economy will create 46.8 million openings; . . . nearly two-thirds of these 46.8 million jobs—some 63 percent—will require workers with at least some college education."[6] Conversely, as Americans have already recognized, college—which used to be an option rather than a necessity for a middle-class life—has become the main gateway to jobs that support a middle-class lifestyle. Policy and public attention have jointly focused, therefore, on the importance of helping many more Americans both enroll in college and earn their degrees.

The new policy focus on higher education is not a bad thing, of course. It has created opportunities as well as problems for those who support liberal education, and we need to hold both the opportunities and the problems in view as we seek to clarify the value and importance of liberal learning for all. In fact, in nearly all jobs, the work environment now is placing a premium on a broader set of skills and abilities along with sophisticated capacities to work in technologically rich environments to solve complex problems with teams of diverse individuals. In the coming years, it is clear that we need more college-educated workers who can succeed in jobs that increasingly require high-level analytic reasoning skills and complex communications capacities.[7] A recent survey of employers commissioned by the Association of American Colleges and Universities confirms that new and existing jobs in today's economy require a broader skill set and higher levels of learning and knowledge. In this study, 91 percent of employers surveyed in late 2009 reported that their company or organization "is asking employees to take on more responsibilities and to use a broader set of skills than in the past"; 88 percent thought that "the challenges employees face within [their company] are more complex today than they were in the past."[8] Carnevale and his colleagues put it this way: "[The] growth in demand for postsecondary education dovetails with two major trends. First, the fastest-growing industries—such as computer and data processing services—require workers with disproportionately higher education levels." Secondly, over time, "occupations as a whole are steadily requiring more education."[9]

These trends are not new, but it is only in the past few years that national- and state-level elected officials have fully grasped the implications of these changing economic conditions for college-going students, especially in light of the nation's changing demographics. We should applaud the fact that many of our nation's governors and our current president appreciate how important college learning is to our nation's future.

Unfortunately, the fact that the economic data are so compelling is also a potential pitfall. The focus on higher education's importance to economic success has dramatically narrowed the public discussion about the aims and outcomes of college learning. The complexity of today's workplace is equally matched in the complexity of the challenges facing Americans as citizens, voters, family members, and community members. But few in America are thinking about the role of a transformative liberal education in preparing students for the challenges of responsible citizenship in a diverse democracy and an increasingly globally interconnected world. In fact, America is the only nation that has a tradition of liberal education that includes the aim of educating for responsible citizenship and for personal and social responsibility at the college level.[10]

Members of the American public do not necessarily know about this tradition, and their elected officials do not seem to treasure it as they should. Many nations around the world—including many emerging and fledgling democracies—are looking to the traditions of American liberal education to transform their own systems of higher education and to broaden their focus beyond workforce development and technical training of leaders.[11]

Within their focus on the role of higher education in economic development, public and policy priorities have focused almost exclusively on increasing the sheer number of college graduates. Policy makers aren't wrong, of course, in asking whether enough students are entering and completing college. We do need many more college graduates than we currently are producing, but as we will see in the next section, the policy dialogue today is all about participation and completion rates. What students need to accomplish in college is barely on the policy horizon.

Complete to Compete:
Measuring Throughput Isn't Enough

It is extremely clear that the public has at least heard the economic message about higher education. Students are flocking to colleges and universities because they understand that a college degree is the ticket to opportunity in today's world. The number of individuals enrolled in college has risen from 15.3 million in 2000 to an estimated 19.1 million in 2010.[12] In one public opinion study, researchers note that "the number of people who thought that a higher education is *absolutely necessary for success* jumped dramatically, up from 31 percent as recently as 2000 to 55 percent in . . . 2009."[13] Policy makers, then, are taking their lead from the public in their unrelenting focus on the macroeconomic imperative of increasing the number of Americans with college degrees. They have listened to the economists *and* their constituents and have looked at *current* rates of college enrollment *and* college graduation and juxtaposed it to job projections and, rightly, "done the math."

They have turned their attention, therefore, to remedying the problem of low graduation rates. This is, in fact, a perfectly reasonable concern and one that our nation's leaders should, indeed, be addressing in concrete ways. Meeting the demands of a changing knowledge economy and helping to drive innovation and economic growth, however, will require much more than just graduating more people by pushing them through the existing system more quickly and efficiently. Those who are pushing this remedy alone are doing so with a limited understanding of what the problem really is and an even more limited sense of what twenty-first-century educational excellence really looks like and what it will take to bring it to many more students.

Initiatives geared toward increasing completion rates are multiplying rapidly. The National Governors Association (NGA), for instance, recently launched Complete to Compete, with the goal of creating state policies that will "improve degree attainment and more efficiently use the dollars invested by states and students." The initiative seeks to "regain excellence in higher education" by increasing the number of college graduates and, therefore, also increasing "our nation's ability to compete internationally." The entire initiative responds to the reality that many other nations now exceed ours in the percentage of young people who hold college degrees and the recognition of the need to compete economically in a knowledge economy. Among other things, the NGA initiative is calling for collection of better "outcome metrics." However, even as the NGA speaks of outcomes, it is, in fact, focused not at all on "learning" outcomes, but instead on completion and student progress metrics (e.g., degrees and certificates awarded, graduation rates, remedial education rates, and transfer rates).[14]

This NGA initiative, of course, builds on President Obama's efforts to reach an ambitious goal. As he stated in his speech announcing the American Graduation Initiative, his administration is seeking, by 2020, to "once again have the highest proportion of college graduates in the world." While he failed to secure all the funding he requested from Congress to launch this initiative, his description provides significant insight into the priorities and assumptions of this administration in terms of higher education. For instance, he hoped to "offer competitive grants, challenging community colleges to pursue innovative, results-oriented strategies in exchange for federal funding." His administration is seeking ways to "fund programs that connect students looking for jobs with businesses that are looking to hire" and to "challenge . . . schools to find new and better ways to help students catch up on the basics, like math and science, that are essential to our competitiveness." Ultimately, the Obama administration seeks to "put colleges and employers together to create programs that match curricula in the classroom with the needs of the boardroom."[15]

In its relentless focus on increasing college graduation rates specifically to increase economic competitiveness and reduce joblessness, the Obama administration also has joined forces with several large philanthropic organizations, including the Bill and Melinda Gates Foundation, which was featured at a 2010 White House Summit on Community Colleges. Melinda Gates spoke at the White House Summit and announced that the foundation was investing $34.8 million over five years to dramatically increase the graduation rates of today's community college students. The news release announcing this initiative quotes the foundation's director of education, Hilary Pennington, noting that the initiative "aims to get community colleges to restructure how they interact with the majority of their students from the moment they enter the college to the time they graduate to provide them the quickest, straightest path to a degree. When that happens, more students finish with a degree, certificate, or credential in hand." According to the foundation, this initiative will focus on "innovative approaches to financial aid counseling, course scheduling, and advising." To date, the foundation has not focused on ensuring that these students also achieve a broad set of learning outcomes.[16]

Other efforts focused on increasing graduation rates include the many initiatives funded by the Lumina Foundation for Education, including its efforts to increase adult degree completion and higher education productivity. In announcing its second-quarter 2010 grants, for instance, the Lumina Foundation noted in a press release that Lumina's grant making reflects the foundation's commitment to three primary goals: "students are prepared academically, financially and socially for success in education beyond high school; higher education completion rates are improved significantly; and, higher education productivity is increased to expand capacity and serve more students."[17] To its credit, the Lumina Foundation is one of only a handful of national foundations that also is attending to the actual content and quality of college programs through its investment in a "degree qualifications profile" and its "tuning" initiative, building on the Bologna Process in Europe. Like other foundations and most policy makers, however, the Lumina Foundation remains primarily focused on a "big goal"—"to increase the percentage of Americans with high-quality postsecondary degrees and credentials to 60 percent by the year 2025."[18]

Training Versus Liberal Learning:
The False Either/Or Choice

Many of the current higher education initiatives being supported by governmental and/or philanthropic efforts—including those sponsored by both the Gates and Lumina foundations—are focused on students who have traditionally been underserved in higher education: first-generation college students and those from underrepresented minority groups. This is, of course, both reasonable and desirable given the changing demographic makeup of America's population and its emerging workforce.

However, many of these first-generation students are being encouraged to pursue narrow training or certificate programs rather than full college degree programs that include both vocational education and the broad outcomes traditionally associated with a liberal education. Students from low-income and minority communities are significantly overrepresented, for example, in for-profit institutions.[19] Most for-profit institutions were never designed to offer a liberal education; their primary focus is on so-called career fields and job training. All students see future employment as an important outcome of college, but we are presenting these first-generation students with a false either/or choice when we steer them to institutions that promise "gainful employment" as the sole result of college study. In so doing, we also may be limiting their career options rather than placing them onto a true ladder of opportunity.

In fact, it is quite clear from data about labor force trends and from employer surveys that all students need both job-specific skills and broad learning that transfers from job to job. The Hart Research Associates 2009 survey found, for instance, that nearly 60 percent of employers surveyed agreed that, to prepare for long-term career success, recent college graduates need *both* in-depth knowledge in a specific field *and* a broad range of skills and knowledge that apply to a range of fields and positions.[20] Employers are interested in this both/and strategy because they know the demands and work environments within their own companies are changing very rapidly. They also know that today's recent college graduate is likely to change jobs very frequently. However, many policy makers seem to be operating with a twentieth-century vision of the economy. They have missed the fact that "Over the past several decades, about 70 percent of the increase in requirements for postsecondary training has stemmed from upgrades in skills demanded by occupational categories that previously did not require higher education. What we called a 'foreman' or 'manufacturing supervisor' in the late 1960s, for example, has morphed into new occupations that now require postsecondary education, including the modern manufacturing engineer."[21]

Despite this new reality, first-generation college students are disproportionately represented in vocational job training programs rather than in the kinds of transformational degree programs described in this volume.[22] They, too, however, deserve the many benefits of a broader liberal education—including a shot at those jobs with the most promise for growth and higher income levels as well as those that require graduate-level education. As Michael S. Roth, president of Wesleyan University, recently wrote in a blog post, "Given the pace of technological and social change, it no longer makes sense to devote four years of higher education entirely to specific skills. By learning how to learn, one makes one's education last a lifetime." He notes that students "should develop the ability to continue learning so that they become agents of change—not victims of it."[23] Policy solutions focused only on increasing students' completion of narrower degrees or certificate programs will shortchange students and our nation's future economic growth.

What Is Broken and What Needs Repair?

All the various higher education initiatives sponsored by major foundations or policy makers—whether focused in the aggregate on increasing graduation rates or specifically targeting underserved students—make several assumptions about the state of higher education and about the most important aims and outcomes of college learning. Wise policy solutions, of course, must rest on accurate assessments of what actually needs fixing.

Policy makers assume that low graduation rates are the result of a combination of structural problems and misplaced priorities within higher education plus a broken K–12 education system. As a result, they are seeking remedies for such things as inadequate academic preparation at the K–12 level; miscommunication or a lack of information about college preparation and admissions; complex financial aid systems; insufficient data collection and analysis on students' progress toward degrees; and a general lack of emphasis on completion as a goal for institutional leaders.

These issues are, indeed, important, but they miss some crucial elements of our national education challenge. A singular focus on college completion—and all that might stand in the way of it—assumes that if a student does succeed in graduating, he or she must have attained the skills and knowledge needed to compete in the global marketplace. There is no evidence to support this assumption, and a growing body of evidence suggests the opposite.

The Association of American Colleges and Universities published a study as early as 2005 noting that "significant percentages of college graduates performed at quite low levels of basic literacy tasks." While we lack many quality national studies measuring students' achievement of crosscutting learning outcomes, those that do exist "contradict students' own rather positive perceptions of their learning gains from college."[24] Studies of students' actual achievement also confirm what employers are saying about the abilities of recent college graduates. For instance, in late 2006, nearly two-thirds of the employers surveyed by Hart Research Associates for AAC&U agreed that "too many recent college graduates do not have the skills to be successful in today's global economy."[25] In the 2009 survey, more than 70 percent of employers also urged colleges and universities to place more emphasis on teaching students such things as critical thinking and analytic reasoning skills, oral and written communication skills, global knowledge, and teamwork skills in diverse settings.[26]

A study conducted more recently by the Social Science Research Council also found that "existing organizational cultures and practices too often do not prioritize undergraduate learning. Large numbers of college students report that they experience only limited academic demands and invest only limited effort in their academic endeavors."[27] This report notes further that "given the limited academic engagement shown by many students, it is not surprising that we find that gains in student performance are disturbingly low." Using results of the Collegiate Learning Assessment, these researchers found that "on average, gains in critical thinking, complex reasoning and writing skills . . . are exceedingly small or empirically non-existent for a large proportion of students."[28] Studies conducted for AAC&U by researchers at the University of Michigan show that large numbers of students also report limited gains on significant personal and social responsibility outcomes from college, such as engaging diverse perspectives, contributing to the wider community, or engaging in ethical reasoning as a basis for action.[29]

Policy makers have finally awakened to the problems of inadequate K–12 preparation for college-level learning and much lower than adequate graduation rates, especially for traditionally underserved students. It is time for policy makers to recognize that the quality shortfall in college is just as urgent as this attainment shortfall. They need to learn much more about the kinds of educational practices that will not only increase retention and graduation rates but also show promise in increasing actual levels of achievement of important college learning outcomes.

There is virtually no discussion among policy leaders, in fact, about two key issues. No one in policy circles is discussing the fact that only *some* college programs are preparing students with the full complement of learning outcomes they need. Policy leaders also are seemingly unaware of the dramatic disparities in student experiences *within* institutions of higher education.[30] They are focused primarily on increasing students' time to degree by improving productivity through better metrics of performance that take efficiency, but not learning outcomes or achievement levels, into account.

Absent from these discussions is the ambitious transformative educational vision at the heart of this book. Not only is this a tragedy because of the effect a liberal education can have on individual students, it is also a dangerously myopic public policy agenda, as it misses the essential message that many college graduates lack the skills and abilities they need to succeed in today's workplace.

High-Impact Educational Practices

We actually now know the kinds of educational environments and practices that increase both the likelihood of graduation and the achievement of key learning outcomes. When AAC&U published its 2007 report, *College*

Learning for the New Global Century, as part of its Liberal Education and America's Promise (LEAP) initiative, it identified a set of effective educational practices that had existed on some campuses for many years but were now beginning to spread to campuses all across the country.[31] These so-called high-impact practices include such things as first-year seminars and experiences, common intellectual experiences, learning communities, writing-intensive courses, collaborative assignments and projects, undergraduate research, diversity and global learning, service learning, community-based learning, internships, and capstone courses and projects.[32] Since that report was first published, AAC&U has also published two follow-up reports that sketch out a much more comprehensive research base demonstrating the impact these kinds of engaged learning practices can have on those students who participate in them. Unfortunately, as George D. Kuh demonstrated in his report, *High-Impact Educational Practices*, "some groups of historically underserved students are less likely to participate in high-impact activities—those first in their family to attend college and African American students in particular." This is true despite the fact that "historically underserved students tend to benefit *more* from engaging in educationally purposeful activities than majority students."[33]

The 2010 report, *Five High-Impact Practices* by Jayne Brownell and Lynn Swaner (who also has a chapter in this volume), expands further the evidence base that suggests the positive outcomes these kinds of educational practices can have.[34] For example, multiple educational studies have shown that one high-impact practice that is increasingly common at both two-year and four-year colleges and universities—the learning community—has a positive impact on grades, persistence rates, ease of college transition, levels of academic engagement, intellectual development, levels of integrative thinking, writing and reading skills, appreciation for and engagement with different viewpoints, and rates of civic engagement. Unfortunately, data from the National Survey of Student Engagement show that only 17 percent of first-year undergraduate students actually participated in a learning community in 2007.[35]

Real Versus Faux Reform

Increasing access to these kinds of high-impact practices must become part of the national policy agenda. Only if this happens can we hope to accelerate "real" versus "faux" reforms—reforms with real promise to increase students' levels of educational, civic, and professional success and contribute to our national economic recovery. Proposals to streamline educational pathways, reduce the need for remediation, increase graduation rates, and reduce students' time to degree, if carefully designed, may be worthy, but they are by no means sufficient.

What, then, would real reform look like from a policy perspective? The educational change efforts described in this volume and the many efforts to spread the high-impact, high-effort educational practices one finds at colleges and universities around the country point the way toward an agenda of real reform.

The nation must begin its efforts to seek excellence in higher education with a set of common reference points for quality that build explicitly on the hallmark outcomes of a twenty-first-century liberal education as previously described. Setting the right goals for excellence must be the sine qua non of higher education quality. The parameters for, and educational pathways to, these reference points, of course, will need to be developed by educators themselves. Policy makers, however, need clarity about these reference points so they can use them to guide their building of appropriate accountability and data collection systems. It is profoundly self-defeating to invest in so-called productivity improvements that leave the actual quality of learning off the table altogether.

The good news is there is an emerging consensus both about what these reference points are and about the need to clearly communicate them to students. Many colleges and universities now have a common set of named learning outcomes for all students. In a recent survey of chief academic officers at AAC&U member institutions, for instance, nearly 80 percent reported that their college or university had common learning outcomes for all students. These lists of outcomes include many of those identified as essential learning outcomes in the influential 2007 LEAP report referenced earlier.[36] The outcomes named by AAC&U member institutions include many of these essential learning outcomes, such as broad knowledge of culture, history, and the physical and natural worlds; intellectual and practical skills; and capacities essential for exercising personal and social responsibility in both work and other settings.[37] Policy makers instituting new accountability and reporting requirements within states could accelerate "real reforms" just by requiring all colleges and universities to name a full set of learning outcomes calibrated to the economic and civic needs of a state, a region, or the nation. Policy makers and accrediting agencies also could use these outcomes and consensus reference points to guide program review and institutional oversight efforts.

Anyone actually on a campus or in the classroom knows, of course, that clarity about outcomes is just a first step. For students to achieve a set of broad learning outcomes, they must pursue these outcomes with intentionality and rigor long before entering college. These essential outcomes, then, need to be viewed as the shared accomplishment of school and college—and of the disciplines and academic fields that are studied both in school and in postsecondary contexts. The set of common core standards adopted by more than thirty states to guide the next generation of K–12 education reform is a good first step. However, as yet, these standards cover only a limited number of learning outcomes in mathematics and language arts and were developed with only minimal input from college educators. Policy and educational leaders at both the K–12 and higher education levels must work much more closely together to develop aligned standards *and* curricular designs that foster a much broader set of learning outcomes and that include more engaged educational practices.

For instance, to prepare students better for responsible citizenship and for workforce success, cultivation of personal and social responsibility depends on a highly intentional educational experience that builds foundational learning at the school level and then immerses students with the complexity of our civic, global, ethical, and intercultural challenges, in general education and in the context of students' chosen majors. One or two courses on global and civic issues in high school and/or college are just not enough. The world is too complex, and students need to learn far more about its complexities than most of our graduates actually achieve. As AAC&U noted in its 2007 LEAP report, only a small fraction of college graduates are globally knowledgeable and competent.[38] This is a dangerous state of affairs.

Most of all, we need to recognize that the commitment to cultivating broad knowledge—of human cultures and the natural and physical world—requires a solid grounding in a whole array of academic studies, foundational experiences in key science disciplines, in U.S. and world histories, in the humanities and cultural studies and languages, and in thematic courses that engage students with the complexity of "big questions," whether these are contemporary questions about issues such as global public health crises or enduring questions about the principles and practices that guide just societies. Employers and civic leaders alike want college graduates who understand today's global realities and contexts, but educating those graduates requires learning that is both deep and integrated, not—as it too often is—fragmented and superficial. Policy leaders must examine curricula to ensure greater levels of engagement and coherence rather than simply counting students and credits earned.

A necessary, if not sufficient, condition for producing a liberally educated graduate is a coherent, engaged, and aligned school-college curriculum. Or, to put it differently, school and college must work together to help graduates prepare intensively for the challenges of a turbulent global economy and the daily difficulties of global and democratic citizenship in a divided world.

Many colleges, universities, and public and private high schools have developed the broad parameters we need to take all these learning challenges seriously and to ensure that students acquire high-level skills, strong knowledge, and an examined sense of their responsibilities to self and others as they progress from school through college. But parameters are just an outline, and we have a long way to go before students even understand the goals they need to embrace, much less actually demonstrate high levels of accomplishment on the full range of essential learning outcomes.

Productive Policy Proposals

Crafting public policy in the context of this national consensus and based on a set of educational reference points related directly to learning outcomes could lead to much more productive changes in educational practice and to real results for real students. Existing proposals such as those offered by the National Governors Association are not built on any notion of learning outcomes and are limited in their focus on graduation rates. However, they do present potentially positive policy directions that can begin to move us forward. For instance, the governors are intent on developing better tracking and data collection systems to enable policy makers and educators to understand how students are making their way through our complex systems of higher education institutions. These developments are spurred by the recognition that the majority of students in public higher education enroll in at least two and often more institutions as they progress toward degrees.[39] Policy makers are right to develop systems that can help us keep track of these peripatetic students from school through college and possibly postgraduate study as well.

Policy makers are also proposing to provide funding to develop policies and programs to increase college completion rates. If those policies are built on the educational research about high-impact educational practices that *both* increase retention and graduation rates *and* increase student achievement of important learning outcomes, these new incentives and the corollary tracking systems will be beneficial. If, on the other hand, policies reward institutions *only* for increasing their graduation rates with no attention to the quality of students' learning experiences, they could be very damaging to national efforts to meet ambitious goals for college learning.

It is quite clear from efforts in the K–12 sector that a sole focus on increasing graduation rates and meeting narrow achievement targets measured by standardized tests can result in the lowering of standards.

Respected Maryland school superintendent Jerry D. Weast argued this point in a meeting with *Washington Post* editors. He noted that the mandates for improvement in the legislation known as No Child Left Behind have "driven states toward lower standards that don't prepare most students for college or careers."[40] This likely occurred because states set low test "cut" or passing scores in order to ensure that most high school students would meet these states' "standards."

As we also have seen in watching K–12 "reform," a focus on just a few learning outcomes can have serious negative consequences. Focusing primarily on language arts and mathematical skills in the establishment of state standards and testing regimes, the K–12 system has, in recent years, seen a serious narrowing of the curriculum that poses dangers to our nation's economic future and to our participatory democracy.[41]

Higher education institutions, too, can all too easily reduce their own requirements in response to a narrowing of policy imperatives or reward systems. They can also increase their graduation rates by, for instance, increasing the selectivity of their admissions—a practice that clearly runs counter to the national need to increase college-going and graduating by precisely those who would be kept out of highly selective institutions given our current admissions practices and their overreliance on standardized tests. Policy leaders must be hypervigilant about the potential unintended consequences of particular accountability and performance requirements or new funding strategies.

Another troubling set of policy proposals are also related to these desires for greater productivity within higher education. These proposals, too, are inspired by the recognition that the United States is falling behind other nations in the percentage of young people who earn degrees. They focus, however, on simply speeding up the process to degree completion by cutting students' time on task. Some have suggested that we shrink the high school curriculum by half and get students right into community college, where they can earn both the high school diploma *and* an associate's degree in four years.[42]

Variants on this theme are flourishing all over the United States. Some are more modest; they propose only to cut high school by one year, since, as some have noted, "the senior year is a waste of time." The assumption is that if students start college in high school, we can get them to a college degree faster. Others have proposed just cutting the requirements for college to only three years of study.[43]

There are a number of problems with these proposals. Proposals to substitute high school course-taking for college-level study take direct aim at some crucial elements in a transformative *college* education: science courses, humanities courses, and problem-centered interdisciplinary courses. These are precisely the subject areas that students can get "out of the way" by selective early college enrollment in high school—with the result that they never get near "science as science is actually done" at the university level. Or, students may never engage the kinds of complex global or intercultural questions that rigorous college classes do so well. These strategies may accelerate the rate of degree production, but they will reliably reduce the quality of American capability. Policy makers, cash-strapped students, and parents all are attracted, not surprisingly, to these "shortened" degree program proposals. They need to know, however, that this approach may indeed save students money, but it may also leave them unprepared for long-term success. It is only possible to believe these kinds of reforms will "work" if one ignores the need for higher levels of learning demanded in this economy and in our society.

Other proposals have focused on reducing remediation rates. These proposals, too, while well meaning, rest on misplaced assumptions about the ability of existing standardized tests to tell us whether students are ready for college-level work and the actual gap between students' current achievement levels and where we need to take them for true success.

Given the realities before us—a complex world that demands ever higher and broader levels of knowledge and skills, and seriously under-achieving students in both school and college—shrinking the time students actually spend on their academic work is exactly the wrong recipe for success. We do, of course, need to ensure that the time students spend in high school or college is not wasted. Instead, it must be spent on more integrative, rigorous, problem-based learning experiences. Few are counting how many of these kinds of experiences students actually have, either in high school or in college. More data could be gathered on these kinds of experiences and their impact on students' actual achievement of learning outcomes.

Proposals to move students through narrow programs more quickly are mounting all around us. With the economic crisis deepening, legislators see these kinds of policy proposals as lifesavers. But they are, in fact, a disinvestment in our future.

Convincing the Public—And Their Policy Leaders

The data cited in this chapter make clear that the public "gets" the growing importance of college in today's economy. They have heard the economic message. Students are flocking to our nation's colleges and universities—both those that are very affordable and those with very high costs. Unfortunately, many members of the public lack a full understanding of the kind of college learning that will really help them and their children reach their own personal and professional life goals. With a public dialogue focused only on helping students "get in" and "get out," it is hardly surprising that families lack good reference points, both for the learning outcomes students need and for the kinds of engaged learning practices that help students develop the needed capacities. To influence policy and move it in productive directions requires support from an informed public. Unfortunately, the academy has work to do to regain the public's trust and confidence. The public's confidence in the higher education sector to actually deliver on the promise of education is waning rapidly. Public Agenda's 2010 study found that "six out of ten Americans now say that colleges today operate more like a business, focused more on the bottom line than on the educational experience of students. Further, the number of people who feel this way has increased by five percentage points in the last year alone and is up by eight percentage points since 2007." The public is also beginning to question whether college is really worth the cost. For instance, "six in ten Americans agree that 'colleges could take a lot more students without lowering quality or raising prices.' Over half (54 percent) say that 'colleges could spend less and still maintain a high quality of education.'"[44]

Those who understand what high-quality education really is—including the power of high-impact educational practices and transformational educational programs—must become far more vocal and must start speaking directly to the public. Forces promoting narrow, vocational learning and more efficient educational practices based on flawed testing strategies are actually very well organized and are "making their case" in policy circles.

The efforts described in this book represent "real" reforms, but they will never reach a large scale if they are not better understood by both policy makers and the public. Educators must take the lead in explaining this new vision for learning and in confronting the myriad forces organizing to subvert it; this starts with clear communications with the public—especially with students, prospective students, and their parents.

The general public and the policy makers who serve that public must hear directly from educators and economists that narrow learning is not enough in an economy that thrives on innovation and that includes a high degree of mobility of workers at every level. They also must understand that college learning—at its best—is different from job training. Vocational training programs are valuable and certainly have their place within our society, but we shouldn't confuse the public by calling them "colleges."

Policy makers and educational leaders all have a role to play in helping the general public understand these realities—and what it will take in reorganization and resources to get the job done right. And until this understanding improves, policy solutions will remain myopic, at best, and destructive, at worst. We need new markers of "success." Retention and graduation rates are only partial indicators of student success—necessary but not sufficient. The college degree is meaningful only when it represents forms of learning that are both valued by society and empowering to the individual. Twenty-first-century metrics for students' success, then, must capture that reality. They need to address evidence about the quality of learning as well as evidence about persistence and completion.

The long-term "college success" question must encompass not only whether students have earned a degree but also whether graduates are in fact achieving the level of preparation—in terms of knowledge, capabilities, and personal qualities—that will enable them to both thrive and contribute in a fast-changing economy and in turbulent, highly demanding global, societal, and personal contexts.

Whatever data systems, accountability frameworks, or funding strategies are developed, they must address not just what courses students take or how many credits they accumulate in a given period of time but also how students actually spend their educational time in college. For instance, how frequently, and with what results, do students actually engage in educational practices—curricular, cocurricular, and pedagogical—that provide them with realistic opportunities to actually develop the kinds of learning they need?

This expanded vision of student success—and how to foster it, assess it, and hold students and institutions accountable for it—provides a far stronger foundation for the future than the policy priorities and investments that now hold center stage. It is a vision that can fuel our economy, renew our democracy, and give all students—not just some—a passport to opportunity.

Those of us who have made liberal education our life's work need to look beyond our individual institutions to the larger landscape of higher education's role in the future of our society. We need to take an active role in building a robust debate about twenty-first-century learning and in creating new societal capacity to foster that learning.

As this book makes clear, we know "what works." We now need to mobilize the determination to make "what works" a shared societal priority.

Notes

1. Woodrow Wilson, *The Papers of Woodrow Wilson*, ed. Arthur S. Link, vol. 18 (Princeton, NJ: Princeton University Press, 1974), 593–606.

2. Carol Geary Schneider, "Liberal Education: Slip-Sliding Away?" in *Declining by Degrees: Higher Education at Risk*, ed. Richard H. Hersh and John Merrow (New York: Palgrave Macmillan, 2005).

3. Association of American Colleges and Universities, *College Learning for the New Global Century: A Report from the National Leadership Council for Liberal Education and America's Promise* (Washington, DC: Association of American Colleges and Universities, 2007), 12, www.aacu.org/advocacy/leap/documents/Global-Century_final.pdf.

4. Hart Research Associates, *Learning and Assessment: Trends in Undergraduate Education* (Washington, DC: Association of American Colleges and Universities, 2009).

5. George F. Zook, *Higher Education for American Democracy: A Report of the President's Commission on Higher Education* (Washington, DC: United States Government Printing Office, 1947); Truman Commission on Higher Education, *Higher Education for Democracy: A Report of the President's Commission on Higher Education*, vol. 1, *Establishing the Goals* (New York, 1947).

6. Anthony P. Carnevale, Nicole Smith, and Jeff Strohl, *Help Wanted: Projections of Jobs and Education Requirements through 2018* (Washington, DC: Georgetown University Center on Education and the Workforce, 2010), 13.

7. Claudia D. Goldin and Lawrence F. Katz, *The Race between Education and Technology* (Cambridge, MA: Belknap, 2008).

8. Carnevale, Smith, and Strohl, *Help Wanted*, 5.

9. Carnevale, Smith, and Strohl, *Help Wanted*, 13.

10. Sjur Bergan and Radu Damian, *Higher Education for Modern Societies: Competences and Values*, Council of Europe Higher Education Series, no. 15 (Strasbourg: Council of Europe Publishing, 2010).

11. Paul Hanstedt, "Hong Kong's Experiment in Integrative Teaching and Learning," *Liberal Education* 96, no. 4 (Fall 2010): 18–23; The World Bank, *Higher Education in Developing Countries: Peril and Promise* (Washington, DC: The World Bank, 2000).

12. U.S. Department of Education, National Center for Education Statistics, *Projections of Education Statistics to 2018* (Washington, DC: National Center for Education Statistics, 2009), table 10.

13. Public Agenda, *Squeeze Play 2010: Continued Public Anxiety on Cost, Harsher Judgments on How Colleges Are Run* (San Jose, CA: National Center for Public Policy and Higher Education, 2010), 3.

14. National Governors Association, *Complete to Compete* (Washington, DC: National Governors Association, 2010).

15. President Barack Obama, "Remarks at Macomb Community College in Warren, Michigan," *Daily Compilation of Presidential Documents* (July 14, 2009): 3–5, www.gpoaccess.gov/presdocs/2009/DCPD-200900565.pdf.

16. Bill and Melinda Gates Foundation, "Foundation Launches $35 Million Program to Help Boost Community College Graduation Rates," news release, October 4, 2010, www.gatesfoundation.org/press-releases/Pages/increasing-community-college-graduation-rates-101004.aspx.

17. Lumina Foundation for Education, "The Case for Improved Higher Education Access and Attainment," www.luminafoundation.org/our_work.

18. Lumina Foundation for Education, "The Case for Improved Higher Education Access and Attainment."

19. Mamie Lynch, Jennifer Engle, and Jose Cruz, *Subprime Opportunity: The Unfulfilled Promise of For-Profit Colleges and Universities* (Washington, DC: The Education Trust, 2010).

20. Hart Research Associates, *Raising the Bar: Employers' Views on College Learning in the Wake of the Economic Downturn* (Washington, DC: Association of American Colleges and Universities, 2010), 6.

21. Carnevale, Smith, and Strohl, *Help Wanted*, 14.

22. Marsha Silverberg, Elizabeth Warner, Michael Fong, and David Goodwin, *National Assessment of Vocational Education: Final Report to Congress* (Washington, DC: U.S. Department of Education, 2004); Xianglei Chen, *First-Generation Students in Postsecondary Education: A Look at Their College Transcripts* (Washington, DC: National Center for Education Statistics, 2005).

23. Michael Roth, "In Defense of 'Learning How to Learn,'" *Good Feed Blog*, October 16, 2010, http://goodmenproject.com/2010/10/16/in-defense-of-learning-how-to-learn/.

24. Association of American Colleges and Universities, *Liberal Education Outcomes: A Preliminary Report on Student Achievement in College* (Washington, DC: Association of American Colleges and Universities, 2005), 6.

25. Hart Research Associates, *How Should Colleges Prepare Students to Succeed in Today's Global Economy?* (Washington, DC: Association of American Colleges and Universities, 2006).

26. Hart Research Associates, *Raising the Bar*, 9.

27. Richard Arum, Josipa Roksa, and Esther Cho, *Improving Undergraduate Learning: Findings and Policy Recommendations from the SSRC-CLA Longitudinal Project* (New York: Social Science Research Council, 2011), 2.

28. Arum, Roksa, and Cho, *Improving Undergraduate Learning*, 4.

29. Eric L. Dey and Associates, *Developing a Moral Compass: What Is the Campus Climate for Ethics and Academic Integrity?* (Washington, DC: Association of American Colleges and Universities, 2010); Eric L. Dey and Associates, *Engaging Diverse Viewpoints: What Is the Campus Climate for Perspective-Taking?* (Washington, DC: Association of American Colleges and Universities, 2010); Eric L. Dey and Associates, *Civic Responsibility: What Is the Campus Climate for Learning?* (Washington, DC: Association of American Colleges and Universities, 2009).

30. George D. Kuh, "What We're Learning about Student Engagement," *Change* 35, no. 2 (2003): 24–32.

31. Association of American Colleges and Universities, *College Learning for the New Global Century*, 12.

32. More information on high-impact practices can be found in George D. Kuh, *High-Impact Educational Practices: What They Are, Who Has Access to Them, and Why They Matter* (Washington, DC: Association of American Colleges and Universities, 2008).

33. Kuh, *High-Impact Educational Practices*, 17.

34. Jayne E. Brownell and Lynn E. Swaner, *Five High-Impact Practices: Research on Learning Outcomes, Completion, and Quality* (Washington, DC: Association of American Colleges and Universities, 2010).

35. Kuh, *High-Impact Educational Practices*, 16.

36. Association of American Colleges and Universities, *College Learning for the New Global Century*, 12.

37. Hart Research Associates, *Learning and Assessment*, 4.

38. Association of American Colleges and Universities, *College Learning for the New Global Century*, 12.

39. Peter Ewell, *The New "Ecology" for Higher Education: Challenges to Accreditation* (Alameda, CA: Western Association of Schools and Colleges, 2010), 1.

40. Daniel de Vise, "Montgomery Schools Chief Says Federal Mandate Is Lowering Standards," *Washington Post*, June 28, 2007, www.washingtonpost.com/wp-dyn/content/article/2007/06/27/AR2007062702845.html.

41. Diane Ravitch, *The Death and Life of the Great American School System: How Testing and Choice Are Undermining Education* (New York: Basic Books, 2010).

42. National Center on Education and the Economy, *Tough Choices or Tough Times: The Report of the New Commission on the Skills of the American Workforce* (San Francisco: Jossey-Bass, 2007).

43. Lamar Alexander, "The Three-Year Solution: How the Reinvention of Higher Education Benefits Parents, Students, and Schools," *Newsweek*, October 26, 2009, 26–29.

44. Public Agenda, *Squeeze Play 2010*, 2.

PART IV

SUCCESSFUL MODELS AND PRACTICES

Introduction to Case Studies

Ashley P. Finley

The case studies written for this volume are not intended to stand alone as exemplars of institutional success, nor are the practices they detail meant to represent *the* definitive models for transformative campus practice. Rather, these cases present something much more universal—and far less commonly documented—voices from campuses of people who have been deeply engaged in institutional change processes; who come from varied campus positions and locales; who have been challenged to write about how they have succeeded, failed, stalled, and been encouraged and where they are going next.

To this end, the authors of these case studies have been guided by two common criteria. First, the case studies needed to be written using a lens that, while necessarily reflective of the institution's journey, could not be static or backward looking. While any case study must reflect upon what has been done and learned, institutional change is governed by the mercurial nature of campuses. The processes of transformation are never finished and are fundamentally dynamic. Thus, the conclusion of each of these case studies should read as an ellipsis: a few dots to indicate the process is never fully complete and that those involved in the process have been best served by looking forward.

Second, guided by a common prospective framing, these pieces have been written to provide an entrée to conversations on campuses seeking similar change efforts. To foster dialogue, the content of these case studies forefronts the activities, processes, obstacles, and structures that highlight qualities of adaptability and transferability across institutional contexts. Too often case studies in higher education rest upon the singularity of campuses, the unique blend of faculty expertise, faculty mission, and curricular gems that make each sui generis—each its own kind, a novelty of experience and process. No doubt the cases presented here offer a range of contexts (a public research university, a private college, a historically black college, a U.S. service academy) and a range of geographic locales that span both coasts and the Midwest. Yet, while each of these institutions is distinctive, the innovation and range of practices detailed among them are malleable enough to be understood and applied across campus milieus. The threads that connect the work of the ten campuses highlighted in these case studies are the same threads likely to be found on campuses across the country.

These points of connection can be categorized into three common areas or facets of institutional change and transformation. First is the harnessing of innovative thinking on campus to link promising practices of pedagogies to motivate larger curricular change. Truly *transformative* innovations go beyond course-level pedagogy to engage the restructuring of existing programs, resources, and policies at the institutional level. California State University at Chico and Georgetown University have both developed inventive pedagogies that have over time garnered substantial institutional attention and embeddedness. Dickinson College and Montclair State University have illustrated how innovation can also be extended to resource allocations, in terms of both faculty time and money for program development.

Second, institutional change involves a vision of multidimensionality. The daily functioning of campuses is dependent upon multiple parts that generally operate independently with separate budgets, tasks, and goals. These entities are often referred to as *silos*—an illustrative term for the distinct nature of the literal and figurative boundaries of these campus components. Institutional change, however, must go beyond the unidimensionality of silos to envision the institution as a collective whole, where spheres of campus life interact and work together to accomplish common goals. This is most clearly demonstrated in the case studies of the Evergreen State College, Georgetown University, and the University of Nebraska, Lincoln, each of which details the productive alignment of curricular and cocurricular dimensions to pursue institutional goals. Wagner College also illustrates the benefit of reenvisioning the "town and gown" relationship to involve community partners and organizations in fruitful and enduring relationships with students.

Finally, institutional change depends upon deliberate and frequent communication. Much of the discussion on campuses around change efforts points to the need to build institutional capacity and involve stakeholders, activities fundamentally driven by effective communication. All the case studies included here in some way identify the role of effective communication in developing institutional change. Morehouse College and the United States Military Academy at West Point highlight the use of assessment to build dialogue. And, perhaps not surprisingly, nearly all the case studies reference the importance of communicating with faculty. Most commonly, this communication focuses on the solicitation of faculty input, consensus building, and active listening. But it can also mean understanding where the conversation has gone wrong and working to develop more effective techniques for outreach and inclusion, as the case study for St. Lawrence University details. Communication also entails developing a transparency of practice and purpose on campuses. Strategies involve effective uses of language and branding as demonstrated by Georgetown; CSU, Chico; and the University of Nebraska, Lincoln. They also involve methods of recognition and gatherings as demonstrated by Wagner College and Morehouse College, respectively. Transparency also means translating the institutional mission in new and productive ways, as demonstrated by USMA, West Point and the Evergreen State College.

The preceding overview is offered only as a guide to what will be found among the case studies in this volume. It is not intended to suggest case studies fit neatly into particular categories of institutional change. Indeed, the rich detail offered within these case studies defies neat categorization or easy summation. The caution of each case study is that change takes time. Beyond this, the lessons to be learned from the stories told here are ultimately left to the interpretation of the individual reader.

1: California State University, Chico

Public Sphere Pedagogy
Connecting Student Work to Public Arenas

Thia Wolf and William M. Loker

Institutional Context

As a public, regional, comprehensive university, CSU, Chico graduates the kind of students that make up the lion's share of baccalaureate students in this country. CSU, Chico is a residential campus, with the majority of students of traditional college-going age and a balanced mix of first-time freshmen and transfer students. Our university has faced its share of challenges in an effort to improve academic engagement and address student wellness issues.

Inspired and fostered by the strong emphasis that president Paul Zingg placed on the civic mission of the university, we considered how best to improve academic and civic engagement in our students. In his inaugural address, Zingg asked if we "dared" as a campus community to "define community values . . . and reward behaviors . . . predicated on service above self, civic responsibility, and high ethical standards." While CSU, Chico has become known for its emphasis on sustainability education and action, Zingg sought the improvement and creation of multiple well-defined outreach efforts that would intentionally tie students' classroom experiences to the creation of civic character.

In collaboration with faculty in several departments over the past five years, the Office of Undergraduate Education, which houses our First-Year Experience (FYE) program, has responded to the president's challenge by creating a new kind of structure in several first-year courses, a structure that assists students in building bridges to the community and in changing their self-view from high school student to emerging adult and successful college student.

We have come to call the method we developed Public Sphere Pedagogy (PSP). PSP has particular characteristics and specific learning outcomes. Courses employing PSP (1) focus on students' reading, class discussion, research efforts, and writing on contemporary—and usually pressing—public issues; (2) connect students' class work to public arenas in order to demonstrate to them through direct experience the relevance of civic studies and scholarly activity to the larger world; (3) place students in dialogue with diverse campus and community members around issues of public importance, providing them with opportunities to behave as adult participants in processes of dialogue and debate vital to the health of a democracy; and (4) encourage students' ongoing civic participation through "next step" activities—such as action plans, further civic course work, and/or commitments to civic activities and organizations. Together, these activities have been shown to increase students' commitments to scholarship and lifelong learning, improve their sense of civic efficacy and personal responsibility, and prepare them for long-term participation in civic life.

One Example of PSP: The CSU, Chico Town Hall

The Town Hall began as a strategy for improving students' engagement in first-year writing courses. In 2006, three composition faculty members teaching the entry-level required writing course responded to the president's focus on increased civic development for students by creating pilot Town Hall sections with a civic dimension. In order to place students in an environment where their research into public issues mattered to a wider audience than their teacher and classmates, the faculty proposed a Town Hall as the culminating work of the course. In this Town Hall, students would present their individual issues-based research projects and lead discussions about the issues they had dedicated their time to understanding. Campus administrators, faculty and staff, and students were invited, as were members of the Chico community.

The first Town Hall consisted of 180 participants, 120 of them students in the sections of the required English course. Students presented key information from their research, then led discussions by starting with a set of their own questions and gradually working in audience questions and concerns.

When students returned to the main hall after two hours of breakout discussions, they spoke ebulliently of their experience, making comments such as "I can't believe this was so interesting"; "Who knew I could enjoy talking about the things my parents discuss?"; "What else can I do that's like this?"; "Now I feel like a college student." Comments of this kind have since been frequently documented in follow-up written reflections, which are now a standard embedded assessment in PSP courses.

Following its initial small-scale success in fall 2006, the CSU, Chico Town Hall grew rapidly. By spring 2007, the event included more than 300 participants, and it now consistently draws over 700 participants. At least 80 "consultants" drawn from the campus faculty and staff and from community organizations participate in a final hour of discussion with small groups of students around public issues. Growth of the Town Hall has occurred organically, first due to growing participation of faculty members and/or to the inclusion of large lecture-style classes.

Public Sphere Pedagogy beyond the Town Hall

Because of the success of the Town Hall, faculty teaching other kinds of courses have worked with the FYE program to revise classes and embed a public event that increases students' engagement. To date, these include courses in American government, public speaking, small-group communication, principles of macro analysis in economics, and university life. For example, in the course Introduction to University Life, students' research and civic work during the semester results in a student-built Civic Dialogue Museum focused on contemporary themes that students have studied (e.g., AIDS and public health issues, global citizenship, and cultural belief systems).

Additionally, the communication studies department has embedded PSP in both their public speaking and small-group communication classes, where students have the opportunity of participating in the Chico Great Debate. The Chico Great Debate consists of a full day of speeches, presentations, debates, and an interactive civic expo, designed and delivered by students in our City Council Chambers. The event is webcast live; students speak to reporters and sometimes appear on the local news. This work represents a full partnership between the university and the city: An evening "main event" debate series is opened by words of welcome from both the mayor and the campus provost.

Finally, an entry-level course in economics, Principles of Macro Analysis, has moved what used to be a set of in-class presentations into a public arena where interested others from all walks of life come to learn from students, to interact with them, and to seek creative local solutions to difficult economic circumstances. As in other PSP offerings, students engage enthusiastically and afterward report a heightened interest in civic activities, including voting, informing themselves on public issues, and participating in community efforts focused on positive change.

What We've Learned

Assessment conducted via surveys, focus groups, narrative analysis of student writing, and classroom ethnographies on the impact of the Town Hall indicates that participation in a PSP course improves students' academic and civic engagement and some features of their wellness. A four-year survey we conducted of students who had been in the first cohort of Town Hall participants indicated significant changes in their positive self-views, their interest in politics, their civic participation, and their belief that "I can make a difference in the world."

Additionally, many faculty members who have been involved in PSP work say, "I could never go back to teaching the old way again," meaning that working in isolation in traditional classroom structures no longer seems as productive or interesting as assisting students to enter the public domain by using their course work to enrich the community. These teachers enjoy the collaborative work of planning the major event together, a kind of planning that reaches back into their classrooms and causes them to compare teaching approaches, research assignments, and learning outcomes. They also enjoy the noticeable impact on their students, who are more able to recognize how their course work matters beyond the boundaries of school.

Public Sphere Pedagogy effectively creates a sense of civic efficacy while bringing home to students the importance of their scholarly endeavors. By inviting students to take part in serious conversations about issues that matter, faculty provide a clear purpose for reading, writing, research, and class discussion that heighten students' sense of agency, involvement, and empowerment. Assessment data have demonstrated both immediate and enduring effects on student attitudes.

One of our most persistent challenges moving forward is to find the institutional structures and resources necessary to sustain PSP. PSP has costs—in terms of organizing the public events critical to the practice's success and in terms of cost on faculty time. In an era of shrinking resources for higher education, any program that does not increase institutional capacity or effectiveness comes under intense scrutiny. We argue that, far from being a "luxury" or an "add-on," PSP has been a proven means of reaching often detached and alienated students and bringing them firmly into the academic enterprise and university community. PSP can also play a key role in reviving the civic mission of the American university. This is an argument that, in the CSU, Chico context, resonates with faculty and administration alike. Whether this support in principle is followed by the modest financial resources needed to sustain PSP—only time will tell.

2: Dickinson College

Engaging Faculty in Learning Communities

Lessons Learned

Shalom D. Staub

A "learning community" is a well documented form of engaged learning pedagogy that has been linked to positive gains in student learning outcomes.[1] At Dickinson College, a small liberal arts undergraduate college, learning communities are composed of linked first-year seminars. Students live together and participate, with their faculty, in campus-based or off-campus out-of-classroom experiences. This case examines the creative processes and interactions of academic administration and faculty integral to the evolution of the learning community experience as an important element of sustained institutional change at Dickinson.

Establishing Learning Communities

Dickinson's faculty embraced first-year seminars as an experience for all incoming students in the early 1980s, with the goal of providing a foundation for college-level writing and research. The current learning community program began as a pilot program in 2003 with two linked seminars to form one learning community. We were specifically interested in creating a first-year student learning experience that linked the academic, campus, and residential experiences. Having the two professors, and particularly their students, report their experiences to the full faculty at the end of the semester was a key step in being able to expand the program to three learning communities with six faculty the next year.

By the fall of 2005, we successfully tapped external funding to provide additional programmatic resources to participating faculty as we sought to expand the program. That year and every year since, learning communities involved approximately ten to fifteen out of forty faculty teaching first-year seminars, working with 160 to 240 students. We have encouraged faculty to explore experiential learning opportunities, such as service learning and field-based learning, to emphasize to students that college learning happens both in and out of the classroom.

Understanding Faculty Resistance

Faculty members had a variety of responses to this new development. "Early adopters" were eager to try this new format, seeing it as an opportunity for high faculty-student engagement, which they viewed as the embodiment of the college's mission. The "opposition," however, manifested in a variety of expressions. One senior faculty member opposed the very term *learning community*, maintaining that the college as a whole and every individual class constitute a learning community. Others said that given our small size and low faculty-student ratio, we don't need this intensive effort. Still others saw learning communities as a ploy to add additional burden to faculty time just after the administration approved a shift from a six- to a five-course teaching load. These faculty members feared that learning community "success" would mean all faculty teaching first-year seminars would then be *required* to teach in this more time-intensive format.

Additionally, we realized that the language we had been using to frame the assessment of the learning community program had unintentionally contributed to faculty resistance. In describing the evaluation of learning communities in relation to individual first-year seminars, learning communities were identified as an "engaged pedagogy." The implicit, though unintended, message was that we had already determined that individual first-year seminars were "nonengaged" learning environments. Thus, we began to shift our language regarding engagement to be much more inclusive,[2] emphasizing that the learning community format alone does not create engaged learning for students. Successful learning communities require strong individual seminars with dedicated teachers, and individual seminars *also* could produce comparable positive effects of academic engagement. Furthermore, we were clearer that learning communities were one form of engaged learning on campus, along with many other examples of high-impact practices—the first-year seminars themselves, faculty-student research opportunities, study abroad experiences, internships, service learning, workshop-based pedagogy in the sciences, and so on.

Collaboration between Faculty and Administration

Overall though, as we sought to recruit first-year seminar faculty in any given year to consider a learning community, we found that the majority neither harbored strong personal opposition nor had a burning desire to jump into an unknown format that promised additional work. We learned that a variety of inducements, for which we had the provost's support, drew faculty into conversation. First, all learning community faculty received a stipend. We also provided access to additional funds to support the out-of-classroom programs at a level significantly higher than the funding available to individual first-year seminars. We provided an upper-class student learning community coordinator to handle all logistics for the supplementary on- and off-campus programming that faculty members designed. Faculty appreciated that we wanted them to focus on developing the experiential learning plan and student interaction. Significantly, we learned that although the stipend and the support were important, a major faculty inducement was the opportunity to work collaboratively with both familiar and new colleagues. Faculty members have reported gaining new perspectives on their own teaching material and generally appreciating the opportunity to work closely with colleagues in other departments and divisions.

We also recognized that there were interested faculty who could not commit the time to the learning community experience. We began to explore alternative models to meet this issue. For example, both a residential and nonresidential cluster of seminars was implemented. Clustered courses linked several courses (rather than just two) sharing a common theme, but without the intensive involvement of faculty. These alternatives provided additional structured opportunities for students to extend their learning out of the classroom without the high demand on faculty time.

These examples contributed to an environment of program flexibility and innovation. Faculty members themselves took the lead for other, related innovations. One year, faculty members linked their learning community seminars on the theme of environmental sustainability to two other courses appropriate to first-year students in relevant disciplines—history, environmental studies, or economics. In this model, eight faculty worked together (four first-year seminar faculty and four additional faculty) to integrate their paired courses. Other faculty, in the humanities, took the idea of linkage in a different direction by creating a common syllabus—Ideas That Shaped the World. In this common syllabus model (without, at present, a shared residential experience), students attend seminar sessions with their individual seminar professors while also attending regularly scheduled plenary sessions and special campus events with invited speakers.

Concluding Thoughts on Institutional Change

The success of learning communities at Dickinson is a story of convergence and amplification. Converging interests of faculty and administrators led to articulating a vision in the 2000 strategic plan. Further convergence of willing early adopters and college resources led to demonstrated value. Participating faculty conveyed the collegial satisfaction and intellectual stimulation they derived from working closely with their learning community faculty partners. Faculty also reported the positive impact on their relationships with students, which benefitted the academic advising role these faculty provide beyond the first-year seminar until a student's declaration of a major. Participating students, even those reluctant or skeptical at the start of the semester, reported high satisfaction with multiple dimensions of the learning community as their first-semester Dickinson experience.

Administrative flexibility, innovation, and careful listening to faculty concerns and interests were necessary elements for building this creative convergence. We learned to capitalize on the "early adopter" interest, to listen carefully to the opposition and be responsive without getting defensive or discouraged, and to explore a variety of ways to engage the potentially interested faculty members. We cannot overemphasize the need to understand and adjust to one's own campus culture dynamic. We are, in fact, a campus that prides itself on a high faculty-student ratio, which creates many opportunities for student-faculty interaction, in and out of the classroom.

Faculty members both responded to administrator-initiated suggestions and amplified the emerging innovation by becoming active initiators in this process. Certainly, this experimental and innovative pedagogy has been built on the foundation of a Dickinson culture that values and supports faculty innovation and pluralism. And yet, the learning community program has been a valuable *catalyst*, with each of the new models amplifying each other. Over time, the campus culture has shifted in that learning communities and other forms of linked seminars now form an established practice. A portion of faculty teaching a first-year seminar in a given year predictably approach the seminar with an interest and openness to explore linkages, both formally and more informally. The openness to experimentation and innovation in this program will undoubtedly continue to encourage faculty creativity and innovation.

Notes

1. See George Kuh, *Experiences That Matter: Enhancing Student Learning and Success*, National Survey of Student Engagement Annual Report 2007 (Blooming-

ton: Center for Postsecondary Research, Indiana University Bloomington, 2007), 14–15, http://nsse.iub.edu/NSSE_2007_Annual_Report/index.cfm.

2. The assessment does actually suggest that successful learning communities produce a different kind of "engaged" learner—self-motivated and personally responsible—and that successful individual seminars more often produce students who described themselves as being engaged "by" their faculty, an external source for their motivation and interest. Ashley Finley, "The First Year Experience and Engaged Learning Initiatives at Dickinson: Findings from Four Years of Research" (unpublished paper, 2009).

3: Georgetown University

Curriculum Infusion

Educating the Whole Student and Creating Campus Change

Joan B. Riley and Mindy McWilliams

Georgetown's development of a wide-scale program of curriculum infusion was motivated by a desire to connect life and learning for our students in a new way—one that both facilitated students' understanding and enjoyment of course material and increased their academic and civic engagement.[1] We knew that curriculum infusion, a pedagogy that involves integrating health issues into academic courses with the aim of changing attitudes and behavior, could be successful in nursing and health promotion courses on our campus.[2] However, we wondered whether curriculum infusion could be used successfully in courses where the link between health topics and academic material was less obvious, and whether enough faculty would embrace this teaching strategy so it would make a campus-wide impact, not only improving students' health and sense of well-being but also engaging students more fully in their academic work. Our aim has been to make an impact on the campus landscape by bringing an important element of our university's mission into the classroom.

With these goals in mind, we developed a model by which curriculum infusion can be used in almost any course. Over sixty faculty in twenty-five academic departments at our university have taught courses using curriculum infusion, reaching approximately 4,200 undergraduate students, or about 30 percent of our student body. We began with courses where the topic seemed like a natural choice—addressing sexually transmitted infections in a biology course, depression in a psychology course, and human flourishing in an introductory philosophy course. As we have grown more confident in the wide applicability of our model, we have expanded the repertoire of courses to less likely ones, such as Managerial Accounting, Economics, and Math Modeling.

319

Here we will discuss four aspects of our project that enabled us to design and implement our program with substantial buy-in from campus stakeholders. These aspects are (1) developing a flexible model of curriculum infusion; (2) sharing ownership and responsibility across university constituencies; (3) collaborating among campus networks; and (4) actualizing our core mission.

Developing a Flexible Model of Curriculum Infusion

The model we developed links academic content directly to students' personal lives through readings, classroom discussions with campus health professionals, and written personal reflections. The careful choice of topic is critical, as is purposeful collaboration between the faculty member and the campus health professional. Due to our belief that the model would not be embraced as a new pedagogical practice unless faculty were able to adapt it to suit their needs, we encouraged each faculty and health presenter pair to implement the model in ways that were grounded in who they were and that integrated with how they already taught. This allowed faculty and health professionals to develop a sense of personal ownership and control over how to apply curriculum infusion in the classroom. Our model encourages freedom and flexibility on the part of the faculty and health presenter and gives them scope to innovate, even if, on the surface, their chosen approach appears to fail to meet the stated minimum requirements of our model.[3]

A flexible model has the added benefit of fostering creativity in course assignments, speaker topics, and course connections that likely would not occur under a strict model. Flexibility is important because students often encounter multiple curriculum infusion courses during their undergraduate careers. Encouraging variety in the model and courses with unique topics and perspectives has enabled us to keep the curriculum infusion experience fresh for students.

Another component of our model is the use of small stipends for faculty and health professionals to provide support and motivation. While the stipends initially served as incentive to participate for some faculty, motivation for continued involvement tended to include improved communication with students, increased student engagement in class as content acquired meaning for students when applied to their lived experiences, and success in connecting students who needed support with campus resources. For health professionals, the stipend served as initial motivation, as recognition that their contributions were as important as those of the faculty member, and as a sign that the university supported their taking time away from individual counseling to participate more fully in the education of all students.

Sharing Ownership and Responsibility

Early on we formed an executive team that included representatives of multiple campus constituencies. Our team included members of the faculty, student affairs professionals, and staff from Counseling and Psychiatric Service (CAPS); Health Education Services; the Center for Social Justice Research, Teaching and Service (CSJ); and the Center for New Designs in Learning and Scholarship (CNDLS), our teaching and learning center. Having such a large group—up to a dozen people at times—share leadership and responsibility presented challenges in terms of coordinating and balancing competing needs and ideas. Yet having so many people invested in the success of the program has helped to share the burden, both workload and financial, of supporting a large multifaceted initiative.

We have come to realize that the program's current design also presents opportunities for student ownership and responsibility that we did not originally envision. Although students do not participate on the executive committee, they do actively participate in the Bringing Theory to Practice conferences and have copresented with faculty and staff at the national level. Students have also demonstrated their engagement with and appreciation for curriculum infusion by including the program in the annual student list of "100 Things to Be Thankful for at Georgetown" and the development of a special-interest student living community called the Cura Personalis House, the Jesuit phrase for care of the person.

Collaborating among Campus Networks

A major goal of the program is to increase the numbers of faculty active in the campus safety net, the coordinated network of campus services and staff that support students who are at risk in a range of ways—from depression and alcohol abuse, to mental health issues, to failing grades because of stress and family burdens. In order to achieve this goal, we needed to challenge faculty, health professionals, and students to expand their notion of their roles in the campus community. The program strives to support faculty and staff in undertaking these challenges by creating a community of collaboration, respect, and opportunities for reflection. Faculty and staff, in turn, support students inside and outside the classroom, in the task of engaging their whole selves in the academic enterprise and in seeking out needed resources.

Through the curriculum infusion program, faculty receive training about what to expect in the classroom when discussing personal issues with students and learn how to connect students with appropriate campus resources. However, we neither want nor expect faculty to analyze students' potential mental health problems nor overstep boundaries into students' personal lives. Rather, the goal is for faculty to be well connected to the health professionals on campus whose job it is to evaluate and find help for students in need.

After participating in the training and teaching a curriculum infusion course, faculty report being more aware of the array of campus resources available, more attuned to student warning signs, and more empowered to act when they believe a student may be struggling. Through class discussions and reflective writing assignments, faculty hear and read about students' stories and struggles. By collaborating with campus health professionals, faculty receive needed support in interpreting these interactions and determining whether follow-up or referral is appropriate. In addition, campus health professionals now enter into classrooms where they encounter all types of students, not just the ones seeking counseling or advice, resulting in increased awareness on all sides and direct connections to support services for students who may need it.

Our program has challenged all of us to be more integrative, more connective, and more synthetic about our lives and showed us how this can be done. Faculty have been challenged to open up classroom conversation and assignments into personal areas with students and to share classroom authority and class time with health professionals. Health professionals have been pushed to leave the comfort zone of one-on-one counseling sessions in order to enter the realm of teaching, where they interact with students in large groups, sometimes up to hundreds of students. Students have been asked to reimagine the boundaries between academic work and the rest of their lives. The impact of the shift in boundaries and roles has been the identification of shared goals for student development and success between faculty and student affairs professionals. Both groups have expressed the sentiment that "we are in this together."

Actualizing Our Core Mission

Engaged learning practices such as curriculum infusion are nurtured and grow in communities that value and seek creative opportunities. Our university culture values creativity and has a history of supporting innovation in teaching, especially through programs sponsored by our teaching and learning center and our Center for Social Justice. This is one reason our faculty and staff were willing to undertake the challenges of this project and to reach across silos to create connections with different members of the university community.

Another reason this program has taken hold is because of a deep-rooted connection of the program's main goals to collectively held values reflected in our university's core mission. Our university, like those everywhere, has a unique set of driving forces based on shared principles centering on the key issues of learning, engagement, and development of the individual student. Other institutions employ the phrases *social justice*, *leadership* or *civic development*, *flourishing* or *preparation for participation in a global society* in their mission statements. Our core values are stated as educating the whole person, the importance of reflection and reflective practice, and care for the person. By using language that our faculty, students, and administrators were familiar with, and by appealing explicitly to institutional values, we were able to position our project as an innovative and concrete way of putting our core mission into practice in the classroom. As universities continue to find new ways to demonstrate commitment to core values and to the transformation of the hearts and minds of students, we hope this program may provide a model for creating effective partnerships aimed at caring for and developing the whole student, within and outside the classroom.

Notes

1. The Georgetown University curriculum infusion program is called the Engelhard Project in recognition of the support provided by the Charles Engelhard Foundation for the Bringing Theory to Practice Project developed in partnership with the Association of American Colleges and Universities.

2. Joan B. Riley, Patrick T. Durbin, and Mary D'Ariano, "Under the Influence: Taking Alcohol Issues into the College Classroom," *Health Promotion Practice* 6, no. 2 (2005): 202–6. This article presents results from a course at Georgetown University that used curriculum infusion and resulted in students gaining knowledge and improving attitudes toward reducing harm related to alcohol use.

3. The minimum requirements for a curriculum infusion course in our model are (1) an assigned reading for students about the chosen student health or personal growth-related topic that also ties in with the academic content of the course; (2) a class session devoted to discussion of the topic, co-led by a campus health professional and the faculty member; and (3) a structured writing assignment (required but not graded) asking students to reflect on the topic in light of the reading and class discussion.

4: Montclair State University

Attempting Organizational Transformational Learning from the Ground Up

Lessons Learned

Valerie I. Sessa

The purpose of this case study is to describe the growth of an institute for leadership development that is currently taking place at Montclair State University and demonstrate how individuals, groups, and the organization interact to both aid and inhibit the implementation of this institute using the lens of organizational learning theory. Although individuals are whole entities, they are parts of groups; and groups, though whole, are also parts of an organization. Thus learning is continuously flowing from individuals to groups to organizations and back again.[1] However, less attention has been paid to what this learning process really looks like in organizations, such as institutions of higher education. This case study demonstrates that the process is less than smooth. Each level (individual, group, or organization) can potentially induce or inhibit learning in its own level and the other levels.

Because individuals and groups tend to be dependent on the organization (e.g., the organization exercises control over individuals and groups by controlling resources, establishing policies, offering opportunities), organizations are more likely to influence individual and group learning than the reverse. Though individuals and groups can induce learning within the organization, this learning is slow and difficult to achieve. The implementation of a leadership development institute at Montclair State focuses on the lessons learned as individuals and groups have attempted to influence organizational learning.

The psychology department (the group) induced the learning by hiring a new faculty member (the individual) with a background in leadership learning and development to take over and further develop a service learning-based leadership course offered within the department for incoming freshmen involved in the Emerging Leaders Learning

Community. The learning community was then managed by the faculty member's counterpart in student affairs, the director of student leadership programs, and the course was staffed using adjuncts who worked for the university in various cocurricular capacities with backgrounds in leadership and leadership development.

As the faculty member began to modify the leadership course, she discovered that, besides the course, there was a rich array of leadership development opportunities at the university. But these were dispersed such that the groups involved did not know they were trying to accomplish similar goals. For example, the course she was trying to change had originated over a decade earlier as a cocurricular program through the Educational Opportunity Fund program. It had been modified into its current form by the director of student leadership programs: a credit-bearing psychology service learning course within a freshman learning community with a living-learning floor in one of the dormitories for Emerging Leaders Learning Community students and alumni. In addition, there was at least one club whose purpose was to develop leaders through service in the community, a number of paid (either through a stipend or an hourly wage) cocurricular positions with an emphasis on leadership development, and an athletic leadership association. Finally, she discovered that the university also had a twenty-year history in community-based learning, including internships, cooperative education, and service learning. The leadership course utilized service learning, a type of community-based learning. However, these groups did not tend to work with each other and did not necessarily know what the other was doing.

The faculty member and the director discovered they had similar visions for leadership development at the university: building and expanding the single course in the Emerging Leaders Learning Community into a recognized institute of leadership development that would serve to promote university-wide leadership development and research. They envisioned a leadership development minor combined and aligned with cocurricular programming as well as faculty research. They also wanted to bring together all the faculty and staff interested in leadership and leadership development into a community of practice to allow leadership development information to flow between the groups.

Lessons Learned

First, if organizational transformation is to be reached from learning at the group level, there ultimately needs to be a motivated and energized nucleus of people who are willing and able to sustain the effort needed.

Additionally, the team needs to have a vision and a loosely formed plan of action. The unified vision serves to attract others, align interests, gain commitment, and guide existing and new team members. The plan of action allows the team to recognize and join with other groups attempting to change the organization along similar lines. At Montclair State, the faculty member and the director formed the nucleus with the vision of an institute of leadership development. The plan of action included developing a leadership development minor and also aligning and enhancing the cocurricular leadership development activities into a coherent whole as a next step.

Second, the team needs to seek and work with other similarly interested individuals and groups to enable learning to flow between individuals and groups. This process creates communication paths for getting work done within or outside the formal organizational structure. It also helps merge visions and plans of action. As more individuals and groups become involved in the transformation, efforts are moved from the fringes to a more centralized location where the institution is more likely to recognize and respond to individual and group learning. The team at Montclair State grew to include faculty, staff, and students from a number of academic, cocurricular, and administrative departments.

Third, it is helpful for the team to fit the transformation into the already existing structure and practices within the organization rather than present it as a wholly new and different initiative. While learning at the individual and group levels can operate on an informal basis and impact each other fairly quickly, learning at the organization level is generally more formal and takes longer time. It involves monitoring and obtaining data about the environment (scanning), translating events and understanding consistent with prior conceptualizations of the environment (interpretation), and formulating knowledge about the relationships between actions within the organization and the environment (learning).[2] Fitting transformation into the current organizational structure and practices facilitates the learning at this level. The team needed to link its desired vision and goals to goals at the organization level and capitalize on top-down initiatives.

Although the team intended to transform the university, it did not "start from scratch." They capitalized on two long-term successful university initiatives—the Emerging Leaders Learning Community and the community-based learning program to create the minor. In addition, they capitalized on the university's strategic plan, which called for three items that fit the vision of the group: development of leadership skills and social responsibility, increasing collaboration among curricular and cocurricular departments, and establishing new cross-disciplinary curricular programs.

Fourth, it is useful for teams to be watchful for the right opportunities to help move their cause forward. Opportunities can present themselves in any number of fashions—funding, internal and external people and champions, and events, to name a few. The faculty member and the director actually tried to move their vision forward twice. The first time they pulled a team together, members, although interested, were unable to commit to the accomplishment of the project. And the project fizzled. The second time, the team found a funding opportunity that enabled them to build the minor and begin to enhance the cocurricular programming. Although the money received from the grant was small, it made public and legitimized the team and the project; it provided energy and motivation to the team; and it held the team accountable for getting the project done, even under difficult circumstances.

Fifth, organizations, groups, and individuals are in a constant flux as they adapt to and change each other. The constant fluxes are not necessarily in alignment with the change the group is trying to enact. Due to these fluxes, transformation does not and cannot occur in a linear progression. Individuals and groups trying to enact transformation in the university must navigate this constantly changing group and organizational environment at the same time they are trying to change the organization, and this takes considerable time and energy. And finally, related to this, other individuals and groups have differing/competing visions they are also trying to enact that can impinge upon the change the group is enacting.

During the time the team developed the minor, they endured two organizational restructurings in less than two years. Both restructures were difficult for the team because they had to adapt to new leaders and lost key members of the team. In addition, at a crucial point in the team's work, as it was trying to get the minor launched, the provost announced his retirement. Although the team succeeded in getting the proposal to him before his retirement, he did not look at it. The new provost was unable to get to it in time and delayed the launch of the minor for six months. Due to the energy spent dealing with these fluxes as well as the energy spent in accomplishing the goal, the team lost momentum and enthusiasm. At the end of this stage of the project, many of the team members dispersed; while their job had been done successfully, they were exhausted.

Next Steps

The minor is thriving—it is now the largest interdisciplinary minor on campus and growing. New cocurricular programs, including a Bonner Leaders scholarship program, a leadership development club, a leadership development conference, and a leadership development camp, are in various stages of growth and development. Thus, key pieces of the transformation process are in place. The team is currently waiting for the right time and right opportunity to move their vision to the next step: to pull all the pieces together into an institute of leadership development that will serve to promote university-wide leadership development programs and research.

Notes

1. Mary M. Crossan, Henry W. Lane, and Roderick E. White, "An Organizational Learning Framework: From Intuition to Institution," *Academy of Management Review* 24, no. 3 (1999): 522–37; Manuel London and Valerie I. Sessa, "Continuous Learning in Organizations: A Living Systems Analysis of Individual, Group, and Organizational Learning," *Research in Multilevel Issues* 5 (2006): 123–72.

2. London and Sessa, "Continuous Learning in Organizations."

5: Morehouse College

Implementation of Peer-Led Team Learning and a Leadership Initiative and Establishment of a New Faculty Track as Examples of Institutional Change

Jann H. Adams and John K. Haynes

This case study describes three reform initiatives: (1) peer-led team learning (PLTL), (2) a leadership development program for faculty and staff in the Division of Science and Mathematics at Morehouse College, and (3) a proposed faculty leadership track as a key revision of the promotion and tenure process. Because both the PLTL and the leadership development program are aligned with the college's strategic plan, numerous campus constituents were involved in their development. These initiatives share a number of things in common: bottom-up organizing efforts, planning groups to foster a consensus-based approach to decision making, institutional support through funding and recognition, and the use of external consultants to assist with evaluation efforts. These initiatives are also connected by the common thread of the institution's dedication to scholarship and knowledge building upon which evidence-guided reform is based. Finally, the lessons learned in implementing PLTL and the leadership development program will help to inform future institutional change efforts, specifically the development of a major revision to the college's promotion system for associate faculty to recognize excellence in leadership.

Peer-Led Team Learning at Morehouse College

Attrition in the sciences and mathematics at Morehouse has been a long-standing concern of faculty and the college. Approximately 60 percent of students taking Organic Chemistry and over 50 percent of those taking Introductory Biology fail these courses. Similar levels of attrition were also noted in introductory courses in the Division of Science and Mathematics. To help combat the attrition of science majors who were switching from one science discipline to another, leaving the sciences to seek nonscience majors, or leaving the college altogether, peer-led team learning was implemented.

Peer-led team learning (PLTL) originated nationally as a learning enhancement strategy in chemistry courses. From its inception, PLTL at Morehouse had strong institutional support and funding. Additionally, a consensus-based approach was used to design and modify the program. Each department had significant autonomy in determining the method of implementation by selecting peer leaders and determining the nature of evaluation. The consequences of these variations in implementation and evaluation, however, resulted in a lack of continuity across departments. The variation in evaluation methods limited the ability to statistically compare the effectiveness of interventions by department. Similarly, departmental support was highly variable, as was the quality of the implementations themselves.

To meet these challenges, over the first three years of the PLTL implementation a number of consultants, including experienced faculty, administrators who had supported and developed PLTL efforts on campuses, and an external evaluation expert, met with faculty and recommended program enhancements. As faculty joined the PLTL implementation group, all were required to attend a workshop for training. A small team of PLTL faculty from each discipline were also recruited to assist the associate dean as part of the PLTL planning group.

Additionally, to encourage faculty support and participation, the Division of Science and Mathematics has provided critical funding and recognition for the PLTL program. Forms of recognition include an annual PLTL recognition luncheon and public acknowledgments of achievement in the PLTL program by the dean during division meetings. Also important to the success of PLTL has been the identification of faculty committed to leading the effort of gaining wide faculty support and initiating the implementation. This process has made it a priority for faculty members to be fully integrated into the PLTL decision-making process and to be accountable to their colleagues for all individual choices (including deviations) in approaches to program implementation.

The Leadership Initiative

The leadership initiative was born from interactions among women faculty with the associate dean of the Division of Science and Mathematics.

Meetings in the division revealed a number of perceived gender inequities, and faculty recommended a number of mechanisms that would be useful in their professional development and in gaining tenure at the college. In response to these criticisms and suggestions, a leadership program was implemented at the college.

In the fall of 2008, a leadership development consultant and a leadership design team composed of junior and senior faculty and three administrators were identified to help guide the early stages of the effort. Identification of key faculty and staff with significant influence in their respective areas was a key component of successful implementation. A division-wide focus group session that included all the division's faculty and staff was organized to gather data on workplace challenges, barriers to advancement, goals, and interest in professional development.

Data from the focus group revealed that administrative assistants, junior faculty, and women faculty found the environment most challenging and sought the greatest support for their professional development and advancement. Presentation of the focus group findings to faculty in a timely manner was seen as a key component of gaining support from chairs, faculty, and staff. An initial curriculum and plan were completed, and an opening symposium was designed for faculty and staff to introduce the curriculum and to tie implementation to feedback gained from the focus groups. Ultimately, the effort was renamed the Leadership and Professionalism Initiative to be inclusive of faculty who may not want to move into leadership positions but who did desire professional development through leadership training.

New Directions for Institutional Change:
A Proposed Promotion Track for Associate Professors

To better prepare faculty members for leadership positions, including chairs, deans, provosts, and presidents, we are developing a new paradigm for promotion of associate faculty to full professor rank. There are two variants of this track. Each variant emphasizes teaching and service but differs according to the role of research. In one variant research is not required, while in the other, research is required but the focus is on pedagogy and/or educational leadership and administration rather than disciplinary-specific scholarship alone.

In the nonresearch variation of this new track, a commitment to service would play the main role (in the absence of a research requirement) in determining whether the faculty member would be promoted. Service includes acting in administrative capacities at the college (e.g., chairing college-wide committees and serving as associate chair of a department and/or associate dean in a division). In addition to the mentoring and on-the-job training that faculty would receive in these roles, they would also be expected to participate in educational leadership training workshops and conferences. In this nonresearch, service-based track, fewer publications would be required than in the traditional track.

We foresee, based on lessons learned in implementing PLTL and the leadership development program, that successful implementation of this new promotion track will be dependent upon several actions. First, it will be important to obtain faculty support by discussing the idea in small and large meetings of faculty, including department-, division-, and college-wide faculty meetings and meetings of the Faculty Council. Second, faculty champions who have credibility among faculty (chiefly senior faculty members) will be sought to help advance the issue among faculty and administrators. Also, since developing leadership skills should be central to faculty development, the Faculty Council will be encouraged to embrace this initiative and incorporate it into the work of its Faculty Development and Faculty Welfare subcommittees.

As with other initiatives developed at Morehouse, administrative support will be critical for success. Because faculty coming up for promotion in this new track will need to be evaluated differently from those in the traditional track, members of the Reappointments and Promotions Committees (RPCs) in different departments and the college-wide Appointments-Promotions-Tenure Committee (APTC) will need to be reeducated to evaluate by new metrics. Additionally, the definition of service requirements will need to be modified and refined to develop greater specificity in light of the new emphasis on this often undervalued area. Workshops will need to be conducted on campus to ensure that all faculty members know how to evaluate this new track and are aware of its importance for achieving the institutional mission. Finally, the new track will need to be included in the college's strategic plan.

Lessons Learned

At Morehouse, institutional change has been governed by several fundamental approaches. First, varying degrees of administrative leadership and faculty-led interest in the initiative are essential to the success of any program that will ultimately create institutional change. In the case of PLTL and the leadership initiative, demand from faculty served as the impetus for these efforts. In the case of the proposed promotion track, senior administrators needed to initiate this effort because faculty members are not sufficiently empowered to alter institutional promotion criteria. While the investment of senior administrators is critical for identifying funds and resources for change, the ongoing involvement of midlevel administrators is critical for setting cultural expectations and examples for faculty performance and participation.

Second, the identification of committed and well-respected faculty members who can influence faculty support is essential for institutionalizing and growing the initiative. Using a consensus-based approach often requires that faculty members be allowed autonomy to make decisions they believe are in the best interests of their work. However, it is also essential that mechanisms to create faculty accountability and incentives ensure that implementation proceeds as agreed and that evaluation data are collected correctly and in a timely manner. The provision of training and development opportunities for faculty is also important to offer faculty access to new programs through the enhancement of their expertise and teaching.

Finally, the use of expert consultants also lends credibility to reform efforts and assists in providing timely, objective feedback and support throughout the implementation of programs. By providing timely evaluation results to faculty and administrators, program implementers received evidence of program effectiveness, and faculty were given helpful feedback for modifying implementations as needed.

6: St. Lawrence University

Listening to the Agents of Pedagogical Change

Catherine A. Crosby-Currie and Christine Zimmerman

Recently, the concept of empowerment was the focus of an article in one of the leading journals in psychology. Although this concept has been around for a while and is a key concept in the particular subfield of community psychology, its consideration in a journal aimed at the entire field of psychology made clear its current vitality for understanding behavior and positive institutional change. This vital concept of empowerment has become a central theme in our work toward institutional transformation at St. Lawrence University. As the term implies, empowerment deals with power—the lack and development of power. In particular, empowerment is about individuals and groups of individuals having the power to create change in the institutions that surround their lives.[1] Others argue that empowerment is about helping those who lack power to find their power and create the change that will promote well-being and reduce stress and negative outcomes.[2]

At institutions such as ours, we typically don't think of our students, especially those who are white and from middle- to upper-class backgrounds, as lacking in "power." But the concept of empowerment is relevant regardless of socioeconomic background because transformative educational experiences do not happen *to* students. They happen because the students *do* something themselves. As educators, we should provide contexts for learning that increase the likelihood that students will have the opportunity *to enable themselves* to transform. As we've found at St. Lawrence, educational experiences that challenge students' preexisting beliefs and knowledge by confronting their preconceptions and lack of knowledge are an important way of providing the context in which educational empowerment and hence transformation can occur.

However, as our case study shows, just as empowerment is essential for student learning, empowerment at all levels is essential for institutional change. When educational institutions discuss creating change, their faculty want to be active, not passive, agents in that change. Hence institutional change that begins with a top-down process is unlikely to be supported by the faculty—even if the change is precisely what the faculty might need or want at the time. On our own campus, the tale of the First-Year Program, a central component of our curriculum for many years, is one that usually begins "It was the idea of the faculty . . ." Unfortunately, our tale doesn't begin that way, and we almost failed because we did not empower those who would ultimately carry out the work. But our tale is also about how we were eventually successful by remembering the importance of empowerment again.

To provide some brief context, the creation of the First-Year Program (FYP) in 1986 was possibly the most transformational change that ever occurred at St. Lawrence University because it completely reconceptualized the first-year experience for our students. Academic advising and communication skills development were now done in the context of a team-taught interdisciplinary course, with the faculty becoming academic advisors for the students in that particular course. In addition, students in a particular FYP course lived together, and the faculty worked with the residential staff to create a holistic, rather than compartmentalized, experience for their students. Within just a couple of years, the SLU experience changed drastically for the students who matriculated there. This case study is about a project that was attempting to transform the educational experiences possible within this long-standing program.

In 2005, St. Lawrence was awarded an initial grant to develop opportunities for engaged forms of learning for our students. This grant had a substantial research component but also supported more community-based learning by creating an institutional structure, the Center for Civic Engagement, and a student-run program, the Community Mentors, both of which bridged the academic and cocurricular and increased the connections between community partners and the faculty and students who were engaged in community-based learning. We subsequently applied for a larger grant to build upon the existing structures and programs and to expand engaged forms of pedagogy beyond just community-based learning and to potentially 100 percent of our first-year students. At the heart of the larger grant was the intentional infusion of engaged forms of pedagogy within the FYP through intensive faculty development. Building on the team teaching and innovative faculty development that have been hallmarks of our First-Year Program since the beginning, the plan was to create pedagogy teams that would explore, discuss, and implement engaged forms of pedagogy in the context of a faculty learning community.

We developed, wrote, and submitted the grant proposal and subsequently received the grant—but we did everything without ever once talking to the FYP faculty about any of it. We can provide several reasons for why we did that: the success of the first grant, a short turnaround time, and a significant leadership transition in the FYP itself. However, our failure to include faculty in the development process was a colossal mistake; it set us up for failure on the project before our work ever began. In the first meeting to discuss the new plan, the faculty resisted through both their verbal and nonverbal behavior. Questions made apparent that we were talking past each other about even the most basic ideas of the plan, such as the meaning of the phrase "engaged pedagogy." After that, the situation just got worse. The project even became the subject of intense debate in our Faculty Senate. Our failure to involve faculty in what was seen as curricular change became an exemplar of what our faculty saw as ways the university and administration disenfranchised the faculty on curricular decisions. Additionally, SLU's climate of using external funding for curricular innovation had already led to faculty feeling stretched to their limits in terms of time and energy; they now saw themselves being stretched even further.

So, we began to ask ourselves whether we should proceed with a plan that the faculty were so against. How could a plan that was met with such resistance ever be successful? How would we get buy-in for the assessment components of the project if we couldn't even get buy-in for the faculty development components—that is, the parts from which the faculty would directly benefit? We were already tired and feeling the weight of the work that lay ahead. In many ways, we simply wanted to quit.

But instead of quitting, we apologized, acknowledging that the faculty were deserving of an apology given that we had disempowered them by our actions. We don't recall if we ever said publically and explicitly "we're sorry," although we certainly did privately and individually, but we clearly were sorry and tried to communicate that fact through our subsequent actions. We also owned up to our mistake. We never publically tried to defend or justify our error of not involving the faculty in the development of the grant; we simply tried to make up for it.

Specifically, we suspended our initial timeline for the plan implementation; we slowed down and backed up to allow faculty time to think about the ideas central to the project and how they might envision the future of teaching and learning within the program. We also made up in every possible way the communication we did not have before. We organized group meetings over meals, talked about the general components of the grant, and put the faculty in attendance in charge of developing and selecting those engaged pedagogies they were most interested in developing. We then communicated those ideas to everyone in the program and sought their input. We also asked faculty for their suggestions of books and other classroom materials, making clear that our role was to provide financial support to implement their ideas, not to generate those ideas. We made it a priority to answer any questions we received related to the process. And we sought opportunities throughout the next few years to keep faculty updated on our activities.

We also listened. We acknowledged their expertise, opinions, and skills by listening. We hired a research associate in the summer between the first and second years of the grant, and she had one primary responsibility for the first few months of the project—listen to the faculty. She asked faculty if she could sit in on their classes, and then she spent many hours talking with faculty teams over tea and coffee—mostly letting them talk about what they were trying to do in their classes, what they were struggling with, and what could help them. As a result of those conversations, we tossed aside the structures we had originally created, in particular the idea of the pedagogy teams, and we began to create informal opportunities for faculty to talk with each other about some of the ways they were trying to engage their students in learning. These *explicit* opportunities for faculty to draw strength from each other, to validate engaged learning practices, and to experience their own transformation as teachers through conversation with each other became the centerpiece of the reenvisioned project. We also restructured some of our budget, having learned that faculty preferred more funds for their teaching (e.g., field trips, workshops, special projects) instead of using the funds for invited speakers or conference attendance. And we developed our assessment instruments based on the conversations of the research associate and in direct consultation with the faculty in the program. All of these actions allowed the faculty to regain power over the project and its future.

Discussion and Next Steps

At St. Lawrence, we discovered our faculty do have an interest in empowering students in their education. But they also need to be empowered in the process themselves. They need to have voice in how institutional change occurs, and they need to have the power to say, "I'm not interested." Just as transformational change does not happen *to* students but *by* them, transformational change in pedagogy does not happen *to* faculty but *by* them.

Our institution has taken our experience to heart and has become much more intentional about inviting faculty into the process of curriculum-related projects and involving them through all planning and implementation stages. We have had several very successful experiences in which widespread involvement in the process has resulted in well-conceptualized grant proposals that have been funded and enjoyed a great deal of institutional support. One project initiated the development of more courses that fulfill our diversity requirement and tools to assess this component of our general education curriculum. A second quite ambitious project is now under way that will expand our curriculum related to environmental education. This project has been an exemplar of inclusivity from beginning to end and has been quite successful in achieving its goals thus far. Looking at these recent successes with plans for institutional change, we realize that our own experience with a plan that almost failed before it began might have actually transformed our institution in ways we never anticipated.

Notes

1. Lauren Bennett Cattaneo and Alita R. Chapman, "The Process of Empowerment: A Model for Use in Research and Practice," *American Psychologist* 65, no. 7 (2010): 646–59.

2. Julian Rappaport, "Terms of Empowerment/Exemplars of Prevention: Toward a Theory for Community Psychology," *American Journal of Community Psychology* 15, no. 2 (1987): 121–48.

7: The Evergreen State College

An Enduring Experiment

Phyllis Lane and Elizabeth McHugh

Though in existence for only thirty-nine years, Evergreen has long been dedicated to student learning and engagement. At the end of the 1960s, Evergreen was funded by the state of Washington as an interdisciplinary public liberal arts college, offering a pedagogical approach to higher education and academics that did not exist within the state. Academic programs were interdisciplinary; a program covenant connected faculty and students as co-learners; a book seminar was placed at the core of the curriculum; narrative evaluations were developed for students and faculty; and a social contract was established for community norms. This is still largely the model being used at Evergreen today on the Olympia (main) and Tacoma (urban) campuses and the Reservation Based Community Determined Program.

Evergreen emphasizes collaboration among faculty, staff, and students to engage as co-learners, creating a transformative and seamless liberal education experience. A critical element for the success and vitality of student learning and engagement at Evergreen is the relationship between academic and student affairs. The collective wisdom, scholarship, and fiscal resources of both faculty and student affairs practitioners have been utilized in transformative ways to blur the lines between these traditionally bifurcated areas. Specifically, student affairs practitioners and faculty share the responsibility for student learning and development. The power of this partnership is in working collaboratively to provide multiple points of support for student success.[1]

Administrative Design and Student Learning

Though the academic deans serve an administrative role, much of what they do translates into active, daily hands-on work with their faculty peers, student affairs colleagues, and students. Offices of the academic deans and dean of students, though in separate divisions, are intentionally located in adjacent spaces to provide ready access for discussion and problem solving. Because the deans are steps away from each other, affairs related to student learning and well-being do not suffer from the usual delays or scheduling conflicts. Having this level of commitment from academics facilitates the best instructional approach for students in crisis or events that can be disruptive to the students' education. This partnership has enhanced the college's capability to act quickly and efficiently to solve problems related to students and classroom climate issues.

Additionally, faculty and student affairs practitioners convene to share critical information and discuss the dimensions of an issue to determine roles and responsibilities for each division in providing emotional and administrative support. This model is used in situations when learning communities experience tragic events, such as the death of a student or faculty member, and to manage the impact of national and natural disasters, such as 9/11, hurricanes, or earthquakes. This model has also been effective when students and faculty in international and domestic settings experience difficulties and need consultation and advocacy. More commonly, the model has been useful in developing the student and faculty relationship within the academic programs. Collaborative program planning includes the partners working on large institutional issues such as integration of high-demand courses into the curriculum, retention and enrollment management initiatives, and the delivery of a curriculum that is planned two years in advance and changes each year. Profound respect and growing understanding of each other's disciplines have emerged from this cross-divisional work, reflecting the egalitarian spirit of collaboration so valued at Evergreen.

Cross-Divisional Products of Collaboration

Transcending the divisional silos experienced by the deans is also evident in how student affairs practitioners are integrated into critical faculty structures and work. Student affairs staff members participate in hiring and orientation for new faculty and are invited to participate in the five-year review process for continuing faculty. Faculty teams teaching core programs (first-year students) and all-level programs (programs open to any student) with a high composition of first-year students are assigned a student affairs practitioner known as a "core connector." The core connector typically attends the academic program twice a week, facilitating inclusion of academic and psychological support within the learning community and extending academic and support referrals outside the classroom. Upon invitation by faculty teams, student affairs practitioners facilitate discussions with students about their experiences in the academic program. This information is then summarized and shared with the faculty team for their consideration. Furthermore, each year a faculty member rotates into an academic advising position in the academic support area of student affairs. Allocation of a faculty line for this position under the shrinking financial resources of the institution underscores the depth of understanding around how this partnership improves student learning through deepening faculty perspective.

There is also a long tradition at Evergreen for faculty development to be an opportunity for faculty and staff to engage in learning communities aimed to increase classroom performance and student learning. Student affairs practitioners often present with faculty in areas focusing on academic support. In recent years, work in summer faculty development institutes has changed the approach to managing behavioral health issues in the classroom, student crises, and developmental issues. Faculty have widely embraced this work, boosting their capacity to connect student well-being with student learning. These institutes often serve as "think tanks" for participants, where ideas may develop into larger college initiatives.

Students as Collaborators in the Learning Environment

One of Evergreen's fundamental beliefs about the purpose of college is linking theory with practice. Nowhere is this more evident than in the role of peer educators. Peer educators are undergraduate students who receive specialized training and are considered staff in the academic support programs. These students provide academic support and social outreach to their peers. Through their work, these peer educators acquire skills and knowledge, and they experience levels of engaged learning that are often in alignment with academic or personal interests. An example of this work includes the preorientation academic learning communities for students of color and TRIO students (low income, first generation, and students with disabilities). Peer educators assist students in their adjustment to campus life and the classroom environment.

Another example is students who are selected, hired, and trained as medical assistants to work as part of a multidisciplinary team of clinicians, thereby developing knowledge and skills, gaining hands-on clinical experience, and providing a visible linkage of academic course work to real-world experience. This model transforms the learning experience for students who are peer educators and those who seek service. And staff and faculty practitioners benefit from the insight and perspective offered by students working as peer educators.

The Challenges of the Partnership

Due to the rapidly changing societal landscape surrounding higher education, the collaborative partnership between faculty and student affairs practitioners must be prepared for a generation of students unlike those we have worked with thus far. Students are coming from more segregated communities. There are access issues for students without financial means or academic preparation. Nationally we might be witnessing the doors of higher education closing due to the increased cost of attendance and shrinking resources. We are at a point in history in which students will incur a lifetime of debt, creating a new cycle of poverty. The academy will become less diverse, and the already fragile pipeline for students, faculty, and staff of diverse backgrounds will dissolve into a de facto disrepair.

As a newer institution, we continue to experience growing pains as part of the maturation process, presenting challenges for change and transformation. Trying to maintain balance between the founding principles and the college's participation in emerging best practices, standards, and pedagogical work in the wider higher education community can create dichotomies within the institution. These areas have included discussion regarding general education, high-demand curriculum, accreditation, and enrollment and retention strategies. Implementing these changes has not been an easy task to undertake. Unlike our older sister and brother institutions, where the interpretations of mission and value statements are based upon the intentions of their founders (which can span centuries), such interpretations at Evergreen are often influentially voiced by the remaining founding faculty and the first generation of faculty hired.

Thus, as institutional change and transformation are considered, there are often tensions within the community about how the change may move the college away from its original mission. To address this tension, Evergreen has a task force structure that provides time and space for this level of inquiry. The Re-Modeling Teaching and Learning at Evergreen task force (RTaLE) is engaged in developing a plan to improve structures that help students gain a better understanding of what an interdisciplinary liberal arts education entails and how to balance this with the need or desire for independent, self-directed work.[2] The work of the RTaLE exemplifies how institutional-level dialogue around change strategies has played out among faculty and between faculty and student affairs. Ultimately these exchanges have led to positive changes for the institution in faculty advising and development of academic plans.

Additionally, building the partnership between academic and student affairs has been achieved through some trial and error. The basis of the partnership has been built on the quality of the relationship and expectations of the leadership (the vice president for student affairs and the provost) in both divisions. Work style, personalities, and role expectations have influenced these relationships. Always challenging to this partnership are faculty changes in their appointments as academic deans every three to six years. Significant accomplishments of the partnership can be lost with the ebb and flow of work styles and personalities of individuals. However, after several years of actively tending to this partnership, processes and protocols have gained momentum and are increasingly working more smoothly. Nevertheless, we know at some point new challenges will emerge to test the endurance of the current partnership structures and practices in place.

Evergreen will continue to demonstrate its endurance through this collaborative and powerful partnership. Additionally, this collaboration in learning across student affairs, faculty, and students will continue to provide a foundation for transformational change within our institution, thus allowing us to continue maturing as the "experiment in the woods." At Evergreen, this is the choice we make, it is how we do our work, and it is who we are!

Notes

1. The 1998 joint report by the American Association for Higher Education, American College Personnel Association, and NASPA identified these powerful partnerships as a critical resource for our college. See American Association for Higher Education, American College Personnel Association, and NASPA: Student Affairs Administrators in Higher Education, "Powerful Partnerships: A Shared Responsibility for Learning" (June 2, 1998), http://naspa.org/career/sharedresp .cfm. Hacker and Dreifus also noted Evergreen's collaborative approach: "Evergreen State College . . . gets our attention for its inventive style, though this school does it in a far more communal way." See Andrew Hacker and Claudia Dreifus, *Higher Education: How Colleges Are Wasting Our Money and Failing Our Kids and What We Can Do about It* (New York: Time Books, 2010), 233–34.

2. Evergreen State College, "Re-Modeling Teaching and Learning at Evergreen DTF" (draft academic statement and advising proposal, October 2010).

8: United States Military Academy at West Point

Building the Capacity to Lead

Lessons Learned in the Evolution of the Leader Development System

Bruce Keith

Leadership is the ability to responsibly influence others to work collaboratively in pursuit of common goals. To the extent that the Army often demands of its leaders the ability to manage others through ambiguous, ill-defined situations, West Point's students (commonly referred to as cadets) must be empowered with the capacity to anticipate and respond effectively to the uncertainties of a changing world.[1] Such emphasis requires the design and implementation of a learning system that empowers students to challenge their existing frames of reference.[2] An empowering learning system will situate student learning in the center of the organization and realign the collegial culture and corresponding support mechanisms around a learning process that is collaborative, creative, critically reflective, actively engaging, and integrative. The assessment of student learning outcomes is an opportunity for all stakeholders to evaluate the level of student competence in each learning sphere and to determine the extent to which the learning system supports students' corresponding development.[3]

West Point has long been recognized as an institution dedicated to the transformation of students into Army officers who are capable of successfully leading others through the ambiguous challenges that confront a changing world. Although West Point's mission—to produce leaders of character for the Army—has changed little in over two hundred years, its approach to accomplishing the mission has changed dramatically, from a pedagogical emphasis on attrition to one more oriented toward development.[4] This case study focuses on the lessons learned at West Point since 1990 in its efforts to design and implement a learning system for leader development.

Three decades of curricular modifications, beginning in 1960 and extending until West Point's decennial accreditation review in 1989, resulted in codification of a new learning system known as the Cadet Leader Development System (CLDS). Following a shift from a wholly prescribed curriculum in 1960 to one that offered electives, areas of concentration, and eventually majors by 1985, West Point realized a dramatic reduction in the number of core courses and a pronounced increase in curricular flexibility and choice.[5] The initial CLDS framework called for an integrated structure of activities to develop West Point cadets holistically and thus empower them to be leaders.[6] Additionally, it established a developmental process in which learning would take place through practice, application, evaluation, and reinforcement.[7] By 2002, the CLDS framework had evolved into a new model centered on three verbs—"Be, Know, and Do." The new model signified the importance of knowledge (Know) and actions (Do) that, when combined with reflection and feedback, possess the power to transform students' sense of identity (Be) into officers who are capable of leading others responsibly through complex challenges.[8]

Lessons Learned from Institutional Change at West Point

West Point's experience in curriculum reform since the implementation of CLDS has taught us five principal lessons. First, the establishment of a framework for leader development—our definition of the educated graduate—provides West Point with a coherent learning system. Once our target for development was identified as "officership," the learning system that supported that development could be described. Specifically, officership was buttressed by six domains (learning spheres)—human spirit, ethical, social, intellectual, physical, and military.[9] The framework acknowledged that the six domains must be standards based and coordinated within the institutional context in ways that provided both cadets and faculty a sense of ownership in evolving the framework.[10]

Second, the learning system must be the product of all stakeholders if it is to enjoy widespread acceptance. The well-intentioned administrators who developed the initial CLDS framework in 1990 did not effectively draw on the insights of the faculty and cadets; consequently, the latter groups had little awareness or sense of ownership of the framework once it was implemented. The successful implementation of a learning system's vision is possible only when the institution actively and repeatedly engages all stakeholders in conversations about the learning system and its desired outcomes. In an effort to more meaningfully coordinate all curricular and cocurricular activities into CLDS, we began to engage representatives from each category of stakeholder through enhanced opportunities for conversations.

Third, conversations with stakeholders must be followed by the intentional design, coordination, integration, and reinforcement of curricular and cocurricular activities. Many of our assessments, including accreditation findings, revealed that the desired learning outcomes were compartmentalized within the six CLDS domains and did not holistically reinforce the critical elements of CLDS—that is, empowering cadets to be informed, confident, responsible, self-directed learners. We found that cadets tended to be risk averse, increasingly afraid of failure and unwilling to take risks that are necessary to push themselves beyond their comfort zones.

To better integrate curricular and cocurricular activities, West Point administrators engaged faculty and staff in a review and revision of CLDS. The intent was to develop in cadets, as graduates, an enhanced ability to understand themselves in relation to others and to engage others responsibly as they seek to resolve the challenges they encounter in multiple contexts.[11] This revised version of CLDS reorganized the priority of the six learning domains, placing identity development (domain of the human spirit), moral-ethical reasoning (ethical domain), and empathy/social interaction (social domain) as the most important aspects of the learning system. The resourced programs—academic, military, and physical—are the conduits through which a set of curricular and cocurricular activities, when coordinated, sequenced, and integrated, can transform cadets from self-centered young adults to selfless leaders of character.[12] Accordingly, we are beginning to recognize that the identity and character components of student development must become the most important learning outcomes around which the institution is structured.

Fourth, students must have meaningful opportunities to develop the ability to assess their own performance throughout the educational process. Such efforts require practice and must be intentionally structured into the learning system. The holistic development of students as leaders of character requires the continuous presence of a corps of persons knowledgeable about theories and applications of human development and capable of intentionally transferring such knowledge to the development of each and every student. At West Point, such persons are referred to as tactical officers—or TACs—and, under CLDS, they have been responsible for helping cadets set and enforce their own standards. In addition to the TACs, there are other institutional agents available to help the cadets, including staff, faculty, and other cadets.

We are struggling to learn a fifth valuable lesson from this process of curricular renewal—that the ability of an institution to successfully manage curricular renewal is contingent upon its willingness to intentionally align strategic planning with the management of resources and assessment of outcomes. West Point continues to suffer from an inability to modify the governance, planning, and resourcing processes in support of CLDS. We have taken a series of small steps to provide stakeholders with a process through which meaningful, informed curricular renewal can function. We developed the definition of an educated graduate and then designed curricular experiences that support these desired outcomes.[13] We created goal teams consisting of representatives from the various stakeholders for each of the intellectual domain's goals; the teams established learning models and gathered evidence. Finally, we established standards for each of the goals—that is, statements of what graduates ought to be able to do—and intensely assessed the cadets' achievements with respect to these standards.

In spite of these accomplishments, West Point's leadership has been either unwilling or unable to reform the institution's governance structure into a transparent, collegial strategic planning process that is aligned with the management of resources and corresponding assessments of institutional effectiveness. This failure to manage governance as a transparent, shared mechanism inhibits West Point from placing its learning system at the center of the institution's operations. As Spady and Schwahn acknowledge, "the main thing is to make the main thing the main thing."[14] To wit, we have yet to make our learning system the main thing.

Concluding Thoughts and Insights

Student empowerment is the vision of a learning system that is supported and reinforced by its organizational context. If the institutional context is not intentionally organized to empower students, then the organizational climate will consist of various stakeholders who are both frustrated and disenfranchised. Presently, CLDS, as our learning system, is squeezed through an institutional structure that is not positioned to effectively address change through a collaborative, forward-looking lens. The effective implementation of a learning system capable of developing cadets' potential to be leaders of character will require a reorganization of institutional governance and the corresponding support structures that is collegial, transparent, and informed by assessments of institutional effectiveness.

Organizing for empowerment requires that institutional leaders develop in others the gift of authorship and the capacity to be actively engaged in collectively empowering all persons who are responsible for the implementation of the learning system.[15] Such leaders need to facilitate conversations, establish a sense of collective ownership over the learning system, and develop in all persons the capacity to self-reflect. In order to realize the transformation of West Point's learning system into one of empowerment, the leadership's absolute control over the process of institutional renewal will need to be relinquished in favor of a more transparent, shared form of governance. Collectively, all persons in the institution need to transfer lessons learned into a continuous process of institutional renewal. Toward this end, West Point's leader development system remains a work in progress.

Notes

1. West Point's learning system for leader development is entitled "Building Capacity to Lead: The West Point System for Leader Development" and can be viewed at www.dean.usma.edu/documents/CLDS2010.pdf. A component of this learning system, the intellectual domain, seeks to ensure that all West Point graduates can anticipate and respond effectively to the uncertainties of a changing world. The operational concept for the intellectual domain is entitled "Educating Future Army Officers for a Changing World," last published in 2007, and can be viewed at www.dean.usma.edu/sebpublic/EFAOCW.pdf.

2. The term *learning system* is intended to connote the intentional structuring and coordination of curricular, cocurricular, and extracurricular activities that lead to the empowerment of informed, responsible, self-directed students.

3. Competence is defined as "the ability to do something consistently and well." William Spady and Charles Schwahn, *Learning Communities 2.0* (Lanham, MD: Rowman and Littlefield, 2010), 59.

4. George S. Pappas, *To the Point: The United States Military Academy, 1802–1902* (Westport, CT: Praeger, 1993); Lance Betros, *Carved from Granite: West Point Since 1902* (Lanham, MD: Rowman and Littlefield, 2011).

5. Between 1960 and 1985, the number of prescribed core courses declined from forty-eight to thirty, representing a reduction of nearly 38 percent. Ten of these eighteen omitted courses were given to cadets in the form of electives for selected fields of study or majors. See George B. Forsythe and Bruce Keith, "The Evolving USMA Academic Curriculum, 1952–2002," in *West Point: Two Centuries and Beyond*, ed. Lance Betros (Abilene, TX: McWhiney Foundation Press, 2004), 378.

6. United States Military Academy, *Cadet Leader Development System* (West Point, NY: United States Military Academy, 1990), 1.

7. United States Military Academy, *Cadet Leader Development System*, 10.

8. United States Military Academy, *Cadet Leader Development System* (West Point, NY: United States Military Academy, 2002), 1, 6.

9. United States Military Academy, *Cadet Leader Development System* (2002), 25–29.

10. United States Military Academy, *Cadet Leader Development System* (2002), 31.

11. United States Military Academy, *Building Capacity to Lead: The West Point System for Leader Development* (West Point, NY: United States Military Academy, 2009).

12. Bruce Keith, "The Transformation of West Point as a Liberal Arts College," *Liberal Education* 96, no. 2 (Spring 2010): 6–13.

13. United States Military Academy, *Educating Future Army Officers for a Changing World*, 3rd ed. (West Point, NY: United States Military Academy, 2007).

14. Spady and Schwahn, *Learning Communities 2.0*, 96.

15. Lee G. Bolman and Terrance E. Deal, *Leading with Soul: An Uncommon Journey of Spirit* (San Francisco: Jossey-Bass, 2001).

9: University of Nebraska, Lincoln

Building Institutional Capacity to Forge Civic Pathways

Nancy D. Mitchell and Linda J. Major

Many have called for higher education to return to its original purpose of preparing graduates for a life of civic engagement through civic learning.[1] A recent survey indicates that "while the majority of students and campus professionals strongly agreed that their campus should be educating students to contribute to community, far fewer feel as strongly that contributing to community currently is a major focus at their institutions."[2] The report concludes that developing an arc for civic learning across the curriculum and cocurriculum and throughout students' college experiences is needed but not yet clearly charted. How can we blaze the trail to close the gap—especially in an environment of limited financial and human resources? We argue that such an endeavor requires rethinking some fundamental assumptions about how we provide education and questioning the boundaries of curricular authority.

Observing that many view the purpose of an education as preparation for a career, campus leaders at the University of Nebraska, Lincoln (UNL) are now asking if students will be equally well prepared to be good citizens. Part of the reframing effort at UNL has been the recognition that institutions of higher education are obligated to develop in their students the knowledge and understanding that will allow them to be productive and responsible members of society.[3] UNL's new general education program calls for increased emphasis on outcomes related to developing individual and social responsibility. This focus on students' general education courses is a great start but not an end in itself. The long-term goal of general education is to guide students in their choices throughout their academic careers and beyond graduation as qualified professionals prepared for citizen leadership.

Mapping the Route through General Education

Building a new general education program can be a journey that is both revolutionary in thinking and evolutionary in its painstakingly slow speed and sometimes messiness, as was the case at UNL. In 2005, the chancellor called for a new general education program at UNL, an institution with about 19,000 undergraduate students and eight undergraduate colleges, each with the power bestowed by state statute to grant its own degrees and govern its own curricula. It was obvious from the beginning of the endeavor that a successful general education reform was going to demand a team spirit. From its inception, the new general education program was a collaborative effort built on mutual trust and respect among all those involved with students' education. Planning committees populated by academic leaders from all eight undergraduate colleges and representatives from critical constituencies, including students, advisors, admissions staff, and various organizations such as the Faculty Senate, haggled over what a graduate of our institution should be able to know and do in the twenty-first century. The result was Achievement-Centered Education (ACE), an outcomes-based program ratified by faculty vote in January 2008 and implemented in fall 2009.

Building Capacity with Cocurricular Experiences

Governing documents for UNL's revised general education program were developed, outlining structural criteria for fulfilling ACE requirements. The documents recognize the importance of activities occurring outside the classroom, such as undergraduate research and study abroad. These activities have the potential to link parts of the students' education—what they learn in their courses with their student life. But despite the best intentions of the planning committee to integrate cocurricular activities into general education (including creating guidelines for counting cocurricular experiences for ACE outcome requirements), only a handful of students applied to get an international study trip to count during the first year and a half of implementation.

A challenge to bridging the in-class and out-of-class experiences stems from the academic reality that faculty members have authority over all matters related to curriculum. How could the faculty's authority over curricular decisions be honored if nonfaculty oversaw the cocurricular component? Practical and structural issues obscured the path, as well. How could cocurricular experiences be tallied in the degree audit system? One recommendation was to make every cocurricular component a course, with faculty signing off on the experience, even if it was a zero credit course. However, this solution raised issues about the distinction between curricular and cocurricular. If each experience became a course, didn't that defy the definition of cocurricular? And if every experience was part of a course, weren't all those experiences curricular by definition?

Overcoming the Curricular/Cocurricular Divide in Student Learning

To start bridging the curricular/cocurricular divide, we rethought how we approached the challenge of including cocurricular experiences. We decided to approach the issue from a different direction. Rather than thinking about discrete areas of authority owned by faculty or student affairs professionals, we thought about how we could reinforce each other's goals for students. Faculty authority over curriculum is not diminished if we think of general education requirements as courses and cocurricular experiences as reinforcing the learning that occurs within those courses. Instead of looking at the issue as a dichotomy, we could embrace the value added by combining both curricular and cocurricular experiences. Thus, if we think about general education as a compass pointing students in the direction of valued learning outcomes—including becoming active citizens—our reframing helped us see how students could benefit from a more cohesive and coherent education that tied learning in the classroom with learning outside the classroom.

Helping to move from thinking to action, colleagues from student affairs proposed collaboration across the campus to enhance the general education program by creating a civic engagement certificate. We worked together to redefine the relationship between academic and student affairs, from independent colleagues to campuswide collaborators. In this collaboration, faculty members represent the formal instruction, and those from student affairs support faculty instruction by guiding students through activities reinforcing civic engagement learning outcomes in courses. Student affairs professionals are thought of as expert partners, joining faculty for the benefit of students. By transforming our own thinking, we were able to envision a road students could take to become active citizens.

Progressing toward the Civic Engagement Destination

Developing the certificate program is an additive process, recognizing the necessary silos of academics/student affairs and building a connection between them in the form of a clearinghouse for ideas and action. One of the objectives of UNL's new general education program, Achievement-Centered Education (ACE), serves as the foundation for this connection by encouraging students to develop the ability to "exercise individual and social responsibilities through the study of ethical principles and reasoning, application of civic knowledge, interaction with diverse cultures, and engagement with global issues."[4] Additionally, two of the ten general education learning outcomes speak directly to this objective: "ACE 8 Explain ethical principles, civic, and stewardship, and their importance to society" and "ACE 9 Exhibit global awareness or knowledge of human diversity through analysis of an issue."[5] The efforts to educate responsible citizens build upon these outcomes.[6]

Starting small, we have used a planning process that reflected what we learned from the effort to revise our general education program. We have worked to be inclusive in our discussions, to communicate transparently and abundantly, and to pay attention to process—carefully negotiating boundaries of who controls what and pushing the edges of possibility. From the beginning, the focus on the civic engagement certificate and its relationship to our general education program has been a joint effort between student affairs and academic affairs. Key elements of the collaborative effort involved gathering faculty, staff, student, and community partner feedback and making feedback accessible and centrally located via Web tools as well as using a pilot model to test the concept.

Being inclusive in decision making is critical to build momentum for sustained success of the project. Recognizing the expertise that exists on and off campus in addition to student affairs and academic affairs yields valuable insights and frankly makes sense in an environment of economic stress. For example, inviting advisers to express their opinion about who might be the student audience yielded good ideas about pockets of students on campus already primed to engage civically, such as preprofessional students, honors students, Greek-affiliated students, athletes, and those in learning communities, and some notion of how we might attract student participation. Ongoing discussions with local community partners add another dimension of credibility, leading to a certificate that will be meaningful to our students while simultaneously addressing needs identified by community organizations and the city, county, or state government.

In the process, we believe we have built a model that ties theory to practice, generating an education that will be more coherent and cohesive on our campus and potentially at other institutions. This thinking has allowed us to build capacity to help students achieve an outcome in their general education program and, more importantly, to make progress toward extending the outcome to lifelong engagement and learning. It allowed us to take advantage of existing precious resources—our staff and faculty.

The Road Ahead

Transformative innovations at the institutional level require the freedom to imagine how collaborative efforts might push boundaries and result in an education in which civic learning can lead to a lifetime of civic engagement. So far efforts to build a collaborative civic engagement certificate have been enthusiastically embraced by student leaders, administrators, and faculty who already recognize the importance of the endeavor. The road ahead is, no doubt, paved with challenges to sustainability of the effort and unseen potholes, including people who remain unconvinced of the value of the effort and others whose involvement is stymied by the precious resource of time. Yet, the promise of helping students become active citizens stimulates and reinforces our commitment to this project. As model citizen Abraham Lincoln said, "Determine that the thing can and shall be done, and then we shall find the way."[7]

Notes

1. For example, see Association of American Colleges and Universities, *College Learning for the New Global Century: A Report from the National Leadership Council for Liberal Education and America's Promise* (Washington, DC: Association of American Colleges and Universities, 2007), and John Saltmarsh, "The Civic Promise of Service Learning," *Liberal Education* 91, no. 2 (Spring 2005): 50–56.

2. Eric L. Dey, Cassie L. Barnhardt, Mary Antonaros, Molly C. Ott, and Matthew A. Holsapple, *Civic Responsibility: What Is the Campus Climate for Learning?* (Washington, DC: Association of American Colleges and Universities, 2009), 19.

3. Patrice Berger, "Thompson Community Dean's List Dinner Speech" (January 29, 2010), http://ace.unl.edu/archive/Berger.pdf.

4. Interim ACE Committee, "ACE Certification" (Lincoln: University of Nebraska, Lincoln, 2008), http:// ace.unl.edu/archive/Certification_working_form.doc.

5. Interim ACE Committee, "ACE Certification."

6. Furthermore, scholarship suggests that service learning and community-based learning models deepen students' understanding of what it means to be a good citizen. See, for example, George Kuh, *High-Impact Educational Practices: What They Are, Who Has Access to Them, and Why They Matter* (Washington, DC: Association of American Colleges and Universities, 2008).

7. Abraham Lincoln (speech in the House of Representatives, June 20, 1848), quoted in "Abraham Lincoln," Wikipedia, http://en.wikiquote.org/wiki/Abraham_Lincoln.

10: Wagner College

Successful Models and Practices

Devorah A. Lieberman and Cassia Freedland

Wagner is a four-year comprehensive college in New York City serving approximately 1,900 undergraduate and 450 graduate students. The mission is to prepare students for life, as well as for careers, by emphasizing interdisciplinarity, integrated learning, civic engagement, scholarship, achievement, leadership, and citizenship.

The college strives to meet this mission through the Wagner Plan for the Practical Liberal Arts. Implemented in 1998, the Wagner Plan integrates liberal arts and professional programs with experiential learning and reflective practice. Within this holistic program, every student participates in a minimum of three learning communities (freshman, sophomore or junior, and senior years) as well as two courses in freshman and senior years that are grounded, as well, in reflective practice. The reflective component of learning communities utilizes reading, writing, discussion, teamwork, and research to develop deep understanding of connections between theory and practice as demonstrated through civic engagement. In addition to learning communities, a new collaborative civic engagement initiative explicitly linking the college and community organizations forms a second cornerstone of the Wagner Plan. Known as Civic Innovations, this initiative has broadened civic engagement to deeply connect academic departments, community agencies, and organizations, with students in full and equal partnership. The goal is to achieve the complementary outcomes of improving services for society and providing students with civic experience in areas directly related to the curriculum as well as career and personal aspirations.

Experiential Learning and Student Development at Wagner College

Every learning community constitutes two separate linked courses, each with clearly defined learning outcomes. The experiential component of linked courses is directly grounded in course objectives and the needs of community organizations or agencies. Faculty work in tandem so that students experience an integration of course content, a connection with their related community engagement projects, and, in a reflective tutorial, the exploration of that which connects theory and practice.

In order to incorporate the most appropriate experiential learning into the course curricula, we have come to understand that a one-size-fits-all experiential learning model is not realistic. We are developing a taxonomy that recognizes two distinct forms of experiential learning and a hybrid of the two. Expected learning outcomes of specific courses, the depth of involvement of students and faculty, and the needs of community partners determine which form best describes the nature of the experience.

1. The *field-based experiences* model brings students into the community in ways that help meet students' learning outcomes but do not impact or benefit the community.
2. *Civic engagement* is a more evolved form of experiential learning. These experiences combine student learning outcomes related to course content with interactions that benefit community partners and community constituents. Traditionally, the weakness in this model has been that many civic engagement experiences are designed by a sole faculty member to complement a single course. The Civic Innovations model of civic engagement addresses this weakness. The strategy underlying Civic Innovations is the development of a sustainable partnership between an academic department and a community organization to address an identified community issue that provides mutual long-term benefit. The portfolio of potential experiential learning opportunities is broad and deep, meeting the needs of students whether they be in their first semester or last. Through Civic Innovations, we establish *community-connected departments* and *department-connected organizations* that withstand changes in faculty, curriculum, and nonprofit leadership.
3. A third category is a *hybrid* including elements of both field-based learning and civic engagement learning.

It should be noted that one form of experiential learning is not necessarily privileged over another. Experiential learning activities embedded throughout a course are dependent upon the student learning outcomes expected by the professor. Field-based experiential learning experiences are usually episodic during the semester and are intended only to enhance course learning outcomes. Civic engagement activities are intended to enhance course learning outcomes and to meet the needs of the community partners. Hybrid experiential learning activities include both field-based and civically engaged activities to enhance course learning outcomes.

Civic Innovations: Strategic and Enduring Civic Engagement

Civic Innovations' two core hypotheses are (1) that students develop deeper commitments to civic engagement and report greater feelings of personal and social responsibility toward the community and a particular organization and (2) that community partners develop greater trust and commitment toward the college.

Prior to our Civic Innovations initiative, it was possible for the students in a single learning community to meet their experiential requirement by volunteering in the community for a set number of hours. Through Civic Innovations, collaborations between institutions and community organizations typically include at least three separate courses from the same discipline, establishing ongoing relationships.

Our data suggest that students participating in Civic Innovations report greater feelings of personal and social responsibility toward the community and their host organization. As well, community partners' needs are being met, and they report feeling more connected to the college. To date, nearly half of Wagner's eighteen academic departments have adopted the Civic Innovations model.

Civic Innovations: Conception, Initiation, and Implementation

It would be tempting for us to take credit for a top-down approach to the development and implementation of Civic Innovations. In fact, the initiative was spawned in collaboration between senior academic administrators and faculty. In 2004, the new provost conducted student focus groups to ascertain the impact of civic engagement activities on student commitment to project sustainability and impact on the community. She found that after the semester concluded, students were only mildly interested in the community partner, and community partners felt "disconnected" from the students. To faculty, she floated the idea of longer-term commitments between the department and the community partner. Faculty were eager to help create a civic engagement model that met the needs of the department, students, and host community organization.

Civic Innovations, or any major new learning approach, would have been unlikely to succeed without faculty participation in conceptualizing, birthing, and developing the initiative. Each department's commitment to Civic Innovations involves a minimum of three or four courses working with the same community partner. This structure has created a model for collegial program development within these departments at Wagner, and the benefits from this have been greater than first realized. For faculty and students alike, expectations for learning outcomes attainment have expanded. For faculty, specifically, this program has accelerated and enhanced the desire to work as a team and to work interdisciplinarily. For departments, a positive sense of synergistic stewardship with their community partners has developed. Additionally, the nagging, and not altogether invalid, perception that the college was benefitting more from community partnerships than vice versa began to dissipate. Finally, the community government and other leaders welcomed the new and much more powerful relationship with the college because they could see long-range value and felt secure with the college's long-term commitment to their organizations.

The Port Richmond Partnership is Civic Innovations' most highly evolved form. Community leaders in an underserved area on Staten Island, Port Richmond, identified four areas of community need: education, health care, economics, and acculturation of immigrants. Civic Innovations now partners with Port Richmond to address these needs through the campus curriculum and departmental integration. These partnerships are creating a campus-community culture of mutually beneficial and mutually shared outcomes.

Institutional Change and Leadership

To maintain frequent and purposeful internal communication among constituencies, the provost has instituted a rigorous program of faculty development. A faculty scholar for teaching and learning assists faculty with the development of teaching strategies and styles. The college provides a mentoring program for new faculty and conducts regular faculty work groups that address scholarship/research and teaching, which often relate to civic engagement.

Wagner has taken steps to reward and recognize campus efforts. Rewards include stipends for faculty heavily engaged in learning initiatives such as Civic Innovations. A fully paid professional development semester (that does not compete with regular sabbaticals) is also offered after the third year in which faculty have taught in the first-year program. Additionally, a day each spring is set aside as Civic Engagement Recognition Day to salute community partners for outstanding achievement.

The college has also been intentional and strategic about the use of external communication through articles in the *Chronicle of Higher Education*, *Liberal Education*, *Change*, and other higher education media, which provides validation for faculty and staff, enhances the college's reputation among opinion leaders, assists in the recruitment and retention of faculty and staff, and facilitates opportunities for fund-raising. The college's broad commitment to internal and external communication fosters the transparency and accountability requisite for successful transformational leadership at all levels within the institution.

Assessment is crucial if we are to understand Civic Innovations' impact on the continuing evolution of Wagner. We continue to examine our deployment of the three models of experiential learning and their impacts on student outcomes, exploring new opportunities for transformation internally and with our partners, and conducting research among alumni to determine impacts on postgraduation community service and careers and feelings of connectedness to the college. The results will lead to further refinement of Civic Innovations, broaden participation among other departments and community organizations, and prove instrumental in securing additional funding.

Index

Contributor Biographies

Jann H. Adams is associate professor of psychology and associate dean of the Division of Science and Mathematics at Morehouse College. She is currently engaged in projects designed to enhance student performance in the sciences through curricular and pedagogical reform as well as interventions designed to support student achievement and exposure to research. She holds degrees from Oberlin College and Indiana University and publishes regularly in scientific journals.

Jerzy Axer, profesor ordinarius, University of Warsaw and Warsaw Theatre Academy, is a classical scholar (Ciceronian studies, the reception of classical tradition in European culture). He is a past president of the International Society for the History of Rhetoric; a member of the Polish Academy of Sciences and the Polish Academy of Arts and Sciences; the founder and director of the Centre for Studies on the Classical Tradition in Poland and East-Central Europe (now the Institute for Interdisciplinary Studies "Artes Liberales"); and the founder of the Interdepartmental Individual Studies in the Humanities and the Collegium Artes Liberales.

Kenneth R. Bain is the vice provost for university learning and teaching, the director of the Research Academy for University Learning, and a professor of history at Montclair State University. A historian whose principle works have centered on the development of U.S. foreign policy in the Middle East, he has been the founding director of four major teaching and learning centers at New York University, Vanderbilt University, and Montclair State. His 2004 book, *What the Best College Teachers Do* won the Virginia and Warren Stone Prize for an outstanding book on education and society.

Randall J. Bass is a professor of English, the associate provost of institutional renewal, and the executive director of Georgetown University's Center for New Designs in Learning and Scholarship (CNDLS), a campuswide center supporting faculty work in new learning and research environments. Working at the intersections of new media technologies and the scholarship of teaching and learning, he is the author, editor, and coeditor of numerous books, articles, and electronic projects, including "The Difference that Inquiry Makes: A Collaborative Case Study on Technology and Learning." He is a recipient of the EDUCAUSE Medal for outstanding achievement in technology and undergraduate education.

Thomas Bender, university professor of the humanities and professor of history at New York University, previously served as chair of the history department, dean for the humanities, director of the International Center for Advanced Studies at NYU, and chair of the New York Council for the Humanities. He is a fellow of the American Academy of Arts and Sciences. His scholarship and teaching have focused on cultural history and the history of academic disciplines. He has been a Guggenheim and a Rockefeller Fellow and a fellow at the Center for Advanced Study in the Behavioral Sciences.

Dessa Bergen-Cico is an assistant professor in the Department of Public Health, Food Studies and Nutrition in the College of Human Ecology. She is a certified addiction specialist and lead faculty for addiction studies at Syracuse University. At Syracuse she has served as the director of the university's substance-abuse counseling and health enhancement programs, director of Sexual Assault Crisis Services, director for assessment for the Division of Student Affairs, and associate dean of students. At the national level she serves on AAC&U's Health and Higher Education National Advisory Board.

Joyce A. Bylander is special assistant to the president for institutional and diversity initiatives at Dickinson College. From this senior-level position, she continues her work on behalf of the college to bridge academic and students affairs and to lead campuswide efforts on diversity. Prior to her appointment at Dickinson, she served at Bucknell University and the College of Charleston in both offices of student and academic affairs.

Kent John Chabotar became the eighth president of Guilford College in 2002. Previously, he served as a faculty member and administrator at Bowdoin College, Harvard University, the University of Massachusetts, and Michigan State University. Since 1983, he has taught in the summer executive programs at the Harvard Institutes for Higher Education and has published widely on finance and strategy in higher education—including the book *Strategic Finance* (2006) and articles on economic crises for *Inside Higher Ed*, *Chronicle of Higher Education*, and *Change*.

Barry N. Checkoway is a professor of social work and a professor of urban planning at the University of Michigan. His research and publications draw from grassroots groups, community agencies, and government programs in the South Bronx, Detroit, Mississippi Delta, and Central Appalachia as well as South America, Europe, Africa, and the Middle East. He worked with the White House in launching AmeriCorps, then as founding director of the Michigan Neighborhood AmeriCorps Program, the Edward Ginsberg Center for Community Service and Learning, and the Youth Dialogues on Race and Ethnicity in Metropolitan Detroit.

Catherine A. Crosby-Currie, associate dean of the first year at St. Lawrence University and an associate professor of psychology, coordinates SLU's comprehensive First-Year Program—a living-learning program with a team-taught interdisciplinary course at its core—as well as the spring First-Year Seminar program. She collaborates extensively with the Office of Institutional Research on a variety of projects and grants related to assessing student academic and personal development.

Richard A. Detweiler is the president of the Great Lakes Colleges Association, an organization of thirteen colleges working to strengthen learning in the tradition of the liberal arts and sciences. A social psychologist, his scholarship includes topics related to intercultural relations and social perception. He is president emeritus of Hartwick College and a Foundation Fellow at Oxford University's Harris Manchester College. Through the GLCA he has founded the Global Liberal Arts Alliance, a multinational organization furthering relationships among liberal arts institutions internationally.

Ashley P. Finley is the senior director of assessment and research at the Association of American Colleges and Universities (AAC&U) and the national evaluator for the Bringing Theory to Practice Project (BTtoP). Through her work with AAC&U and BTtoP, she helps colleges and universities develop, implement, and communicate meaningful assessment strategies that facilitate depth of learning at the student, faculty, and institutional levels. Before joining AAC&U, she was a member of the faculty at Dickinson College.

Cassia Freedland is currently the director for the Center for Leadership and Service at Wagner College. She is committed to helping community organizations fulfill their missions and sees college-community partner-ships as a potent engine for bringing about positive change. She has served as a key member of the Wagner demonstration site for the BTtoP Project.

Richard Guarasci is president of Wagner College. He served as provost and vice president for academic affairs at Wagner prior to his selection as the College's eighteenth president. A graduate of Fordham and Indiana University in economics and political science, he encouraged the develop-ment of a comprehensive four-year undergraduate program required of all Wagner students that links interdisciplinary course clusters with ex-periential learning and civic engagement. During his presidency, Wagner has become a practice-centered liberal arts college.

Donald W. Harward, president emeritus of Bates College, served as VPAA at the College of Wooster, Ohio, and as a faculty member in philosophy at the University of Delaware, where he founded and led the university honors program. He serves on the boards of national education, philan-thropic, and social service organizations and is a frequent contributor and consultant to professional discussions regarding liberal education and civic engagement. As one of its founders, he directs the Bringing Theory to Practice Project.

John K. Haynes, David Packard Professor in science and dean of the Di-vision of Science and Mathematics at Morehouse College, is a teaching scholar in the area of developmental biology—his doctoral work from Brown University. Prior to his appointment as dean, he served as chair of the biology department at Morehouse for 16 years. He is actively involved in reform of undergraduate science education.

Debra Humphreys is the vice president for communications and public affairs at AAC&U, overseeing the association's public affairs programs, outreach, media relations, publications, and marketing efforts. With de-grees from Williams College and Rutgers University, she has taught and published on trends in undergraduate education, employers' views of college learning, and nineteenth-century African American and women's literature. Humphreys was the founding editor of AAC&U's quarterly, *Diversity Digest*, now published as *Diversity & Democracy*.

Bruce Keith, professor of sociology and associate dean for academic affairs at the United States Military Academy, West Point, New York, is one of the principal leaders of work undertaken on the Military Academy's learn-ing system for leader development. The system serves as an important national model for undergraduate education, which has been enhanced by and distributed through various AAC&U consortia and conferences.

Adrianna J. Kezar, associate professor of higher education administration at the University of Southern California, publishes widely on leadership, organizational dynamics, change, and educational reform. A scholar of higher education reform, her work has been used in multiple BTtoP and AAC&U conferences and is published in leading educational research journals.

Julie Johnson Kidd is president of the Christian A. Johnson Endeavor Foundation in New York, which supports liberal arts education in the United States and Europe, the arts, and American Indian causes. As chairman of the Museum of the American Indian, Mrs. Kidd negotiated the agreement that led to the creation of the Smithsonian's National Museum of the American Indian, for which she received the James Smithson Medal. She has served on a number of college boards of trustees, in the United States and abroad, and is currently the founding chair of the European College of Liberal Arts in Berlin.

Phyllis Lane is the dean of student and academic support services at Evergreen State College. Her administration experience includes positions at public research institutions as well as denominational and private liberal colleges. She has been an active participant in BTtoP conferences and AAC&U summer institutes, including the Boundaries and Borderlands project and the Greater Expectations project. Her work as an administrator includes K–12 to higher education alignments, diversity, student retention, and engagement initiatives.

Peter L. Levine is the director of research at the Jonathan M. Tisch College of Citizenship and Public Service and the director of CIRCLE (Center for Information and Research on Civic Learning and Engagement) at Tufts University. His books include *The Future of Democracy: Developing the Next Generation of American Citizens* (2007) and *Reforming the Humanities: Literature and Ethics from Dante through Modern Times* (2009).

Devorah A. Lieberman, president of the University of La Verne, California, was formerly provost and VPAA at Wagner College. Her extensive involvement and leadership with national initiatives include increasing civic and community engagement; shaping institutional transformation; balancing graduate, professional, and liberal education; focusing on student and faculty development; increasing internationalization; and enhancing campus diversity. Her dedication to these initiatives on the college campus has also informed and shaped her scholarly agenda, national presentations, and publications.

William M. Loker, cultural anthropologist and dean of undergraduate education at California State University, Chico, has, in concert with leadership from his administration and faculty, overseen the acclaimed work of a university deeply examining, and then achieving, a purposeful civic mission directly connected to the institution's focus on civic learning and student success, especially among first-generation students.

Theodore E. Long is president emeritus of Elizabethtown College, where he served for fifteen years until his retirement in 2011. Prior to his appointment at Elizabethtown, he was provost at Merrimack College and a faculty member at George Washington University, Hollins University, and Washington and Jefferson College. As a trustee, he chairs the student affairs committee at Capital University. He is a frequent facilitator for the Association of Governing Boards' Education and Consultation Service.

Linda J. Major serves as assistant to the vice chancellor for student affairs at the University of Nebraska, where she is responsible for coordinating a comprehensive approach to address high-risk behaviors on campus and in the community, cocurricular leadership, and division-wide assessment and professional development. She has been recognized by both the American Public Health Association and the U.S. Department of Education's Network Addressing Collegiate Alcohol and Other Drug Issues for her work in college-based programming.

Michael V. McGill has served as superintendent of the Scarsdale Public Schools in Scarsdale, New York, since 1998. He writes and regularly speaks on the national school reform movement's implications for liberal learning and on the place of public education in a democracy. A graduate of Williams College and Harvard University, he served previously as a school superintendent in Massachusetts and New York State, as well as an independent school head in Connecticut.

Elizabeth McHugh, director of health and counseling services at the Evergreen State College and adjunct member of the faculty, is responsible for leadership of the Health Center, the Counseling Center, and the Office of Sexual Assault Prevention. Elizabeth teaches in a campus program (the Student Medical Assistant Program: A Practical Approach) and has been involved with the Bringing Theory to Practice Project for the past six years. She is Evergreen's senior leader for the National College Depression Partnership.

Mindy McWilliams is assistant director for assessment at the Center for New Designs in Learning and Scholarship at Georgetown University, where her work focuses on assessment and research to improve student learning and teaching practice across the university. She has served as a key member of the Georgetown leadership team for the BTtoP/Engelhard curriculum infusion program, contributing to programmatic design and assessment of the program's effect on student learning outcomes and on faculty practice.

Nancy D. Mitchell helped create and implement the outcomes-based Achievement-Centered Education program as director of general educa-tion at the University of Nebraska. She balances this responsibility with her appointment as professor of advertising in the university's College of Journalism and Mass Communications.

Sally Engelhard Pingree is committed to the support of public health, mental health, substance-abuse issues, education, and environmental af-fairs. She has pursued these passions through a variety of board affilia-tions, including the Charles Engelhard Foundation, the African Wildlife Foundation, Boston College, the Carter Center's Mental Health Task Force, the National Gallery of Art, the Potomac School, and St. Andrew's School. She is the founder of the S. Engelhard Center, which focuses on projects and initiatives that address the intellectual, emotional, and civic develop-ment of today's students.

Alice (Jill) N. Reich served as vice president of academic affairs and dean of the faculty at Bates College from 2000 to 2011 and continues to serve there as a professor of psychology. As an administrator, teacher, and re-searcher, her work has encompassed the opportunities and challenges of approaches in higher education that are inclusive of engagement with the community. At Bates, she oversees the college's Harward Center for Com-munity Partnerships, nationally recognized for the scope and range of its work linking the faculty and curriculum to the community.

Joan B. Riley, assistant professor in the human science and nursing departments at Georgetown University School of Nursing and Health Studies and nurse practitioner in the on-campus Student Health Center, teaches courses on health promotion and disease prevention. Her health promotion efforts focus on college students, persons with disabilities, and health literacy. She has been a co-investigator on the BTtoP Project at Georgetown since its inception in 2002.

Daniel Tad Roach, a founding member of the BTtoP Project, has served as the headmaster of St. Andrew's School in Middletown, Delaware, since 1997. A Williams and Middlebury graduate, he regularly addresses issues of transition from school to college, admissions policies, and student learning as he leads, and was a member of the faculty of, a most highly regarded private residential school.

Carol Geary Schneider has been president of the Association of American Colleges and Universities (AAC&U) since 1998, the leading national organization devoted to advancing and strengthening undergraduate liberal education. AAC&U's emphasis, Liberal Education and America's Promise (LEAP), is a ten-year public advocacy and campus action initiative designed to engage students and the public with the needs of a college education for the twenty-first century and to identify comprehensive, innovative models that improve learning for all undergraduate students. She is a graduate and member of the Board of Trustees of Mount Holyoke College.

David M. Scobey is executive dean at the New School of a new division organized around interdisciplinary engagement and the integration of liberal learning with social and professional practice. As a cultural historian at the University of Michigan, he created the Arts of Citizenship Program and served as the founding director of the Harward Center for Community Partnerships at Bates College. He is the author of *Empire City: The Making and Meaning of the New York City Landscape* (2002), as well as numerous publications on American history, civic engagement, and higher education.

Valerie I. Sessa, associate professor of industrial and organizational psychology at Montclair State University, focuses her research and teaching on how students can develop and learn to be better leaders and community citizens. Other research interests include the interconnections between individual, group, and organizational learning. She has served as a key member of the Montclair leadership team for multiple BTtoP projects.

Shalom D. Staub, associate provost for first-year programs and first-year class dean at Dickinson College, is responsible for first-year seminars and the learning community program for first-year students and has worked with faculty to develop Dickinson's service learning and community-based research programs. He regularly teaches courses cross-listed in sociology, religion, Judaic studies, and Middle East studies.

Catharine R. Stimpson is a university professor and dean emerita of the Graduate School of Arts and Science at New York University. She writes on cultural, literary, and educational issues, with a special interest in the subject of women and gender. She is a past president of the Modern Language Association and of the Association of Graduate Schools, a founder of the interdisciplinary journal *SIGNS*, and the former director of the MacArthur Foundation Fellowship Program.

William M. Sullivan is a senior scholar at the Center of Inquiry in the Liberal Arts at Wabash College, where he is directing a study funded by the Lilly Endowment. He has previously directed studies of professional and liberal education as senior scholar at the Carnegie Foundation for the Advancement of Teaching. His books include *A New Agenda for Higher Education: Shaping a Life of the Mind for Practice* (with Matthew S. Rosin) and *Work and Integrity: The Crisis and Promise of Professionalism in America.*

Lynn E. Swaner has served as faculty member of the Graduate School of Education, C.W. Post–Long Island University, as the national grant evaluator for the Bringing Theory to Practice Project, and as an academic and student affairs administrator at Columbia University and C.W. Post–LIU. Holding a degree in higher education from Teachers College, Columbia University, and a counseling degree from C.W. Post–LIU, she is also a licensed mental health counselor. Currently she consults and regularly publishes in the areas of teaching and learning, faculty development, and accreditation.

Thia Wolf is the director of the First-Year Experience program and a professor of English studies at California State University, Chico. She works with faculty, with students, and with student affairs staff to design and implement programs that engage first-year students in the public sphere. Her attention to student learning and development is reflected in Chico's nationally recognized program in linking the civic and liberal education.

Christine Zimmerman is the director of institutional research at St. Lawrence University. For over a decade, she has provided leadership and support in the areas of survey research, strategic planning, and learning outcomes assessment. She regularly partners with the associate dean of the first year at St. Lawrence on projects related to the assessment of student academic and personal development.